SEVEN BLACK PLAYS

SEVEN BLACK PLAYS

THE THEODORE WARD PRIZE
FOR AFRICAN AMERICAN
PLAYWRITING

Edited by Chuck Smith

With a foreword by August Wilson

NORTHWESTERN UNIVERSITY PRESS
EVANSTON, ILLINOIS

Northwestern University Press
www.nupress.northwestern.edu

Printed in the United States of America

10 9 8 7 6 5 4 3

ISBN-13: 978-0-8101-2045-7
ISBN-10: 0-8101-2045-3

LIBRARY OF CONGRESS CATALOGING-IN-PUBLICATION DATA

Seven Black plays : the Theodore Ward Prize for African American
    Playwriting / edited by Chuck Smith ; with a foreword by August Wilson.
        p. cm.
    ISBN 0-8101-2045-3 (trade paper : alk. paper)
    1. American drama—African American authors. 2. African Americans—
Drama. I. Smith, Chuck, 1938–
PS628.N4S485 2004
812'.54080896073—dc22

                                                            2004004725

∞ The paper used in this publication meets the minimum requirements
of the American National Standard for Information Sciences—
Permanence of Paper for Printed Library Materials, ANSI Z39.48-1992.

This volume of Seven Black Plays
is dedicated to the memory of Lorraine Hansberry,
Theodore Ward, and Clarence Taylor.

Special thanks to associate editor Tracye Graves;
to Barbara Gaynor and Natalie Moore,
who have served as prize community readers
for fifteen consecutive years;
and to the 1983–2003 Columbia College
Chicago Theater Department faculty.

CONTENTS

FOREWORD

August Wilson

There is a moment in Carlyle Brown's *The African Company Presents Richard III* when the company is jailed for performing William Shakespeare's plays, and as they wrestle with the demand that they stop, one of the characters agrees, saying, in essence, that Shakespeare is not the only one who has a tongue.

This volume is ample evidence that we do indeed have tongues of our own and they speak in a variety of voices with a clarity that honors a tradition which has many luminous points gained by will and daring. Art is made out of the spiritual resources of the people who create it. Out of their experiences, the sacred and the profane, is made a record of their traverse and the many points of epiphany and redemption. To have a black American art on the field of tradition and history that upholds and promotes the values of its ancestors empowers and provokes a sense of self that speeds development and progress in all areas of life and endeavor.

For me, and I suspect it's the same for others, writing a play is like walking down the landscape of the self, exploring what D. H. Lawrence called the "dark forest" of the soul. It is a place rife with shadows, a place of suspect quality and occasional dazzling brightness. What you encounter there are your demons, which you have fed trying, as Hansel, to make your way back home. You find false trials, roads closed for repairs, impregnable fortresses, scouts, and armies of memory. It is a place where the cartographers labor night and day remaking the maps. The road is sometimes welcoming, and its wide passages offer endearment with each step only to narrow to a footpath that has led you, boatless, to the edge of a vast and encompassing ocean. Occasionally, if you are willing to negotiate the perils, you arrive, strong and brighter of spirit, to a place that sprouts yams and bolls of cotton at your footfall. To begin that journey is an act of faith. It is, in another guise, heroics of a fierce resolve. Each of these plays is a performance, an artistic rendering of sensibility guided by aesthetic concerns, in which that faith is rewarded.

Our literary accomplishments are not without peer, but they demand a proper accounting on their own terms. All language, whether the language of theater or music, the language of mathematics, of painting or architecture, describes the idea of the one who is speaking it. When we, as black Americans, sit down to create in the formal language of theater, we are describing our ideas about the world. We are making an aesthetic statement that makes use of ourselves in total. Our history, our experience, our culture, our ideas about pleasure and pain, our concepts of beauty and justice, our ideas of story and song. It doesn't leave any part of ourselves out of the equation. Our approach to aesthetics is informed by our sensibilities, which have been shaped by our culture. Our response to the stimuli and phenomena of the world that we encounter is a cultural response. To the extent our culture is different from any other culture, it follows that our witness and aesthetics are also different. Since we are making this art out of the solitary confines of our imagination and memory, it must stand that it is made up out of ourselves as a way of defining and celebrating that self, a way of bringing it closer to the divinity.

The making of art is a daunting task. The song turning back in on itself, empowering itself with its own discoveries, its own energies. "In the language of the day I will say eternal things," writes Jorge Luis Borges in the poem "Browning Resolves to Be a Poet." To write for the ages is within our capabilities, which are as wide as God's closet and embrace much finery. This volume is witness and testimony.

SEVEN BLACK PLAYS

THE LAST SEASON

Christopher Moore

First-Place Winner

1987–1988

PLAYWRIGHT'S STATEMENT

As a playwright who works also as a historian, I am very fortunate to once have been in the company of some of the last century's greatest athletes. Many summers ago, as a young playwright—supporting myself then as a sportswriter—I attended a gathering of active and retired professional baseball players. On this special July 1977 night in New York City, after a Major League Baseball All-Star Game that had been dedicated to the thirtieth anniversary of Jackie Robinson's entry into the major leagues, several players, members of the press, and VIPs all took the team bus back to a posh Manhattan hotel to attend a private reception.

At the crowded party suite were Henry Aaron, Rod Carew, Reggie Jackson, Ken Griffey Sr., Pete Rose, Johnny Bench, and many other great players. We listened as former players like Roy Campanella, Willie Mays, Larry Doby, and Monte Irvin spoke about their memories of "Jackie" and the experiences each had in the old Negro Leagues, where, like Jackie, they had once played. So privileged did I feel to be a part of this special event, listening to and partying with these amazing athletes, that I barely noticed the presence of some elderly black men in the room. They, too, were all former baseball players who had been invited to the All-Star Game as "special guests" of Major League Baseball.

Though I had been a baseball fan since I first saw Mays make a basket catch in the late 1950s, the faces of these old men were not at all familiar to me. I watched as Doby, Irvin, and Mays, who appeared to know the older men as friends, treated them with extraordinary respect. A circle of people gradually grew around the old men as Campy coaxed them to tell their stories to everyone. By midnight, the seniors were doing most of the talking and almost everyone younger than seventy had many questions about their lives as young men in the old Negro Leagues.

For me, that was the event that inspired *The Last Season.*

PRODUCTION HISTORY

The Last Season, by Christopher Moore, was first presented by the Columbia College Chicago Theater Department at the New Studio Theater in February 1988. It was directed by Ivory Ocean, with set design by Brice Williams, costume design by Julie Jackson, and lighting design by David Nolan. Sheryl Carter was the dramaturge, and Beth Hirsch was the stage manager.

Rockford "Rocker" Mills	Glen Bradshaw-Collins
Lewis Fowler	Thomas W. Green
Willard "Young Boy" Mount	Jonathan Kuykindoll
Sam Foster	C. Lewis-Chatman
Rudy Easton	L. M. McIntyre
Bellman Barkum	Evan Lionel Smith
Sugie Brookfield	Senuwell Smith
Henry Simmons	David J. Thibodeaux
Elrod Payne/Old Man	Ray A. Thomas

The play was subsequently presented by theater companies including ETA in Chicago, Plowshares in Detroit, and the Robey in Los Angeles. The Robey Theatre production was coproduced by Legacy Productions, a Chicago-based touring company, at the Stage 52 Theatre in Los Angeles in September 2001. It was directed by Chuck Smith, with set design by Ed Haynes, costume design by Naila Aladdin-Sanders, lighting design by Doc Ballard, and sound design by Anthony Carr. Sherrie Lofton was the stage manager, and John Freeland Jr. was the production stage manager.

Rockford "Rocker" Mills	Glen Bradshaw-Collins
Rudy Easton	Karl Calhoun
Sam Foster	Ben Guillory
Willard "Young Boy" Mount	Amad Jackson
Sugie Brookfield	J. J. Marshall Jones
Henry Simmons	Harry Lennix
Lewis Fowler	Dwain A. Perry
Elrod Payne/Old Man	M. Darnell Suttles
Bellman Barkum	Frantz Turner

CHARACTERS

Old Man

Rudy Easton, early thirties, self-satisfied, center fielder and team captain

Lewis Fowler, late twenties, small and youthfully enthusiastic, shortstop

Rockford "Rocker" Mills, late thirties, family man and the team's oldest player, first baseman

Sugie Brookfield, late twenties, stocky and badly dressed, second baseman

Henry Simmons, late twenties, confident and ambitious, pitcher and occasional outfielder

Bellman Barkum, early thirties, lanky and sharply dressed, third baseman

Sam Foster, well-preserved disciplinarian of the game, coach

Willard "Young Boy" Mount, eighteen, team rookie, right fielder

Elrod Payne, late twenties, solitary, left fielder

Ennis Little, catcher

Announcer

STAGING

The Last Season is a play for nine or ten actors. Casting an actor to portray the catcher, Ennis Little, who may appear in the team photo or at team celebrations, is optional. The characters of Old Man and Announcer may be doubled with team members.

Varying levels from left to right connect three primary sets on the stage. At the rear center of the stage is the team room with locker room–type open stalls for each player. Above the stalls hang two large banners depicting the Negro League Champions of 1945 and 1946. In the team room are three long benches, a bulletin board, and a small mirror on the wall.

A 1930s vintage bus interior, serving as the office of Coach Sam Foster, is farthest stage right. The original bus seats are removed, and the office is furnished with a desk, file cabinets, and two chairs. Baseball mementos are scattered throughout the office.

A dugout, elevated slightly with an overhanging roof, is downstage left. A single bench is in the dugout. Over the roof is a sign: HOME OF THE MONT-GOMERY BLACK KINGS BASEBALL TEAM.

Downstage is suggestive of the out-of-doors and roadside. This area contains a few large stones and shrubs and is a natural walkway. Lighting of the set should accurately define each playing area and enhance the temperament and time definitions of the play.

ACT 1

[Fall 1946, Montgomery, Alabama. A fairground and ballpark on Dexter Avenue. The stage is dark as the play opens and begins with a prologue. Light rises softly to reveal a figure entering from the area next to the dugout. He appears to be an OLD MAN *dressed darkly in a long coat and wearing a hat. His face is not recognizable, and he seems not to have been in this setting for a very long time. The* OLD MAN *reaches under the dugout bench and retrieves a baseball bat. The bat is old and dusty. He brushes off the bat, examines it for a moment, takes a few slow swings, and then gently sets the bat down. There is a fallen sign atop the dugout roof. He pushes the sign—*HOME OF THE MONTGOMERY BLACK KINGS BASEBALL TEAM—*back to its original position. He quietly studies the sign for a moment. He stands motionless as there is the sound of an offstage "call."]*

PLAYER I *[singing]*: Call yourself a Montgomery King!
ALL *[singing]*: King's my name, and King I sing!
PLAYER I *[singing]*: Play them fellows, black or white!
ALL *[singing]*: Beat them fellows, day or night!

[Beneath the Negro League banners on the rear wall, light begins to rise on a celebration. Before the light is up, the OLD MAN *is seen moving out of view. Shouts and laughter drown out the song as the celebration continues. Six baseball players are in the midst of a victory party. All are members of the Montgomery Black Kings. They are celebrating their second straight Negro League championship. Present are* RUDY, LEWIS, ROCKER, SUGIE, HENRY, *and* BELLMAN. *All are in their after-game clothes and are drinking or drunk. They fall out laughing as they interrupt their call, shouting to a crescendo of "Kings! Kings! Kings! Woooeee! Two! Two! Two! Two in a row, y'all! Two!"]*

RUDY: Three!
ALL: Three!

[Laughter.]

LEWIS: Damn! This liquor is gettin' to me.
ROCKER: Drink up! We the best damn team to ever play this game. Drink, I say, drink!
SUGIE: Coach Sam—where you? Coach Sam, come over here and say somethin'.

[*Enter* SAM.]

You the head of this outfit. Speak up! Speech!

[*Others join* SUGIE.]

Speech! Speech!
SAM: Shut up and I'll speak.

[*Players quiet down.*]

I'll say two items. First, you all are drunk and you stink.

[*Laughter.*]

Second, you played a hell of a game.

[*Cheers.*]

Quiet down. Quiet down. Kings have won two straight championships.
ALL: Two!
SAM [*topping them*]: We will be the first team in history to take this banner for three straight! I spoke.
ALL: Three!
LEWIS: We got it, Coach! Three!
ALL: Three! Three!
SAM: Yo. One more word, y'all. One more. Be proud of what you did out there today—be proud of what you did all season. Ain't nobody better than what you showed me. This ain't no footloose clown ball club. You fellas did each other well—all of us. You showed good pride and showed good playin'.

[*All drink to their victory.*]

And yo, we got one more matter here to take care of. Can't overlook this.

[*He withdraws the Owner's Trophy from a canvas sack.*]

Henry Simmons, front and center.

[*Players begin a slow round of applause.*]

Brother Simmons, you know us colored folk ain't got a whole lot of frivolous money, but Mr. Clarence Stoner, who owns this ball club—

[*Groans are heard.*]

Stoner—

BELLMAN: Where the heck is he anyway?

SAM: He got other businesses. He ain't got to be here. You might be the better for it. Stoner, Mr. Simmons, has asked me to present the Owner's Trophy for an outstanding season. Brother Simmons, this belongs to you.

LEWIS: Go on, Henry.

HENRY: You sure Stoner wasn't drunk when he figured to give me this?

BELLMAN: He was drunk—'cause he didn't give it to me.

[*Players laugh and ad-lib congratulations.*]

HENRY: I want you to know I feel proud to have this trophy. I'm proud, too, to be a member of this team and have a piece of that banner. Like Sam says— proud we play the best ball bar none.

LEWIS: Negro League is the best league.

BELLMAN: Colored ball is the best ball.

ROCKER: Shoot, ain't nobody hold a stick to us.

SUGIE: If they don't believe this after two banner years, they is blind and dumb.

[SAM *watches as all show excitement.*]

LEWIS: We gonna give it to them three times!

[LEWIS *stands on the bench and grips the banner proudly.*]

SUGIE: Three times!

ROCKER: Kings!

BELLMAN: Champeens! We the champeens!

SUGIE [*singing*]: Call yourself a Montgomery King!

BELLMAN [*overlapping*]: Ennis got a truck. Let's get Enny's truck!

PLAYERS [*singing*]: King's my name, and King I sing!

BELLMAN: We gonna take the banner into town.

SUGIE [*singing*]: Play them fellows, black or white!

[*Players take down the banner.*]

LEWIS: White folks is gonna say, "Who are them crazy coons?"

PLAYERS [*singing*]: Beat them fellows, day or night!

SUGIE: We going to tell them just that: "We are the Montgomery crazy coons— Kings!"

BELLMAN [*singing*]: King's my name, and King I stand!

PLAYERS [*singing*]: Champions throughout the land!

BELLMAN: They might say we crazy, but we the best baseball team they'll ever lay eyes on. Come on, Sam, Rudy.

SUGIE [*singing*]: Call yourself a Montgomery King!
RUDY: I'll be with you—
PLAYERS [*singing*]: King's my name, and King I sing!
RUDY: —we'll be there.
ROCKER: Hold her high!
BELLMAN: We is coming!

[*Laughter and yelling as players depart.* RUDY *and* SAM *remain.*]

SAM [*calling to the players*]: Don't get yourselves shot up now! I don't need to lose a whole team to some sheriff who thinks you're fixin' to scare all them good white folks half to death—or scarin' colored folks, too!

[*He takes a bottle of home brew out of a canvas sack.*]

[*To* RUDY] Now this here's the real stuff. Have some 'shine.

[RUDY *declines.* SAM *drinks.*]

Rudy?
RUDY: Yes, Sam?
SAM: Shake my hand.
RUDY: Two championship banners back-to-back.
SAM: How about it? Next to Savannah, we're the only club ever to win two in a row.
RUDY: Savannah couldn't swallow the third.
SAM: Savannah couldn't handle it. We can. The war took some of their boys, but it took some of ours, too. And don't forget, last year was a war year—most of it was—and we won even without all our best. No, winning three in a row ain't for sure. But there weren't no war this year and there ain't none now, and if them boys don't get shot tonight, we're going to make it next year, too.

[*Heard in the distance, players shout,* "Three! Three! Three!" SAM *and* RUDY *savor the sound.*]

Two championships and a new grandbaby. A new grandbaby boy.

[RUDY *shakes* SAM's *hand.*]

RUDY: Hey, that's good for you. Tell everybody.
SAM: He ain't the only baby. But he is mine.

[*He takes a drink.*]

How did you like our trophy man? He had some series, huh?

RUDY: Henry has come a ways. I'm glad he got it. He did a good job.

SAM: You all did. I did, too. We played together, that's why we won. I guess I'm just concerned about winnin'.

RUDY: Winnin' and hollerin'. Sam, you are the holleringest coach I ever saw.

SAM: I don't holler.

RUDY: More hollerin' even than when you was playin' all the time.

SAM: You coach a team full of us, you'd holler, too.

RUDY: You must be doin' somethin' that is correct.

SAM: I ain't going to argue with you.

RUDY [*raising his drink to toast* SAM]: To Coach Sam. To old Coach Sam.

SAM: To Rudy—who ain't gettin' no younger. Rudy, these two seasons past, they been two good years—coachin', winnin'. The Lord's been good to me—to us. And you—you, Rudy—

[*Anticipating a compliment,* RUDY *becomes a bit uncomfortable.*]

No, no, hear me out. You, boy, got a lot to do with how this team turns out. Some of the others—they're all good players but they like their foolishness, too. You're their team captain. Don't be too casual. They could be the most wonderful of all teams. We can be. Sometimes we are, but you got to keep at 'em.

[*He takes a drink.*]

You know what keeps us from being just any other club? Pride. Not boastfulness. We can't be clowns. We are a proud team. You can't win diddly without it. We are the Montgomery Kings, Champions of the Negro Leagues and whatever else as far as I am concerned. We got to know it. Drink one for the team.

RUDY: To this season and the next.

SAM: Three in a row.

RUDY: As long as there ain't no war, we'll be OK.

SAM: To hell with a war. Nothin' ain't going to stop us, Rudy. We ain't gonna be stopped—for war or nothin' else.

[*Lights fade as the two men exit downstage right. Lights rise on the team room. The players are in various stages of dress and undress. Most are seated.* BELLMAN *is at the mirror, studying himself. It is the new baseball season.*]

SUGIE [*reading a newspaper*]: Woooeee. Yo, hear this here on Kansas City. They busted them boys' hind parts over in Jackson last week.

ROCKER: Jackson ain't a bad team this year.

SUGIE: KC ain't beat Jackson in four tries and they ain't beat us.

ROCKER: There you go, countin' them chickens—anybody say "banner year"?

[*Others respond in unison, "Banner year!"* BELLMAN *and* ROCKER *confidently exchange the team handshake.*]

LEWIS [*to* SUGIE]: That the new paper?

SUGIE [*ignoring* LEWIS]: Who else is good? Mobile? *Maybe,* Mobile, but you know they gonna choke.

ROCKER: Birmingham.

SUGIE: They ain't beat us. This go-around looks like it's us and the Jacks, here on.

[LEWIS *tries to read over* SUGIE's *shoulder.*]

Yo, boy, can't you see I am readin'?

LEWIS: I want to see if they got the Dodgers in that paper.

ROCKER: Last I heard, he was doing pretty well. You can't hardly find any word on the boy 'less you readin' the colored paper.

LEWIS: What they got, Sugie?

ROCKER: I hear all the papers everywhere in the South cut his name right out. White folks don't want to know the boy.

LEWIS: What they got, Sugie?

BELLMAN: Read our game. I want to hear what they got to say about me. Three home runs I had last week.

ROCKER: What they got?

SUGIE [*reading haltingly*]: "The—Brooklyn—Dodgers—staged—a—dramatic—fin—ish—today—"

LEWIS [*continuing*]: "—as they defeated the New York Giants 2 to 1."

SUGIE [*concentrating*]: Today, now what day is that? Colored paper don't never give you what day it is.

LEWIS: Go on, Sugie.

SUGIE [*reading*]: "The Dodgers scored the winning run as colored speedster Jackie Robinson stole home—"

ROCKER: Stole home!

SUGIE: The boy stole home on 'em!

LEWIS: He won it for 'em. He's done it a couple times now.

BELLMAN: I do it all the time. Heck, who beat the Dodgers in exhibition? We did.

SUGIE: Says here, too, "Robinson, the swift ebony gazelle, also scored the Dodgers' first run—"

LEWIS: He scored 'em both?!

SUGIE: "The Sepia Samson—"

BELLMAN: Sam who? Seep what?

SUGIE: "—then stunned the Giants as he scored all the way from first on a single by Pee Wee Reese."

LEWIS: Damn, they only had two runs and he scored both.

[RUDY *and* HENRY *enter from upstage entrance.*]

Jackie Robinson's the one who won it for 'em!

ROCKER: Rudy, Jack Robinson is bustin' them up. Two hits and scored two runs.

LEWIS: He won the game for 'em!

RUDY: All right, I knew we'd show them folks somethin'.

ROCKER: Never thought I'd see the day.

BELLMAN: He ain't doin' no more than what we can do.

HENRY [*to* SUGIE]: They got any more on him down there? He was hittin' pretty low last I saw. He got a few hits but they ain't goin' to keep him if he ain't hittin'.

LEWIS: He's hittin'. Colored ballplayer in the big leagues and he's bustin' 'em.

BELLMAN: Lewis, ain't nobody here surprised. We been knowin' this for a long time. Last month when we played them two white teams? Busted the both of 'em, didn't we? We'd a busted a third if that peckerwood umpire hadn't a called back Sugie's hit—

SUGIE: A home run it was.

BELLMAN: —right down the left-field line, clean inside, and the red-nose bastard called Sugie a foul ball. No, that boy ought to do good. I'd go up and kick his young sepia ebony black butt if he didn't.

[*He snatches the paper.*]

The hell with Jack Robinson. What's this paper got on us—me?

ROCKER: You ain't gonna find no better play than right here with us. Now, I can't say what else they doin' to Jack Robinson up there, but the boy played some ball with us in this league, so I ain't worried about him. He only been playin' there three or four weeks. You I am worried about.

[ROCKER *turns and points to the bench farthest left in the team room. Seated there, almost out of view, is* YOUNG BOY. *There is a shy innocence about him.*]

Come out here where we can see you.

SUGIE [*ignoring* YOUNG BOY]: How much time 'fore we get on the bus?

ROCKER: Where was you throwin' that ball out there today? We'd a had the runner if you'd brung the ball down about twelve feet. It almost cost us the game.

HENRY: I want a beer. [*To* SUGIE] You goin' to the store?

SUGIE [*rising to exit*]: Nope. The bus.

ROCKER [*lightly patronizing* YOUNG BOY]: The idea is to win ball games.

BELLMAN: Explain the game to him, Rock—

ROCKER: We play two games today. The first, here, which we won—

BELLMAN: It's over.

ROCKER: —and the second game we play in Mobile tonight.

BELLMAN: We ain't played that game yet.

ROCKER: You got to control that throw!

RUDY [*to* YOUNG BOY]: Remember what we told you, line it up.

LEWIS: They treatin' Jack Robinson pretty bad up there, I hear.

BELLMAN: So how'd you think they was gonna treat him?

HENRY [*to* YOUNG BOY]: Yo. Young Boy. Run to the store. We got a policy here, a rule you may have ain't read yet since you been here. Young boy on the team runs for beer after every game. Young boy goes and gets the beer.

[*Others nod.*]

True, boy.

YOUNG BOY: When this all start?

HENRY: It's been started. It's a tradition, though for a while we been overlookin' it.

[*Others nod.* YOUNG BOY *is tentative about the "tradition."*]

LEWIS: We'll all give you money.

HENRY [*to* YOUNG BOY]: You ain't think we were goin' to make you cover it. No, Young Boy, we all put in.

[HENRY *collects a few coins from each of the players. He gives them to* YOUNG BOY.]

There you go. You got some change in your hand now. You fly and we buy.

[YOUNG BOY *starts his exit.*]

Right fells, we buyin' and you is flyin'.

[YOUNG BOY *exits.*]

Ballantine boy! Or Jax! Don't come back here with none of that Florida pee water.

BELLMAN: Ballantine cost two cent a can extree.

HENRY: Boy don't know it but he flyin' and buyin'. He don't look like he be around here all too long anyways.

ROCKER: Boy got an arm like a rifle, but he got to control it.

RUDY: He's havin' a slow start. We all have had them.

LEWIS [*picking up the newspaper*]: There's got to be more colored playin' in the big leagues.

BELLMAN: The heck there does.

ROCKER: They got one. That's all they want.

HENRY: They got the wrong one at that.

LEWIS: I don't think I'd want to go nowhere where they don't want me.

BELLMAN [*disbelievingly*]: Shoot.

LEWIS: I ain't got no call to want nothin' what don't want me.

BELLMAN [*to* LEWIS]: If you want a good-lookin' woman and she don't want you, you still don't want her?

LEWIS: Nope, not if she don't want me.

ROCKER [*ignoring* BELLMAN *and* LEWIS]: Rudy, do you think Jack Robinson will keep makin' good?

BELLMAN [*incredulously*]: You don't want a good-lookin' woman?

LEWIS: Nope.

RUDY: The few times I saw him—he's—he's a good ballplayer. He can play.

[ROCKER *picks up a very large leather shoe from one of the stalls.*]

ROCKER: Where this come from?

SUGIE: That's Lewis's.

LEWIS: Uh-uh. That ain't mine, that's yours.

SUGIE: We picked it up. Somebody left it behind at some ballpark.

LEWIS: That clown team—

BELLMAN: Them foolish boys—

LEWIS: What's their team called? The Buffoons or Buffuns, some kind of dumb name—

ROCKER: Do they put feet in them things?

LEWIS: From up Memphis, ain't they?

[*He takes one of the shoes and puts his hat on sideways.*]

You put your hat on cock-square—and do a little jig.

[*He does a few steps.*]

SUGIE: And they play games looking like that.

ROCKER: That's mess to me.

[LEWIS *tosses the shoe back to* SUGIE.]

HENRY: I remember Jack Robinson, too, and he ain't look that good to me. To tell the truth, I ain't think he was even the best on Kansas City when he was playin' there.

LEWIS: Can you imagine, every time he gets up to bat, somebody's callin' him a name.

ROCKER: Got to be Christian.

LEWIS: Got to be crazy.

BELLMAN [*to* LEWIS]: What, you ain't been called no names?

LEWIS: If somebody called me nigger every time I got up—

BELLMAN: Somebody called you a nigger every time what? You'd keep right on playin'. Man been callin' you that word since you come out your mama. You'd get used to it.

ROCKER: What time we headin' out?

RUDY: Four o'clock.

ROCKER: I'm takin' these old bones to the bus.

BELLMAN: Me, I'd rather play in Mexico or stay all the time in Cuba like we do in the winter before I'd want to play with the white boys. I'm going to Mexico next year anyways. They're payin' good money. Mexicans and Cubans treat you all right. I'm goin'.

ROCKER: Wake me up when we get to Mobile. If Young Boy ever gets back, put my beer in my glove. Don't drink it.

[ROCKER *exits.*]

LEWIS: Name-callin' or not, it must be somethin' to be playin' in the big leagues. At least you stay in them fancy hotels. They ain't sleepin' on no bus. I hear they got beds two feet thick and soft as a fat gal's butt. And all of them got a new car. I seen them boys when they come down here.

RUDY: We got cars, Lewis.

LEWIS: Not like the cars I seen them boys drivin'. Big spankin' new car cars. I seen one with a span' new Cadillac. New! A '47! Pure white with silver all around. V-8. We got buggies, Rudy. This man had a car.

BELLMAN: Mexico is so where I'd go if I wasn't playin' here. Good money, pretty gals.

RUDY: Mexico is not a bad deal from what I hear.

BELLMAN: Shoot no.

LEWIS: Maybe you'll tell me somethin' 'bout this Mexico idea. I can't speak none of that shit stuff—Spinach.

BELLMAN: We get our third banner, and I'll be gone. If we don't, I'll still go. Only my gal friends is keepin' me here now, and I might cut them loose.

LEWIS: I hope we do win three. That would be nice.

BELLMAN: Nice? You see all of them gals who come around after we won our second banner? Woooeee. That's why I'm here.

LEWIS: Gals do treat you better when you win. Most niggers can't win at nothin'. Them gals meetin' men who ain't nothin'.

BELLMAN: Well, I don't know about this, Lewis. But here we are champeens twice, and we gettin' twice as much sugar. I can't handle twice. Three times is like to kill me—or my johnson. And if he dies, I better be dead.

LEWIS: They do like themselves a Montgomery King!

BELLMAN: These women—they ain't used to meetin' a man who is at the top of his profession. Most women ain't got a whole lot to choose from when it comes to champeens. [*To* LEWIS] Do you care why they like you?

[LEWIS *first shakes, then nods, his head.*]

LEWIS: Jack Robinson must be havin' a time with the ladies.

BELLMAN: I ain't doubt it. Only colored in the league and all, I suspect he's got his share.

HENRY: He's married. Wife and boy.

BELLMAN: Is that right? Oh. Too bad. 'Cause I know it's out there for him if he wanted it. But, if he's like me, he don't mess around on his main woman. No sir.

RUDY: You a dog, Bellman.

[*Players laugh and tease* BELLMAN *as* SAM *enters.*]

SAM: I hate to see a group of grown men sittin' around doin' nothin'. What are you still doin' dillydallyin' around here. Bus is ready to pull out.

LEWIS: I thought it don't leave until four.

SAM: Four, huh? How in hell do you expect to get to Mobile by tonight? We got to get that bus goin' like lightnin' as it is. You the only ones left? Let's move. Where's Young Boy?

HENRY: We sent him to the store.

SAM: Sent him? He's the rookie on this team, but he's still a equal like every-man else. He's got trouble enough without you all runnin' him for errands.

How long did he leave? He ain't here, he ain't goin'. Are you goin' to leave them bats here, Mr. Fowler? Then load 'em on the goddamn bus. You's actin' like you's won it all. First place this time of year don't mean nothin'. We got a few games more, then you act lazy.

[RUDY *remains as the players exit.*]

Rudy, you're team captain. Keep some standards set for them, why don't you? Sittin' around here—I know you all sent that boy off there for beer and they can drink it after the late game. They ain't going to drink it before. You don't maintain discipline, you know what'll happen. You got a job in this, too. Bullshootin'—shootin' the shit. All I hear when I walk in here—talkin' women, broke-down cars, and the Robinson boy—everything but what they're here for. You're their captain, Rudy—talk about what's going on here.

[YOUNG BOY *enters carrying a package of beer bottles.*]

Bus is leavin' now, boy. Get your gear. Come on, move it. You better learn somethin'—first place this time of season don't mean nothin'. Nobody drinks them beers until after the game.

[YOUNG BOY *hurries out with the package and his gear.*]

Any other year, maybe I wouldn't care neither, but this season they got a chance at history. Three championships, Rudy, that's what I want. Drinkin' before a game. Rudy, you know better.

RUDY: Heck, I wasn't drinkin', Sam. They thought they had some time.

SAM: In this hot weather? You drink one now, game time they'll be half asleep. Coloreds is like Indians, they can't hold no liquor. Just like Indians.

[*Lights fade as* SAM *and* RUDY *exit. The deep rumble of the bus engine is heard.*]

Start it up, driver! Let's move.

[*Music from the last stanza of the national anthem—"and the home of the brave"— fades as lights rise on the dugout, where* ELROD *is seated. He wears the uniform of the Montgomery Kings. He wears his uniform and cap constantly throughout the season. He is seated alone, as it is his nature to be by himself. He addresses players both on and off the field. Sometimes he speaks to himself. Today he yawns and dozes.* SUGIE, *poised as the on-deck batter, tosses a baseball glove at* ELROD's *head before sprinting to the batter's box (offstage).*]

ELROD: What?! OK, let's go. Let's go. Come on, Rudy! Come on, Rudy—

[*Someone at the unseen end of the dugout yells, "You fool, that's Sugie! Fool."*]

What? "Come on, Sugie!" That's what I said—"Come on, Sugie." I ain't say "Rudy." Yes, I said "Sugie"! Yes, I been sayin' "Sugie"! Yes, I am awake!

[ELROD *returns his attention to the game.*]

Come on, Sugie—damn you. We're up by eight runs—

[*Loud crack of the bat.*]

—nine. Yes, Sugarman, good hit. We got another run—damn—ten runs ahead—15 to 6. Why don't you all go home—let me go home. Ain't nobody here. [*Yawning*] She is, huh—sittin' up behind me? She is sittin' right up behind me in the stands, and you want me to look, huh? You want me to turn around and look, huh? What's Lena Horne doin' at a baseball game—with no clothes on? Oh, she *looks* like Lena Horne. And you look like a big black mule. Three games we played today—two yesterday—two Friday. Ain't we got nobody who can make an out? Young Boy is up. Let me get my stuff. We goin' home.

[*He sees* YOUNG BOY *swing and shakes his head.*]

Good swing, Young Boy! Shoot—damn, Young Boy cain't buy a hit. Most of these folks gone home. There wasn't too many folks today, was there?

[*Pause.*]

Mmmmmph. Least he let the umpire do the callin' on that pitch. All right, I'll be quiet. Let me hush. *What you swingin' at, Young Boy!?* How did he get on this team?

[YOUNG BOY *strikes out.*]

He's gone. Yeah, all right, it's almost over. We gonna win this one like we're goin' to win all this year. Three championships. Ain't nothin' changes. Not around here. And it's a good thing it don't.

[ELROD *exits as light fades on the dugout and the voices of* HENRY, LEWIS, *and* SUGIE *are heard approaching. Lights rise on the open path area downstage. It is early evening and the players are dressed to go to a local colored roadhouse.*]

HENRY: I'm telling you—Brooklyn Dodgers or no, the boy ain't that good. Yo, he only went one for twelve against the Cardinals over the weekend. One for twelve. One stinkin' hit in twelve times at bat. Give me a chance, I'd show them what a colored man can do.

LEWIS: He got more than one hit.

HENRY: You sayin' the paper's lying? One hit. Me and Sugie played against him. Tell him, Suge, when Robinson was playing in the league here. I'm the pitcher and he ain't do a gotdamn thing off my ball, he'd swing, nothin', swing. Not a gotdamn thing. Tell him.

SUGIE: He was a good ballplayer, Henry. He wasn't the best I ever seen, but he was all right.

HENRY: Shoot. I don't want to hear it. I can put Robinson in my back pocket and you can, too. He's so good that's why they lookin' for somebody else.

LEWIS: Huh?

SUGIE: You sure you heard right on this?

LEWIS: What you talkin' about? Somebody comin' down here?

HENRY: Lewis, this might be better if we keep it on the quiet for a while—

SUGIE: I don't believe it. They actin' like they don't want to keep the one colored they got. Why they goin' to now look for somebody else.

HENRY: Maybe they ain't satisfied with the one they got. One hit in twelve times up?

LEWIS: Who, Henry? Which one?

HENRY: Boston Red Sox. They already had a man lookin' at our games. We don't want to spill this out, Lewis, not just yet. Some of the fellas might not—do well, knowing this type of information. But I figure y'all can know.

LEWIS: You sure, Henry? Where you hear this?

HENRY: They have already been here. They have seen us play. Look, my sister cleans up at the Claxton Hotel. She heard the man when he checked out yesterday. He said he was from the Boston Red Sox—he was lookin' at ball-players—and he said he'd be comin' back from time to time. She told me before we got on the bus to come here.

SUGIE: He supposed to be here in Birmingham?

[HENRY *shrugs.*]

LEWIS: He said he was lookin' for colored?

HENRY: He didn't say he wasn't. He *was* in Montgomery.

SUGIE: Montgomery got a white team, too.

HENRY: Ain't none of theirs goin' no place. My mama would call them white boys "wasted white." They white boys but they might as well be niggers. No, they ain't goin' nowhere.

LEWIS: He say he saw us yesterday? I got two hits yesterday.

HENRY: He'll be seeing us again anyway if he didn't.

SUGIE: I still don't know what to make of this. First, when they got Robinson I thought we'd all be up there, since they first signed him, and ain't nobody else up there. Nobody but a couple of fellas in their what-they-call minor league. And I ain't goin' to sign up for no minor league.

LEWIS: This fella you talkin' about say minor league?

SUGIE: We makin' more money here than they do in their minor league. Heck, we got some of their major-league boys beat on that score—with our exhibition money and down in the islands in the winter—

LEWIS: I don't want to play in no minor league myself. Colored or white.

HENRY: Keep on the quiet.

SUGIE: I tell you, most times I think we're better off here.

[SUGIE *sees* BELLMAN *approach.* BELLMAN *enters, dressed in the best finery of 1947. His appearance is resplendent.*]

BELLMAN: Who's better off what? Ain't nobody better off than what you see here.

LEWIS: Go on, Barkum!

SUGIE: You bought that suit.

BELLMAN: Of course I did. You think they just give it to me 'cause I'm good-lookin'?

SUGIE: You knew I was fixin' to get one like that.

BELLMAN: Yeah, yeah. You been fixin' to get a whole lot of clothes, but you keep wearin' them. [*With disgust at* SUGIE's *appearance*] You goin' to the place lookin' like that? Boy, how long you been with this team, you ain't in the cotton no more—you a professional ballplayer. Take him home, I ain't goin' nowhere with him.

SUGIE: I look fine. I'm OK.

BELLMAN: Uh-uh. I look fine. Their two suits is OK. You a mess. Go on back to the hotel.

SUGIE: These clothes is fine. Besides, we in Birmingham, we ain't in Chicago. Gals here go for me if I was in my drawers. Matter of fact, we'll be in Chicago next week, then you'll see me in some clothes. I got my eye on that same suit.

BELLMAN: Brother Brookfield, Chicago is not the place to start lookin' good. You got to start lookin' good in the smaller cities and towns. Chicago is like New York. They are the top-tip. This is a new suit and I am wearin' it tonight in Birmingham. I don't have to. I could wear any of my twenty-one other suits, but I am startin' it off in Birmingham because next week it will be in Chicago. And I want it to be ready. Do you understand?

HENRY: Where are we goin' anyways?

LEWIS: We goin' to that same piccolo joint, Bark?

BELLMAN [to SUGIE]: You are on a team called the Kings. It is important that you dress like one. Look at the way you dress. Do you make your own clothes? Do you find them? You don't buy 'em, do you? Somebody better burn that store down.

LEWIS: Let's go, y'all. That same joint, Bark, Chrystals?

SUGIE: Get off me.

BELLMAN: Yeah, Chrystals.

HENRY: We go there every time we're in this town. Let's go someplace else, why don't we.

LEWIS: I like Chrystals. Them gals don't never see no ballplayers in there. Every time we go in, we is set.

BELLMAN: Brother Lewis, we are set wherever we go. We are the Kings. [To SUGIE] Let's me and you take a walk back to the hotel. I might got somethin' you can put on.

SUGIE: You ain't dressin' me.

BELLMAN: No, I'm not. You going to dress yourself. But you ain't goin' nowhere with me wearing that boll weevil jacket. Now come on to the hotel. Be glad we in a town where we got a hotel to stay. Least you can do is look right. You on the best team there is and you can't look no better? Stoner is payin' you, ain't he?

LEWIS: We'll see y'all up at Chrystals.

BELLMAN: Rudy says he's comin'—and Young Boy. [To SUGIE] You walk on up ahead. I don't want to be seen with you.

SUGIE: You ain't got no twenty-one suits.

[SUGIE exits.]

BELLMAN [calling after SUGIE]: No, I got more. But your woman is holdin' some of them for me at her house—for when I stop by.

[SUGIE returns and grabs BELLMAN in a threatening bear hug.]

[Diffusing the situation] I'm only joshin'. Let's go. You know a tease, don't you?

[SUGIE and BELLMAN exit.]

LEWIS: Barkum is crazy for lookin' good, ain't he?

HENRY: Yeah. But I don't know why any of us wants to look so good for some of the joints we go to.

LEWIS: What's wrong with where we go? Chrystals is nice. Like Barkum says, we got Chicago, Kansas City, New York. We go to some nice places.

HENRY: Nice colored places.

LEWIS: I like 'em fine. As long as there is girls. Like we say, they do like them a Montgomery King.

HENRY: Yes, they do. But guess awhile about how much they might like you if you was a Brooklyn Dodger?

LEWIS: Hmmm. I don't know though. We doin' pretty good. There ain't many colored men makin' the money we do. Folks like us wherever we go. At least the colored do.

HENRY: Don't always be willing to settle on colored, Lewis. We're better than colored. That fella from Boston takes a good look at us, he'll know what I mean.

LEWIS: Maybe. But I bet he don't show. I remember two years ago when they first signed Jackie and we all thought they'd be comin'. Ain't nobody showed.

HENRY: He will come, Lewis. They all will come. You see, they know some of us can play with them. Maybe not all of us, but some. They got Jack Robinson but they know there is better ones right here.

LEWIS: Do you know what this here Boston team might be lookin' for?

HENRY: I reckon a bat—they know we can run, heck, even Jack Robinson can run—a good bat, or an arm. Sam ought to be workin' us more at the plate, throwin' some more practice before games.

LEWIS: Oh, we're all hittin' pretty good. Don't get Sam started on workin' us to death. He'll do it.

HENRY: Work is what we need, Lewis. You want to look good out there, don't you? You're playin' pretty good, Lewis. You be just the one they see and grab Jack Robinson's job.

LEWIS: Go on, Henry. [*Laughs.*] Me playin' in the white league be like a kitty cat playin' in the doghouse. Meow. Woof. Woof. No—well, maybe. I believe I can now.

HENRY: Sure you can. A lot of us can, Lewis, if they let us. I ain't got no doubt.

LEWIS: I'm hittin' pretty good this year.

HENRY: Yes sir. I see you, Lewis. Doin' real well.

[HENRY *and* LEWIS *begin to exit downstage right.*]

Who we waitin' on? We might as well head on over.

LEWIS: I think we're waitin' on Rudy—and Barkum said Young Boy is comin'.

HENRY: Young Boy got clothes more like a boll weevil than Sugie. Come on, let's go. Rudy knows how to get there.

[*They leave as* YOUNG BOY *enters from downstage left entrance. He is dressed for a night on the town. Light holds on the clumsy* YOUNG BOY *for a few moments as he watches in silence as they leave without him. Light fades as he runs to catch up with them. In the dugout,* ROCKER *is seated as* ELROD *enters.* ELROD *stares ominously at* ROCKER.]

ROCKER: Ain't you up this inning? What's wrong with you?

ELROD: You know that's my seat.

ROCKER: Ain't you up this inning?

ELROD: How long you been seein' me in that spot? Since 1938, when I got here—eight years, minus two for the war. Now, I'd like to sit down.

ROCKER: You was probably sittin' in the war, too.

ELROD: I was sittin'—sittin' with a bazooka right in the heart of Germany with the Redball Express . . . fightin'est group of colored truckers this world will ever see. Baseball? Pssshaw, Redball. Someday, someway, somebody gonna tell what *we* did in the war.

ROCKER: Someday, someway.

[ROCKER *shifts to give* ELROD *his seat.*]

Meanwise, I got another proposition. Lend me some money.

ELROD: What? I'm talkin' about near dyin' in the world war and you're—

ROCKER: You ain't die, did you? You alive as me. Let me hold two dollars until Friday. I'm the one here's got a family. Maybes God let you live to be here to loan me a few dollars.

ELROD: Ain't you up this inning?

ROCKER: If you get a hit.

ELROD: I don't carry no money on the field.

ROCKER: Yes you do. It's in your shoe. Everybody knows where you put your money. . . ain't nobody stole it yet, has they?

ELROD: I ain't got but two dollars myself.

ROCKER: You got twelve dollars, at least. I saw you put it in your shoe. You might have more. I saw a ten and at least a couple of ones. I'm good for it, Elrod . . . you know me.

[ELROD *secretively withdraws money.*]

Thank you, Elrod. If I'd a known me and my wife was going to have eight children, I'd a named one after you.

ELROD: Lord knows you probably workin' on nine, so remember E-l-r-o-d.

ROCKER: Thank you kindly.

[*Loud crack of the bat.*]

Yes, Henry!

ELROD: Henry got a pretty fair bat these days.

ROCKER: He must want to make sure any big-league spies in the crowd, they see him.

ELROD: Spies.

[*They both chuckle.*]

And you say "crowd"? There ain't no crowd here today.

ROCKER: Wonder where they all are? It's a pretty nice day. [*At the field*] Look at him. Henry's waitin' on them there Boston folks.

ELROD: I ain't see 'em.

ROCKER: Neither me.

ELROD: Big league, shoot. What are we, the small-boy league? Our ball is fine with me.

ROCKER: Me too. My oldest boy has started to sayin' he wants to play up north. Boy knows more about Jack Robinson than he does me. He got a radio hooked up to hear their games. My wife says he cuts out darn near every word the papers got on the boy. She says she got to get to the paper first before he goes to cuttin' out pieces about Jack Robinson.

ELROD: Two kids I thought was after my autograph the other day asked me if I knew Jack Robinson.

ROCKER: What'd you tell them?

ELROD: Told them, "Yeah, I'm his brother."

ROCKER: You up next.

ELROD: I'm watchin'. Come on, Young Boy . . . *What you swingin' at, Young Boy?!* It's up to me.

[*He takes a few practice swings.*]

I'll show them the reason this team won two championships.

[*He starts for the batter's box.*]

Stay out of my seat.

[*Dugout darkens as lights rise on the team room.* LEWIS, SUGIE, *and* HENRY *are in the midst of a conversation.* BELLMAN *is seated off on a bench by himself.*]

LEWIS: You see that big old red-face man behind the backstop? Red-face man, white shirt, sittin' right close? He could have been somebody . . . maybe that Boston fella?

BELLMAN: He ain't nobody. He sells the pop and stuff to the refreshment stand. You all keep lookin' for Henry's man from the big leagues. We all heard about your man, Henry.

[HENRY *ignores* BELLMAN *but cuts a sharp look at* LEWIS.]

HENRY: I been keeping a look at the box on Boston to see where they might be needing the most help. Lewis, they got a boy playin' shortstop who ain't playin' too good. Oh for four Sunday, and the way I figure it, this boy ain't had but three hits in two weeks.

SUGIE: Looks good for you, Lewis. How's their fella at second base doin'?

HENRY [*checking the newspaper*]: Second? Man went four for four.

SUGIE: Four for four.

HENRY: That's a tough spot. He's good.

LEWIS: I'm glad I don't play there. Sounds like they are set at second.

HENRY: Bark, their man at third don't look too good from this here.

SUGIE: At second, how's his glove?

HENRY: It don't say.

BELLMAN: I don't know why y'all believe they got some different kind of game. I don't give a ding what they got. I told you, I'm going to Mexico . . . or the Caribbean. Mexico man's money better than colored or white.

SUGIE: Their boy's hittin' good, but I want to know how his glove is. You got to be able to field, too. A lot of folks can do one.

LEWIS: There was 'nother fella here today I noticed I ain't never seen before. Did you see a heavyset man in a blue shirt? Bright blue. Heavyset—

BELLMAN: Do you think every strange white man at our game got to be somebody?

HENRY: When we get back on the field, show me where he was sittin'. I might have seen him myself.

BELLMAN: Yo, what they got on our games in there? Read me somethin' on us.

LEWIS: This is the white paper. You know they ain't got nothin' on us, Bark. They say the man who owns the Dodgers—what's he called, Branch Rickey?— they say he's steady catchin' hell for puttin' Jack Robinson on the field.

HENRY: He ought to catch hell. He's playing a colored man on the field, but he's playin' the wrong colored man.

SUGIE: Let them look at us. We'll show them what we can do.

LEWIS: Who's better? Does Boston play Brooklyn?

HENRY: They're not in the same league.

LEWIS: Boston be the best all around, if they had some coloreds.

[ROCKER, RUDY, and SAM enter. They are all dressed in uniform.]

SAM: All right, you all quiet down.

LEWIS: Coach, you got any word on a fella from Boston seeing today's game?

SAM: Who?

[HENRY and SUGIE try to hush LEWIS.]

LEWIS: The Boston Red Sox are comin' here—

HENRY: There's supposed to be a man coming around looking for colored ball-players.

SAM: Good for him. Put the paper away and listen up.

[Some of the players continue to talk softly.]

I said shut up. You want to talk about playing with white boys, you do it on your time, not this team's. Are you playing white boys this evening?

[All are quiet as SAM takes center position.]

We are in first place. Lord knows why—and we don't deserve it—and we ain't going to stay in first place unless some changes—attitude changes—are made around here. Them two champeenships we got didn't come easy, or from any one man on this team. They come from the work of all of you all. You are a team, but I am starting to see some misdirection in you. You are acting less than yourselves. You're not pulling for the next man. You are showing bad signs—of a lack of team pride. My job is to maintain you all as a group, keeping you all pullin' towards the same goal. Ain't nothing else that happens got beans to do with our job. Lots of clubs go right down the pipe when they stop pulling together. It ain't going to happen here.

[Pause.]

On the field, it's each of y'all's responsibility to work as a unit. Each man pulls for the next. No letup, Fowler. Pride and discipline. Off the field, pride and discipline. Rocker, no drinking unless you are inside an establishment. I seen you and I won't have it. Brookfield, you are to be dressed well at all times. I mean decent. Simmons, I don't want to see no undershirts or bare nothin' when you are off the bus—it ain't never too hot. On the road all this goes doubled. Play up to your best and act your double best. You wear a King uniform. You ain't a clown team. You are an ambassador out there. You represent the team and all the colored in this city. Any man who can't follow these rules is a man I don't want. We want to win. We want to do ourselves proud, and we want to keep folks coming to the ballpark.

[*He is about to leave.*]

Mason group has invited us all to their lodge for late supper after our next game. I want us all there. Savannah ain't here yet. Their bus broke down. Probably be here in a couple hours.

[SAM *exits.*]

RUDY: Coach Sam has spoken.

BELLMAN: What's he hollerin' for? We in first place, ain't we?

ROCKER: Eatin' with the Masons tonight ain't a bad deal. This is what I like about our league. Somebody's always feedin' us. By the by, the lady bring over any more of them church cookies?

RUDY: So you think this here Boston fella is gonna come sign you all up.

BELLMAN: I ain't seen no Boston man.

ROCKER: They lookin' to find somebody for Jack Robinson to talk to.

[*He continues his search for cookies.*]

We can play with anybody.

SUGIE: Ain't nobody arguin' here.

ROCKER: Shoot, we been provin' this in exhibitions for years.

BELLMAN: They barnstorm on us and we keep rainin' hell back.

RUDY: Why y'all sniffin' up to play in them big leagues?

BELLMAN: 'Cause they's white and we is colored. What other reason niggers got to run out on their own?

HENRY: I want to show them what a colored man can do is all. You all know the boy they got ain't the one who should be representin' us. I want folks to know how good a ball we play here in our league. We're the ones who's the best—and I'm with Sam on what he said about what we got to be doin'. We got to play hard and best, we can't let up.

ROCKER: You all done eat up them church cookies.

HENRY: I'm with Sam on that score. We all ain't pullin' our weight around here. If this Boston fella is lookin' for players, we got to show him something.

BELLMAN: To hell with what he's lookin' for. He'll see a team what knows how to win.

ROCKER: Pure and simple—I shoulda been the one done the integratin'.

HENRY: Hey, if this fella's goin' to be here, maybe for the next game, why don't we get in a little practice session—some workout before the game? Savannah ain't here yet, we got time.

ROCKER: We know how to play ball, Henry. I'm goin' to try and find one of them churchwomen to bake me some more of them cookies. My woman cannot make a decent cookie to save her life.

BELLMAN: Why don't you come help me fix my car now like you said? You know cars.

ROCKER: I'm lookin' for cookies.

BELLMAN: Hell with a cookie! You said you'd work on my car—and you owe me some money, don't you? Yeah—and you ain't pay Elrod back, neither. I'm gonna remind him, too.

[ROCKER *goes reluctantly.*]

It's parked out back. Come on!

[ROCKER *turns.*]

Please!

[BELLMAN *and* ROCKER *leave.*]

HENRY [*as* BELLMAN *and* ROCKER *leave*]: What about some workout—? Rudy, you're team captain. Can't you get them to work out for a time?

RUDY: Man's home for one day, Henry, he wants to get his car fixed. Everybody ain't here anyway.

HENRY: Maybe the four of us—

RUDY: I'm going over and give Sam a hand on his clerical work—he's gettin' backed up. Like you say, I am team captain.

[RUDY *leaves.*]

HENRY: Everybody got time for everything except making us look like bigleague ballplayers.

SUGIE: Henry, you really guess this Boston fella is comin'?

HENRY: I know he is.

SUGIE: You say they ain't got the right shortstop.

HENRY: Not according to the paper. He ain't got no bat.

LEWIS [*with satisfaction*]: That's my spot.

SUGIE: And the man at my slot, second base, he's hittin'. That ain't right. I ain't never hit less than .300 in my life and they got a man in my slot. You still want to get in some workout, Henry? Before the game? Maybe pitch to each other—hit a few balls on the ground. Least we can keep sharp for the game.

[SUGIE *and* HENRY *exit the team room.* LEWIS *rushes to join them.*]

LEWIS: Hey, that's my spot!

[LEWIS *exits. Lights rise on the coach's office.* SAM *is rummaging through his bookkeeping.* RUDY *walks up the steps to the office and enters. Music on the radio plays softly, then fades.*]

SAM: We got to cut down on expenses. Equipment, transportation, that bus, you boys. This stuff adds up, Rudy. We got to pay for this.

[*He hands* RUDY *some files.*]

Look these figures over for this month, will you? Folks ain't comin' out for the games like they should be. Smaller towns ain't been bad, but some of our stops—smallest cut we had there since I can remember.

[*He hands* RUDY *more paper.*]

RUDY: A lot of folks still lookin' for work since the war, Sam.

SAM: I ain't blaming nobody for working or lookin' for work.

[*He tosses more files at* RUDY.]

One thing I've learned, Rudy, folks will come if you give them a good game. Stoner, our big-time Negro owner, he's back on his publicity thinkin'. Tells me he wants to start using all this commotion around this Jack Robinson. He tells me he wants to start publicizing you boys is on your way to the big leagues—the next Jack Robinsons. Thinks more folks will come out if we publicize that way. He got plans to build a bigger ballpark, a stadium maybe. May be talk, may be what we do, we'll see. He figures this should be our best year.

RUDY: Stoner's a hard man to make a few dollars. Stoner and attendance.

SAM: We'll give him good baseball. We got a reputation here, Rudy. Folks come to see our games, they see a good game—and they keep comin' back. Couple of years ago, attendance numbers started slippin', and Stoner come up with another big idea. He wanted to change our uniform, paint us up to look like clowns. I said we got plenty of clowns all right, but this team ain't gonna be one. I said you want a clown team, you go off and get a clown team—they are out there. But on this team and in this league, there ain't going to be no circus. I won't have it. A lot of folks that don't know us think that's all we got anyways. A few weeks later, the attendance numbers go up—Stoner shuts up. Because we was winnin'. Took the first of our two banners that year. That's the reputation I want.

[*He tosses* RUDY *another sheet of paper.*]

RUDY: What do you want me to do with this?

SAM: Look it over.

[SAM *reaches for a bottle and offers* RUDY *a drink.*]

Some 'shine?

[RUDY *declines.*]

I ought to get some gal in here to take care of this stuff. You know when I first come in the league, we didn't have this kind of bookwork. We had a schedule—a piece of paper. Which didn't mean nothin' 'cause we was stoppin' anyplace anybody had a challenge. And sometimes, if we had a game Monday and we didn't get there to Tuesday, heck, that was fine. But now we're organized. We got a game date, we get there. White folks ain't the only ones who can organize. And as far as this league is concerned, I'll wager you can't find one operation run by colored or Negroes which has got the organization we got. In this country! I'll bet you.

RUDY [*still examining the papers*]: Looks OK to me, Sam.

SAM: This league has come a long way, Rudy—and there ain't all that much we're having to rely on from them folks these days. Look at what we're doing with rooming. Sure, there's times we're sleepin' on the bus. What colored man ain't—in a bus or in his car—they don't want us. But we got it mapped out now with knowing where a colored rooming house is set up almost every two hundred miles. Way I figure, we ain't never no more than four or five hours from a place to sack out for the night, if we want. People put a door in your face, you go around it. It ain't perfect, but it's gettin' better, Rudy.

RUDY: Your figures seem OK.

SAM: You know some of the teams are having trouble keeping together ever since this Robinson thing. We got some who think the floodgates are going to open up for everybody to go pourin' in. Two weeks ago, the Monarchs had to forfeit a game 'cause half their team ran off for a tryout they heard was going on. Forfeit their game. And the fellas who left for the tryout? They got there, and the white man told them to go home—said they heard wrong. If they want colored, and a colored player wants to play for them, fine, that's their business. But it ain't happening yet. Not enough to cause commotion and bust up our league.

[*He takes a drink.*]

Henry out there. Shut him up, why don't you. Runnin' his mouth about some Boston fella he heard supposed to be here any day now. We don't need no fairy talk on this team. We got a championship to win—and defend. There's two, I want the best one. Talk to them, Rudy, keep them occupied with winning ball games. It ain't always my position to tell them they can be the best, but you can. You know them rules of behavior I hollered at 'em? Well, I wrote them down. I'm posting them on the board first thing tomorrow.

RUDY: Sounds good to me.

[*Slight pause.*]

You through needin' me, Sam? If I get a minute, I want to run down to my place. My people say they ain't seen me in a month.

SAM: Sure.

RUDY: How's that new grandbaby?

SAM: He's sick. Daughter's watchin' him, they got a woman there with him, too. I trust he'll be fine.

[*Pause.*]

[*Softly*] Give me the papers.

[*He takes the files from* RUDY.]

RUDY: Still don't have much on where you're going to cut down.

SAM: I'll work somethin' out.

[RUDY *starts to leave as* SAM *begins to put away the files.*]

One more . . . one more matter, Rudy. Stoner wants me to consider letting a man go. You got any ideas?

RUDY: What? We got few enough as it is. Sam, we can't play another man shy.

SAM: I say the same. Sometimes I think Stoner's more interested in money than he is in winning. I'll figure it out—I don't want to lose another man. Go on, while you got time.

RUDY: Yeah, Coach. See you over at the field.

[RUDY *leaves as* SAM *stands silently for a moment.*]

SAM [*softly*]: Yeah.

[SAM *resumes tidying his files as light fades. Light brightens on the team room, where* LEWIS, HENRY, *and* BELLMAN *are seated. They are between games of a double-header and are only half undressed when* SUGIE *enters.* BELLMAN *watches as* LEWIS *and* HENRY *play cards.* SUGIE *comes in marching, singing a rhythmic military cadence.*]

SUGIE: Another game left to-day—your right. Another home run for me—tonight. One, two, three, four. One-two, three-four. Two games today, two games t'morry. If it wasn't fo' da money, I'd sho' be sorry! One, two . . .

[*He puts away his glove.*]

HENRY: You playin'?

SUGIE [*singing intensely and hovering over* LEWIS]: Playin' every day, playin' very ha-ard. Deal me a ca-aard, deal me a ca-ard. One, two . . .

LEWIS [*annoyed*]: Sit down, boy.

SUGIE [*still singing*]: Don't call me boy, I ain't yo' toy—

[HENRY *laughs as* SUGIE *begins to mock-strangle* LEWIS.]

   Break yo' head w-ide, the young man di-ied! One, two . . .

BELLMAN [*picking up the cadence*]: One, two . . . Sound off!

SUGIE: Yo' mama was home when you left—

BELLMAN [*marching*]: Your right!

[HENRY *joins the march.*]

SUGIE: Yo' sister was home when you left—

BELLMAN AND HENRY [*marching*]: Your right!

SUGIE: Yo' woman was home when you left—

BELLMAN AND HENRY [*marching*]: Your right!

BELLMAN [*breaking up laughing*]: Let's not talk about yo' woman—

SUGIE: Sound off!

SUGIE, BELLMAN, AND HENRY [*marching*]: One, two—one, two, three, four!

HENRY [*knowingly*]: And where did y'all get that tune?

SUGIE: U.S. Army, Service and Supplies!

BELLMAN AND HENRY: Your right!

SUGIE: We march fifty miles a day to that march.

BELLMAN: Don't make me remember.

[BELLMAN *and* SUGIE *shake hands as* SAM *enters unnoticed.* SAM, *carrying a handful of pay envelopes, looks toward the players, then looks at the bulletin board located at the rear of the team room. He takes his time as he distributes the envelopes to each man.*]

HENRY [*to* SUGIE]: Couple of hits make you feel good, huh?

SUGIE: Couple of home run hits do!

BELLMAN: You wasn't too bad in the field there—for a change.

HENRY: Reachin' left—reachin' right.

SUGIE: Why thank you, Henry, Bellman—

LEWIS [*interrupting*]: Some of them balls was pretty much my way, Sugie.

SUGIE: —I like to think I was doing my job.

[SAM *turns to the players and motions toward the bulletin board.*]

SAM: Did you all give this a gander?

LEWIS: What you got there, Coach?

SAM: Read it—all of you.

[LEWIS *gets up from the card game and walks to the bulletin board.*]

It's the rules. They been up there all day.

SUGIE: Why ain't nobody posting over averages on the board? I been hittin' every day for two weeks, Coach.

HENRY: I know why our averages ain't being posted around here. Old Sam's trying to save someone from being embarrassed.

SAM: Mind your own business. There is somethin' more important up there for you to read.

SUGIE: When my average is up, I want to see it up.

HENRY: Some folks on this team might be cryin' if they see on paper what they been hittin'.

BELLMAN: Or what they ain't been hittin'. They ain't talkin' about you, Lewis.

SAM: I said mind y'alls own business. I manage this team. Read them rules.

SUGIE: Everybody knows, Sam. Why not let the boy see for hisself.

BELLMAN: You didn't hit so good when you come in the league.

SUGIE: That ain't make no difference with old Coach Willy Goode, he put the numbers up.

SAM: Just abide by them rules up there.

HENRY: You see him that last time up? Three balls—not a strike on him—and he swings at the next three worst damn balls I ever saw. Least he could have walked. I don't think the boy's ever actually been to first base—has he? Sugie, why don't you walk Young Boy out to first base before the game? Show him where it is.

SUGIE [*jokingly taking a step forward*]: This is first base.

[*Others laugh.*]

SAM [*angrily*]: He's a rookie—just like you all once was. We give you time, we'll give him the same. Sugie, the bat you broke yesterday comes out of your pay.

SUGIE: What? What bat?

SAM: The bat you broke. That's three you broke this month. They ain't free.

SUGIE: It snapped right off in my hand!

SAM: That ain't no excuse. Every man here knows how to hold a bat properly 'cept you. Next man who breaks one pays for his, too.

SUGIE: Young Boy broke one—he going to pay for his?

SAM: Now how's that concern you?

SUGIE: I want to know we is all being treated equal.

SAM: You are. He broke one and you broke three. Is that equal? And why you got him on your mind all the sudden? One minute, if you're not wantin' to rub his nose in his mistakes, the next you want him to pay for the one bat he broke since he's been here—and you broke three.

[RUDY *and* YOUNG BOY *enter behind* SAM.]

Leave the boy be and tend to yourself. He'll work out fine.

[*He sees* YOUNG BOY.]

I told them—I'm telling everybody—next man who breaks a bat pays for it. [*To* YOUNG BOY] Goes for you, too.

[*He gives pay envelopes to* RUDY *and* YOUNG BOY *and starts to leave.*]

There's a notice on the board about behavior rules around here. Read it.

[*He turns before leaving.*]

You all keep winning and put some people in the stands, you won't have to be paying for no bats.

[*He exits.*]

SUGIE: Paying for broke bats. Don't that beat all.

BELLMAN: We hit a home run into a lake, we going to have to pay for the damn ball?

YOUNG BOY: I'm sorry if this is for what I did—

HENRY [*cutting him off*]: What he did. He ain't done nothin' since he been here, now he's worrying about something he did do. [*Laughs.*] He ain't going to Boston. No, Young Boy, don't none of this here concern you.

RUDY: You don't talk about the man like he ain't here, Henry.

HENRY: I didn't say nothin'—

SUGIE [*interrupting*]: It's Sam, Rudy! Paying for some damn bat! This team ain't got no money? We got to pay for a damn bat!

BELLMAN: You hold the bat right, you wouldn't pay for it. I could see that coming by the way you hold your bat.

RUDY: Sam's getting the squeeze from Stoner. Stoner wants to cut down spending.

SUGIE: So he takes money out of my pocket.

RUDY: It's either that—or cut a man down.

SUGIE: Well, that ain't no kind of fair—make me pay for gettin' a hit.

BELLMAN [*tossing a ball to himself*]: Just hold your bat right. You lucky the ball hits it anyway.

SUGIE: No, the only place they do this kind of mess is here with niggers.

BELLMAN [*continuing to toss the ball as he leaves*]: I'm hungry.

[BELLMAN *exits.*]

LEWIS: I ain't never heard of nobody paying for a bat before.

HENRY: Yo. Come on, let's us get in a few swings. I feel like throwing.

LEWIS: It's hot, Henry.

HENRY: Let's go—unless you want to be paying for bats for the rest of your life.

[*He beckons to* SUGIE.]

Sugie? We might be better off if they did cut a man.

[*He directs his attention to* RUDY.]

You and Jack Robinson going to stay here?

[RUDY *nods.*]

Suit yourself.

[SUGIE *grabs his glove and follows* HENRY *and* LEWIS *out. Offstage,* SUGIE *is heard laughing, "This is first base!" Others are heard laughing.* YOUNG BOY *is seated alone.* RUDY *stands, watching him silently.*]

RUDY: If you want, you can get a few swings in off my throws before the game.

YOUNG BOY [*pausing slightly*]: Thanks, Rudy.

RUDY: Yeah. Come on. I'll throw you some. Be good for you to get the feel of a few cracks with that big swing of yours.

[YOUNG BOY *remains seated.*]

You OK?

YOUNG BOY: Rudy—I ain't workin' out. I can't do it.

RUDY [*reassuringly*]: Being young boy with the Kings ain't the easiest place to be. You got to give yourself some time—Sam is—give yourself some. Heck, you're one of the youngest ever to make the team. You the youngblood. That's sayin' somethin', ain't it? You like being a King, don't you?

YOUNG BOY: You all are a great team, Rudy.

RUDY: All right then. And you are with us.

YOUNG BOY: I wished my whole life I could play with you all. I growed up just over the hill from Montgomery. My daddy—my daddy used to take me here.

RUDY: Yeah, he like to see you play?

YOUNG BOY: He ain't never seen me with the Kings before. He's old and he wants to, but he's got to keep back to the house. My daddy showed me how to play this game—but I think he taught me a whole lot better than what I been showin'. He told me better . . .

RUDY: Sounds like he played some ball himself.

[*Pause.*]

YOUNG BOY: He played for the Kings—right here. Don't nobody remember him. He was on the first Kings team there was. Sam heard of him. He was playin' good and somethin' bad started happenin' to his eyes. He got the blue in 'em, and his eyes went poorly. He don't see so good. He couldn't play ball no more so he went back to where he come from. He can't hardly see at all, even when I was little, but he could play with me. We had a stick and some twine that made an old ball, and he'd throw to me, and he made me play up to him. I wasn't any good then, but he showed me. He said I had to if I wanted to be a ballplayer special. He was good, Rudy. He got pictures of when he played—I got 'em. He was good—he was a King. Sam says it. My daddy wants to come to a game—to hear it, I guess. He said he's gonna come today. He always says it. My daddy—my father taught me, but I ain't doin' him right. Man who wears the uniform ought to contribute.

RUDY: Do you feel you'll get better?

YOUNG BOY: I do, Rudy.

RUDY: It ain't easy for nobody startin' out. Some of 'em been around here a long time and, for them, it still ain't easy—especially when you're trying to make your living like these fellas—like us, double especially, like us.

YOUNG BOY: But you all are winners. Before I got here you won two banners. I want to contribute for a third—and fourth and forever.

RUDY: Then don't try to do it all in one day, or one week, or one swing. We got one of us now up in what they call them major leagues—Jack Robinson. You think you got a load of troubles, at least you got your battle among your own. Your own don't hate you—they ain't supposed to. But him, he got folks hating him whether he gets a hit or no. We're all behind you. We are all the same, so we are with you.

[YOUNG BOY *rises as* RUDY *begins to walk with him to the door.*]

If you was a Japanee, or some Nazi trying to get back in the fight, we'd be gunning against you. But you're one of us, Young Boy, so don't worry, we'll stick with you. Your pops will, too.

[*As the two men leave,* RUDY *hands* YOUNG BOY *a bat. They exit as light dims on the team room and rises on the dugout.* ELROD *is seated alone in the dugout. He begins by extending his greetings to an unseen woman in the stands.*]

ELROD: How do! How do-de-do! [*To himself—and others*] You can't beat these gals in Savannah! They want themselves a gentleman. "Sweet baby blossom, let your hair down low. Pick up your dress, let your big legs show." Woman got thick legs. Thick. Like ham. More folks would have came out here today if they'd a known you was gonna be here. Somethin' about Georgia makes a woman different—fatter, sweeter. I'm going to marry me a Georgia woman—once I find one. Young Boy up. You got it, Young Boy.

[*Slight pause.*]

Sweet baby blossom—big, round, 'n' firm, nuff to make me squirm. Make you squirm. [*Leeringly*] How do—yes, yes. Must be one of them Savannah boy's woman, but why she lookin' so hard at me. They do like them a Montgomery King. [*Slightly under his breath*] How do. How do.

[*He sees he is being watched.*]

What's this Savannah first baseman lookin' at? Is he lookin' at me? Yes, he is—must be his woman. Better leave me to watch Young Boy strike out. Go, Young Boy . . . *What you swingin' at, Young Boy!?* . . . He ain't holdin' his hands right . . . you can see that.

[*His attention turns toward first base.*]

Don't keep your eyes over here at me! I'll bust you up and take your woman. Dingy-heady Negro. Come on, Young Boy! Put it to this Savannah fool . . .

[*Watching* YOUNG BOY *swing and miss, he shakes his head in disappointment.*]

Damn, Rudy got him using that big bat and it's too heavy for him. Ball ain't going to get no better than that. Come on, Young Boy! Show this pretty lady something. Show my woman—yeah, my woman—my squirmin' woman, you simpleminded Savannah fool! Yes she is! Show us, Young Boy! Show us—

[*Loud crack of the bat.*]

Goooooood Loorrd—good-bye!

[*Cheering crowd is drowning him out.*]

Reverend Abraham Absolom Jones Junior Young Boy! You see that, fool, even your woman is jumpin' for our Young Boy! Yes ma'am! You keep right on jumpin', darlin'. Right on!

[*Cheers continue as light fades on the dugout. Briefly, lights rise softly on the team, and* BELLMAN *can be seen congratulating and celebrating with* YOUNG BOY. *Light fades on team room and dugout.*]

ACT 2

[*A few weeks later, midsummer 1947, in the team room.* ROCKER, BELLMAN, *and* YOUNG BOY *are standing by the bulletin board. They are quietly reading an* Ebony *magazine article posted amid clippings from the* Montgomery Advertiser *and the* Alabama Journal. HENRY *silently watches them reading.* RUDY, *seated at the bench, is greasing his fielder's glove. All have just come in from a workout.*]

BELLMAN [*reading*]: *Ebony* magazine! Does this boy own all the colored papers and magazines?

RUDY: Got more stuff on Jack Robinson, huh?

BELLMAN: You can't turn around, you see his face on somethin' or another.

ROCKER: Here the cracker papers, too. I never seen them on our board. "The blue-black leopard." "Leopard"—them white papers always call him some kind of animal.

BELLMAN: What's this about "five more colored players are poised to enter organized baseball"?

HENRY: That's all of them that they got waitin' in their minor league. Their minor league ain't nothin'.

ROCKER: Jack Robinson.

[SAM *bounds into the team room.*]

SAM: All right, you all, good workout. Good workout!

BELLMAN: We ain't got enough games? We got to work out?

SAM: Keeping you in tune, Barkum, keeping you tip-top.

[ROCKER *and* YOUNG BOY *are still standing at the bulletin board.*]

What y'all got, a girly picture up there? [*Laughs.*] You ain't old enough, boy . . . Rocker, I told you about girly pictures and you . . . Get away from that wall, Rocker, before she jumps out and kisses you!

RUDY [*to* SAM]: You're feelin' good.

BELLMAN: He ain't been sweatin' in the sun.

[*There is a small commotion as* LEWIS *and* SUGIE *enter loudly.*]

SUGIE: Why don't you calm down, boy—

LEWIS: I know where I am, I know where you are!

SAM [*cutting them off*]: Listen up, you two.

LEWIS: I know what you're trying, Sugie!

SAM: Quiet up—you two talk later. [*To all the players*] Listen here. Good work-out. We needed it. Them Kansas City boys is staying close—no need for them to be on our necks—and Savannah ain't far behind. I want to get in one of these drills, maybe once a week.

BELLMAN: Sam, why the hell do we need to work out? We in first place.

HENRY: He told you. I been sayin' we need workouts all along.

BELLMAN [*to* HENRY]: We playin' two sometimes three games a day. How you figure we need workouts?

SAM: Bark, check your schedule. We got games coming up on the northern swing—and I don't want to break stride. Don't think them Giants is going to lay down for you. Black Giants is the ones we're most like to meet for the banner. They might be the ones stand betwixt us and three championships.

HENRY: Giants got an eight-game win streak, Sam. They're goin' to be tough.

SAM: Henry's right.

HENRY: This game ain't just the body, it's the mind, too. We got to think quick.

SAM: Right again. We got to show we got the stronger mind, too. Anyways, our World Series is still a ways down the road, but we're going to be ready.

[*He gets ready to leave.*]

Stoner ain't quieted down none, neither. He keeps bellyaching about atten-dance. But we'll take care of him, too. We get a eight- or ten-game string of wins together, we'll generate some excitement. He'll be turning folks away. We'll get folks back to the games. Boys, this is going to be like last season!

[*He turns to* YOUNG BOY *as he is about to leave.*]

You, mister—you're startin' to look like a ballplayer. It's about time.

[*Players acknowledge his progress.*]

Now, did you carry all the equipment off the field like you're supposed to?

[*Embarrassed,* YOUNG BOY *shakes his head.* SAM *replies with mock anger.*]

Get it!

[SAM *exits.* YOUNG BOY *follows hurriedly.*]

BELLMAN: Workout—I don't care what y'all say, I ain't for this.

RUDY [*smiling*]: Your bones can't make it, Bark?

BELLMAN: My bones? [*Grins.*] I'm out all night.

ROCKER: Ain't his bones. Is his bone.

BELLMAN: I found a cute little sugar lookin' for some King play. I stumbled into this. Big legged ... big hipped ... big tittied—I like 'em big or small—this gal wasn't foolin' ...

ROCKER [*sliding closer*]: This gal wasn't foolin'.

BELLMAN: And lookin' hard for a Montgomery King—any one of us—

ROCKER [*entranced*]: Any one of us.

BELLMAN: But I'm the only one out ... What am I gonna do? And I'm tired ... tired.

ROCKER: She must want the bone. Did you dog?

BELLMAN: Dog.

[*Slight pause.*]

You from the old school—that sounds nasty.

ROCKER: I mean did you dog? Like she the cat and you get that mouse she got and then you the big dog—and you commence to gettin' some kitty—

BELLMAN: You don't tell no woman today you want her mouse or her cheese—or she's some kind of cat. Times is changin', ol' Rock.

SUGIE: Rock, you don't ask for no mouse or no cheese.

BELLMAN: Some pussycat maybe. No, men are more sophisticated today. What you tell 'em, Suge?

SUGIE: You tell 'em you want they booty. Bootyful beautiful booty!

BELLMAN: Uh-uh, you take that booty, like you the pirate.

ROCKER: I say what I say.

BELLMAN: You a married man. Why you talkin' about these matters?

ROCKER: I am married, but I ain't dead.

BELLMAN: You like to scare your woman with your nasty ways. That's why you ain't gettin' none. Correct me, you with eight kids, you gettin' more from Clarisse than you need or less than you want, one.

[ROCKER *laughs.*]

Last night, I was tired, yes. But I did it for the team—for you all.

LEWIS [*confronting* SUGIE]: You got a problem remembering where you supposed to be playin'? You play second base—balls hit to me at shortstop is played by me. If you'd a done that in a real game, we'd a lost two runs.

SUGIE: You couldn't make the play. I crossed because you couldn't make it. Who got the ball? Answer me that. Who got the ball?

LEWIS [*angrily*]: You play second base. The shortstop on this team is me.

SUGIE: Don't tell me where I am. Boy, I'm the one played shortstop here before you ever got to this team. Don't tell me "I play second base and you play shortstop." I'll be going to anywhere the gotdamn ball is and I can make the play. Heck, I got the chance, you might just see me go from second out to the gotdamn left-field fence.

RUDY: Calm down, Sugie, Lewis—

LEWIS: Boston team ain't lookin' for no second baseman, that's why you're on my spot.

SUGIE: I know where I play. You better work on your own ability. Like Sam and Henry say, you one of them here need to be workin' out.

HENRY: Lewis, Sugie make a good play on the ball. Let's leave it at that. I seen it, it was out of your range.

LEWIS: Out of my what—

HENRY: Man closest to the ball is always the one who should get it. Plain and simple. [*To* SUGIE] You looked good out there. You could be teaching Jack Robinson a few tricks.

LEWIS: You ain't doing nothin' I can't do! I know what he's up to. Henry tells him Boston Red Sox need a shortstop and he's tryin' to move me out. He knows them Red Sox ain't lookin' for no second base, they got one.

SUGIE: Talk to me, if you want to talk.

LEWIS: I ain't saying nothin' but what I know.

ROCKER: Leave it be, y'all.

HENRY: It's competition, Lewis. It makes everybody work a little harder at their jobs. That's all.

LEWIS: Boston ain't lookin' for no second baseman and he knows it. You want the white man to see you, don't you? See you at my spot. Why don't you get on off the Kings and go play someplace else? Kings don't need you.

SUGIE: Kings don't need a man who can't do his job.

BELLMAN: Oh shit.

[LEWIS *lunges at* SUGIE, *but he is caught by* RUDY.]

RUDY: You all hush up! Y'all know where you play. Lewis, you're our shortstop, and, Sugie, you play second base. Y'all trifling over nothin'.

HENRY: The real idea here is to practice! Keep having workouts to improve at our positions individually. That's the way you're going to get better.

LEWIS: Ain't nobody better at my spot but me!

BELLMAN [*overlapping*]: Forget this workout mess. I play games!

ROCKER: We just had one extree workout.

HENRY [*cutting them off*]: We need more. Every game we ought to be doin' more.

BELLMAN: You ain't the one to be calling workouts. That's Sam's job, or Rudy's.

HENRY: Sam's the one who called today's workout.

RUDY: Then let Sam call another one, and only Sam. He seemed satisfied.

BELLMAN [*to* HENRY]: You ain't the leader here.

[*Momentary silence.*]

RUDY [*to* LEWIS *and* SUGIE]: You all know where you play now? Right? We ain't gonna win no kind of championships if you don't stay together. Sugie, we in the Negro League—you better be playin' for them colored folk. Lewis, come on with me and fix up some chow for the ride tonight. We ain't gonna have no time later.

[*He starts to leave.*]

The rest of you ought to do the same. We're ridin' long tonight. C'mon, Lewis.

[*He leaves as* LEWIS *begins to lace up his civilian shoes.*]

ROCKER: Ride, ride, ride . . . don't you wish we had an aeroplane?

BELLMAN: Amen.

HENRY: You all have to wait for Sam to call a workout every time we need one?

BELLMAN: Rock? After our next banner, I'm going to see if they do this much ridin' in Mexico.

LEWIS: Henry, your workouts are for you. You pitch and you want all the swings. We throw balls to you. We catch balls you hit. Only one getting any practice out there is you.

[*He finishes lacing his shoes.*]

Here on, I'm working out only when Sam calls it. Don't ask me to work out with you no more.

[*He rises and leaves.*]

HENRY: Suit yourself, Lewis. You don't need no practice. You're the best there is.

SUGIE [*smiling sarcastically*]: He an all-star almost every year, ain't he?

ROCKER: Will you all quit quibblin'. There's talk around here like we're some kind of dog team. We in first place still.

HENRY: Yes, we're in first place. But that fella from the Boston Red Sox might not care what place we're in. He wants to see the best ones we got and we want to show him what we got.

ROCKER: Boston, huh? [*Chuckles softly.*]

BELLMAN: There he come with the invisible man again.

HENRY: He's coming, Barkum.

BELLMAN: I ain't seen him, Henry. Where is he? He over in your room?

[ROCKER *laughs.*]

Henry got Red Sox on his brain. We ain't playin' for no Red Sock, Henry. Man who pays my salary name is Stoner—yours, too. Little black-face bald man—you seen him? He got half a dozen funeral homes and one baseball team. Ain't nobody gettin' a pay envelope from nobody else. Red Sox. You know where I believe your Boston man is, Henry? Boston.

[BELLMAN *and* ROCKER *roll with laughter.*]

HENRY: You're a clown, Barkum. Just like one of them damn circus fools. This game is just a big damn joke to you.

BELLMAN: I can't laugh if I want to? Who you, the sheriff? Sheriff Henry.

HENRY: I ought to be your damn daddy, if you don't begin to take this game seriously—

BELLMAN [*overlapping, smiling*]: Sheriff Henry. You going to fire me? Huh, Sheriff? Sheriff Henry going to fire me.

HENRY: Why we always got to be the fool? Them suits you got—white man laughs at you just for the way you look. You need a damn daddy.

[*Short pause.* BELLMAN *lunges at* HENRY. *He is restrained by* ROCKER.]

BELLMAN: Who you talking "daddy" to me? My father's name is Whitlow Barkum and you don't look a damn sight like him. You might can bust over someone else's head round here, but you ain't bustin' over mine, boy. You can wait on this Red Sock peckerwood all you want, but I ain't waitin' for no man to tell me what I am.

HENRY: All I'm saying is we got to keep sharp. We got to play hard.

BELLMAN: For who!?

ROCKER [*to* HENRY]: Playin' hard don't mean forgettin' who we are. We as good as any team there is. You ain't the one to be telling a man who is serious and who plays hard. That's Sam's job—not yours. Far as I'm concerned, them folks ain't want me when I started out, and I ain't dreamin' to play for them now. Quiet down your bickerin' and tend to your jobs of winnin' this league's title again.

[*He begins to coax* BELLMAN *out.*]

C'mon, let's rustle up some food for the ride tonight. Y'all remember, we got a champeenship to win. This year ain't over yet.

[ROCKER *and* BELLMAN *exit.*]

SUGIE: They were getting pretty tough on you.

HENRY: You too. Sugie? I will never understand us. Sometimes I wonder how we ever got what little we have.

SUGIE: I don't think they believe anybody's goin' nowhere—or anybody's lookin' at us.

[*Short pause.*]

HENRY: You looked good out there today. You could have taught Jack Robinson a lesson.

SUGIE [*laughing*]: I don't know . . .

HENRY: Really. I seen him play. They had him at shortstop when he first broke in—down here. But he couldn't handle it. You got better hands. You move the ball better.

SUGIE: They say he's pretty fast.

HENRY: I'm faster than him, and I know he can't throw a curveball. A pitcher is a lot more valuable to a team than what he's doing. A lot of us is fast as him—and plenty faster.

SUGIE: Like I say, I can't remember much of him playin' when he was in the league, but the way I feel—I'm playin' good ball.

[*Light dims gradually on* SUGIE.]

HENRY: You are, Suge.

[*Slight pause.*]

You and me.

[*Pause.*]

Jack Robinson. Jackie. [*Laughs.*] We're baseball players. Jack Robinson, he's a baseball player, too. But where is he playin'? He's playin' for the Brooklyn Dodgers and we are here in the Negro League. White folks call us the coon league . . . They think we're dirt. Niggers playing ball with other niggers. They laugh at us. And don't think almighty Jack Boy ain't laughing right on with them. The white folks and him, they're lookin' at us like we are small boys. Small boys who you leave out the house while grown folks talk and conduct their business. A grown man want to conduct his business he talks to another grown man, he takes his business and he goes face-to-face. Jack Robinson. He's the man and we're the boys. They think they got a ballplayer. They got a nigger. The rest of them they got in them two-bit minor leagues is niggers, too. [*Speaking as if* SUGIE *were no longer present*] Let me get the chance. Let me. I swear to you like I would swear before God. Give me a chance, and they'll send his nappy head back to the cotton. He's laughing now—wearing his little white-boy uniform—I know he is. But when he's down in the mud where his little black butt belongs, I'm going to laugh—right to his face. And I'll tell him, "Nigger, you was up there, but now I'm there and I'm good boy! They had the wrong nigger! I'm good boy."

[HENRY *is suddenly startled by* SUGIE'S *presence.* SUGIE *seems not to have heard a word.*]

All I want is I want to go face-to-face, eye to eye, and show any man on this planet I am great, too. You can stay here and get left behind, if you want. But I'll swear with God again, I ain't stayin' here with you.

[*Lights rise slowly on* SUGIE.]

Yes sir, Suge. You been playin' good ball—you and me.

[SUGIE *nods.*]

SUGIE: They say Jack Robinson is a college boy. I ain't go to college, but who says you got to be a college boy to play ball? He ain't got nothin' on me, Henry.

HENRY: I been telling you.

SUGIE: They ain't going to be taking many coloreds. Maybe one a team. But they got the wrong one now.

HENRY: I been telling you, Sugie. I been telling you.

[*Lights fade as the two men exit. Offstage a single voice is heard singing, as if off far away: "Call yourself a Montgomery King. King's my name, and King I sing. Play them fellows, black or white. Beat them fellows, day or night. King's my name, and a King I stand. Champions throughout the land." Lights rise on the area directly in front of the dugout.* SAM *is standing next to the dugout.* RUDY *enters and seems to search for some lost objects. He is unaware of* SAM'S *presence. It is a day off for the team.*]

SAM: There ain't no game today.

RUDY [*surprised by* SAM'S *presence*]: Hey, Sam. My little nephew collared me into goin' fishing down to the river, but he ain't got no string. I saw some out here someplace. I got a taste for fish myself.

[*He continues to search for string.*]

Say, what are you doin' here? You got a day off, too.

SAM: Team tryouts.

RUDY: Oh, shoot! Tryouts! Let me get out of here then before them young boys run me out. [*Grins.*] You going to see what kind of new blood you got to take our places, huh, Coach? What time you startin'?

[SAM *does not answer.*]

Sam? What time you startin'?

SAM: It's started.

RUDY [*surprised*]: Yeah? You ought to tell them boys if they going to play professional ball, they better get here on time. You ain't a professional if you're late.

SAM: They ain't late. They been here and they're gone. Two fellas showed. This is a new day, Rudy.

RUDY: Wait a minute. They got the day right? . . . The time?

SAM: They knowed it. It's a new day, I'm telling you. Time was, King tryouts and damned if every colored ballplayer or supposed-to-be ballplayer in the state didn't show up. You couldn't get in, there was so many. Right now fellas be pushin' and shovin' just to line up. King tryouts was the biggest event could happen for a colored who wanted to play ball—just trying out. Two fellas showed, Rudy—two. And one wasn't no kid—Will Davis—you know him. Will ain't but a few years younger than me. Two—and one who ain't got no business even thinking of playing ball. Heck, I sent them on home— told them they had the wrong day—wires was crossed. The two of them left here with their heads down. They wanted like hell to join, though.

RUDY: We ain't publicizing enough. You said it yourself.

SAM: Publicizing ain't got nothing to do with this, Rudy. There is some kind of changes going on here. You see it?

RUDY: King tryouts and two folks show.

SAM: It ain't just tryouts—it's our tryouts—our league. Them boys who would have been here today are scraping up every nickel and penny they got to go off any place they can for them white team tryouts. Country boys, too.

RUDY: They're runnin' after a fairy tale is all it is. Their game ain't ready for them kind of changes.

SAM: Maybe not. Maybe neither is ours. Where's our boys gonna be then? When them white folks see too many colored folks now, them white folks get jittery—some even when there is one! Colored boys, to them, is backwood or rock headed—and they get mean as the dickens, mean faced to them colored boys. It ain't the same no more, Rudy. I guess most folks figure there ain't nothin' colored worth taking part in anyways.

[*He reaches down and picks up some loose string and offers it to* RUDY.]

You going fishin' or no? Better not keep that young fella waitin'. My daughter's baby boy, they say he was just feelin' a little ill. Doctor say he might be sickly for a while. I might want to get him a little fish pole too one day. I ain't been home much myself. I'm calling a workout for tomorrow, Rudy. Everybody shows—no excuses. We still got a few folks who pay good money to see our games. We ain't going to let them forget that no team in this league ever won three. We'll let them chew on that for a while.

[SAM *and* RUDY *leave as lights rise on the roadside waiting area for the team bus. A few players have entered and await the team bus. It is a hot day.* ELROD, *still in uniform, has taken a seat at the top of the platform. He is quietly eating from a mason jar.* ROCKER *and* YOUNG BOY *have also found places to sit. They are in civilian clothes, as is* BELLMAN, *who is standing over* ELROD. HENRY, *wearing his shirt around his waist, keeps a pacing watch for the arrival of the bus. All are visibly hot.*]

HENRY: How long are we going to be waiting for this dang bus?
ROCKER: He was supposed to be here half an hour ago. [*Smiles.*] Elrod, you always eatin' them beans.
BELLMAN: Sardines and beans. Everything you eat makes me sick.

[*Short pause.*]

HENRY: Elrod, you ever take that uniform off?

[*He does not answer.*]

BELLMAN: He ain't got no sense.
ROCKER: Wearing the uniform is all right by Sam, Henry, but he's going to jump you if he catches you without your shirt.
BELLMAN: Bean-eatin' fool.
ROCKER: Carrying his own beans might not be a bad idea for this trip. We going through Tennessee. Ain't no colored stops through the whole state, it don't seem. Hey, you buy them beans or you bring them from home? Where you get them?

[*He does not answer. He continues eating.*]

YOUNG BOY: Elrod ain't talkin' when he's in them beans.
HENRY: Yo, Young Boy. Get on down the store and pick up some beer, hear.
ROCKER: Elrod is serious eatin'.
BELLMAN: Lookin' at you eat makes me sick. Why don't you take your jar back behind the bushes where nobody sees you?
HENRY: Yo. Young Boy. You hear me?

[*He takes out some money.*]

Pick up something for yourself while you're gone.
YOUNG BOY [*ignoring* HENRY, *smiling*]: Bark, you ain't got to look at him.

[HENRY *pushes money toward him.*]

Go on, Henry.
HENRY: I said treat yourself, too.

[*He continues to push money at* YOUNG BOY.]

YOUNG BOY [*unthreateningly*]: I said go on, Henry. I ain't playin' with you. You see I got my own pop. Go on and look for your Red Sox man.

[*Others laugh.* HENRY *looks at him quietly.*]

HENRY: Young Boy feelin' beside himself these days, ain't you, Young Boy? Barkum, ain't you thirsty?
BELLMAN: I ain't goin' nowhere. [*To* ELROD] I know why you're sittin' there. You think you're gettin' the backseat, but you ain't. I see you. Ain't nobody cares if you are first on the bus. We been down this road before.
HENRY: Rock, go and get a couple of beers for me and you.

[ROCKER *shakes his head.*]

Y'all a bunch of lazy butts. The bus ain't going to be here for another hour and one of you got a chance to earn a couple of free cold beers for yourself.
ROCKER [*stretching*]: Take too long to get to the store and back.
HENRY: And then you get on the bus.
ROCKER: It's too hot, Henry.
BELLMAN [*to* ELROD]: I ain't playin' about the seat.
ROCKER [*slowly*]: Hot, hot, hot. I am so tired. You best to get that shirt on before Sam sees you.
YOUNG BOY [*looking up from the* Chicago Defender *newspaper*]: This paper says

about colored boys in the big teams—this paper says nine fellas are signed to major-league teams—

HENRY: That ain't right.

YOUNG BOY: They ain't all with the, you know, big league, though. Nine guys. That's somethin'. That's somethin', ain't it?

ROCKER: It sure is. Nine? That's sort of hard to believe.

HENRY: This ain't all nine playin' with the big teams.

YOUNG BOY: Uh-uh, like it says, seven of 'em are in their minor leagues.

ROCKER: Nine.

HENRY: It's not nine. It's two—and they had Thompson and Brown up there and they let them boys go. It's two. It's Robinson and Doby—and they gonna make Doby go back. He ain't doin' nothin'—and I know Robinson's gonna mess up.

BELLMAN [*interrupting*]: Shush! Larry Doby, he's the one ought to be there. He played good in this league. What they say on Larry?

ROCKER: Now that's a boy should do good. He can hit 'em.

HENRY: I'm telling you, he ain't hittin' up there.

BELLMAN: What you got, Young Boy?

YOUNG BOY: Jack Robinson and Larry Doby. This paper say they ain't hardly using Doby. It says he ain't hittin' but he ain't gettin' no chance—"Since his arrival more than a month ago, Doby has seen little activity. He has been used sparingly."

HENRY: Go on. Read why they're "sparing" him. I read it. He's struck out half the time he's been up. He's been up twelve times, and he struck out six—swingin'. Tell me they're going to keep him. Shoot, you'll see him again but he'll be wearing colored clothes.

YOUNG BOY: But the fella writin' this says, "Doby does not look comfortable." Like maybe he don't feel he belongs yet. My daddy tells me, sometimes if you don't feel comfortable, you can't do your job. He got to ease up like you told me, huh, Rock?

ROCKER: I suppose so. It can take time to, uh . . . make the grade. Like I say, I really ain't remember much of some of these fellas. They really ain't the ones I thought was going to be the first. I really don't know where they're lookin' for some of these guys. With nine, I would have thought one of us—one of you all—

HENRY: It's two.

ROCKER: Somebody say Doby went to college, too. Robinson was a college boy. I don't know what kind of way they figure out who they want. Some folks is goin' though. Even if most of 'em is in their minor league. That uh—minor league ain't no big deal, huh?

YOUNG BOY: How you like them Brooklyn Dodgers? They must like coloreds— they signed the most. They got guys in their minor league who they say may be joinin' Jack Robinson next year, maybe. What do you think, Rock? Do you think they can stick?

ROCKER: I—What you askin' me for, boy? [*Sharply*] I don't know.

BELLMAN: Where is this mule-legged bus?!

HENRY [*to* YOUNG BOY]: Boy, get your head out of the paper and go to the store.

[*He snatches at the paper.*]

BELLMAN: Damn!

HENRY: Young Boy, yo, store is nice and cool, now go on.

[HENRY *pushes money at* YOUNG BOY.]

Come on. Get some exercise so you can be like your favorite nigger in the big league. He is your King Coon, ain't he? He is your Jesus, ain't he?

ROCKER: Lord's name in vain.

HENRY [*ignoring* ROCKER]: I said go to the store.

YOUNG BOY: Get your money out of my face, Henry.

[HENRY *flippantly knocks* YOUNG BOY's *hat to the ground.*]

HENRY: Go to the store—

YOUNG BOY [*trying to push the money away*]: Go on.

HENRY: Shit, nigger, go to the store!

YOUNG BOY [*pushing* HENRY *to the ground*]: Don't call me no names!

HENRY: The sun must be puttin' crazy thoughts in your head. I'm gonna hurt you now.

YOUNG BOY: You ain't givin' me no chores.

HENRY: I'm gonna hurt you now. Get on your knees, [*aside to others*] you and your nigger pops.

[HENRY *lunges at* YOUNG BOY *and pins him to the ground. He grabs a large stone and raises it dangerously above* YOUNG BOY's *head. Players show their horror but do not physically move to stop the attack.*]

You bastard! You raggedy bastard! Who you sayin' no to?! Who?!

[SUGIE *and* RUDY *enter.*]

RUDY: Henry! You ease off!

HENRY: I ain't gonna kill him, Rudy. I'm gonna teach him his place. Who you talkin' back to!? Who!?

[HENRY *brings his arm down to strike* YOUNG BOY. YOUNG BOY *frees his hands and stops the blow. They tussle and* YOUNG BOY *has gained the advantage before the fight is broken up by* RUDY *and* BELLMAN.]

RUDY: Hold off—

BELLMAN: He ain't do nothin' to you, Henry!

HENRY: This nigger is the rookie on this team! You run when I tell you.

RUDY: He ain't got to run for nobody, Henry! I don't know what your beef is, but you better keep it off this team. It ain't going to help us if either one of you busts up the other. Get your shirt on! We got travel rules! If you're hot, go find some shade!

[*He turns to the others.*]

What happened here stays here—with us. Sam don't need to be hearing stories about this—nonsense! Nobody does. Go on and walk, Henry! Walk it off and don't bring it back—and take your time. Bus ain't going to be here for another hour, anyhows.

[SUGIE *and* HENRY *leave.*]

ROCKER: What is in that boy's head?

BELLMAN: Woooeeee! Young Boy ready for Joe Louis!

ROCKER: He ready for grizzly bear!

BELLMAN: You was down, then you was up! Are you part Indian? I only seen Indians fight like you.

ELROD [*to* YOUNG BOY]: You want some beans?

RUDY [*to* YOUNG BOY]: Yo, there ain't going to be no more fightin', you hear. I'm surprised at you, lettin' Henry get to you. There's worse than him around. You going to be stickin' everybody who gets on your back?

BELLMAN: Aw, Henry had it comin', Rudy. 'Sides, we ain't had a good tussle on this team in a long time.

ROCKER: Fight can put some fire under this ball club—help clear the air.

RUDY: Not on this team it don't. We ain't never won nothin' scrappin' amongst ourselves. [*To* YOUNG BOY] Henry ain't the only man you'll run into who'll get you mad. Keep some control over yourself now, Young Boy.

ROCKER: Well—it was a good tussle to me.

BELLMAN: Yes sir.

RUDY: Sam don't know nothin' about this.

ROCKER [*excitedly*]: Yes sir. I had a fight like this once—with a white man. I beat him good. Yes sir-ree boy, you're somethin'!

[ELROD *rises and places his jar where he has been seated. He starts to leave upstage right.*]

BELLMAN: I had a couple tussles like this myself. [*Laughs.*]

ROCKER: Yo, Elrod. Where you goin'? You goin' to the store?

[ELROD *leaves.*]

[*Calling out*] Run on past my house on your way. Yo! See if my wife got any food for me. Yo!

BELLMAN: Yo! Boy!

[BELLMAN *laughs. Others are quiet as* ELROD *returns and stops directly in front of* BELLMAN.]

Man here wants you to, uh, go by his house. See if his wife got any food for him.

ELROD [*to* ROCKER]: I ain't goin' to your house. [*To* BELLMAN *ominously*] Don't go nowhere—I'll be back.

[*He turns and leaves.*]

ROCKER [*calling out*]: It's on your way, pigheaded cuckoo clock. I ought to slap that boy silly. Let me see I can't get some food—some chicken—[*glaring at* BELLMAN]—for this ride. Good fight, Young Boy.

[ROCKER *exits.*]

RUDY: Y'all pick a worse day to scrap. It's hot. This weather might be enough to make me turn to tusslin'.

BELLMAN: Too bad we can't take the train to Memphis—make our few game stops on the way. Be a whole lot cooler on the train.

RUDY: I don't know about today. I passed by the station this morning. A whole lot of folks were pilin' in them cars.

BELLMAN: Oh yeah. I saw them. Colored climbin' all over them cars. I said where the hell are that many Negroes goin' on one train?

RUDY: They's on their way to St. Louis.

BELLMAN: What they got, a big colored church affair goin' on there?

RUDY: No sir. St. Louis is where a certain—what you call 'em—big-league team is playin' tomorrow. Folks want to see themselves a Jack Robinson.

BELLMAN: Rudy. Ain't nobody riding no train no six or seven hundred miles to see nobody play no baseball. No. I don't care what color he is. No! [*Laughs.*] We got a ballpark right here in Montgomery and they ain't hardly showing up.

RUDY: They're going to St. Louis. Folks ain't stopped going to see everybody's games.

YOUNG BOY: Hard to believe folks go that far to see one man play.

RUDY: These are colored fans and they got a colored ballplayer.

BELLMAN: Well, what are we? For a boy who ain't much of a ballplayer, he sure is ridin' in the big car. He's got it all. I'm almost scared to want what he got.

RUDY: Bark, he's playin' white ball. He ain't white—and they lettin' him know it.

YOUNG BOY: You know what I can't figure? How come there ain't no Montgomery King?

[*Short silence.*]

BELLMAN: Shoot. Don't think they don't want us.

[*Slight pause.*]

I'm going south south to Mexico—out of the country—next year, so I don't care what they do.

[*Slight pause.*]

It's simple. We ain't lookin' for them.

RUDY: How many of their teams we beat?

BELLMAN: Yeah, count them up. It's Stoner! He likes them banners too much. I call them Stoner's banners!

RUDY: Banners make money—most years—and he's made a lot of money off us.

BELLMAN: That's it. He wants to keep them goin'. We're his pride and joy. He ain't goin' to let them pick the apples off his tree. No way. He's too proud of us to let them take us away. I bet he don't even let them in to watch our games.

YOUNG BOY: Must be it—because we the best team there is.

RUDY: Colored ball—there ain't nothin' wrong with being here—right where we are.

BELLMAN: Me, I don't care what they do or who they want. We know what we are. Next year this time, I'll be in Mexicoland or Cuba. They want whatever kind of man you are, they want you. Yes sir. I'm goin' to have me a trunk full of pesos and barrel of Mexican whiskey.

RUDY: You goin' to take the money then, huh, Bark?

YOUNG BOY: Would you go, though, Bark? If they asked you to?

BELLMAN: I might would consider it. Give Jack Robinson somebody to talk to. It don't seem he's got nobody to do that with now. Boy must be talkin' to his glove. I figure I'm good enough to play with him. I am. I ought to be able to play with anybody.

YOUNG BOY: Everybody talks like they got some kind of different game.

RUDY: It's the same game—leastways on the field it is. Only a lot of folks still don't know it—they don't know a lot about us. Around here, don't forget, a lot of us don't believe we're worthwhile until they tell us we are. You got men who have been through this league here and ain't nobody knows their name except the people who saw them or played with them. And can't nobody tell them or me that they didn't make this little boy's game look like it was something awful important and good. Colored game? Colored fans? All colored—Negro from bus to mule. We're still good. We do important things, too. Barkum ought to be able to play? He can play ball with anybody—even ugly as he is. Rocker, Sugie, Henry, you, boy. Don't look now, but you're playing on a big-league team. They'll be lucky one day if they're as good as us now! And we can play side by side and together and every which ways.

[*Slight pause.*]

YOUNG BOY: We're playing big-league ball now.

RUDY [*smiling*]: Yeah.

[*He laughs—and they all laugh.*]

BELLMAN: Look at us. We some big, big, *big*-league ball-playin' Negroes! Put my face in that *Ebony* magazine! Let's us advertise something. They got Jack Robinson's picture sellin' everythin' in *Ebony*. Cigarettes . . . baby food.

YOUNG BOY: Ain't no baby going to eat what you eat.

BELLMAN: I could get them babies to eat pork chops, chitlins, ham bones, and buy them cigarettes. I could get a baldhead man to buy Dixie Peach. I'll be the first colored man selling hair tonic to white folks. Yes I could! I can see my face in the magazine picture now—me and a supersize can of Brylcreamum. Like on the radio, "Use Brylcreamum—"

RUDY: Brylcreem!

BELLMAN: "A little dab will do you." I use a big dab! I'll show them what a colored man is capable of.

RUDY: Anythang!

BELLMAN: Lord, you knows it.

RUDY: Amen! Ain't it the truth. You know, in the army, in the war, I'd tell them I was a ballplayer back home. They'd look at me like I was crazy.

BELLMAN [*smiling*]: They knew all their guys but we weren't nothin'.

RUDY: You know what surprised me? Some colored didn't know.

BELLMAN: They knew the Yankees and Joe DiMaggio—Ted Williams.

RUDY: Ted Williams—yeah. We played against him a couple of exhibition games in the war.

BELLMAN: He's a good ballplayer.

[*Pause.*]

What time's our game? That bus ain't never gonna show.

RUDY: Six o'clock.

BELLMAN: Might as well get some food to pack along myself. Another hot day in Montgomery waitin' for a bus that won't show.

[*He begins to leave.*]

Whatever happened to our Boston fella?

RUDY: You know who started that fairy tale.

[BELLMAN *has almost gone.*]

Don't get nothin' too heavy or greasy . . . we got a game.

[*Lights fade on the players as the sound of a public address* ANNOUNCER *begins to play over a loudspeaker.* LEWIS *is seated alone in the dugout. He sits quietly as the* ANNOUNCER *is heard.*]

ANNOUNCER: We want to thank you all for comin' out here today. The final score, Montgomery Kings 6, Birmingham Barons 1. We got more good games comin' up in the next few weeks. Homestead will be here next week— on the twenty-eighth—that'll be two games on that day—Homestead's the first game . . . and the second game, that one features Mr. Satchel Paige and the Monarchs, Mr. LeRoy Paige. Him and the rest will all be out here from Kansas City—Satchel Paige. That's a doubleheader on the twenty-eighth— Homestead and Mr. Satchel Paige. We got another announcement here. Don't forget, any ball you bring to the ticket window will get you in free. So, before you leave, you might want to look out behind the fence, or by the river, for a home run ball or a foul ball. Any regulation baseball—still in good condition—will get you in the game. Them at the ticket door will decide if the ball is good. So bring them on in—and come early. Ladies' Day is also on the twenty-eighth.

[LEWIS *continues to sit silently as* ELROD *enters the dugout.* LEWIS *quietly rises and* ELROD *sits. Slight pause.*]

LEWIS: Old Satch ain't had it today.

[*He is undecided whether to leave or stay.*]

You coming?
ELROD: It's cool out here. I'm going to sit a spell. You can go on in.
LEWIS: It is some kind of little chill.

[*He picks up a bat and takes a few swings.*]

We started late. They can't be holdin' up games waitin' on a couple of stragglers to get to the park. Folks can't get here on time—they don't get here—you can't be holdin' up a game.
ELROD: You want to get your pay, don't you?
LEWIS: I sure do. There was a few folks here today, but I'd a figured a whole lot more for Satch. Compared to last time we was home, I bet there was more here today. Do you think there was more folks here today? Rod?
ELROD: Yeah.
LEWIS: That's good then, huh? We want to keep 'em comin'.

[*Slight pause.*]

It is cool out here. It is summer, ain't it?
ELROD: Go on in then.
LEWIS: No . . . no. I just want to stay awhile . . . sit here. You ain't got a bad spot—this part of the bench. I don't usually sit down this far. You get to think over here, huh? Or watch gals.

[*Short silence.*]

You—you been playin' pretty well.
ELROD [*shrugging*]: Average.
LEWIS: Your average is better than mine. Mine is getting better. As long as mine ain't the worst.

[*He smiles and his mood lightens a bit more.*]

Sugie been ridin' the ball, ain't he? Young Boy—look how far he's come, boy. It's them big arms he got. I reckon, farmin'. That's a tough job . . . on a farm. I did it when I was growin'. It didn't put much on me though. I didn't much like farmin'. I always wished to be doin' just what I'm doin'. Did you wish this, too—Rod?

ELROD: I don't wish nothin'.

LEWIS: I did. I ain't as . . . I ain't as sure of myself . . . as you . . . you all. I don't know what I'd do if I wasn't playin'. I wish people would keep comin'.

[*Slight pause.*]

I wish I was like you. You keep to yourself. Nobody understands you. [*Smiles.*] Are you sure you weren't kicked in the head by a mule? You know, some of the fellas think you're touched—crazy! [*Laughs.*] I do, too—think you're cuckoo sometimes. Last season, after we won, you didn't play in the winter in the islands with us. You stayed—you stayed here and worked—on some kind of outside job, didn't you?

[ELROD *nods his head, then turns away.*]

You are crazy. It's fun in the islands. Beaches, palm trees, gals—gettin' gals and gettin' drunk! It's winter here, but it's like summer there. Ain't nobody workin'. [*Smiles.*] I'm gettin' kind of old to be doin' that stuff myself. It can be fun, though. You ain't never with the gang. [*Smiles.*] El . . . what do you get out of being cuckoo?

[LEWIS *begins to call* ELROD's *name but stops. There is a quiet moment as* LEWIS *looks at* ELROD, *who has not moved. Light begins to fade on the dugout.* ELROD *seems unaware of* LEWIS, *who rises slowly and leaves. Sound of swing music builds as lights rise on the upstage landing area to a nightspot exterior. A neon sign—*EBONY TER-RACE—*glows brightly.* HENRY *appears as the music builds. He ducks back in to get* SUGIE.]

HENRY: Sugie, come on out here.

SUGIE: Didn't you see me talkin' to a woman, Henry? What do you want? You can't tell me inside? Come on back. Barkum! Get your hands off my woman!

[*Music begins to fade.*]

What's out here, Henry? I got a gal in there—

HENRY: I got somethin' to tell you, Sugie—

SUGIE: Tell me inside.

HENRY: I got to tell you in private. This is about women, too. Plenty of women, if you listen. It's about Red Sox.

SUGIE: This Boston mess again, Henry? C'mon, let's—let me go.

[*He starts to leave.*]

HENRY: He's here, Sugie!

[SUGIE *returns.*]

The man is here! I have spoken with the man, Sugie. I know you all been mockin' for sayin' he is coming, and he is here. He was here today. This is important, Sugie. And I'm telling you because you can make the right moves. He come up to me after today's game. He come to me! He said—he said he's been here before—he's seen a lot of our games. He said he's seen talent—good talent.

SUGIE: He say anybody's names?

HENRY: Yeah, he said names . . . but he said he's—he told me he's not the man who can make the decision. Some other folks got to do that. We got to go to them.

SUGIE: Where's this leave us?

HENRY: It leaves us with this: he can't do the signing, but he told me where we got to go to get to the men who do the signing.

[*He takes a worn envelope from his pocket.*]

There is going to be tryouts, Sugie. He wrote me down where they is going to be, and this here will get us in. It's in Louisville . . . Saturday coming. This is a special invitation.

SUGIE: Louisville?

HENRY: There's only a coal train running Friday night. We'll have to take that— we can be hobos.

SUGIE: We got games—

HENRY: We'll be back. Half a day, we can—

SUGIE: Half—

HENRY: *A day.* We got the invite!

SUGIE: Henry—we got games.

HENRY: We'll be back. Let's see who's laughing now. Them niggers don't be- lieve nothin' until it cracks them up alongside the head.

SUGIE: Get back how? When, Henry?

HENRY: We'll get back! I'm telling you about the biggest chance of your life.

SUGIE: We'll miss games. We can't jump the team.

HENRY: We ain't jumpin' nothin'. A couple of games. They don't need us to beat Mobile. Sugie, the man was here.

SUGIE: But he didn't sign nobody—

HENRY: He can't!

SUGIE: We heard about tryouts before. You're talkin' about jumpin' the team.

HENRY: I ain't talking about jumpin', and you ain't heard nothin' all year that sounds like what I am tellin' you today. Suge, this is a white team. We know the spots they need, and we can fill 'em. The men who can hire us will be there.

SUGIE: Ain't they got no other day?

HENRY: No. It's all on the paper—directions and all. They want us.

SUGIE: They want us, but we got to go to Louisville and miss games? What about what we got to do here, Henry? We workin' on our third championship, Henry. Ain't no team won three. Sam and the fellas—what are they gonna think of us? Tell the man—tell him we'll come up in a while after the season. You said it yourself, he seen us play. He can wait, can't he? Let's get this season over with, then we'll go. We got about only three weeks, we'll win the World Series and we'll get the banner—

HENRY: Whoa—what series?

SUGIE: Our World Series—

HENRY: You call what we play—

SUGIE: It's what they call it.

HENRY: Who?! Who calls it a World what?! World what?! We have to let white folks laugh and laugh and laugh at every stupid thing we do. Do you really believe the—them banners—are important?

SUGIE [*slowly*]: Yes. They're important, Henry—to me.

HENRY: Then you—you're a black fool. Negro World Series—Negro Leagues— any type of group or organization of colored folks that you can think of—Negro churches, Negro doctors, nurses, the Negro Ladies Society, Negro heaven and Negro hell! I fought in the war for this country, and I want a little more than "Negro" pinned on my chest. I'm so tired of that word—them words. "Negro," "Afro"—I ain't no African—"colored," "black"—makes me sick. You don't even want to call yourself a Montgomery Black King—that's our name—nobody does. I don't know what's in your head, but I know what's in my head. They didn't always let us do what they did, but they're lettin' us now—some who are quick are gettin' in! Don't lie about this team. All of 'em ain't goin'—all of 'em ain't good enough. Rudy—you—and me, we're the only ones who can play out of this league and stick. And Rudy ain't got sense to go—so it's you and me.

[*Short pause.*]

SUGIE [*quietly*]: It's you—you got the sense.

HENRY: You asked me if the man today told me names. You're one of them. Is that enough to get you to go?

SUGIE: I ain't goin'.

HENRY: Well, brother, maybe you better stay here. I don't think you're going to be alone. [*About to leave*] You talk about jumpin'. More people are jumpin' on them trains or listenin' to their radios to see your boy—your Dodger boy—than are ever gonna see one of this team's games. Everybody knows where he is. Everybody knows who he's playin' next month. You go back in your club, you ask somebody who you played today. I'm going. If you change your mind—

[SUGIE *has started to walk back to the club.*]

—you let me know.

[*Swing music rises as* HENRY *walks off and exits. Music continues as an inebriated* SAM *enters his office and stumbles. He is bleeding from his forehead. He puts his hand to the wound and discovers the small trail of blood.*]

SAM: Shit. I'm bleeding.

[*He is carrying a bag. He puts the bag down and does a little jig as the music plays to its end. He falls, sits, and laughs.* RUDY *enters.*]

RUDY: Sam? What the heck happened?

SAM: Is that you, Rudy?!

RUDY: Sam, what do you call yourself doin'?

[*He tries to help* SAM *up.*]

SAM [*pushing* RUDY's *hand away*]: I ain't drunk! I . . . I . . . I'm bleeding . . . How in hell am I bleeding?

[*He studies the blood on his hand, then laughs.*]

I ain't drunk. I was workin' out! [*Laughs.*] Don't you work out, Rudy? Practicing. We didn't need no damn extree practice. Why? Huh? Why?

RUDY: Let me help you—

SAM: Them workouts was a bad idea. Some—yes!—some. I eased off on them, though, didn't I? Training like the devil. Stoner didn't have no hand in it. You boys are men—you ain't no damn racehorse. My job is to coach, Rudy. My job is to win—here, in this league, here. And my main job is to feed my family—ain't that any man's main job?

RUDY: We're winnin', Sam. This year, what King team's won as much as we have?

SAM: We ain't! We ain't won yet! Why can't we win? We can't be clowns. We won't be clowns. I ain't drunk, Rudy. I'm sick.

RUDY: You—you was supposed to meet with Stoner tonight?

SAM: I saw him. I said I'm sick.

RUDY: Is everything square? He ain't gonna mess with the team?

SAM: You like a drink, Rudy?

RUDY: He ain't got more silly suggestions.

[*Slight pause.*]

What is it, Sam?

[SAM *reaches for the bag and takes out a package. It is neatly wrapped. He begins to open it.*]

SAM: Something I want to show you here—an idea from Stoner. A order from Stoner. Something he wants you all to have.

[*From the package, he removes the gaudy shirt and trousers of a baseball uniform. The two pieces are garishly designed. It is, essentially, a clown suit constructed of a shiny golden fabric.*]

Pretty, ain't it?

[*He takes out a cap. It has an elongated bill and is styled ornately. At its crest is a crown emblem.*]

Here's a hat to go with it. A crown. Got a whole carton of this shit. Here, I'll wear it.

[*He puts on the shirt and cap.*]

Not too bad, huh? I'm a real king now. He wants us to wear this outfit. Do you believe it? Folks don't want to see us unless we're in this getup. He wants to attract attention.

RUDY: He ain't serious.

SAM: Serious as sin.

[*He takes a drink.*]

He wants everybody to get a good look at you. He wants you all to be seen. Stoner knows what is goin' on. Me and him had a long talk—or he talked to me. I listened. There is more to this Jack-Robinson-integratin'-the-big-leagues than meets the eye, Rudy, a whole lot more. Stoner showed me. You know them boys who been signed so far—big-league clubs have to pay for them boys. If they want colored, they got to pay for 'em—from those who has got 'em. Colored owners didn't want to sell, not at first, but they're sellin' now. Right now here in this league, some of the owners are gettin' five, ten—one of 'em got twenty thousand dollars for sellin' a colored ballplayer. A year ago, you couldn't give them colored. "Why would anybody want colored people?" they'd say. We come a long way, ain't we? One day they can't give you away and the next day they can sell you. Which brings me to the crux of my meetin' with Stoner. He ain't made a dime. He says, "I got the best team—two goddamn banners—and nobody wants 'em." And he can't understand why. He don't know what a team is.

[*He staggers a bit more.*]

Says you boys ain't bein' appreciated—say you boys ain't gettin' the attention you deserve—say these uniforms ought to help bring folks to the game. Boost yous. Set fire to the team, he say. Folks see fire, they go! Other folks follow! Big-league folks! White—

[*He abruptly stops and tries to tear the uniform from his body.*]

Get me out of this! Get me out! You ain't wearin' it! Nobody on this team is wearin' this! I told Stoner. He put out his stinkin' cigar and he looked at me and he give me the package. He told me there was three weeks left to the season after which I would have to find another job.

RUDY: We're worth more to him there than we are here. He lose you, Sam, he's losin' them banners, and we got it this year, it's sure almost.

SAM [*taking a drink*]: I don't know about that, Rudy. But one thing sure, he don't care. He don't. Folks don't—Stoner don't.

[*He offers* RUDY *a drink.*]

He ain't a dumb man. He's losing money so he's got to make changes. He's a smart man.

[*Cross light*—SUGIE *can be seen seated in the dugout.* SAM *picks up the uniform.*]

He's lookin' out for himself. You can't blame him—can you?

[*Lights fade on* SAM's *office.* ELROD *enters the dugout. He glares at* SUGIE *to get up from his seat.* SUGIE *rises and paces nervously.*]

ELROD [*taking his place on the bench*]: That was easy enough. Don't expect me to thank you—it's my seat.

[SUGIE *continues to pace. He is looking for someone.*]

You better hurry on out if you want to get in a few swings before the game starts. Boy, what the heck you lookin' for? There some woman out there?
SUGIE: No.
ELROD: Then sit down. You are unnerving me.
SUGIE: Elrod—Henry ain't here.
ELROD: I know. Sam's lookin' for him now. He better show soon—
SUGIE [*interrupting*]: Henry ain't here! He went to Louisville.
ELROD: What?
SUGIE: He went up to try out with a big-league team. He must have took the train last night. He wanted me to go with him. Damn. He's gone.
ELROD: What's he figure we do without him? He's pitchin'. Shit! He run out? He jumped the Kings? Sam don't know, and you better tell him. Boy, you better tell him!
SUGIE: I ain't tellin' Sam nothin'. I thought he might have changed his mind. He told me about this two days ago and he ain't spoke since. Goddamn, he jumped the team.
ELROD: You better tell Sam. Is he comin' back?
SUGIE: I don't know—
ELROD: Then tell Sam! He jumped the team. Who do he think we got to play his spot? He better not come back, that nigger. Boy, you go tell Sam. Go on! Tell him!

[SUGIE *leaves.*]

Tell him that creep run out! Shoot! Season almost over, and Henry got to do this mess. Nigger. Shit.

[*Light holds for a moment on* ELROD *as players enter the team room. It is quiet. An occasional low remark breaks the silence. They speak, but to no one in particular. Each glares at* BELLMAN.]

BELLMAN [*holding a baseball*]: Don't look at me—I ain't a pitcher. You do it.

ROCKER [*moving toward the water pail*]: No damn water! You finish the bucket, you fill it up!

RUDY: Thirty minutes before the next game.

LEWIS: Of all days, we don't need two games.

SUGIE: We get to lose two in one day.

BELLMAN: You want to lose? Jump the team like your friend.

LEWIS: We're not the only team in first place now. Some of our games comin' up, though—some of them teams is broke down. They ain't got nobody neither—we can beat them.

RUDY: Quiet up.

BELLMAN: The last thing I'm going to have is Henry Simmons laughing off, wherever he is, about how we can't win without him.

YOUNG BOY: We got another game today, and two more tomorrow, then the season's over. We win them and then the series against the Black Giants and we got it all.

SUGIE: Four games in two days.

ROCKER [*sternly*]: Hey, that's the way it is around here.

BELLMAN [*to* SUGIE]: You hear from your friend?

LEWIS: I don't give a damn if we never hear from him. Let us win our World Series. We win the . . . World Series . . . he'll wish he was here. I ain't heard of him signin' for no team.

ROCKER: We don't need him.

YOUNG BOY: Amen.

SUGIE: I still don't believe he ran out. He jumped the team. He's been with us most as long as anybody—except Rock. It's hard to believe a person can be almost a—a brother to you and then—run out.

BELLMAN: Shoot.

RUDY: Forget him. He's gone. We got to take care of ourselves now.

BELLMAN: We seen 'em like Henry before—all my life. We knew it. He'll be with you—until the sun comes shining up someplace else. He don't think of nobody but hisself.

LEWIS: That kind of creep—he don't care about you. He ain't going to do good nohow. He ain't no good. He ain't going to make it up there. I could do a better job than him. Hmmph. He thinks he can play with them.

[HENRY *appears in the doorway. All are silent. He is dressed in street clothes and carrying a satchel.*]

BELLMAN: Well—lookee here.

[*Short silence.*]

Ain't you got a game in the big time now?

HENRY [*to* SUGIE]: It didn't work out.

ROCKER: And you come back? Get the hell out of our team room.

HENRY: Rock—

ROCKER: Get out of here.

RUDY: Henry, you got your reasons why you left, but you better talk to Sam.

HENRY: Yeah. I was, uh, lookin' for Sam. I couldn't find him. I ain't stayin'.

BELLMAN: Good.

HENRY: I had to come back to town for a minute—and I'm gone.

[*He turns to* SUGIE.]

It didn't work out, Suge. It was good you didn't go. Tryouts was supposed to be Saturday, but they didn't have them till just yesterday. I been a week waitin' on a tryout.

LEWIS: We don't care.

BELLMAN: Sugie, take your boyfriend on out of here.

HENRY: There was—I'm goin', Bark—[*turning again to* SUGIE] I wanted to tell you what happened. We were all in Louisville for the Red Sox tryouts. There was about two hundred ballplayers—all colored. They wouldn't let us go on the big field, like the man told me said. We had to go to a high school field—a colored high school, all junky with rocks and big stacks of war surplus tires piled up behind home plate and junk surplus trucks out in the field. There was so many of us, we had to break down into groups. Eighteen in a group—nine playin' nine—and we each played a one-inning game till everybody come to bat one time. One time. Nobody had time to get nothin' goin'. They didn't even let me throw. It came my turn to hit and this pitcher they had—pitcher?—a raggedy-headed nigger, couldn't throw worth a damn. I don't know where they got this fool. Bad thing was, he couldn't get the ball across the plate. He was scared to death of the white man watching him, I guess. He didn't give me nothin' worth swinging at, and with one chance, I had to swing. I swung at three of the worst damn balls. I had to! It was my only chance and the nigger wouldn't give me a pitch worth hitting. I struck out, yeah. This skinny black black bastard—I called that nappy-headed son of a gun everything I could think of—

[SAM *enters and stands silently behind* HENRY.]

—I told him, "You no good raggedy black!!!"

[*He turns suddenly to see* SAM. *The room is quiet.*]

Sam—I want to say—

SAM [*cutting him off*]: Shut up! I don't want to hear nothin' from you. [*Yelling to the others*] We got a game! Suit up! All of you all! We got a game!

[*Others begin to exit quickly.*]

LEWIS: The nigger you said was pitching to you—should have broke your skull.

BELLMAN: He ain't playin' with us.

SAM: Shut up! All y'all! We got a game!

[*Others exit.*]

HENRY: Sugie.

[SUGIE *exits.* SAM *and* HENRY *stand alone in the room.* HENRY *starts to empty his locker.*]

SAM: Henry, boy—

HENRY: Sam—

SAM: Shut up. I don't know what to make of you. I'd call you one for the books, but I think I've met you before. I've known you someplace. How long you been with the Kings? Six or seven years? Back then, we was building. We won some, but, basically, we was just startin' to see this team as it could be— as we—as we are. I know it don't mean nothin' to you, but a lot of folks worked for this. What the other man got ain't always what it seems, Henry. Sometimes you got to make your own—maybe you don't even want to— and you have to—sometimes. You ain't the only one who wants you up in the big leagues, Henry, but there ain't no more jumpin' or runnin' out. You got a contract with this team. Anybody wants you can have you, but they got to buy you—from Stoner. Remember, after Brooklyn took Jackie, colored owners got smart—said they ain't going to give you boys away. You got a contract says you're Stoner's property—but he'd sell you in a minute—a second. And I can't say I'd blame him. I want you up there, too. I want you all up there—after this year—because there ain't going to be much left here.

[*Light begins to rise in the dugout, where* ELROD *is seated.* SAM *pauses in thought for a moment.*]

You, uh—you suit up. You're playing—not for you, but because you owe the team. It's your debt. Pay it up—and you get the hell out. We come in a team, Henry. We're gonna try to go out one. Get dressed.

[SAM *turns and places a ball on the bench. He leaves as lights fade on the team room and rise fully on the dugout.* ELROD *is seated silently as an assortment of hand clapping, whistles, an occasional cowbell, and a horn are heard in the background. In his desire to help a rally begin, he makes whooping sounds and methodically twirls white socks or a towel above his head.*]

ELROD [*whooping*]: Whoop. Whoop. Whoop it up! Whoop. Whoop. You the King, Rocker! Let's go! You the King! Whoop, whoop.

[*His whoops take on a cadence of a chicken clucking or a whooping crane. It is spell-like.*]

Whoop, whoop. [*Talking to someone*] I'm whoopin'. You ain't heard nobody whoop before? You better whoop, too. Come on, Rocker! Whoop, whoop—shooooot!

[*Pause.*]

We got to score here! One out and bases loaded? We going to win this or not? Them stands is full for a change—World Series full. Let's go. Sugie. Yes sir, one run's all we need, one. Straight out, Sugarman. One, and we all go home! [*Softly*] Whoop, whoop, whoop, whoop, wh, wh, what! Strike! Bugs a strike! Come on, ump! Got eyes like a damn possum! [*Softly*] Whoop, whoop, whoop, whoop, whoop, wh, wh, why you swing at that, Sugie?! Damn! Both y'all got possum eyes. Look 'em over, Shoog.

[*Background sound of bells, et cetera, grows again.*]

Ain't we going to get nobody in? Look at all these folks. Where y'all been? They come out for a World Series, don't they! Sugie, Shoog!

[*Crowd noise builds.*]

Whoop. Whoop. Sugie, Shoog. Whoop. Whoop. Sugie, Shoog. Sugie. Sugie. Sugie.

[*Loud crack of the bat. For a brief moment there is an almost deafening silence until, just as suddenly, the sound rushes back into the ballpark.*]

Sh! Sh! Holy shoot! Sugie! Sugie! Sug-gie! Sug-gie!

[*Chant of "Sug-gie! Sug-gie!" as players enter the team room.* ELROD *remains in the dugout.*]

Sugie. Sweet Sugie. Sugie done took us all home! Three! Three!
ALL: Three! Three! Three!

[*Players are all in the team room, each dressed in civilian clothes and some wearing their uniform tops or bottoms. They continue to chant "Three! Three!" Chants fade and there is low laughter heard.*]

ELROD: Sugie done put us in the record books. Heck, we all did. I guess I did,
    too.
LEWIS [*calling out from the team room entrance upstage*]: Elrod! Get over here!
ELROD: Yeah!

[*He has started to change from his uniform to his civilian clothes in the dugout.*]

LEWIS [*calling out*]: Elrod!? What the hell are you doing?
ELROD [*continuing to dress*]: Mind your own damn business.
LEWIS [*returning to the others*]: That fool is out there dressing in the field! Cuckoo
    clock!

[*Players laugh.*]

ROCKER: Crazy Elrod.
ELROD: I always dress out here after we win a championship—a banner. It's a
    personal tradition. Tradition. We ain't got much of that anymore. But I'll
    never miss a banner party, especially for our third. Most anybody else had
    was two. Ours was—history.

[*Players greet* SAM *as he enters the team room. Players applaud and whistle as* SAM *goes to each one and shakes hands. Each has a dark brown beer bottle.* HENRY *is alone.*]

SAM: Good game. Good series.
ROCKER: We got 'em all now, Coach.
SAM: Good job.
BELLMAN [*drunkenly*]: I'm gonna tell 'em all about you in Mexico—'bout
    Coach Sam!
SAM: Oh yeah. You better learn to speak somethin' down there—Spinach.
SUGIE: You shut Stoner up good, Coach!
ROCKER: He want you back now.

[SAM *goes to* RUDY.]

RUDY: It's all like you wished, Coach!

BELLMAN: Call yourself a what?!

PLAYERS [*joining in loudly*]: Call yourself a Montgomery King! King's my name, and King I sing!

[YOUNG BOY *bursts in the room.*]

YOUNG BOY: Did y'all hear?! Jackie! Jack Robinson! They done made Jack Robinson Rookie of the Year!

[*Players react: some are pleased, some are hesitant.*]

SAM: What?!

BELLMAN: Hot damn!

SAM: Ain't that somethin'. He's a good one, Robinson is. What's he going to do next? Rookie of the Year, huh! Boy's had a helluva season. That's good. That's real good. Makes me proud.

LEWIS [*calling out from the team room entrance*]: Elrod!

YOUNG BOY: A King banner and Jack Robinson Rookie of the Year!

LEWIS [*turning and yelling to* SAM]: How about it, Coach—next year, too, huh? For us.

[*Players continue to mill about.*]

ELROD [*fully dressed and still seated*]: It was good we got this last one in. Sam was right, though, wasn't nobody talkin' about four. Half the team was gone by the spring. [*Smiles.*] Rudy. Rudy Easton.

[*Players continue their celebration.*]

He did OK. Rudy played about four or five years—up there. He was a little late gettin' started. Henry. Henry Simmons. Henry came back with us, then he left—he got signed. He played for a while, but he couldn't seem to stick with a club. He played for two or three of them teams, then they finally let him go. He was a good player. Never heard of him again. Sugie. I wouldn't tell him this, but he was one of the strongest men I ever saw.

[SUGIE *demonstrates his smooth swing for* YOUNG BOY.]

They give him one chance—and it didn't work out. Young Boy. Our Young Boy. There was the surprise—not to me. He went up all right, shoot, he went up. White folks ended up calling Young Boy one of the greatest ballplayers anybody's ever seen—who ever played the game. They put him in their Hall of Fame. I saw him play once—he sent me a ticket. He was good. He was real good.

[*He rises and starts to cross to the team room.*]

The rest of us? Till the team and the Negro Leagues busted up and died out altogether, we hung on—we had to, most of us. [*Smiling and shaking his head*] Jackie. He ain't do too bad, neither. Rookie of the Year and they put him in their Hall of Fame. Nobody could ever tell me different about Jackie. Jack Robinson was one of our best—one of.

[*He completes his cross to the players.*]

BELLMAN [*drunkenly*]: He musta put some real colored stuff on them!
SUGIE [*very drunkenly*]: I'm gonna show 'em some myself. They seen a little bit. I'm gonna show 'em a whole lot!
RUDY: You gonna show 'em power, Suge?
SUGIE: Power? When I get to one of them white teams, I'm gonna hit that ball soooo faaarrrr!

[*He pretends to have a bat in his hands, swings, and falls down laughing. Others laugh.*]

ROCKER [*to YOUNG BOY*]: Some day, you gonna be smackin' them up there, too. [*Laughs.*] Like I woulda. I shoulda done the integratin'.

[SAM *takes a drink of beer and stands quietly.*]

BELLMAN [*staggering over to embrace ROCKER*]: You? You couldn't integrate your-self—[*Laughs.*]
SAM: Listen up.

[*Conversations continue.*]

Listen up here before y'all get too drunk to know what you just did. Come on over. Line up. We're going to raise one for the team.

[*Overlapping follows as players slowly make their way toward SAM.*]

LEWIS [*prematurely lifting his glass bottle*]: To number three.
SAM: Hold on there.
BELLMAN: Don't forget it!
SAM: All of us in here! All of us.

[*Players begin to form a line to either side of SAM.*]

LEWIS: Raise 'em up.

RUDY: Get over here, Sugie—

BELLMAN: Montgomery Kings.

LEWIS: *Champeens!*

ROCKER: Folks will be talking about this team for a long time.

BELLMAN: Forever.

SAM: Move in here.

BELLMAN: When Kings do battle, it's a short war. Call yourself a what?

SUGIE: A King. [*Laughs.*]

SAM: Straighten up here.

LEWIS [*starting to whistle*]: I can't whistle. [*Laughs.*]

SAM: We had a good year here. We showed—some pride. We started slow but we hung in—

ROCKER [*over SAM's remarks*]: Let's go into town in Enny's truck.

BELLMAN: Get the truck, Ennis.

LEWIS [*cutting him off*]: Raise 'em up!

[*The players each raise a bottle.* ELROD *follows the gesture, as does* SAM. SUGIE *beckons* HENRY *to join the toast. A single comment is heard from* SAM—"Come on, son." HENRY *joins the line of nine men and raises his bottle.*]

HENRY: Champeens.

[*Light lowers as players lift their bottles and then lower their arms to their sides. For a moment, their position takes on the likeness of a faded team picture. Unhurriedly, the players begin to leave the team room. Light remains low as they all exit.* SAM *says quietly, "Let's go. Let's go." Only* ELROD *remains in the room, darkened with age. He puts on his dark hat and glasses and stands silently for a moment.* ELROD/OLD MAN *looks about the room, turns, and leaves. He walks slowly to center stage. The whistling sound of the team "call" is heard softly. He stops and turns. He walks slowly until he stands in the area immediately in front of the dugout. He looks up and enters the dugout. He sits, then edges his way to a spot on the bench where he is most comfortable. He leans back and smiles. He remains quietly motionless as light fades to black.*]

FATHERS AND OTHER STRANGERS

Jeff Stetson
First–Place Winner
1988–1989

PLAYWRIGHT'S STATEMENT

The relationship between fathers and sons is a complex and fragile one. A child sees a man who serves as his role model and mentor. A man sees a child who is more than a reflection of himself but who he hopes encompasses his own set of dreams and aspirations for the future. All fathers want the best for their children. All children expect to be able to depend on their fathers for guidance, nurturing, strength, support, and love.

The relationship between black fathers and their sons is a particularly delicate one. The baggage of racism is carried and passed on from one generation to another. The psychic damage that occurs to a man who has been treated as inferior and feels he has nothing of value to offer the people who love him creates the possibility for dysfunctional behavior. In the context of a family, such behavior can, and often does, have a detrimental and, perhaps, devastating effect on children, who internalize the pain of their fathers and make it their own.

Fathers and Other Strangers was written to explore such a dynamic. A hardworking man, ashamed of his accomplishments, victimized by a system of oppression that sees him as irrelevant, raises his son in silence. He believes he can offer his son nothing of substance and remains in the family only to serve as an example of what his son should never become. Unable to express love, incapable of believing he deserves love, he dies hoping only that his son will be driven to do more, be more.

The play is about that son, his success, his pain, and ultimately his discovery of the meaning of love and how it can cure even the legacy of the past.

PRODUCTION HISTORY

Fathers and Other Strangers, by Jeff Stetson, was first presented by the Columbia College Chicago Theater Department at the New Studio Theater in February 1989. It was directed by Chuck Smith, with set design by Bill Decker, costume

---

design by Andrew Wycislkak, and lighting design by Patricia "Cookie" Baucum. Courtney Nicholson was the stage manager.

Mr. Peter Nelson	David Doston
Dr. Douglass Angoff	Mitchell Eisenberg
Mrs. Mary Nelson	Keli Garrett
Mr. Donald Davis	Jeff Hess
Edward "Ted" Nelson	Hoover Lewis III
Dr. Paul Janis	Keven Locke
Mr. James Stefano	Bill Roumas

The play was subsequently presented by the Chicago Theater Company at the Parkway Theater in February 1990. It was directed by Chuck Smith, with lighting design by Patrick Kerwin, costume design by Glenn Billings, and sound design by Corbiere T. Boynes. Natalie Moore was the properties and assistant stage manager, and Edward D. Richardson was the stage manager.

Dr. Douglass Angoff	Darwin R. Apel
Dr. Paul Janis	David Barr
Mr. Peter Nelson	Kristian Chanin Crawford
Mrs. Mary Nelson	Bonnie DeShong
Mr. Donald Davis	Larry Jahn
Mr. James Stefano	George Kiefer
Edward "Ted" Nelson	Dwain A. Perry

CHARACTERS

Mr. James Stefano, middle-aged, white

Dr. Paul Janis, late thirties, African American

Mr. Donald Davis, middle-aged, white

Dr. Douglass Angoff, middle-aged, white

Mrs. Mary Nelson, middle-aged, African American

Mr. Peter Nelson, middle-aged, African American, Mary's husband

Edward "Ted" Nelson, teenage, African American, son of Mary and Peter

ACT 1

[*In a dimly lit office, two people sit within three or four feet of each other. One has something that looks like a notebook in his hand. The other is in a slightly reclined position.*]

MR. STEFANO: Don't you think we need more light?

DR. JANIS: Why?

MR. STEFANO: So you can see my problems.

DR. JANIS: I'm here so you can see your problems.

MR. STEFANO: Then why am I paying you a hundred and fifty bucks an hour?

DR. JANIS: It's a living.

MR. STEFANO: Live with a little more light.

[DR. JANIS *rises and moves toward the light switch. He flicks the lights on and takes his seat.*]

DR. JANIS: Happy?

MR. STEFANO: Would I be here?

DR. JANIS [*reaching into his jacket pocket*]: Mind if I smoke?

MR. STEFANO: I'm fucked up. Why ask me?

[DR. JANIS *pulls out a gold case and takes out a joint.*]

That's dope!

DR. JANIS: I won't take that personally.

MR. STEFANO: You're gonna get high while I'm bleeding about my problems?

DR. JANIS: I should suffer 'cause you're fucked up? Anyway, it mellows me out . . . makes me more sensitive to my environment.

[*He lights up.*]

MR. STEFANO [*looking at* DR. JANIS *curiously*]: You sure you're a psychiatrist?

DR. JANIS [*pointing to the certificates on the wall*]: Bought and paid for.

[*He passes* MR. STEFANO *the dope.*]

Here, take some of this. It will help you to relax.

MR. STEFANO: I don't think I should take it.

DR. JANIS: It'll be good for you . . . Trust me.

MR. STEFANO: I'm Catholic.

DR. JANIS: You go to confession?

MR. STEFANO: Yes.

DR. JANIS: You're covered . . . Ten Hail Marys, fifteen tops . . . Go ahead.

[MR. STEFANO *looks doubtful but takes the joint and proceeds to take several very deep, long drags.* DR. JANIS *impatiently waits with his arm extended for the return.*]

Am I going to get it back?

MR. STEFANO: Huh?

DR. JANIS: Back. [*Slowly*] Am . . . I . . . going . . . to . . . get . . . it . . . *back*?

MR. STEFANO: Oh, sure. Here.

[DR. JANIS *looks at the little that's left and decides to place it in the ashtray.*]

DR. JANIS: And you wonder why I charge one fifty an hour? You got any idea how much that stuff costs?

MR. STEFANO: I heard all you high-paid shrinks were into cocaine.

DR. JANIS: No. That's for white doctors . . . nostrils are smaller.

MR. STEFANO: Oh, yeah . . . I never thought of that.

DR. JANIS [*shaking his head in disbelief and giving a trace of a smile*]: Let's get back to you. How are things with the wife?

MR. STEFANO: You really know how to wreck a high.

DR. JANIS: What do you want to talk about, Mr. Stefano?

MR. STEFANO: Look, Doc, can't we quit that "mister" stuff and just call me James?

DR. JANIS: OK. If you prefer, James.

MR. STEFANO: Yeah. I guess I'll talk about her.

DR. JANIS: Fine.

MR. STEFANO: No, Doc. She ain't been "fine" in years.

[*Pause.*]

Bet you're surprised I know those expressions!

DR. JANIS [*looking puzzled*]: What expressions?

MR. STEFANO: You know. "Fine" and stuff like that.

DR. JANIS: I'm impressed.

MR. STEFANO [*pleased with himself*]: Right on!

DR. JANIS [*just a bit cynically*]: Far out.

MR. STEFANO: Hey, I didn't know you people used that.

DR. JANIS: On rare occasion. Just as a cultural-exchange experience.

MR. STEFANO: I can dig it.

DR. JANIS: Now . . . about your wife?

MR. STEFANO: Yeah, my wife. Doc, nothing I do seems to make that woman happy. I bust my butt at work. The kids get everything they want. She gets her nails done twice a week. I don't know why, she doesn't do enough work around the house to get them chipped.

[*Pause.*]

Doc?

DR. JANIS: James.

MR. STEFANO: What's a good husband?

DR. JANIS: One who asks the question.

[*Beat.*]

At least, it's a start.

MR. STEFANO: I've tried, Doc. I really have.

[*Pause.*]

We used to have a really nice home over on Lakewood Drive about five years ago. Then the nig . . .

[*Uncomfortable pause.*]

DR. JANIS: Niggers moved in?

MR. STEFANO: Gee, Doc, I didn't mean . . .

DR. JANIS: It's OK, James. Sooner or later we'll deal with that, too.

MR. STEFANO: You know, I was going to Doc Harris for three years before he retired. He was real impressed with you. Told me not to worry about him not being around anymore . . . said you were a terrific psychiatrist. He never said anything about you being . . .

DR. JANIS: Black?

MR. STEFANO: Yeah. That first session we had, I didn't think it would ever end. Here I was getting help from someone I'd try to keep out of the neighborhood.

DR. JANIS: And would you try to keep me out now?

MR. STEFANO: Hell, you'd raise the property value. But it did take time.

DR. JANIS: Yes. I know. It's been seven months and I finally got permission to drop the "mister."

MR. STEFANO: Think I can drop the "doc"?

DR. JANIS: No. I'm not ready for that.

MR. STEFANO: Fair enough. You know, I don't think of you as black anymore.

DR. JANIS: Am I supposed to be flattered?

MR. STEFANO: I didn't mean . . .

DR. JANIS [*sharply*]: Yes, you did!

[*Pause.*]

Mr. Stefano, James, we can continue this, but it's not going to get us to deal with your wife.

MR. STEFANO: I want you to like me, Doc.

DR. JANIS: I know. And you want your wife and children to love you.

MR. STEFANO: Is that wrong?

DR. JANIS: Depends on why you need it and how you go about getting it.

MR. STEFANO: Sometimes it's easier to buy.

DR. JANIS: If that were true, you wouldn't be here.

[*Pause.*]

You want to talk about Christmas night?

MR. STEFANO: You have a way of raising unpleasant memories.

DR. JANIS: If you're around to remember them, they can't be that bad.

MR. STEFANO: That's only 'cause I screwed that up, too.

DR. JANIS: Most people who try to commit suicide are often looking to be saved, to have someone say, "No. I won't let you die."

MR. STEFANO: What happens when no one says anything at all?

DR. JANIS: You come to someone like me.

[*Beat.*]

MR. STEFANO: When the kids opened the presents they got angry at me 'cause I forgot to get the batteries to run the damn things. And Sarah, she complained about the coat being the wrong size and the necklace being too "gaudy." It was the only one I saw in the store that had that many diamonds, so I thought I couldn't go wrong.

DR. JANIS: And you tried to make it right by going into the garage and . . .

MR. STEFANO: And inhaling the fumes from my dear wife's Jaguar. The bitch never forgave me for messing up her exhaust pipes. I had the sensation of life leaving me with every breath. Breathing and dying, the deeper each breath, the closer death. I guess I didn't breathe enough to die. I remember her screaming at me, something about what did I do to her car . . . I would have cut my wrists, but all I had were Atra razors. [*Laughing*] Headlines in the local paper: "James Stefano Nicked to Death with Double-Edged Safety

Blades". . . one blade pulls your hair while the other cuts your wrist . . . slowly . . . very slowly.

[*Pause.*]

[*Bitterly and with pain*] So I messed up my wife's exhaust pipes instead.

DR. JANIS: You started seeing Dr. Harris shortly after that?

MR. STEFANO: Yeah. I had to. My priest told me to seek some help and I had met Dr. Harris in the hospital anyway. Seemed like a good enough egg. It'll be four years this Christmas.

[*He reflects on some thought.*]

Christmas.

[*He shakes his head.*]

I give the family money now. Let 'em buy their own presents.

DR. JANIS: What happened after you got home?

MR. STEFANO: You mean after the hospital?

[DR. JANIS *nods yes.*]

Nothing. It was like it never happened. No one was supposed to talk about it. Sarah had the car fixed. Oh, but the garage door was taken off, only garage in the town without a door.

DR. JANIS: Did you ever think of trying again?

MR. STEFANO: No. Didn't have to. I had gotten my answer.

DR. JANIS: Then you knew you were asking a question?

MR. STEFANO: Yes. I knew.

[*Silence.*]

Did you get me high so we could talk about this again?

DR. JANIS: Would I do something like that?

MR. STEFANO [*smiling, then seriously*]: Doc, about the . . . you know . . . trying to explain where we used to live. I really feel bad about . . .

DR. JANIS: That's good, James. You should feel bad. Who knows, after we're through, I may have succeeded where others have failed.

MR. STEFANO: In doing what?

DR. JANIS: In making you feel guilty about the right things, James.

[*Pause.*]

Look, if it makes any difference, five years ago, I wouldn't have wanted you in my neighborhood either.

[*Long pause.*]

MR. STEFANO: Doc, do you like me? I mean, do you really like me?

[*The lights fade slowly on* MR. STEFANO. DR. JANIS *turns and moves toward his desk. He looks at the area where* MR. STEFANO *had been. He stares for a moment and then speaks.*]

DR. JANIS: It is more than the neighborhood, James. So much more than the neighborhood.

[*The lights rise and* MR. DAVIS *is standing in the vacated spot.* DR. JANIS *puts on his professional smile and moves to greet him.*]

Mr. Davis, nice to see you. How have you been?

MR. DAVIS: Dr. Janis, you're looking well. Business is fine. I may even take a vacation soon.

DR. JANIS: Sounds like a good idea. Oh, by the way, congratulations on that Rotary Club award.

MR. DAVIS [*surprised*]: Did you read about that?

DR. JANIS: No.

[*Long pause.*]

MR. DAVIS: How did you learn about the award?

DR. JANIS: Mr. Greenly told me.

MR. DAVIS [*concerned*]: You know Mr. Greenly?

DR. JANIS: Yes.

[*Uncomfortable pause, which* DR. JANIS *lets build.*]

MR. DAVIS: I suppose you do business at one of his banks?

DR. JANIS: No . . . Charges too much for checking accounts.

[*Beat.*]

So, would you like to start our session?

MR. DAVIS [*puzzled*]: Yes. Of course.

[*He fidgets.*]

DR. JANIS: What would you like to talk about?

MR. DAVIS: How long have you known him?

DR. JANIS: Who?

MR. DAVIS: Mr. Greenly.

DR. JANIS: Long time.

MR. DAVIS: Well?

DR. JANIS: Well, what?

MR. DAVIS: I mean, do you know him well? Mr. Greenly?

DR. JANIS: We play golf occasionally. As a matter of fact, we were playing golf last Saturday and he happened to mention he was going to a banquet that evening in your honor . . . That's how I learned of the award.

MR. DAVIS [*curiously*]: I see.

DR. JANIS: Don't worry, Mr. Davis, I didn't violate any confidences. He doesn't know you're a patient.

MR. DAVIS [*unconvincingly*]: Why, of course, I never would have thought that. I guess I was just a bit taken back, I mean surprised, that you knew Mr. Greenly so well.

DR. JANIS: Yes. I could see where you might be.

MR. DAVIS: But please be assured, Dr. Janis, I have the utmost confidence in your professionalism. I wouldn't be seeing you if that were not the case.

DR. JANIS: I wonder if you really know why you're seeing me?

MR. DAVIS: I beg your pardon?

DR. JANIS: Do you know why you're here?

MR. DAVIS: I don't know what you mean.

DR. JANIS: Do you know why you're seeing me, not any psychiatrist, but specifically me?

MR. DAVIS [*fumblingly*]: You came highly recommended.

DR. JANIS: From someone you know well?

MR. DAVIS: I don't really remember who . . .

DR. JANIS: Was there any particular reason why you wanted a black psychiatrist?

MR. DAVIS: I don't understand.

DR. JANIS: I think you do.

[*Beat.*]

You selected me because I was a black psychiatrist. Or more to the point, you chose me because I wasn't a white one.

MR. DAVIS [*somewhat embarrassed*]: Well, I try to be open regarding my relationships, professional or otherwise.

[*Pause.*]

I'm a lifetime member of the NAACP.

DR. JANIS [*sarcastically*]: Do you attend their meetings?

MR. DAVIS: Well, no. But I would if . . .

DR. JANIS [*sharply*]: Stop it, Mr. Davis! Please. You're not in a public board-room now, and no one's giving you any awards for your civic and community achievements.

MR. DAVIS [*upset*]: I think this is highly unusual. I would appreciate it if we could get to the issue at hand.

DR. JANIS: The issue at hand is whether or not we can deal honestly with any issue.

[*The two men look at each other for several tense moments.*]

You travel forty extra miles away from your home and away from your business to meet with me. Do you have any idea why you do that?

MR. DAVIS: I don't object to the travel . . . in fact, I rather enjoy the time to . . . help me unwind.

DR. JANIS [*disgustedly*]: You travel here so that no one will know you have a psychiatrist. And you have me because you thought there would be little chance that I might know anyone in your precious little social circle. Oh, but that's not all. There's one more reason, maybe the most important of all.

MR. DAVIS: This has gone quite far enough. I don't need to pay you—rather handsomely, I might add—to put up with your vulgar assumptions.

DR. JANIS: You can consider this visit on the house, Mr. Davis. And if you want to leave, please do with my best wishes, but, before you do, at least know this . . . I know you're seeing me because you couldn't face the possibility of sharing your insecurities and your problems with someone who looked like you. I have no intention of being your professional mammy!

MR. DAVIS [*shaken*]: I'm sorry if you misunderstood my . . .

DR. JANIS: Fuck you!

MR. DAVIS: What?

DR. JANIS: I said fuck you and your mama.

MR. DAVIS: Why, you arrogant black bastard! Who the hell do you think you are to address me that way? I didn't expect some street talk from a man in your profession. I have a good mind to . . .

[DR. JANIS *starts laughing, quietly at first, then uncontrollably.* MR. DAVIS *is startled by it.*]

I fail to see the humor.

DR. JANIS [*waving his hands to stop him or to explain*]: It doesn't matter who you are or what you are. When someone talks about your mama, the truth has a way of coming out.

[*Pause.*]

You're right, Mr. Davis, you do have a good mind. I think it's time you used it for more than reviewing the profit and loss columns of your business ledgers. You want a new psychiatrist? Get one. I'll be happy to recommend a good white doctor close to home.

MR. DAVIS [*concerned*]: I never said I wanted a new . . . perhaps I need to consider, to place this in a proper context.

DR. JANIS: I don't want you to put this "in the proper context"! Act! Act, Davis! Even if in acting your lips say what your proper context finds too vulgar. "Black bastard" is what you felt. It's what you meant! Compensate for that by writing a check to the NAACP.

[*The lights fade on* MR. DAVIS. DR. JANIS *moves to center stage. He looks back toward his darkened office.*]

Fuckin' asshole! Blue-blooded hypocritical bastard. I don't need your bullshit or your money! Condescending son of a bitch. I ought to take out an ad in the *Wall Street Journal:* "Davis the Dickhead Seeks Cure from a Nigger with an M.D."! That'd get the good ol' boys from the country club talkin'. Might even take your Rotary award away. How'd you like that, Davey? [*Mockingly*] "Well, I've always been a contributor to the NAACP. How was I to know it stood for Nappy Afros Against Caucasian People? Why just the other day, I patted a colored child on the head for luck and gave him a quarter. I've always been open in my relationships."

[*Pause.*]

Only relationship you've ever been open with is a wallet; pictures of value-less old white men on devalued currency. *Act, Davis! Act!* [*Bitterly*] There have been far too many people who wouldn't.

[DR. JANIS *moves stage right as the lights rise on* DR. ANGOFF's *office.* DR. ANGOFF *is seated and smiles at* DR. JANIS *as he enters and takes a seat.* DR. ANGOFF *gives him a long look.*]

DR. ANGOFF: Angry?

DR. JANIS: You got it!

DR. ANGOFF: Same issue?

DR. JANIS: How'd you guess?

DR. ANGOFF: I read my notes from our last three sessions. White patient . . . black psychiatrist . . . racial conflict gets in the way of curing penis envy.

DR. JANIS: The real conflict continues to be this contradiction: my psychiatrist is white and I'm expecting understanding.

DR. ANGOFF: I can handle Oedipus conflict, child molestation, schizophrenia, subliminal perception, and why little Johnny wears his sister's panty hose, but racism is too complex for me?

DR. JANIS: Do you still put stock in the Oedipus conflict?

DR. ANGOFF: Well, I'm a closet Freudian with Skinnerian tendencies.

DR. JANIS: How do you handle it?

DR. ANGOFF: I suppress my inner feelings through behavior modification and rationalize it as the only normal approach to use.

[*Pause.*]

Tell me about the patient.

DR. JANIS: A guy named Davis. Lots of money.

DR. ANGOFF: Who else could afford us?

DR. JANIS: Tries to be liberal and other lies his father told him.

DR. ANGOFF: Is his father a significant factor?

DR. JANIS: Yeah . . . What? . . . Are you going to try to draw another analogy with my . . .

DR. ANGOFF: If the Rorschach fits. You know the reason psychiatrists have psychiatrists is not so we can test out theory among the elite. It's to prevent us from internalizing all the pain. Particularly that pain that has a striking resemblance to our own.

DR. JANIS: I thought we were supposed to cure the patient, not let them get us dysfunctional.

DR. ANGOFF: We stay with our patients a long time, Paul. We had better make sure their problems don't stay with us after they leave the office.

DR. JANIS: Maybe we should learn to cure them more quickly.

DR. ANGOFF: Every patient who has a physical problem knows that if he waits too long, his risk of not being cured is increased. If you detect cancer early enough, you've got a chance; however, smoke a few more cartons before your next visit and, hey, don't blame the doctor. But emotional or psychological problems, fifty years of repressing that you hated your mother or you were molested by kindhearted Uncle Joe as a child and you can't enjoy being touched at age thirty-five, those problems we're expected to fix in six to eight sessions. Paul, you can't cure that kind of pain with two aspirin and some vitamin C.

DR. JANIS: I don't know, they say that vitamin C is some powerful stuff.

DR. ANGOFF: You know what Freud said about jokes, particularly bad ones?

DR. JANIS: It works for Henny Youngman.

DR. ANGOFF: Let's not get ethnic, shall we.

DR. JANIS [*with a poor Jewish accent*]: So, I should suffer so you should be happy?

DR. ANGOFF: Look, I won't do Richard Pryor if you won't do Henny Youngman. Agreed?

DR. JANIS: Agreed.

DR. ANGOFF: Good. Now, how did you blow your cool?

DR. JANIS: I happened to mention that I knew one of Davis's associates. It almost made him piss in his silk drawers. He doesn't want to deal with the fact that he's seeing me because it's safer for him.

DR. ANGOFF: Is it ever really safe?

DR. JANIS: Depends on what you fear most.

DR. ANGOFF: You resent him?

DR. JANIS: It bothers me that he plays this game with himself and thinks I don't know it.

DR. ANGOFF: Then you resent his silk drawers?

DR. JANIS: Are we getting Freudian again?

DR. ANGOFF: No, we're getting back to you and, yes, your father.

DR. JANIS: Sounds like Freud to me.

DR. ANGOFF: OK. So I lied. It's Freud.

[*Beat.*]

This Davis, is his father like yours?

DR. JANIS: Like mine? Christ, they couldn't be more different.

DR. ANGOFF: How?

DR. JANIS: Try bank accounts.

DR. ANGOFF: I didn't know that made you different.

DR. JANIS: You didn't?

DR. ANGOFF: Contrary to popular belief, money does not prevent personality disorder, the fear of rejection, or the need to be loved.

DR. JANIS: Tell that to poor folks.

DR. ANGOFF: I can't. They're too busy taking care of rich folks and their guilt-driven anxieties.

DR. JANIS: Did you ever play the dozens?

DR. ANGOFF: No, but I studied major British writers one semester. You have any idea how insulting *The Canterbury Tales* can be?

DR. JANIS: If they were insulting to you, just think how I must have felt.

DR. ANGOFF: Why is it always so difficult to talk about your father?

DR. JANIS: Are we back to the dozens or is it *The Canterbury Tales* you wish to play?

DR. ANGOFF: What kind of father was he?

DR. JANIS: What kind of father was he? What's expected from a father, Doug? Paying the rent? Being a provider? Being an example to his children?

DR. ANGOFF: And was he a good example for you?

DR. JANIS [*after a long reflective thought*]: The night my father died, the family visited him in the hospital. We knew it was just a matter of time. I think he knew it before the rest of us. He asked everyone to leave the room, except for me. And when they were all gone, he reached out his hand to me. I put mine in his, and he brought me closer to him.

[*Pause.*]

It was the first time I had ever seen fear on my father's face. It was the first time I had seen much of anything . . . looking at my father was like looking at a blank page or a stone that had much of its character worn away by storms, or other forms of abuse, or just time. He said the only thing he could ever do for me was to serve as a bad example, to be the kind of person I would never want to be like. He hoped he had at least been successful in that.

[*Silence.*]

A few moments later he just stopped living, or breathing, to be more exact.

[*Long pause.*]

I hate the thing that made my father despise himself. I hate the system that made my father die thinking he was a failure.

DR. ANGOFF: I think you hate something much more than that, Paul. I think you hate the fact that you let him die thinking you believed it.

DR. JANIS [*shaken by this, but quickly getting control*]: I did believe it. I believed the man who worked two menial jobs and took abuse after abuse, without ever getting angry or killing somebody, I believed with all my heart that he was a failure. And he was right about me not wanting to be like him. I vowed I would never be poor, would never clean up behind some rich white cat who was too lazy or stupid to pick up after himself. I let my father die as quietly as he let white folks walk over him, without ever raising a single protest.

DR. ANGOFF: And what would have happened if he had protested?

DR. JANIS: Maybe he would have died without that look on his face. I suppose that would have been worth being unemployed.

DR. ANGOFF [*studying* DR. JANIS]: Why did you become a psychiatrist, Paul?

DR. JANIS: The truckers' union wouldn't let me join.

[*The two men look at each other.* DR. JANIS *becomes serious.*]

I thought it was the easiest way to change the world, at least the world of the black child. I wanted to hold a mind here.

[*He extends his arm as if to cradle some fragile thought in the palm of his hand. He stares at it.*]

To wash the pain away, to hold it up to the light and prove there was nothing wrong with it. I wanted to repair all that psychological damage produced by distorted truths and quiet lies and nights that lasted too long . . . And now, I treat rich white folks or a few black ones that want to be.

DR. ANGOFF: Rich white folks need love, too.

DR. JANIS: They have the stock market.

DR. ANGOFF: It closes at four.

[*He rises and walks near his desk.*]

When you were talking about your father, you almost started crying. Why'd you hold yourself back?

DR. JANIS: Black men don't cry. Didn't you know that, Doug? Anyway, when was the last time you cried?

DR. ANGOFF [*thinking for a moment*]: When I saw *E.T.* Did you see it?

DR. JANIS: Yeah.

DR. ANGOFF: And you didn't cry?

DR. JANIS: I refused to. Sitting around all those folks with tears in their eyes over a damn ugly robot.

DR. ANGOFF: It's a story about compassion.

DR. JANIS: It's science fiction.

DR. ANGOFF: Paul, does it bother you to help white people?

DR. JANIS: That's my profession.

DR. ANGOFF: That's not what I asked.

DR. JANIS: What was the question?

DR. ANGOFF: Does it bother you to help white people?

DR. JANIS: Not as much as it bothers them.

DR. ANGOFF: Why would it bother them?

DR. JANIS [*laughing*]: You ask that as if you really don't know.

DR. ANGOFF: I don't know . . . Maybe I trust people more than you.

DR. JANIS: Trust? What the hell do you know about trust, Doug? You could be a damn quack and the first day a patient walked through that door, he'd believe in you. He'd take one look at that face and he would tell you fears he wouldn't tell his own mother.

DR. ANGOFF: Or father?

DR. JANIS [*ignoring the comment*]: The same person would walk through my door and see a color. Not a doctor who might be able to cure that pain, that torment.

[*Pause.*]

You know the patient, Stefano, the one who tried to commit suicide?

[DR. ANGOFF *nods yes.*]

He's been seeing me for over seven months now. I've tried everything to get him to open up with me. Today, I darkened the room so that my color wouldn't stand out so much . . . I even gave him some cabbage to smoke . . . told him it was dope . . . I thought that would help . . . That's what I have to do in order for a person to see a psychiatrist and not a color, a color that blinds him from everything else, including himself.

DR. ANGOFF: What do you think Davis saw when he left your office?

DR. JANIS: I don't know. Maybe he felt he saw a man for once.

[*Pause.*]

You know what I told him? I said I wasn't going to be his professional mammy.

DR. ANGOFF: I think I'd give anything to be that.

DR. JANIS: Any particular reason you want to be a mammy? Besides the fact that you were fond of *Gone with the Wind*.

DR. ANGOFF: It's the closest thing to being there to help without the threat, without the power to be embarrassing. It's like being invisible and yet you're there to furnish some strange but important sense of support. Isn't that what Ellison meant, in part, when he wrote *Invisible Man*?

DR. JANIS: You've read Ellison and you cried at *E. T.*? By God, Doug, will you never cease to amaze me? And I think you ought to read him again. His theme was a bit more complicated than that.

DR. ANGOFF: You still haven't answered why you stopped yourself from crying.

DR. JANIS [*firmly but without anger*]: I should cry before you and not my father when I had the chance to? I could have made a difference to him. He could have died knowing I didn't want him to. He could have known that then. What's the use now?

DR. ANGOFF [*softly*]: I don't care if you let out your emotions here or not, as long as you do it someplace. I also think it might help if you didn't do it alone.

[*Pause.*]

You didn't kill your father, Paul. He died. Maybe he died too soon. Maybe you should have acted differently. I don't know. But you aren't responsible for his death.

DR. JANIS: How do you measure responsibility, Doug? Did I have to cut him, or was it enough simply to let him bleed? He had grown accustomed to insults from strangers. He just never got over silence from his family.

DR. ANGOFF: Insults from strangers?

[*He thinks briefly of some distant memory.*]

When I was a child, I remember walking to school with some of my friends. One of the kids pointed to this black man who was washing some windows of a bank and said, "Look, there's a nigger." They all started laughing, and so did I. But I didn't know what was so funny. I had never heard the word before and so when they left, I walked over to this man and asked him what a nigger was.

[*Pause.*]

As long as I live, I will never forget the way he looked at me. I never thought it was possible for a face to have so many expressions over such a short period of time. He told me that a nigger was someone who was always trying to prove himself, except he never could, because there would always be another test, always another challenge. Then he smiled, for the first time, and said he didn't have anything to prove, so he must not be a nigger.

[*He looks at* DR. JANIS *for a moment.*]

I thought it was a good definition.

DR. JANIS: You think I'm trying to prove something?

DR. ANGOFF: Maybe.

DR. JANIS: Suppose I'm not proving it for me?

DR. ANGOFF: Then maybe you're making someone else a nigger. Do you really want to do that?

[*Silence.*]

Why don't we leave here, get something to eat?

DR. JANIS: No thanks, Doug, I've got a session tonight.

DR. ANGOFF: You're working this late?

DR. JANIS: It's a favor to my aunt, some neighbors of hers; family problems, I think.

DR. ANGOFF: Aren't they all?

DR. JANIS: You weren't kidding, were you? You really are a Freudian.

DR. ANGOFF: Freudians never kid. They just have impure thoughts, usually incestuous.

DR. JANIS: At least they keep it in the family.

[*He rises and begins to exit.*]

Talk to you later.

DR. ANGOFF: Give me a call for drinks.

[DR. ANGOFF *attempts to give* DR. JANIS *a "soul" handshake but fails miserably.* DR. JANIS *does little to help him and appears to enjoy the failure.*]

DR. JANIS: Why don't you work on that for our next session, and then we'll go on to even greater forms of communication.

DR. ANGOFF: I might have gotten it, if you had helped a little.

[DR. JANIS *exits as the lights fade on* DR. ANGOFF *and rise on center stage.* DR. JANIS *stops, lost in thought. He hears* DR. ANGOFF*'s voice: "Paul, does it bother you to help white people?"*]

DR. JANIS: I made a promise, sealed in silence between a dying father and a son that knew nothing of life, a promise that I would never be like you. Never be some servant who catered to folks too dishonorable to pick up their own dirt and too deceitful to admit that it's theirs.

[*Beat.*]

But what have I become instead, a servant to the lies men believe about themselves, a keeper of the discarded recollections of people too afraid and ashamed to remember their own pain. You picked up white people's garbage—I clean up the lies they create to make life more bearable. Which one of us really deals in dirt?

[*He extends his arm; his hand is cupped, gently. He stares at it for several beats.*]

To hold a mind here. To wash the pain away. To steal the memory that makes it ache.

[*Pause.*]

To change the world of a black child grown old.

[*After a moment or two, the lights rise on* DR. JANIS's *office. He seems to follow the light to that office as lights on center stage dim slowly. He becomes occupied with office matters as the Nelsons arrive.*]

MRS. NELSON: Excuse me, we're looking for a Dr. Janis.
DR. JANIS: Yes. I'm Dr. Janis. You must be the Nelsons. Please, come in.

[*The Nelsons move toward the center of the office.*]

MRS. NELSON: Why, thank you. This is my husband, Peter.

[MR. NELSON *shakes hands with* DR. JANIS *but appears reluctant to do so.*]

And our son, Edward.

[EDWARD *shakes hands with* DR. JANIS *but is even more reluctant and has a degree of defiance.*]

I'm Mary.
DR. JANIS: Pleased to meet all of you. Why don't you sit down and make yourselves comfortable. Can I get you some coffee? [*To* EDWARD] Or soda?
MRS. NELSON: No. No, thank you. Doctor, I appreciate you taking this time to see us. Your aunt Florence is always talking about you.
DR. JANIS: I hope it's good.
MRS. NELSON: It's beyond that.
DR. JANIS: Well, my aunt has been known to exaggerate.

[*He studies* MR. NELSON *and* EDWARD, *who seem to be uncomfortable or, in the case of* EDWARD, *indifferent.*]

Now, let's see, what gives me the feeling that not everyone is happy to be here?

[*Silence.*]

MRS. NELSON [*looking at her husband and son and then, a bit embarrassedly, at* DR. JANIS]: I'm sorry, Dr. Janis. You were nice enough to see us, and the least we could do . . .

DR. JANIS [*holding up his hands to stop her, then to* MR. NELSON]: Mr. Nelson, do you want to be here?

MR. NELSON [*hesitantly*]: Meaning no disrespect, sir . . . Doctor . . . but I just don't see the point. I did this to satisfy my wife.

EDWARD: You mean to stop her from complaining.

MR. NELSON [*sharply*]: Don't refer to your mother as "her"!

EDWARD: Well, she's a "her," ain't she?

MR. NELSON: You mind your tongue, young man. Edward, don't let me have to warn you again.

MRS. NELSON: Peter, please, not here. Doctor, I did push my husband and son into this, but I just didn't know what . . . I thought we were growing farther and—

EDWARD [*interrupting and mockingly*]: Farther apart. I just don't know when it all started. I've tried my best but Edward just persists in attempting to be black . . . and we've tried so hard to . . .

MR. NELSON: That's quite enough! You think this is a joke? Well, I assure you . . .

DR. JANIS: Excuse me, Mr. Nelson. Let me offer a suggestion. Perhaps I could speak with you and your wife separately and then I'd like to see Edward. After that we'll see where we are. Is that OK with each of you?

EDWARD [*already standing*]: Suits me fine. I'll be out in the waiting room. Hey, Doc, you got any *Sports Illustrated* out there? *Players* would be better but . . .

[*He looks around the office.*]

You look more like the *Playboy* type.

MR. NELSON: Edward, I—

DR. JANIS [*cutting him off*]: I think you'll find something to keep your interest.

EDWARD: Later, all.

[EDWARD *exits.*]

MR. NELSON: I apologize for my son's . . .

DR. JANIS: Don't. Don't apologize for anyone else, Mr. Nelson. It's not needed and, generally, it isn't satisfactory.

MR. NELSON [*taken aback a bit*]: Yes . . . of course.

[*Pause.*]

DR. JANIS: Now, why are we here?

[*Silence.*]

Mrs. Nelson, why did you want your family to see me?

MRS. NELSON: We don't seem to be a family anymore, Doctor. I thought, I hoped we could rectify that.

MR. NELSON: Mary, don't be so overly dramatic. We are a family and we're experiencing what every family experiences.

DR. JANIS: And what is that, Mr. Nelson?

MR. NELSON: Communication problems . . . a teenage boy who is trying to be a man too soon . . . confusion over different values, different circumstances.

MRS. NELSON: Dr. Janis, we just seem to argue all the time or, worse, sometimes we don't talk at all.

DR. JANIS: Who do you mean when you say "we"?

MR. NELSON: She means my son and me, usually. And if my wife and I argue, either in silence or otherwise, it more often than not is about or over him.

DR. JANIS: What seems to be the problem?

MR. NELSON: My son sees himself as a "revolutionary," which is to say, he sees himself as antieverything or, to be more precise, anti–everything I represent.

DR. JANIS: And what do you represent?

MR. NELSON: I'm the principal of the high school my son attends. I guess that means I'm the establishment. It may also mean I'm not black enough for him. He would like me to be more militant. I think it would also help if I were poorer. That way he could identify with the oppressed more easily.

MRS. NELSON: Peter, you're being unfair. He's not that extreme or that superficial. He's just committed, and a bit confused; and sometimes, very, very hurt.

DR. JANIS: How is he hurt?

MRS. NELSON: Edward used to be very different than the way he is now, Doctor. He and his father got along wonderfully. We all did. He was a star athlete in junior high school, an A student, popular with all his classmates. He was voted class president in the eighth grade; the first black ever elected to that position in the history of the school.

DR. JANIS: He went to a majority white school?

MRS. NELSON: There're very few blacks at the school, either as students or staff.

DR. JANIS: When did Edward start to change?

MR. NELSON: When he got older. The girls he used to play with got older, too.

DR. JANIS: White girls?

MR. NELSON: That's all there were.

MRS. NELSON: When he was thirteen, he was going to his first prom, with a lovely girl named Susan. Her family and ours had been friends for years. He was so excited. We had rented a tux for him and he looked so handsome . . .

[*The lights fade and* EDWARD *appears dressed in a tuxedo and holding a corsage. He is both nervous and excited and looks at his parents, who are now standing in silence. They look at each other for several moments.*]

EDWARD: Well, how do I look?

[*Pause.*]

   That bad, huh?

MRS. NELSON [*moving toward him*]: You look wonderful.

EDWARD: Mom, do you think these flowers will go OK with Susan's dress? She's wearing an off-blue, and the florist said the contrast would be . . .

MR. NELSON [*cutting him off*]: Susan's not going.

EDWARD [*startled*]: What?

MR. NELSON: I said, she's not going.

EDWARD: But why? Is something wrong with her?

MR. NELSON: Not with her.

EDWARD: Then what's the matter?

MRS. NELSON: Her father doesn't want you taking her. He doesn't approve of the two of you dating.

EDWARD: Doesn't approve? Susan and I have always been friends. He's never . . .

MR. NELSON: You were children then. It's different now.

[*They stare at each other in silence.*]

   I have a colleague named Mr. Jackson. He teaches at Fairmont. He has a very pretty daughter about your age. I thought something like this could happen, so I checked to see if she would be available. We'll be a bit late getting to the prom, but we'll get there, if you still want to go.

EDWARD [*looking at his father in disbelief*]: You thought something like this could happen?! And you've arranged to import some stranger from across town. You think 'cause we're the same color, we'll be able to party OK!

MR. NELSON: She's a lovely girl.

EDWARD: I don't know her! You take strangers to a movie, or out for some ice cream, not a goddamn prom!

MR. NELSON: Don't you swear in this house!

EDWARD: That's what bothers you . . . that I swear? Did you make a backup plan for that too? Have a priest waiting outside to bless the house?

MRS. NELSON: Edward, I know you're upset. But I think you ought to go to the prom anyway. Show them all that this won't stop you from . . .

EDWARD: Show them! I don't have to show them anything! That's for you and Pop . . . I don't believe what a jerk I've been. I'm running around like I'm just one of the gang. The principal's son, a shining example of what you can be when you stop being what you are!

[*Pause.*]

And you knew it all the time. Everyone knew, except me. I was the only one too busy worrying about whether or not the flowers were the right color, and it wasn't the color of the flowers that mattered at all.

[*He throws the flowers toward the back of the stage.*]

It's easy to forget you're black in this house. I'll tell you one thing, I'll never forget it again.

[*He exits as the lights return to* DR. JANIS *and the office. The Nelsons look at him and each other.* MRS. NELSON *breaks the silence.*]

MRS. NELSON: Edward had never confronted racism before. We had protected him from that for as long as we could. It wasn't just the prom night, but what happened afterwards. Susan was hurt as well, and feeling guilty and ashamed. She wanted to make it up to Edward, but he was feeling too much pain to care about anyone else's.

MR. NELSON: Susan tried to take her life, Dr. Janis. She failed, but her parents sold the house and moved the family to another state. For all we know, it could have been another country.

[*Pause.*]

We lived in a rather small community and the word had spread pretty quickly.

MRS. NELSON: Friends didn't help the matter at all. Some tried to console Edward but just made things worse. Others tried to understand but were so awkward in their attempts. And others . . . others said some vicious things. I never knew young people could be that cruel. They must have been taught well.

DR. JANIS: Did Edward blame himself?

MR. NELSON: He did just about everything. First he wondered what was wrong with him. Then he wondered what was wrong with us. Later he just got angry at everyone.

DR. JANIS: How did the two of you handle the prom incident and then the suicide attempt?

MRS. NELSON: Peter?

MR. NELSON: Evidently, not very well. You see, I had been principal of the school for some time, and I guess I had grown accustomed to separating school issues from family concerns.

DR. JANIS [*surprised*]: You saw this as a "school issue"?

MR. NELSON: In some ways I guess I did. As I said earlier, it was a rather small community, and I really didn't have many options to exercise.

DR. JANIS: Options to exercise? Mr. Nelson, forgive me, but I don't understand how your son's pain couldn't have been separated from your work responsibilities.

MR. NELSON: Doctor, I just didn't know what to do or say to him. I couldn't run a race relations clinic for the school. There weren't enough of us there to even give the term "relations" any meaning.

DR. JANIS [*changing the subject, but still a bit aggravated*]: When did Edward begin to be a . . . "revolutionary"?

MR. NELSON: Almost immediately. He quit basketball. He said he wasn't interested in using his skills for the benefit of the "Man." His whole behavior changed.

DR. JANIS: What about dating? He's a young man. Did he take anyone out to parties or school events?

MRS. NELSON: He would go out occasionally with girls at the school, white girls. But he would always sneak around. He never stayed with anyone long. He almost seemed to use the people he went out with, nice girls at first, but later, he would go out with . . .

MR. NELSON: Tramps!

[*He looks sternly at his wife.*]

Well, that's what they were, Mary. Tramps. He seemed to enjoy bringing them by the house. He would sneak around with nice girls, but the others he would put on public display. When he turned sixteen last year, I bought him his own car. I thought that might give him a sense of responsibility. He could drive into town and be around more black kids. But that just made it worse. Last month he tried to paint the car black, green, and red.

DR. JANIS [*failing to stop a smile*]: Tried to?

MR. NELSON: Thank God I saw the paint and could stop him before he started.

DR. JANIS: Why would you stop him? I thought you said it was his car.

MR. NELSON: Dr. Janis, you can't be serious. I'm principal of a small conservative high school and my son is going to park in the lot with a "back to Africa" automobile that's an advertisement for black power!

DR. JANIS: Was it his car?

MR. NELSON: Well, hell yes, but within limits.

[*Pause.*]

DR. JANIS: Mr. and Mrs. Nelson, I think I should see your son now. Would you mind waiting outside for a few minutes? I promise I'll be as quick as possible in getting us all back together.

MRS. NELSON: Would you like us to send in Edward?

DR. JANIS: Please.

MRS. NELSON [*rising and looking at her husband, who is lost in thought*]: Come on, Peter.

MR. NELSON [*rising slowly, somewhat confused*]: Doctor, may I ask you a question?

DR. JANIS: Of course.

MR. NELSON: Should I have let him paint the car?

DR. JANIS: I don't know, Mr. Nelson. Maybe your son just wanted to see if he could. Sometimes, at sixteen, you feel very powerless and, sometimes, very much alone.

[MR. NELSON *thinks about it.* MRS. NELSON *touches him lightly on the arm. They both exit. A few moments later,* EDWARD *struts in.*]

EDWARD: You want me to sit in the shrink chair, Doc?

DR. JANIS: Whatever makes you comfortable.

EDWARD: Solid. I'll take the couch.

[*He flops down.*]

Did you fix the folks for me?

DR. JANIS: Do you think they need fixing?

EDWARD: You did talk to them, didn't you?

DR. JANIS: What would you like fixed?

EDWARD: Is there a cure for Negroitis?

[*He looks around the office, then at* DR. JANIS.]

Or am I asking the right person?

[*Silence.*]

This is quite an office, Doc. What do you get, eight to ten bucks an hour? Or do you charge by the type of problem?

DR. JANIS: No. Flat rate.

EDWARD: Yeah, well, if it works. Look, Doc, can we speed this up? I've already missed the *Soul Train* awards. I'd like to get home in time for reruns of *Hill Street Blues.*

DR. JANIS: You're pretty tough, aren't you?

EDWARD: I can hang.

DR. JANIS: You think you're tough enough to talk to your father?

EDWARD: About what?

DR. JANIS: About anything important.

EDWARD: Wrong, Doc. If it's important, I handle it alone.

DR. JANIS: Alone is not always the best place to be.

EDWARD: Depends.

DR. JANIS: Have you heard from Susan?

EDWARD [*startled for a moment but regaining his cool*]: So, that's what you talked about. What did they tell you?

DR. JANIS: They told me about a prom you never attended.

EDWARD: I didn't miss anything.

DR. JANIS: Have you heard from her?

EDWARD: She wrote a couple of times.

DR. JANIS: What did she say?

EDWARD: I don't remember.

DR. JANIS: Do you still have the letters?

EDWARD: Why would I keep the letters from a sick chick?

DR. JANIS: Why do you think she was sick?

EDWARD: Hey, is it normal to try and kill yourself? No. I never kept them.

DR. JANIS: What did she write, Edward?

EDWARD: I told you! . . . I don't remember.

DR. JANIS: Why did you quit basketball? I heard you were quite an athlete.

EDWARD: One slave in the family was enough.

DR. JANIS: Are you referring to your father?

EDWARD: He's in charge of the plantation. Principal Nelson, the chief servant of Western High School.

DR. JANIS: Being principal of a high school isn't quite comparable to being a slave.

EDWARD: You works the field or you works the house; a slave is a slave, Doctor.

DR. JANIS: Up until Susan, you seemed to think differently about your father.

EDWARD [*bitterly*]: Up until Susan, I never had a reason to think.

DR. JANIS: You think your father let you down?

EDWARD: He let himself down. I'm just a natural consequence.

DR. JANIS: He loves you.

EDWARD: Did he say that?

DR. JANIS: He didn't have to.

EDWARD: He has to for me, and even then I wouldn't believe him.

DR. JANIS: Why not?

EDWARD: He had his chance to show me.

DR. JANIS: How? By letting you paint your car black, red, and green?

EDWARD: They told you that, too?

[*Silence.*]

No, Doc. I'm not a kid. In ways that would have made a difference.

[*Beat.*]

I heard him on the phone, talking to Susan's father. I'm dressed like a damn penguin, hoping the flowers wouldn't wilt before I picked her up, and he's talking to his buddy about how the kids have planned this and promising nothing would happen. Then I heard him pleading with this asshole, begging him not to do this. I got a father whose best friend is a hypocritical bigot and he wants him to forget it for one night!

DR. JANIS: What would you have wanted him to do?

EDWARD: I don't know. Maybe we were the ones that should have moved.

DR. JANIS: Would you really have wanted your father to run at the first sign of trouble?

EDWARD: He was running to stay there. Maybe he should have stopped trying so hard to please white folks.

[*Pause.*]

DR. JANIS: Do you know what my father did for a living?

EDWARD [*looking at* DR. JANIS *for a moment*]: I know he wasn't president of the country. I'm sure I would have read about it in *Ebony*.

DR. JANIS: He was a janitor. I used to be ashamed of that because I thought he kissed ass to keep his job. You think your father does the same to keep his. Edward, I don't know your father. I don't know any of you. But I do know that pain sometimes forces us to act differently, to see things in ways that are not always true. You think your father failed you, or himself. What do you think your father faces every day from teachers at his school who would love to see him fail; from some staff who are doing whatever they can to see that he does; and from parents who may not have wanted him there in the first place?

EDWARD: Like you said, Doc, you really don't know any of us.

DR. JANIS [*rising, somewhat frustrated*]: I'm going to ask your mother to join us. Is that OK with you?

EDWARD: Is that my punishment for not answering the questions right?

[DR. JANIS *gives* EDWARD *a glance over his shoulder.* EDWARD *is preoccupied as the look from* DR. JANIS *turns slowly from a hint of anger to a smile of admiration, or fondness, or simply understanding. He exits for a moment, then reenters with* MRS. NELSON, *who seems both concerned and curious. She takes her seat.* EDWARD *ignores them both.*]

DR. JANIS: Do you get along with your son, Mrs. Nelson?

MRS. NELSON: Why, yes.

DR. JANIS: Edward?

EDWARD: What?

DR. JANIS: Do you get along with your mother?

EDWARD: We don't play ball together or anything, but yeah, we do fine.

DR. JANIS: Why?

EDWARD: What do you mean, "Why"?

DR. JANIS: Well, she's married to someone who you don't seem to hold in the highest regard.

EDWARD: Everyone's entitled to one mistake.

MRS. NELSON: Edward, that's enough! You ought to be proud of your father. He's accomplished a great deal. He's done it for us, for you. He deserves your respect.

EDWARD: For what? For being the first "Negro" principal of Western High?

MRS. NELSON: Do you have any idea what it means to be the "first," Edward? It means you are, absolutely and totally, alone. And when you're alone for a long time, it changes you. You learn to be quiet because no one would listen anyway. And if for some reason you have to scream, no one, not a single person around you, would understand why.

[*Pause.*]

Yes! He deserves your respect for being the first and not losing his mind.

EDWARD: How do you know he hasn't?

MRS. NELSON: Because I sleep with him! I feel the tension in his back and see the pain in his eyes. I can tell the type of day he's had by how much he turns in his sleep. [*Softly*] I know how many times he got angry and couldn't let anyone know by the way he makes love. All that pain, all that anger, it lets me know that he hasn't gone crazy.

[*Pause.*]

And, Edward, I know how strong he is by the way he can tolerate what he sees in your eyes when you look at him, but I don't know how much more of that he can take. [*To* DR. JANIS] Maybe that's why I wanted to meet with you, Doctor. I was afraid what would happen to my husband if he could no longer face his own son. Most of all, Edward, I'm afraid of what will happen to you if you're the reason he can't face himself.

[*Silence. After several moments,* MR. NELSON *appears.*]

MR. NELSON: I think I know what it feels like now when students are waiting outside to see me. I'm sorry for interrupting, but I . . .

[*He notices that his wife is upset, in tears.*]

Mary? Are you all right? [*To* DR. JANIS] Look, I didn't come here for you to upset my family any further than we . . .

DR. JANIS: Mr. Nelson, do you love your son?

MR. NELSON: I beg your pardon?

DR. JANIS: I asked you if you loved your son.

MR. NELSON: Of course I love him.

DR. JANIS: When was the last time you told him?

MR. NELSON: I try to every day, in everything I do. If anybody should be asked about whether or not they love, I'm afraid it's my son.

DR. JANIS: Edward, do you love your father?

[*Silence.*]

I asked if you love your father.

EDWARD: I plead the Fifth.

[MR. NELSON *looks at the floor, obviously hurt by the response.*]

MRS. NELSON: Edward, how could you say that?

EDWARD: I didn't say anything.

MRS. NELSON: That's exactly what I mean.

MR. NELSON: It's all right, Mary. You can't force your own son to love you. It wouldn't mean much that way in any event.

DR. JANIS: Mr. Nelson, on the night that Susan's father stopped her from going to the prom with your son, what did you do?

MR. NELSON: I tried to talk him out of it, for the sake of the kids. I didn't want either one of them hurt because of his prejudice. But after he refused I went over to see him.

[EDWARD *looks at his father, surprised.*]

Ted had gone to his room. I knew he was crying. I could hear him even though he was playing his music loudly and trying to act as if it was no big deal.

DR. JANIS: What happened when you got to Susan's house?

MR. NELSON: He said he didn't want this event to interfere with our friendship. I told him that we had no friendship anymore, that my son was home crying, that I could hear Susan doing the same, and that those tears had cost us so much. I had hoped that they wouldn't cost us any more. We got into a heated exchange.

DR. JANIS: And then?

MR. NELSON [*slowly*]: And then, Doctor, he spit in my face.

[*There is total silence.* MRS. NELSON *looks at her husband as if there is more to tell and expects it to be told.* EDWARD's *stunned look turns gradually to disgust.* DR. JANIS *turns away, embarrassed and disappointed.*]

EDWARD: He spit in your face? You let someone do that to you?

MRS. NELSON: Peter? Tell him.

EDWARD: Tell me what?! That he let some asshole spit in his face and he did nothing!

MRS. NELSON: You don't know what you're saying.

EDWARD: And you don't know who you're living with!

MR. NELSON: I've had enough of this. Mary, I think it's time we left.

EDWARD: Like you did when he spit on you? What did you do, Pop, look at your watch and excuse yourself for staying too long? Or did you beg him for something to wipe it off with ... something used, of course.

[*By this time he is standing directly in front of his father, in confrontation.*]

MR. NELSON: I said it was time to leave.

MRS. NELSON: Peter, for God's sake, tell him!

MR. NELSON: No! I don't have to justify my life to you . . . to some doctor . . . not even to my own son!

EDWARD: How do you justify it to yourself?

[MR. NELSON *attempts to leave but* EDWARD *blocks him. They stare at each other. After several moments, the silence is broken.*]

I asked you a question.

MR. NELSON: And I told you we were leaving . . . Now, get out of my way.

EDWARD: If I were a white man, would you speak to me that way, or would you wait for me to spit on you, too?

[MR. NELSON *takes a step into his son, as if to strike him, but stops himself. He looks at his son with anger, then disappointment, and finally hurt. He moves slowly away from him as* EDWARD *bows his head in shame, wishing that his father had struck him.* MRS. NELSON *moves toward her son, makes him look at her, then speaks.*]

MRS. NELSON: He hit him.

MR. NELSON: Mary!

EDWARD: What?

MRS. NELSON: Your father hit him, Edward . . . He hit Susan's father and almost killed him.

MR. NELSON [*softly*]: Mary . . . I asked you never to tell him that.

MRS. NELSON: I can't let you keep that from him any longer, Peter . . . not now, not thinking what he thinks.

MR. NELSON: And what do you expect him to think now? That's it's OK to strike someone, to lose control, like some thug on the street?

[*Pause.*]

Mary, do you need me to prove myself, too? After all this time, don't you at least know who I am?

[*He walks away.*]

It doesn't matter . . . I know . . . It's the only thing that makes me take it . . . I know who I am . . . I know what I do . . . And I know why.

EDWARD: You hit him?

[MR. NELSON *moves toward* EDWARD.]

MR. NELSON: *Yes!* I hit him! I lost control and let a bigot get the best of me, and I'm not proud of that.

EDWARD: It's something I could have been proud of.

MR. NELSON: Why?

EDWARD: Because you would do that for me.

MR. NELSON: I didn't do it for you! I did it for me. That's what I'm ashamed of, that I finally let one of them get to me . . . finally let one of them prove what all of them thought anyway. When I hit Susan's father, I felt what he and a thousand like him had always failed to make me feel . . . "dirty." I had never felt that before, not even after he spat on me. But, once I lost control, there was no difference between us. That's when I really felt spat upon.

EDWARD: You should have told me. I had a right to know.

MR. NELSON: I had a right for you to believe in me, without knowing.

[*Pause.*]

EDWARD: I needed to see a man.

MR. NELSON: I wanted you to see a father.

EDWARD: Pop, do you really think there's a difference?

MR. NELSON: I don't know, but I'd like to believe that one punch shouldn't have to prove either one. [*To* DR. JANIS] Or do you think differently, Doctor?

DR. JANIS [*lost in thought but not unaware of the question*]: One punch? It may not prove a father or a man, Mr. Nelson, but I suppose it's important for a son to know that a father is capable of throwing one, if provoked enough.

MR. NELSON: And what about a father? What's important for him to know about how a son loves him . . . and why?

[*Pause.*]

DR. JANIS: I'm afraid I can't answer that. You need to discover that for yourself . . . or look into your son's eyes to see what's there now that wasn't there three minutes ago . . .

[MR. NELSON *looks at his son.*]

Or three years ago.

[MR. NELSON *looks at* DR. JANIS; EDWARD *continues to look at his father while* MRS. NELSON *looks at her son.*]

MR. NELSON: Is that really what it takes, Doctor . . . one punch?

[*The lights fade on the Nelsons and rise on* DR. JANIS, *who walks to center stage. The lights fade rapidly on the office and are now intense on* DR. JANIS.]

DR. JANIS: See, Pop, how simple it is . . . one punch; a little slap, that's all. It doesn't take much. A fuckin' principal could do it. A high school principal, Pop! Those guys don't even fart when they're alone! But the colored one hit somebody. Even he was pushed beyond reasonable limits . . . reasonable limits . . . limits, goddamn it! The point when you fight back. The time you say, "No more"! The place where you become a man. Where you do something that makes your kid take notice and feel proud. Pop, you know anything about pride? You know anything about pain? My pain . . . my pride! How could you ask your own son to be ashamed of you?

[*Pause.*]

What did you care about? Cleaning some fucking floor and dirtying your name; washing windows that cursed your own reflection. Windows that shouted: "Clean me, boy! Take the stain off me and place it on yourself." [*Sighs.*] Even the fucking window could feel clean.

[*Long pause.*]

One punch . . . one little slap . . . one "Clean your own fuckin' window" or "Mop your own goddamn floor." Just once . . . once, and you could have gotten your son back instead of eyes that cursed your reflection louder than the windows. Instead of a voice more quiet than that broom you pushed so lightly, so often, and so well. One fuckin' punch! One act of defiance. One tiny little statement of manhood, and I would not have lost my father; I would have not lost myself. One goddamn *punch*!

[*On the word "punch,"* DR. JANIS *takes a violent swing, which leaves him turned slightly away from the audience. There is an immediate blackout.*]

ACT 2

[DR. JANIS *and* DR. ANGOFF *are seated in* DR. ANGOFF's *office. They are in conversation as the lights begin to rise slowly.*]

DR. JANIS: So, when I separated the boy from his parents, it all started to come out.

DR. ANGOFF: The young Nelson?

DR. JANIS: Edward.

DR. ANGOFF: Yes. You don't honestly believe he's going back home and be the good and loyal son.

DR. JANIS: He'll have problems, but nothing he can't handle.

DR. ANGOFF: He's hurting inside.

DR. JANIS: He'll be all right.

DR. ANGOFF: With help ... a great deal of help.

DR. JANIS: What? Would you put him in therapy for a few years?

DR. ANGOFF: And what would you have him do, hit somebody every time he had the urge? Would that solve anything?

DR. JANIS: It might be one of many acceptable alternatives.

DR. ANGOFF: Come on, Paul ... You know that's not an answer.

DR. JANIS: Depends on who's asking the question.

DR. ANGOFF: What's that supposed to mean?

DR. JANIS: Well, Doug, let's put it this way: What would Charles Bronson do? Or Clint Eastwood? ... Or John Wayne?

DR. ANGOFF: What would someone like Martin Luther King do?

DR. JANIS: Junior or Senior?

DR. ANGOFF: Junior.

DR. JANIS: I don't know, Douglass ... Actually, I've always been fascinated as to what might have happened to the civil rights movement if, let us say, Dr. King might have snatched just one redneck cracker by the back of the neck and slapped him till he started singing for Jesus.

DR. ANGOFF: A Negro spiritual, I presume.

DR. JANIS: I think not ... Aretha might be more appropriate ... something like "R-E-S-P-E-C-T, find out what it means to me."

DR. ANGOFF: I think the civil rights movement would have ended.

DR. JANIS: I think it would have begun, but let's not discuss politics. Or was that religion we were dealing with? Anyway, your concern for Edward is touching, but he's stronger than you think.

DR. ANGOFF: He's a kid.

DR. JANIS: He stopped being a "kid" a long time ago.

DR. ANGOFF: Kids don't stop being kids. They just lose some of their freedom to act the part.

DR. JANIS: We're not dealing with a teenybopper from Long Island.

DR. ANGOFF: No. And we're not dealing with a younger version of you, either.

DR. JANIS: I don't know about that. He's pretty sharp.

DR. ANGOFF: But he doesn't hide his pain quite as well.

DR. JANIS: What is that supposed to mean?

DR. ANGOFF: It means I was thinking about our last conversation.

DR. JANIS: I hope you learned something.

DR. ANGOFF: Oh, I think I did. Your story about your father's death, it was moving, eloquent . . . so much so that I hadn't realized how controlled it was . . . how highly intellectualized. I needed time away from you so that the Janis mystique could be less compelling.

DR. JANIS: Do you have a point to this? I mean, before my compelling mystique starts to unduly influence you again.

DR. ANGOFF [*a bit annoyed*]: Sometimes I wonder whether there is a point to anything we do, other than to further perfect a ritualistic dance we should have given up a long time ago. But since we didn't, or couldn't, yes, I have a point to this. I was wrong.

DR. JANIS [*smiling*]: I could have told you that.

DR. ANGOFF [*clearly annoyed, but regaining composure*]: It wasn't so much that you let your father die thinking he was a failure that hurt you, that continues to hurt you. It was that you had let him live thinking that. You might think it's the same thing, but it's not. With the former, you can dismiss it as a quick error in judgment, an emotional block that couldn't be removed quickly enough. But with the latter . . . with the latter, you have to accept responsibility. It had to be deliberate. It had to be intentional. And it had to be an indictment; even from an eleven-year-old boy, whose indictments are often more absolute.

[*Silence.*]

DR. JANIS: I think Edward will be fine. If I were you, I'd say a prayer or two for Susan.

DR. ANGOFF: We weren't talking about Edward or Susan.

DR. JANIS: We weren't talking.

DR. ANGOFF [*angrily*]: We were talking. We weren't listening, but we sure as hell were talking!

DR. JANIS: I'm sorry about last night, Doug.

DR. ANGOFF [*confusedly*]: What about last night?

DR. JANIS: I couldn't make dinner; something came up at work.

DR. ANGOFF: You're working too hard. Maybe you need to get yourself a partner.

DR. JANIS: I'm saving that for when I have a son.

DR. ANGOFF: What if he doesn't want to be a psychiatrist?

DR. JANIS: Then he can be an astronaut.

DR. ANGOFF: And if he doesn't like heights?

DR. JANIS: I'll lower the moon.

DR. ANGOFF: Now, why didn't I think of that?

DR. JANIS: You're too conventional.

DR. ANGOFF: How did we get from your father and hiding your pain to lowering the moon for a son you don't have yet?

DR. JANIS: Douglass, you have to pay attention to the flow of the conversation.

DR. ANGOFF: Why do I have the feeling that you could have a conversation without me?

DR. JANIS [*siting back in the chair, then seriously*]: I see. Tell me, how long have you had this insecurity . . . this feeling that the world goes on without you?

[*Pause.*]

DR. ANGOFF: Did you love him?

[*Silence.*]

Did he love you?

DR. JANIS [*looking away, walks toward the desk, then turns*]: He loved everyone but himself.

[*He looks at his watch.*]

I'd love to continue this, but I'm late.

DR. ANGOFF: For what?

DR. JANIS: I have a session with Davis.

DR. ANGOFF: Even time seems to be on your side.

DR. JANIS: I'm happy to see you're finally dealing with an acceptance of reality.

DR. ANGOFF: In the end, the acceptance you take is equal to the reality you make.

DR. JANIS: Is that from a Beatles song?

DR. ANGOFF: With a change here or there.

DR. JANIS: You should listen to jazz.

DR. ANGOFF: I do, but it's harder to paraphrase.

DR. JANIS: Then listen to the blues. You can repeat it as is, and it still means different things.

DR. ANGOFF: I can't identify with the blues. I've never had a woman leave me.

DR. JANIS: In that case, sing it from the woman's perspective. I'm sure they suffered terribly.

DR. ANGOFF: Funny. Very funny. Stop by after the session with Davis. I'll buy you a drink.

DR. JANIS: I've got some notes to go over tonight. But I'll stop by before then.

[DR. ANGOFF *puts his hand up high, as to wait for a high five from* DR. JANIS, *who looks at* DR. ANGOFF *somewhat awkwardly. After a moment or two,* DR. JANIS *responds as if to pacify* DR. ANGOFF, *who appears delighted that he has discovered a new communication technique.*]

You've been watching too much basketball, Doug.

DR. ANGOFF: It seems to work for a team.

DR. JANIS: Do you know why teams wear different colors, Doug?

DR. ANGOFF: To tell them apart.

DR. JANIS [*pointing to him in agreement*]: Don't forget it.

[DR. JANIS *exits as the lights fade on* DR. ANGOFF. DR. JANIS *pauses at center stage. He hears* DR. ANGOFF's *voice: "Did you love him? . . . Did he love you?"* DR. JANIS *looks back toward the darkened office as the lights rise on* DR. JANIS's *office and* MR. DAVIS. *After a beat,* DR. JANIS *proceeds to his office and greets* MR. DAVIS.]

Hello, Mr. Davis.

MR. DAVIS: Doctor.

[*Long pause as he takes a seat.*]

Before we start, I owe you an apology. My behavior during our last meeting was inexcusable.

DR. JANIS: I think the debt is even, an apology for an apology.

MR. DAVIS: No, you were right. You don't need to apologize for the truth.

DR. JANIS [*taking a seat next to* MR. DAVIS]: The truth can always be packaged differently, so it can be swallowed easier or held more comfortably.

MR. DAVIS: I've had things a little too comfortable for a while now. I think your truth was packaged just fine.

DR. JANIS: What would you like to talk about, Mr. Davis?

MR. DAVIS: The truth.

DR. JANIS: Packaged, or out of the box?

MR. DAVIS: How 'bout a little of both.

DR. JANIS: Ready when you are.

MR. DAVIS: You know what I wanted to be when I was a kid? A kid, hell, I was twenty, but I guess that was a kid to my father. I wanted to be a writer, a creative writer. But it had been preordained from birth. I had to assume my father's business. I was the only child, you know. After that was accomplished, Father and Mother moved into separate rooms. I think the closest they ever got was at dinner. But the table was quite long, and Father would be at the head, while Mother would sit at the opposite end. I was in the middle. [*Smiles.*] I guess in more ways than one. They never really had to talk to each other or to me, not even to pass the butter or salt and pepper. We had a butler and several servants, and we seemed to talk to each other through them.

[*He looks at* DR. JANIS *for a beat.*]

You were right, you know.

DR. JANIS: About what?

MR. DAVIS: I did have a mammy.

DR. JANIS [*smiling*]: I never doubted it.

MR. DAVIS: She was the only one I could ever feel comfortable with. I think she was the only one who ever held me when I cried.

DR. JANIS: And she never told anyone.

MR. DAVIS: No. Never.

DR. JANIS: Should she have?

MR. DAVIS: Father would have had her fired. He would have fired me, if he could have.

DR. JANIS: And your mother?

MR. DAVIS: I never knew what she wanted, if she wanted anything at all. At my father's funeral, it was the first time I had seen her out from under his shadow.

DR. JANIS: And what did you see?

MR. DAVIS: I don't know really. By that time, I had become just like him. I think she noticed and decided that being under one shadow had been quite enough. She sold the house and everything in it, and then she disappeared.

DR. JANIS: Did you ever hear from her?

MR. DAVIS: Several years later I was notified of her death. She donated all her belongings to charitable organizations. But she did leave me one thing. I received it in a small brown package. It was the only manuscript I had ever written. I thought my father had thrown it away. But evidently Mother had kept it, probably rescued it from the trash. When I opened it and recognized what it was, I cried.

[*Pause.*]

It's odd, I didn't cry at being notified of her death. I cried for some silly story written years earlier. She gave me back a part of my past, and I cried about it.

DR. JANIS: Do you remember what the story was about?

MR. DAVIS [*laughing*]: It was about a successful businessman.

DR. JANIS: Did it end happily?

MR. DAVIS: Very.

DR. JANIS: What happened?

MR. DAVIS: He sold the business, and lived.

DR. JANIS: Tell me about your father, Mr. Davis.

MR. DAVIS [*bitterly, and with pain*]: A cold man. I never remember him laughing. Never. Oh, he had that business laugh. You know, the one that's meant to take up space, or follow the boss's bad jokes; but never the real one. The one you can't stop because it comes naturally. The one that's contagious and causes others to feel it, too.

DR. JANIS: Did you . . .

[*He stops for a moment, realizing the question he's about to ask has been asked of him.*]

Did you love him?

MR. DAVIS: Oh, yes. All the way to the funeral. And then I realized I didn't have to anymore. He couldn't punish me if he thought I was no longer behaving properly.

[*Pause.*]

Didn't you get angry when I called you a "black bastard"?

DR. JANIS: I was angry at myself.

MR. DAVIS: Why?

DR. JANIS: By that time I had offered to pick up the cost of the session. Calling me "black bastard" at one hundred and fifty dollars an hour is one thing, but when it's free . . .

[*Both laugh. Pause.*]

MR. DAVIS: Is it wrong not to love your father?

DR. JANIS: Always.

MR. DAVIS: I didn't love him.

DR. JANIS: We learn not to love, Mr. Davis. Sometimes the ones who teach us are the ones we want to love most of all.

MR. DAVIS: My father never taught me much of anything . . . He seemed never to have the time. Whenever I tried to make it, I felt like I was disturbing him. Either that or else I'd mess things up.

[*He is quiet for several moments, thinking of some memory.*]

I remember my father was in the den working on some account. I was playing in the hallway leading to the den. I must have been seven or eight at the time. I kicked this big red ball too hard and it went into the den, rolling toward the desk my father was working behind. I ran to try and stop it before it hit the desk, but I tripped into it instead and knocked a cup of coffee over. It spilled across the desk and onto the ledger sheets. My father got up furiously and grabbed me by the shoulders. He had enormous hands and fingers and I was quite convinced my life was about to be crushed out of my body. But just as suddenly as he had grabbed me, his grip softened and he was holding me, looking at me. It seemed like it was forever, or maybe I just wanted it to be. He picked up the red ball and handed it to me. Then he gave me a little pat on the rear end.

[*Pause.*]

I left the den feeling my father had played with me. I kept that red ball for a very long time. I had forgotten all about that.

[*Silence.*]

DR. JANIS: Do you still think you don't love him?

MR. DAVIS [*close to tears*]: I wanted to love him . . . he just never let me.

DR. JANIS: There are many things we can blame our fathers for, but they can't control that, even if they wanted to.

[*There is a long silence as* MR. DAVIS *cries softly.*]

MR. DAVIS: I would give all that I have to be in that room with my father again. To have him hold me one more time. To have one more chance.

DR. JANIS: All of us would like another chance, Mr. Davis . . . all of us.

[*He looks away and begins to speak as if he were alone, reflecting on his own situation.*]

A chance to show parents the power they have over the lives of their children; a chance for children to say the right things to their fathers before they die. A chance to explain the silence.

[*There is a long pause as both* DR. JANIS *and* MR. DAVIS *are lost in thought.* DR. JANIS, *finally realizing* MR. DAVIS's *presence, moves toward him, touching him lightly on the shoulder.* MR. DAVIS *grabs* DR. JANIS *and begins to sob.* DR. JANIS *attempts to make a comforting motion but doesn't seem to know how.* DR. JANIS *stiffens uncomfortably and then becomes suddenly professionally distant and cold. The lights in* DR. ANGOFF's *office begin to rise slowly.* DR. ANGOFF *is looking in the direction of* DR. JANIS *and* MR. DAVIS, *a long and cold stare. After several moments,* DR. ANGOFF *moves toward his desk and sits, still looking into* DR. JANIS's *office.*]

MR. DAVIS [*pulling away from* DR. JANIS]: I'm sorry . . . I don't know what came over me. I apologize . . . [*With an embarrassed laugh*] That's two apologies in one day.

[*Lights begin to fade on* MR. DAVIS *as* DR. JANIS *proceeds slowly to center stage. He appears uncomfortable, shaken. He looks back at his darkened office.* DR. ANGOFF *is still watching as* DR. JANIS *speaks to himself.*]

DR. JANIS: "Two apologies in one day" . . . it ain't enough . . . It ain't hardly enough.

[DR. JANIS *proceeds to* DR. ANGOFF's *office as lights fade on center stage and rise brightly on* DR. ANGOFF, *who is now preoccupied with some papers on his desk and generally trying to avoid* DR. JANIS. DR. JANIS *waits for some form of recognition, but none is forthcoming. After several moments,* DR. JANIS *breaks the silence.*]

I think Davis and I are doing better now.

[*There is no response from* DR. ANGOFF.]

Did you hear me? I said . . .

DR. ANGOFF: I know what you said.

DR. JANIS: Well, what do you think?

DR. ANGOFF: Since when has that mattered to you?

DR. JANIS: What are you upset about?

DR. ANGOFF [*cynically*]: Am I upset?

DR. JANIS: You're not a good liar.

DR. ANGOFF: Thank you. It comes from not practicing.

DR. JANIS: Are you trying to tell me something?

DR. ANGOFF: I've learned I can't tell you shit, Paul!

DR. JANIS: Look, what the fuck is it with you?

[DR. ANGOFF *pushes the paper to the side of the desk and looks at* DR. JANIS *for the first time.*]

DR. ANGOFF: He needed you, man.

[*Pause.*]

And you couldn't respond.

DR. JANIS: What are you talking about?

DR. ANGOFF: He reached out for you. He touched you . . . and needed to be touched back. You could have done that, Paul. No one would have thought of you as less black. You could have held the poor son of a bitch and made him feel as if you were in the same fuckin' room . . . that you gave a good goddamn about him. But not the invincible Dr. Janis! Not the world's first perfect psychiatrist. The one that cures white patients in a single visit . . . without the laying on of hands.

[*Pause.*]

Do you really despise us that much?

DR. JANIS: What, did you have a hard day at work or something? Your dog die?

DR. ANGOFF: It wasn't the dog that died, Paul. Maybe it was our friendship. No, that couldn't be . . . something has to live before it dies, and you wouldn't let that happen. We exchange some pleasantries, an occasional glance of admiration here or there . . . But if it gets too close . . . too human . . . it's time for you to leave.

[*He rises and begins to pace.*]

"Want to have drinks, Paul? . . . Oh, I'd love to Doug, but can't today . . . Dinner next week? . . . Sure, Doug, I'll give you a call."

[*Pause.*]

But the call never comes. You can't let me be part of your world, your social life. It doesn't matter if it's because of my skin color or yours. It's the same madness. I was hoping there were some of us left who had somehow managed to remain sane . . . I give you a little intellectual stimulation, a little entertainment between other experiments on the human condition . . . No, Paul, it wasn't the dog that died.

DR. JANIS: What is it with you people?

DR. ANGOFF: Whoa! Did Captain Courageous, the Phantom of Psychiatry, slip up and use a euphemistic phrase like "you people"! Not the great freedom fighter, spokesperson for equality, justice, and ham hocks in every kitchen!

DR. JANIS: It wasn't a "slipup." And don't get so goddamn cute! You wouldn't know a ham hock if it snuck up and raped your rice!

DR. ANGOFF: Can give but not take? Tsk. Tsk.

DR. JANIS: You people need to be loved . . . or forgiven . . . or both. Would it make you feel safer at night . . . would you sleep more comfortably if you knew we weren't angry anymore? That we aren't in some back room plotting a strategy to take over . . . to get even? Or maybe we should be in the fields singing songs of praise, shuffling happy feet?

[*Pause.*]

You know what's troubling you? You resent seeing a black man who doesn't need your help . . . your couch . . . your artificial wisdom refined by a dozen extra years of educational distortion and cultural manipulation.

[*The two men look at each other for a long time, and then* DR. ANGOFF *begins to speak with a sad frustration.*]

DR. ANGOFF: Tell me something, Paul. Do you date white women? Ever think of dating white women?

DR. JANIS [*amused*]: Oh, Doug, you disappoint me. I never thought you would give in to such kinky interests.

DR. ANGOFF: Why don't you try answering the question, Paul?

DR. JANIS: But, Doug, don't you know that's all I think about . . .

[*He starts to speak with a thick accent, meant to depict a slave-type response.*]

I means I cants hardly controls myself. When I sees me a white woman, Dr. Doug, sur, well my minds jus' goes a younda and den I preys: "Oh, Lawd, cants I have me a white woman jus' dis once!"

[*There is a long pause as the two men stare at each other.* DR. JANIS *finally breaks the silence, this time harshly.*]

No, Doug, as much as this may surprise you, I do not date white women.

DR. ANGOFF: When you see a white woman, what do you see?

DR. JANIS: To tell you the truth, Massa Angoff, I don't see much of anything.

DR. ANGOFF: No? I'm rather surprised. I thought you'd see something. Probably something pathetic, or confused, or sinister, or untouchable, or some fucking image symbolically corrupt.

[*Pause.*]

I want to know when you look at a white woman . . . I mean, if you just happen to see one walking down the street one day, whether or not, just for the sake of things, just once, in this goddamn fucked-up world of dos and don'ts . . . just once . . . you might see a person. Someone who might care for you . . . who, as strange and bizarre as this might seem . . . who, one day, you might care about. A woman, Paul! A person! Because if you can't see that . . . if there is no possibility of ever seeing that . . . then what in God's name do you see when you see me?

DR. JANIS [*with a curious look*]: Why, Doug, I wouldn't want to date you either.

DR. ANGOFF: Stop it! Just stop . . . [*Shaking his head*] I can't take this anymore. You win. You're better than me. You're quicker . . . sharper. I can't compete with you. You want to score points? You want to frustrate me? OK. You've won.

[*He looks at* DR. JANIS *for several moments in silence.*]

You know, for all that knowledge trapped inside you, for all that talent blocking out the sensitivity that could make you human, you're really just a frightened and scared man, with a pent-up rage that will destroy you and those who want to be a part of you.

DR. JANIS: Don't talk to me about rage, Doug . . . You know shit about rage! When you leave here tonight and decide you need to get home a little quicker than the speed limit allows, what do you have to worry about if a cop stops you? A little inconvenience? A fuckin' ticket? That same cop stops me, I have to wonder if there's a police call for a well-dressed black man that might get me killed. Or if he's in a bad mood and resents seeing a nigger making more money than he does . . . I have to wonder, should I smile and make this motherfucka think I'm not showing enough respect or look serious and risk being thought of as arrogant or uppity or cocky . . . If a cop stops you, it costs you a few minutes or a few dollars. If he stops me, it could cost me my life! So don't talk about rage to me!

[*Pause.*]

Last week, a black teenager . . . a goddamn kid . . . gets shot and crippled for the rest of his life because he wanted to pay for a pizza and some off-duty assassin thought he was trying to rob the store . . . A kid, Doug . . . a fuckin' kid reaches in his pocket to pay for some food, and a cop thinks he's going for a gun . . . His crime was being hungry, and poor, and black, and don't ever talk to me about rage! When I first met you, I wanted to put my foot up your ass . . . You're seated behind your desk, looking over my papers, wondering whether or not you had the time to be my mentor. You look up at me and say: "Well, you appear to be quite bright . . . quite intelligent . . ." Two degrees from Harvard, one from Yale, and you have to tell me what you would feel too foolish telling a white boy with the same credentials . . . as if my intelligence needed your validation . . . Or maybe you needed to shock your own value system into some type of sensibility that would help you to accept my existence, my legitimacy . . . As long as you live, don't you ever talk to me about rage.

[*Pause.*]

You want honesty? You think you're really ready for that? Well, here's a dose of truth for you . . . You don't cure your patients, Doug . . . You become friends with them . . . Good ol' Dr. Angoff, for two hundred dollars a week, they get someone to talk to. And so you're frustrated 'cause I won't be your friend for free. Certainly, the most exotic one you'd have, which is why you wanted me to begin with . . . You're not really very different from Davis. He wanted me because he had no one else he could admit failure to. While you, you needed me to round out your menu of personal experiences.

DR. ANGOFF [*obviously taken aback and a bit shaken*]: I never knew the resentment ran that deep . . . the pain . . . I had no idea.

DR. JANIS: No . . . You never did . . . You never could . . . It's the grand delusion. Give 'em enough education, and they're bound to love you. Have them read, Dylan and Keats, and they'll make your problems their own.

DR. ANGOFF: And so, what have we created, Paul, a modern-day Bigger Thomas, whose rage is impeccably dressed in a three-piece suit and whose violence is hidden in the language of the articulate?

DR. JANIS: So, you've read Richard Wright, too. I must say, you understand him better than Ellison.

DR. ANGOFF: I'm not sure I understand anything anymore. I'm not sure I want to.

[DR. ANGOFF *walks toward his desk and picks up a file. He walks to* DR. JANIS *and hands it to him.*]

You might as well take this. It's your file. You may find it interesting reading.

[DR. JANIS *glances at the file quickly, disinterested, and then takes the pages out and flings them across the office.*]

DR. JANIS: Like you said, you probably don't understand anything anymore.

DR. ANGOFF: Anything else you'd like to toss? Come on, Paul, it's about time for you to lose control. Here, why don't you kick a chair over.

[DR. ANGOFF *kicks a chair over, then looks at* DR. JANIS.]

No? You don't want to kick? OK, then, how about we throw some more paper around the office?

[DR. ANGOFF *takes some sheets of paper off his desk and begins to toss them around the room.*]

You don't want to do that, either? Fine. Let's see . . .

[*He takes the wastebasket and hands it to* DR. JANIS.]

Why don't you just empty that, Paul?

[DR. JANIS *holds the wastebasket and then slowly, while looking at* DR. ANGOFF, *turns it upside down.* DR. JANIS *shakes the basket slowly and, when all the trash is on the floor, tosses the basket to the side.*]

DR. JANIS: Are you satisfied?

[DR. JANIS *reaches into his jacket, pulls out his wallet, takes out a twenty-dollar bill, then places the wallet back inside his jacket.*]

Here's twenty dollars. Pay somebody to clean up this mess.

[*The two men are facing each other.* DR. JANIS *has his hand extended with the money.* DR. ANGOFF *does not take it.*]

DR. ANGOFF: The office comes with a janitor. It's included with the rent.

[DR. JANIS *stiffens.*]

What's the matter, Paul? Does the word offend you?

[DR. JANIS *places the money slowly into his pocket. He then begins to go around the room, picking up paper and generally cleaning up.*]

DR. JANIS: This is what you'd rather me do, anyway, isn't it, Doug? I mean, doesn't this seem more appropriate to you?

DR. ANGOFF: You are a bit overdressed.

DR. JANIS: Janitors have better wages now. It happened when the whites integrated.

[DR. JANIS *continues to straighten up the office and places his papers back into his file. After several moments, while on one knee, he reads something on one of the sheets of paper that catches his interest. He rises slowly and walks toward* DR. ANGOFF *with the single sheet of paper in his hand. He studies it and then begins to read it aloud.*]

"Paul is a victim of self-hate, not unlike many blacks, who have internalized the factors which contributed to their victimization."

[*Silence.*]

How many blacks have been inside this office, Doug? How many patients do you have who are black?

DR. ANGOFF: Not many.

DR. JANIS: How many?

[*Pause.*]

DR. ANGOFF: None.

DR. JANIS: If I were to open your phone book, besides myself, how many black people could I call?

DR. ANGOFF: I don't have the phone numbers of any other blacks in my book.

DR. JANIS: None? Well, your knowledge of us must have come from someplace . . . How else could you know so much about our "self-hate"? Did you hang with a lot of black folks at Yale in the early fifties? No, I guess not.

[*Pause.*]

You haven't been to Harlem recently, have you? No, somehow I don't see you on the A train. [*Pointing in recognition*] I know, *Life* magazine, right? That's where you learned about us. [*With doubt*] Of course, there was a while there when *Life* wasn't publishing. But, what the hell, you probably kept the back issues. You know, the ones with the "Negro Problem" on the covers.

DR. ANGOFF: That's enough, Paul. You've made your point. But I'm still a psychiatrist. And I'm competent to judge problems, independent of race.

DR. JANIS: "Independent of race"? Well, why didn't you describe my self-hate, independent of race? Did I make a mistake reading it?

[*He looks at the paper again.*]

No. There it is. "Self-hate, not unlike many blacks." Was that a typo, Doug?

[*Long pause.*]

You asked me earlier if I ever wanted to date white women. Now, what was it, exactly, that made you ask that?

DR. ANGOFF: I already explained.

DR. JANIS: I was into my "self-hate" at the time, so I couldn't hear you. Would you mind telling me again?

DR. ANGOFF [*slightly frustrated and uneasy*]: I was making the point that if you couldn't see women—

DR. JANIS: White women.

DR. ANGOFF: As potential lovers, or partners, then you've allowed racism to affect relationships in such a way as to—

DR. JANIS: Why use that example, Doug? You could have used a hundred others. You could have asked if I've ever gone to the movies with a white friend . . . or if I bowl with the psychiatrists' league on Tuesday nights. Or if I enjoy punk rock concerts. But you didn't do that. You wanted to know about me and white women. You have any idea why you wanted to know that?

DR. ANGOFF: I told you why.

DR. JANIS: To you, the trained psychiatrist, the competent judge of persons independent of race, blacks hate themselves and love your women. You got the problem and the solution all neatly tied together into one hell of a distorted and arrogant vision of the world that validates any lie you create.

[*Pause.*]

I have to hand it to you, Doug. In fact, our whole profession is to be commended. There's no way of ever winning an argument with a Freudian. If I want to sleep with my mother, they already knew it. If I don't, I'm into rejection and denial. And if I want to sleep with your mother, I'm manifesting projection. Now, how can you beat a perfect system like that?

[*Pause.*]

You don't know shit about me, or black people, or your goddamn self! You've been looking to find out what a nigger is ever since you asked that black man fifty years ago. And when you couldn't find one, you did what everyone else does, you created your own. It made it easier to explain something you couldn't understand.

[*He approaches* DR. ANGOFF.]

Would it make you feel better if you called me a nigger?

DR. ANGOFF: I'd rather call you a cab.

DR. JANIS: Cabs don't pick up black men this late.

[*Beat.*]

Have you ever called someone a nigger, Doug?

[*Pause.*]

Have you?

DR. ANGOFF [*softly*]: I'm sure I have.

DR. JANIS: To their face?

DR. ANGOFF: Probably not.

DR. JANIS: Were you wearing a hood at the time?

DR. ANGOFF: I didn't deserve that, Paul. You may not accept the term "self-hate" as appropriate or accurate. But hating your father is just an extension of that.

[DR. JANIS *looks at* DR. ANGOFF *with disbelief, then sadness.*]

DR. JANIS: You haven't heard anything I've said, have you? I never hated my father, Doug. I hated the fact that I loved him.

[*Pause.*]

I loved him in the only way I could, as a child, not fully allowed to be a son. He loved me in the only way he knew how, as a black father, not fully allowed to be a man . . . But we loved each other. Even he knew that, which is why he asked me not to. For some reason, he believed if you loved someone, you would try to be like them . . . He wanted more for me. And maybe he was afraid he couldn't help me get it.

[*He moves closer to* DR. ANGOFF.]

I once told him that I wanted to be a lawyer. I didn't even know what a lawyer did, I just thought it would impress him. I think it hurt him instead. I saw this glimpse of pride on his face rapidly turn into fear, to doubt, to his own sense of reality. It is a terrible thing, to see a child's dream die on a father's face.

[*Pause.*]

From that time on, I never told him what I wanted to be.

[*He looks at* DR. ANGOFF *to wherever common truth can be found.*]

But we did love each other. He loved me enough to risk losing me . . . I loved him enough not to tell him.

[*Silence.*]

I wish I hadn't loved him so much.

[*Beat.*]

Good-bye, Doug.

[*He begins to exit but stops at* DR. ANGOFF's *voice.*]

DR. ANGOFF: Paul, will I see you . . . again?

DR. JANIS: Do you have any idea how much contempt I feel for you?

DR. ANGOFF: Because I'm white?

DR. JANIS [*sadly*]: No. Because you want me to be.

DR. ANGOFF: I've never wanted that.

DR. JANIS: You've never known how to want anything else. You think of it as an honor, like being admitted into your private club or getting a key to the executive restroom. It's amazing what lengths men will go to in order to keep their piss private.

[*He looks at* DR. ANGOFF *with some regret.*]

Do you know what a maid knows?

[DR. ANGOFF *looks puzzled.*]

Everything . . . She does your laundry, so she knows when your ass ain't clean. She knows about the house and every secret in it. No one analyzes the maid, Doug. No one.

[*Beat.*]

I just wish the fuck I knew who the maid goes to for help.

[*He suddenly grabs* DR. ANGOFF's *hand and begins to shake it.*]

That's how I shake hands, Doug. I've always shaken hands that way.

[*Pause.*]

Haven't you?

[DR. JANIS *exits. The lights fade quickly on* DR. ANGOFF's *office and rise on center stage, where* DR. JANIS *stops.*]

One punch. Everyone has the right to throw one punch, Pop. The problem is, sometimes you just don't know who to hit.

[DR. JANIS *proceeds to his office. He is lost in thought as* EDWARD *enters. For a moment, he goes unnoticed, and then he startles* DR. JANIS, *who recovers quickly and makes an attempt at a smile and greeting.*]

Edward? Well, this is a pleasant surprise.

EDWARD: I needed to see you . . . I'm not a liar . . . I guess I'm a lot of things, but I'm not that.

DR. JANIS: Did anyone say you were?

EDWARD: I remember what was in those letters . . . from Susan . . . I kept them, at least, until yesterday.

DR. JANIS: You don't have them now?

EDWARD: Nobody has them now. I suppose I didn't want them anymore. Well, I just wanted to tell you that.

[*They look at each other for several moments.*]

DR. JANIS: You want to have a seat?

[*He motions to the chair.*]

EDWARD: No . . . Makes me feel like a patient . . . Did I interrupt something? You look kinda upset.

DR. JANIS: Oh, just had an argument . . . no big thing.

EDWARD: With one of your patients?

DR. JANIS: No, with another psychiatrist.

EDWARD: Is he a brother, too?

DR. JANIS [*smiling*]: No.

EDWARD: Do psychiatrists fight with each other a lot?

DR. JANIS: All the time. I think we resent seeing each other for free.

EDWARD: You didn't cut nobody, did ya?

DR. JANIS: I didn't bring my knife.

EDWARD [*after studying* DR. JANIS *for a moment*]: You don't look much like a knife carrier anyway. Maybe a small derringer . . . with a pearl handle . . . Yeah, that seems more like you.

DR. JANIS: Guns are considered phallic symbols . . . Would you mind very much if you saw me as a .357 magnum?

EDWARD: You're all right, Doc.

DR. JANIS: You want to sit there?

[*He points to his own chair.*]

EDWARD: You mean your chair?

[DR. JANIS *nods yes.* EDWARD *sits and begins to feel how the chair suits him. He seems to be undergoing a change in power and status as he looks around the room and then motions to* DR. JANIS.]

Why don't you have a seat?

[DR. JANIS *smiles and then takes a seat next to* EDWARD. *They sit in silence for several moments and glance at each other a number of times before* EDWARD *finally speaks.*]

You got any kids?
DR. JANIS: No.
EDWARD: Why not?
DR. JANIS: I never wanted to be evaluated that honestly.
EDWARD: If you got nothing to hide, the truth shouldn't matter.
DR. JANIS: I'm not bothered by the truth. I'm bothered by honest evaluations.
EDWARD: Is there a difference?
DR. JANIS: Only in the accuracy, not the outcome.
EDWARD: What made you want to be a psychiatrist?
DR. JANIS: I couldn't play basketball.

[*Pause.*]

EDWARD: What do you do when patients don't answer questions?
DR. JANIS: I keep asking them.
EDWARD: What made you want to be a psychiatrist?
DR. JANIS: I had a terrible hook shot.
EDWARD: What made you want to be a psychiatrist?
DR. JANIS: Too small for power forward.
EDWARD: What made you want to be a psychiatrist?

[*Beat.*]

DR. JANIS [*smiling warmly*]: I thought I knew something about silence. The pain that causes it. The fear that perpetuates it . . . Being quiet can hurt a lot of people.
EDWARD: Were you quiet?
DR. JANIS: When I shouldn't have been . . . When it would have made a difference not to be.

EDWARD: Was your father really a janitor?

[DR. JANIS *nods yes, then takes a wallet from his jacket and removes a picture.*]

DR. JANIS: Here's a picture of him.

[EDWARD *takes the picture and studies it.*]

My mother used to think he looked a lot like Paul Robeson.

EDWARD [*handing the picture back to* DR. JANIS, *who places it on his desk*]: Who's Paul Robeson?

[*Pause.*]

DR. JANIS: Played football at Rutgers.

EDWARD [*taking out his wallet to hand a picture to* DR. JANIS]: That's a picture of Susan.

DR. JANIS [*looking at it*]: Is that you under the lampshade?

EDWARD [*shrugging*]: I learned to party white.

[*Pause.*]

You think it's strange that I kept her picture?

DR. JANIS [*handing the picture back*]: Depends on why you kept it.

EDWARD: I never wanted to be that stupid again . . . that naive . . . You know, after what happened with Susan's father got around the school, I started to learn about other things . . . why parties were canceled after I was invited . . . why friends never introduced me to their sisters . . . I kept the picture 'cause I wanted to remember what to hate.

DR. JANIS: Your memory that bad, you had to keep a picture for three years?

EDWARD: What were you quiet about?

DR. JANIS: My father.

EDWARD: Why?

DR. JANIS: I didn't know how to tell him I loved him . . . I didn't think he wanted me to.

[*Pause.*]

Why'd you keep the picture so long?

EDWARD: Couldn't find a frame that fit.

DR. JANIS: Why'd you keep the picture so long?

EDWARD: Forgot it was in my wallet.

DR. JANIS: Why'd you keep the picture so long?

EDWARD: What picture?

DR. JANIS: Why'd you ...

EDWARD: Because I cared! [*Painful smile, then softly*] Because I cared ... Now that is strange, isn't it?

[*Pause.*]

How long were you quiet?

DR. JANIS: As long as it gets.

EDWARD: How long is that?

DR. JANIS: While my father was dying.

[*Beat.*]

You really think it's strange to care about someone?

EDWARD: You help many white people?

DR. JANIS: They're most of the people I see.

EDWARD: What's their hang-up?

DR. JANIS: Dear Abby takes too long to respond to their letters.

EDWARD [*smiling*]: I like you, Doc. You don't take things too serious. You're not like my father. He worries whether or not he tips the newsboy enough ... Of course, the newsboy is white, and Daddy wants to please all of them ... even the little ones.

DR. JANIS: Black principal of a school attacks a white man in a small town. You think they give promotions for that?

EDWARD: If they did, a lot of blacks would move into the neighborhood.

[*Pause.*]

Doc, if someone had spit in your face ... what would you have done?

DR. JANIS: Depends.

EDWARD: On what?

DR. JANIS: On whether I was carrying my knife or my derringer.

[*Pause.*]

What were in the letters, Edward?

EDWARD: Just that Susan was ashamed of her parents and that she wanted to stay in touch.

DR. JANIS: Did you ever answer her?

EDWARD: No. Well, actually, yes. But I never mailed it. So, I guess that means no, doesn't it?

DR. JANIS: That means no.

EDWARD: I tried calling her one day. It was right after she tried to—you know, take her life.

DR. JANIS: What happened?

EDWARD: Her father took the phone from her. He said he hated me. Told me I had destroyed his family. Then he said he wished I was dead and hung up.

[*Beat.*]

I kind of figured after that we weren't gonna be drinkin' buddies.

[*Long pause.*]

DR. JANIS: What did you do after that?

EDWARD [*shrugging*]: I don't know. I remember holding the phone for a long time. I guess I cried.

DR. JANIS: You guess?

[EDWARD *looks at* DR. JANIS *for a beat.*]

EDWARD: It really messes with you when an adult tells you he wishes you were dead.

[*Beat.*]

Yeah. I cried.

DR. JANIS: And then?

EDWARD: And then I hated.

[*Pause.*]

Doc, am I screwed up?

DR. JANIS: Do you think you are?

EDWARD: I don't know who to hate anymore. I've tried it with everyone and it hasn't helped.

DR. JANIS: Edward, if you've learned that much, then you're a lot less fucked up than the rest of us.

EDWARD [*studying* DR. JANIS *closely*]: Did you swear to impress me?

DR. JANIS: What do you think?

[*Long pause.*]

EDWARD: I think it's not strange to care about someone . . . just stupid sometimes.

DR. JANIS: Only if you don't let them know.

EDWARD: And when you let them know, what happens then?

DR. JANIS [*moving to his desk*]: Maybe nothing. Maybe you get hurt. Or you get loved. But the one thing you never have to worry about is having to live with not saying it.

[*Pause.*]

So what do you do with your life now?

EDWARD [*shrugs*]: I don't know . . . Too small to play power forward.

[*Pause.*]

You loved him a lot, your father?

[DR. JANIS *looks at him softly.* EDWARD *rises.*]

I better be getting home. I have some things to say. Not all of it will be good, you know?

DR. JANIS: Just let it be honest . . . and fair.

[*The two shake hands firmly, then look at each other.* DR. JANIS *suddenly brings* EDWARD *to him. They hug like father and son, or older and younger brother, or friends.* EDWARD *takes a step back and looks at* DR. JANIS *oddly before questioning him.*]

EDWARD: Hey, Doc, you're not . . . funny or anything, are you?

DR. JANIS: Edward, I'll tell you what, if it makes it easier, think of me as a teammate who just scored the winning touchdown.

EDWARD [*thinking for a moment*]: Oh. Well, that's OK then.

[*They give one more embrace, then part.* EDWARD *begins his exit but turns halfway in the light and darkness.*]

This Robeson . . . he was more than a football player, wasn't he?

DR. JANIS: Much more.

EDWARD: See you, Doc.

DR. JANIS: Take care, Edward.

[EDWARD *exits.* DR. JANIS *is left in the office looking at the area that* EDWARD *has just vacated. He smiles, but it is a sad smile, a smile that eventually turns to a distant recollection. He moves slowly to his desk, sees his father's picture, picks it up gently, and walks to his seat. He sits, arms on knees, both hands holding the picture. He looks at it for several moments.*]

Do you remember when you used to hold me on your lap? You would blink your eyes, then I would blink mine. We'd keep doing that, and smiling, and before you knew it I would fall asleep. I remember one time, I thought I would fool you and not really fall asleep. So I closed my eyes, for a long time. Then I opened them, real quickly to try and catch you.

[*Pause.*]

I saw you looking at me . . . staring through me. You were crying. No sobs. No noise. Just tears, streaming from your face to mine. I closed my eyes so you wouldn't know I had seen you. But I will never forget how those tears felt on me.

[DR. JANIS *is crying. No sobs. No noise. Just tears, falling on the picture of his father.*]

They burned . . . and in a way, they cleansed. I knew those tears were for me. I just never knew why.

[*Pause.*]

Pop? It's the tears that you don't see that really burn. [*Holding his father's picture*] To hold a mind here. [*Holding his father's picture extended*] To wash the pain away. [*In tears*] To steal the memory that makes it ache. [*Standing*] To forgive the silence for being so loud. Silence! No stronger indictment than that. No more painful response than no response. No more cowardly response than the failure to speak, to reach out, to touch . . .

[*Pause.*]

To change the world of a black child, grown old. *I love you, Pop!* . . . [*Softly*] I love you . . . Can you hear me? *I love you!*

[*He studies the picture for an answer.*]

Does it make a difference, now? Does it still matter? I love you . . .

[*He wipes his tears away. A moment passes.* DR. JANIS *then sees* MR. STEFANO *standing there, smiling sheepishly.* MR. STEFANO *is dressed in a loud tropical shirt, Bermuda shorts, and argyle knee socks, with penny loafers. He has a camera strapped around his neck and is wearing a fishing cap.*]

MR. STEFANO: Hi, Doc.

DR. JANIS: James?

MR. STEFANO: Bet you're wondering why I'm dressed like this, huh?

DR. JANIS: The . . . thought had occurred to me.

MR. STEFANO: I'm leaving my wife . . . Well, I was going to leave my wife, now I'm not sure.

DR. JANIS: And you dressed like that to make up your mind?

MR. STEFANO: Oh, no. I dressed like this when I thought I was going. You see, I've always wanted to travel. You know, visit Tahiti. Plus, I always wanted a camera; the thirty-five-millimeter jobs, not those little Instamatics.

DR. JANIS: And you're not thinking of going now?

MR. STEFANO: When I told the family, I was expecting a celebration.

DR. JANIS: You didn't get one?

MR. STEFANO: They seemed upset, not angry, or anything like that. I mean, really upset. That's why I came here. I wanted to know if you thought I was doing the right thing?

DR. JANIS: I don't know, James. I really don't know. What do you think?

MR. STEFANO: I thought I knew. I guess I'm just getting cold feet. That's to be expected, isn't it, Doc?

[Pause.]

Shit, Doc, I'm scared! What should I do?

DR. JANIS: They teach good psychiatrists never to answer those kind of questions.

[Pause.]

Let me be less than a good psychiatrist, straight-out, man-to-man.

MR. STEFANO: Man-to-man.

DR. JANIS: I think you ought to do everything you can to make your kids and your wife love you . . . not with any goddamn toys that are tossed aside before the batteries run down . . . not with any coats or jewelry . . . just you. And once you've done that, if it's not enough, tell them all to go to hell and go find yourself a new family, only do it right this time . . . And anyway . . .

MR. STEFANO: What?

DR. JANIS [laughing]: You look ridiculous in that fuckin' outfit.

MR. STEFANO: I never did have the legs for shorts.

DR. JANIS: Your color coordination leaves something to be desired, too.

MR. STEFANO: I don't really want to go to Tahiti . . . I sunburn too easily.

[Beat.]

Guess you wouldn't know about that, would ya, Doc?

[*Uneasy pause.*]

Did I say something stupid again?

DR. JANIS: Forget it, James. It's been a long day.

MR. STEFANO: You want to buy a camera?

DR. JANIS: Keep the camera . . . You always wanted it, didn't you?

MR. STEFANO: Yeah . . . I always wanted it.

DR. JANIS: Keep the things you've always wanted.

[DR. JANIS *moves to the wall and places his father's picture in the corner of his graduation certificate, which is hanging on the back wall. He turns to look at* MR. STEFANO.]

My father.

MR. STEFANO [*studying the picture*]: Good-looking man . . . What type of uniform is that? Was he in the service?

DR. JANIS [*smiling*]: You might say that.

MR. STEFANO: What branch?

DR. JANIS: Domestic surveillance.

[*Pause.*]

He died a hero. But no one ever knew.

MR. STEFANO: I suppose it's like that with undercover work.

DR. JANIS: James?

MR. STEFANO: Yeah, Doc.

DR. JANIS: Do you like me?

MR. STEFANO: Hell, Doc, if you lowered your prices, I'd love ya.

DR. JANIS [*smiling*]: You in the mood for something to eat?

MR. STEFANO: I'm starving.

DR. JANIS: I know this great soul food place. Specialty is fettucine with chitterlings.

MR. STEFANO: Am I dressed OK?

DR. JANIS: Oh, yeah. The chitterlings will love ya.

MR. STEFANO: Before we go I have a confession . . . I knew that wasn't real dope you gave me. But I appreciate you would do that for me.

DR. JANIS: It isn't nice to fool a psychiatrist, James. You might get the wrong problem fixed, then you'd really be fucked up.

[*He places his hand on* MR. STEFANO's *shoulder, ready to exit.*]

MR. STEFANO: Can I drop the "doc" now?

[DR. JANIS *looks back to the picture of his father, then to* MR. STEFANO.]

DR. JANIS: Not a chance.
MR. STEFANO: Yeah, well, I can dig it.

[*The two men exit. The lights fade very slowly on the office, except for one spot that is focused on the picture within the frame. When all the rest of the lights have faded, that one remaining light also begins to fade slowly to black.*]

JELLY BELLY

Charles Smith
Second-Place Winner
1988–1989

PLAYWRIGHT'S STATEMENT

I first met Jelly Belly in Chicago on a hot August night in 1982. I had finished my first year of graduate school and had stopped by to visit with my brother Michael before heading back to Iowa City. That night, I sat on the front porch of my brother's house, drank beer, and listened while Jelly Belly discoursed on his system of values. He had assessed all human life in terms of cartons of cigarettes and time spent in jail. According to Jelly Belly, killing an uneducated black man would probably get you probation. If you killed an educated white man, you would have to serve at least ten years of a twenty-year sentence. A white woman with a family would probably get you the death penalty.

What shocked me was not that Jelly Belly had very calmly and openly admitted to murdering several people on several occasions, many of whom had been his friends. What shocked me was the fact that each time he had been convicted of murder, he had spent no more than six months in jail.

I immediately decided that Jelly Belly was an aberration, a freak of society who had slipped through the cracks of justice. As the night wore on, I slowly came to understand that Jelly Belly was no more of an aberration than I was and that his system of values could not exist without a concrete foundation to serve as a basis for those values. I began to realize that Jelly Belly's system of values was not his own but rather one that he had inherited from a power far greater than himself. He was not the actual perpetrator of the unending cycle of violence but an unknowing and helpless perpetrator.

PRODUCTION HISTORY

An earlier version of *Jelly Belly* titled *Jelly Belly Don't Mess with Nobody* was awarded the 1985 Cornerstone National Playwriting Award and was produced by Penumbra Theatre Company in St. Paul, Minnesota, in 1986.

Jelly Belly received its world premiere production at Victory Gardens Theater in Chicago on January 21, 1989. It was directed by Dennis Zacek, artistic director, with set design by Linda L. Lane, costume design by Glenn Billings, lighting design by Larry Schoeneman, and sound design by Galen G. Ramsey. Doug Thompson was the production stage manager. Marcelle McVay was the managing director.

Bruce	Donald Douglass
Mike	Charles Glenn
Kenny	Oscar Jordon
Jelly Belly	A. C. Smith
Barbara	Diane White

Jelly Belly was produced off-Broadway by Chicago's Victory Gardens and the New Federal Theatre in New York in 1990. It received the NBC New Voices Award and an Audelco Award nomination for new work. The play was produced by Woodie King Jr. and directed by Dennis Zacek, with set and lighting design by Richard Harmon, costume design by Judy Dearing, and sound design by Jacqui Casto. Jesse Wooden Jr. was the production stage manager.

Bruce	Donald Douglass
Kenny	Ramon Melindez Moses
Jelly Belly	A. C. Smith
Mike	Weyman Thompson
Barbara	Gina Torres

CHARACTERS

Barbara, early twenties, has been around the block a few times, sometimes called Miss Mike

Mike, midtwenties, construction worker doing the best he can, married to Barbara

Bruce, cool and smooth junkie whose drug of choice is angel dust; moves almost like a dancer—leans, dips, and turns but never falls; clothes a bit outdated but immaculate—except for the dirty collar and the rip in his pants at the knee

Kenny, friend to Mike, innocent and amazed by the smallest wonders of the world

Jelly Belly, a large man with a belly that shakes like jelly

STAGING

The play is set on a summer night in 1980 on the South Side of Chicago. The setting is the high porch of an old narrow two-story wood frame house on a block in a neighborhood where dozens of other narrow two-story wood frame houses, exactly like the first, line the street. There is very little room at the top of the porch, forcing anyone sitting in front of the house to sit on the steps. The other houses, which are only suggested, are too close together, creating a strong feeling of territorial claustrophobia. People remain only on their own tiny tract of sidewalk or porch, careful not to stop or stand in front of anyone else's sidewalk or porch unless invited to do so. Children are playing, and music can be heard off in the distance.

[*As the lights come up,* BARBARA *is sitting at the top of the stairs drinking a beer. After a moment, something out of the corner of her eye catches her attention.*]

BARBARA: Hey, boy. You. I'm talking to you. No, not you, the other one. The little nappy-headed boy. Don't try and act like you don't know who I'm talking to. What you doing messing with that car? I said, what you doing messing with the door on that car?

[*Beat.*]

Do I look like a fool to you? Boy, you know good and goddamn well that ain't your car. You ain't old enough to pee straight, how you gonna be old enough to own and drive an automobile? Why don't you gone on away from here and leave that car alone? You don't live around here.

[*Beat.*]

What? Wait a minute, ain't you that little Patterson boy? Your mama Evon Patterson? Don't try to lie to me, I know who you are. I know your mama, knew her from back when before she got pregnant with you. What did you say? I'll tell you one thing, if I got to come down off this porch, I will kick your little ass. I'll beat your ass, take you home, and then your mama will beat your ass. That's right. Now take your little butt on home and leave people's property alone. That's right, go ahead.

[*Beat.*]

Goddamn juvenile delinquent.

[MIKE *enters from the house.*]

MIKE: Who you out here talking to?
BARBARA: Little hardheaded hoodlum from across the way.
MIKE: No Kenny yet?
BARBARA: Not yet.
MIKE: Wanna 'nother beer?

[MIKE *hands* BARBARA *a beer.*]

BARBARA: Mikie asleep?

MIKE: Went straight out.

BARBARA: That was quick.

MIKE: He was tired.

BARBARA: He was tired? Shit, what about me?

MIKE: He kept talking about school—man, it was funny. You know what he calls it?

BARBARA: Don't tell me, let me guess. Kenny's garden.

MIKE: Don't you think that was funny?

BARBARA: Yeah, well we almost didn't make it to Kenny's garden. Little boy wore me out. First he started with the questions. "Is Kenny's garden real big, Mommy? Mommy, will there be other kids there? How come Kenny's garden is inside, Mommy? Mommy, will they have bathrooms there?" When we got there, he looked around and didn't see no Kenny. That's when he folded his arms, nodded his head, looked up at me, and said, "Thank you, Mother. I'm ready to go home now." I tried to explain to him, "No, Mikie, this is kindergarten, remember? You have to stay." But he wasn't having none of that.

MIKE: Did he cry?

BARBARA: At first.

MIKE: Man.

BARBARA: Until I told him that if he wanted to be like his daddy, he couldn't cry.

MIKE: I wish you wouldn't tell him that.

BARBARA: Whatever works.

MIKE: Look at that.

BARBARA: What?

MIKE: There. That little boy messing with that car.

BARBARA: That's that little Patterson boy.

MIKE: Hey, boy!

BARBARA: Little delinquent.

MIKE: What you doing messing with that car?

BARBARA: Juvenile delinquent.

MIKE: You better get away from that car!

BARBARA: I done told him once.

MIKE: Somebody ought to talk to that boy's mama.

BARBARA: And what you think that's gonna do?

MIKE: It'll do something.

BARBARA: That woman don't care about that boy. If she did, he wouldn't be out here.

MIKE: Go on home, boy! Go watch TV or something. Go ahead!

[MIKE *and* BARBARA *watch the boy leave.*]

Damn shame.

BARBARA: That boy is sliding on a slippery road to hell.

MIKE: I'm going to call Kenny.

BARBARA: For what?

MIKE: See what happened.

BARBARA: Will you stop worrying about Kenny? Kenny's going to have to learn how to take care of himself. Now sit down for a minute. Chill out.

[MIKE *sits.*]

I called my father today.

MIKE: For what?

BARBARA: Just to talk.

MIKE: Shit.

BARBARA: Mike . . .

MIKE: I wish you wouldn't have done that.

BARBARA: He's my father.

MIKE: Yeah.

BARBARA: I'm allowed to talk to my father, ain't I?

MIKE: Depends.

BARBARA: On what?

MIKE: On what you two talked about.

BARBARA: We didn't talk about nothing. We just talked.

MIKE: Yeah, OK, just talked.

BARBARA: Mike, if you don't want to go back, you don't have to.

MIKE: Right.

BARBARA: You could find another job.

MIKE: Where?

BARBARA: Anywhere. There are places out there that would hire you in a heartbeat.

MIKE: Everybody's cutting back.

BARBARA: But you got experience.

MIKE: Everybody's got experience.

BARBARA: You don't have to take this shit from them, Mike. With all of the construction going on in this town, you could find a job paying twice what you're making now.

MIKE: Where?

BARBARA: Anywhere.

MIKE: I already looked. There was nothing in the newspaper. I went down to the unemployment office, but there was a line. I can't see myself standing in line all day.

BARBARA: Then I'll get a job.

MIKE: You?

BARBARA: Damn right. Me.

MIKE: Doing what? Working with your father?

BARBARA: I don't have to. I can do other things.

MIKE: Work as a receptionist.

BARBARA: They call it administrative management, baby. Director of inter-office communications.

MIKE: Receptionist.

BARBARA: Don't knock it. Receptionists make lots of money.

MIKE: Yeah, like your last job.

BARBARA: That's not quite what I had in mind.

MIKE: Call her. I'm sure she'll be glad to have you back.

BARBARA: That bitch was crazy, Mike.

MIKE: Tell me about it.

BARBARA: Come rubbing up on me telling me how I can increase my cash flow.

MIKE: You should've told her something.

BARBARA: I did. Told her she didn't have enough cash to be getting into my flow.

MIKE: So call her. Yeah, that'll be nice. You call up the dyke and I'll quit my job and stay home with the kid.

BARBARA: I'm serious, Mike. You don't have to go back. If worst came to worst, I could always go to work for my father.

MIKE: See? That's what I thought.

BARBARA: Come on, Mike . . .

MIKE: That's exactly what he wants. For you to go to work for him. His little girl. No. Absolutely not.

BARBARA: So I can go someplace else.

MIKE: Why you so set on getting a job? You don't have to go to work. Not unless you really want to. I mean, if that's what you want to do, say so. It's fine, by all means, go right ahead. But you told me you wanted to stay home with Mikie. And I mean, hell, we're doing all right. We got a little money in the bank, we don't owe nobody nothing. We are three steps ahead of everybody else who are two blocks behind. I mean, we're not doing that bad, Barbara.

BARBARA: I just want to make sure you don't have to do anything you don't wanna do.

MIKE: You ain't got to worry about that. I'm going back tomorrow and act like nothing ever happened. I'm going to be all smiles, handshakes, and grins, 'cause right now, that's exactly what I wanna do and exactly where I need to be. But the day is going to come when I won't need them anymore. The day is going to come when I'm going to be my own boss, have my own company, and that's the day I'm going to walk into that office and tell them to kiss my black ass. But until that happens, I cannot quit, I will not quit. It's going to take a lot more than this to knock me down.

BARBARA: Does this mean I have to stay home now?

MIKE: Not if you don't want. You can go back to work for the dyke if you want.

BARBARA: Well, you know . . . she and I did have a certain rapport.

MIKE: So call her.

BARBARA: You don't mind?

MIKE: Course not.

BARBARA: You sure?

MIKE: Positive. You just have to find you someplace else to live, 'cause you sure the hell ain't staying here.

BARBARA: Boy!

[BARBARA *slaps* MIKE *about the head.* MIKE *tries to duck, then freezes.*]

MIKE: Wait.

BARBARA: What?

[*She freezes.*]

MIKE: Shit.

BARBARA: What?

MIKE: Look.

[BARBARA *looks.*]

BARBARA: Shit.

[BRUCE *enters. He is blasted out of his mind. He walks slowly and smoothly, leaning to the side. Taking three steps forward and two back, he moves across the stage, past the point where* MIKE *and* BARBARA *are sitting.*]

MIKE: Good. He didn't stop.

[BRUCE *stops. He starts to take three steps backward and one forward until he is once again standing in front of the porch.*]

Damn.

[BRUCE *slowly melts at the foot of the steps and lapses into a stupor.*]

BARBARA: You know what this means, don't you?
MIKE: What?
BARBARA: Jelly Belly's out.
MIKE: No.
BARBARA: Why else would Bruce be here?
MIKE: It hasn't been that long.
BARBARA: Six months.
MIKE: No.
BARBARA: I'm telling you, Jelly Belly is out and is here, somewhere near.
MIKE: Bruce.

[*Beat.*]

Hey, Bruce!

[*Beat.*]

Bruce!

[BRUCE *wakes, looks around, and looks back at* MIKE.]

BRUCE: Yo, Mike. Brother man, what you doing here?
MIKE: I live here, Bruce.
BRUCE: What?

[*He looks around, then back at* MIKE.]

That's right. Glad to see you're on top of things, brother man. Right on.

[*He starts to lapse back into a stupor.*]

MIKE: Bruce.

[*Beat.*]

Hey, Bruce!

[*Beat.*]

Bruce!
BRUCE: Yo, Mike. Brother man.
MIKE: What you want, Bruce? What you doing here? You looking for somebody?

BRUCE: Nah, Mike. I'm just . . . you know . . .

MIKE: No, I don't know. What do you want? You don't live around here.

BRUCE: You know, Mike, say like . . . I know that. But what happened was, see . . .
   I come to check you out, Mike. Yeah. I come to see what was happening.

BARBARA: There ain't nothing happening.

BRUCE: Well you know, that's cool too.

[*He starts to nod off again.*]

MIKE: Bruce!

BRUCE: Goddamn, man. What you want?

MIKE: I want to know what you're doing in front of my house.

BRUCE: I just told you. Damn.

[*Beat.*]

   Didn't I just tell you?

MIKE: You ain't told me nothing.

BRUCE: I just told somebody.

BARBARA: You ain't been around here in six months, Bruce. What're you doing
   around here now?

BRUCE: Hello, Miss Mike.

BARBARA: I asked you a question.

BRUCE: You did?

MIKE: What you doing here, Bruce?

BRUCE: I wanted to stop by and check you out, Mike. You and your fine lady.
   Why don't you let me have one of them beers, Miss Mike?

BARBARA: Ain't no more.

BRUCE: Why don't you let me have a swallow of the one you got then?

[BARBARA *drains the can, then shakes it.*]

BARBARA: It's empty. Nothing left but some spit. You want that?

BRUCE: Let me check it out.

[*He takes the can, turns it up, drains it, then looks at the can.*]

   That was all right.

MIKE: There's nobody here and nothing to get high on.

BRUCE: You don't want me in front of your house or something? All you got to
   do is say so. If you don't want me here, just say so and I'll leave. Shit. I can
   take a hint.

MIKE: I don't want you in front of my house.

BRUCE: You ain't got to be subtle with me, Mike. I can pick up on the nuances.

MIKE: Then leave. Good-bye. So long. See you on the rebound.

BRUCE: I mean, shit, man. You know? I ain't got to hang out around here. I can find someplace else to go. It don't matter to me, Mike. You know why? 'Cause I got . . . a strong mind.

BARBARA: Here we go.

MIKE: What'd you want to do?

BARBARA: What can we do?

MIKE: We can go in the house.

BRUCE: Man . . . I was walking down the street and the motherfuckin' police came up to me and said, "Bruce, we ought to lock your monkey ass up." And you know what I told them? I told them, "Go ahead, motherfucker. You can't hurt me by putting me in jail. You won't hurt me one bit. 'Cause I got a strong mind." Motherfucker got out of his car and knocked me down, Mike. Kicked me in the head and shit. Said, "Are you hurt now?" And you know what I told him? I told him, "Nah, man, you still ain't hurt me. You ain't killed me so you ain't hurt me. I still got my life." You know what I mean, Mike?

MIKE: Yeah, Bruce.

BRUCE: See, you can be in jail, or you can be on the street, or you can be in a mansion with lots of money and a woman and shit, but if you got a strong mind, it's all the same, Mike. It's all the same.

BARBARA: Let's go in the house.

KENNY [*from offstage*]: Mike! Hey, Mike! Mike!

[KENNY *enters carrying a roll of blueprints under his arm.*]

Jelly Belly's out! He's down the street, Mike. He's on his way down here.

BARBARA: I told you.

KENNY: What you doing around here, Bruce! Get away from here! Go back out on the boulevard or something!

BRUCE: I'm waiting on Jelly Belly.

KENNY: Well go someplace else and wait 'cause we're going in the house, ain't that right, Mike? Jelly Belly can come but won't nobody be here.

MIKE: I'll be here, Kenny.

KENNY: But Jelly Belly's coming.

MIKE: So?

KENNY: So, let's go in the house, Mike.

MIKE: I'm not running from Jelly Belly.

KENNY: We're not running, Mike. We're just going in the house.

MIKE: Remember what I told you, Kenny?

KENNY: Yeah, Mike, I remember.

MIKE: Jelly Belly's a man, Kenny. Just like you and me. You don't have to be afraid of him. Now, you finish up the blueprints?

KENNY: Finished.

[MIKE *takes the blueprints from* KENNY, *opens them, and then begins to examine them.*]

BARBARA: You get it right this time, Kenny?

KENNY: Think so. Been working on it all day. Worked on it during my lunch break at work and worked on it after I got home from work. You know, Mike . . . it gets dark out here nowadays.

[*He looks up to the sky.*]

It's dark out here now. You might go blind, Mike, trying to see, it's so dark out here.

MIKE: We're not going in the house, Kenny.

KENNY: OK, Mike. That's cool. No problem. Any beer?

BARBARA: Fresh out.

MIKE: You wanna go get some?

KENNY: Don't want no beer that bad. Jelly Belly's out. What happened to you at work today, Mike?

MIKE: Nothing.

KENNY: You wasn't there.

MIKE: I told you I wasn't coming.

KENNY: You said you were going to be late, Mike. That's what you said.

MIKE: I said I might take a sick day and that's what I did. I took a sick day. You fix all the problems with the foundation?

KENNY: Yeah, Mike. It was easy.

MIKE: Good.

KENNY: So you were sick today, Mike? Is that what happened?

MIKE: Ain't that what I said?

KENNY: You said you took a sick day. You didn't say you was sick.

MIKE: Well I was sick, OK?

BARBARA: He had the stomach flu, Kenny. A twenty-four-hour bug. He had to get it out of his system.

KENNY: I had the stomach flu once. Throwing up and stuff. Diarrhea. It was something. You had that, Mike?

MIKE: Yeah. Stomach flu.

KENNY: That's bad.

MIKE: Yeah, bad. Come here, Kenny, look. You don't need collar beams and the ceiling joists.

KENNY: Yes, I do, Mike.

MIKE: Look. The ceiling joists will give you all the support you need. See?

KENNY: Yeah, Mike, I see that.

MIKE: See where the tension is?

KENNY: But suppose I wanted to finish the attic? Suppose I wanted to put an extra room up there?

MIKE: Then you would add collar beams.

KENNY: How?

MIKE: You clamp them onto the ridge boards, Kenny.

KENNY: But you won't be able to get to the ridge boards. See? See what I mean? Look. You'd have to tear up the whole roof just to get to the ridge boards.

MIKE: I didn't see that.

KENNY: So I figure, you put in the collar beams now. That way, you have a good, strong roof. Tornado comes, hurricane, you got nothing to worry about. You know that house we pass on the way to work? The one that got the caved-in roof? I went in there, Mike. I went inside and looked around. And you know what? No collar beams.

MIKE: I like this, Kenny. This is good.

KENNY: On the way to work this morning, I showed Mr. Perkins and you know what he said? He laughed. He said I was stupid to try to do something like this.

MIKE: Well, Perkins don't know what he's talking about.

KENNY: Mike? I don't want to ride with Perkins no more.

MIKE: You won't have to.

KENNY: One time was enough for me.

MIKE: I'll come and get you in the morning.

KENNY: You're not going to be sick tomorrow?

MIKE: Nope.

KENNY: You and me, we can ride together again?

MIKE: Just be ready when I come and get you.

KENNY: I'll be ready, Mike. Five o'clock in the morning, right?

MIKE: Right.

KENNY: Just like always, right, Mike?

MIKE: That's right. Just like always.

KENNY: So can we go in the house now?

MIKE: What did I tell you?

KENNY: OK, Mike.

BARBARA: I'm with Kenny. The man gives me the creeps.

MIKE: You want to go in? Go ahead. Ain't nobody stopping you.

BARBARA: You want something to eat, Kenny?

KENNY: No, ma'am. I already ate. Mama cooked lots of food tonight. Cooked it all on that old stove. You know what I'm going to do? I'm gonna get my mama a new stove. New house, new stove. Yeah. New refrigerator too. She cooked beans and rice, pork chops. I ate so much, I couldn't move. Couldn't work on the blueprints. Couldn't do nothing but lay there and look at TV.

BARBARA: Got a big pan of lasagna in the house.

KENNY: Lasagna?

BARBARA: That's right. Even got a loaf of French bread. I could put some garlic and butter on it . . .

KENNY: You got any of that cheese in a can?

BARBARA: Parmesan cheese?

KENNY: Yeah. You got any of that?

BARBARA: Sorry.

KENNY: Don't matter. Hey, Mike, let's go in and eat some lasagna. Then we can play Monopoly. I'll be the shoe.

MIKE: No.

KENNY: Then you be the shoe.

MIKE: I'm not playing Monopoly, Kenny.

BARBARA: Come on, Mike. Let's go in.

MIKE: We got business to finish.

BARBARA: Finish it later. Let's keep tonight to ourselves.

MIKE: I'm not putting it off.

BARBARA: You wasn't here when that woman came by. I ain't never seen nothing like that before. She couldn't stop shaking, couldn't sit down. She would jump every time the phone would ring or a car drove by. It scared me, Mike.

MIKE: So go in. You don't have to stay.

KENNY: Come on, Barbara. Let's go eat.

MIKE: You are staying out here.

KENNY: OK, Mike. I'll stay.

MIKE: You got the money?

KENNY: Yeah, Mike, I got it.

MIKE: When he gets here, I want you to give it to him, OK? Just give him the money and it'll be all over.

KENNY: But what should I tell him, Mike? What should I say about what happened?

MIKE: Don't say anything. Just give him the money and shut up.

KENNY: But what if he asks?

MIKE: He ain't going to ask. And don't you go volunteering any information either.

BARBARA: Yeah, Kenny. Just give him the money and keep quiet.

MIKE: You're a grown man, Kenny. You don't have to answer to nobody.

KENNY: OK, Mike. Just like at work, right?

MIKE: That's right.

KENNY: You know what happened to me today? The foreman came up to me while I was eating my lunch and said, "Kenny, I want you to go dig out that septic tank." And you know what I told him? I told him, "I'm eating my lunch right now. You wait until I get through eating my lunch and then I'll go dig it out."

MIKE: Good for you.

KENNY: 'Cause I'm a man, right, Mike?

MIKE: That's right.

KENNY: And they got to respect me, right?

MIKE: Right.

KENNY: But they won't respect me if I don't stand up for what's mine. I got to stand up and be a man and can't let nobody push me around or let nobody tell me what to do, 'cause if I don't, I'll get used, right, Mike? They'll use me and I'll never have a life of my own.

MIKE: Yeah, Kenny, now shut up. OK?

KENNY: I'm sorry, Mike.

MIKE: And don't start apologizing.

KENNY: I piss you off or something, Mike? I don't want to piss you off.

MIKE: No, Kenny, you haven't pissed me off.

KENNY: You're still not feeling too good, are you, Mike?

MIKE: No, Kenny, I'm not.

KENNY: Mike's not feeling too good, Bruce, so get away from here! Go on! Leave him alone! Go home or something.

BRUCE: Fuck you, Kenny. You always jacking off at the mouth. Jackety, jackety, jackety, jackety, jack. You worse than an old ho, always bumping your gums.

BARBARA: I'm going in. I'll see you when you get through.

[BARBARA *exits into the house.*]

KENNY: You better watch who you talking to, boy. I'll rearrange your face for you.

MIKE: Cool it, Kenny.

KENNY: I'll send you to the moon.

BRUCE: You ain't going to do shit but talk, 'cause that's all you know how to do. You worse than a motherfuckin' politician, I swear.

MIKE: Leave him alone, Kenny.

BRUCE: Yak, yak, yak.

MIKE: Just ignore him.

BRUCE: Motherfucker get tired of hearing you yak all the time. In my ass like a goddamn hemorrhoid.

KENNY: You just better be glad Mike is out here. That's all I can say. Junkie motherfucker.

MIKE: No need for all of that, Kenny. Don't let him get you upset. Look at him. You're better than he is. Don't let him pull you down to his level.

KENNY: You ain't nothing, Bruce. Get away from me.

[KENNY *pushes* BRUCE *to the side as* JELLY BELLY *enters.*]

JELLY: Mike! Brother man!

BRUCE: This is what I'm talking about.

JELLY: What's happening? Jelly Belly's here and it is time to roll.

BRUCE: Jelly!

JELLY [*indicating* BRUCE]: I don't believe this shit. Somebody tell me I'm dreaming. Motherfucker's got a nose like a bloodhound. Get out of my way, boy!

BRUCE: I'm sorry, Jelly. I was just standing here.

JELLY: Well, go stand someplace else. You make me sick. I don't want you around me, and Mike don't want you around him either, do you, Mike?

MIKE: He's not bothering me.

KENNY: Well, he's bothering me! Go back out on the boulevard, Bruce! Hang out with the Puerto Ricans or something.

JELLY: That's right, boy. Your presence is bringing down the value of the neighborhood. Go on! Get away from here!

[BRUCE *stumbles to the edge of the space and instead of falling flat on his face, as it appears he will do, he softly glides to rest and lapses into a stupor.*]

Sorry motherfucker. So, Brother Mike. Tell me about it. What's been happening? How you been? What you been doing?

MIKE: Working.

JELLY: Same ol' Mike.

KENNY: I've been working too, Jelly.

JELLY: You?

KENNY: That's right.

JELLY: Doing what?

KENNY: Construction. Mike got me a job with him. I've been working with Mike.

JELLY: I don't know how. You ain't smart enough to do shit but get high and steal.

KENNY: I don't like it when people call me dumb, Jelly Belly.

JELLY: You never minded it before.

KENNY: That was then and this is now.

JELLY: Time don't change ignorance.

KENNY: I'm telling you, Jelly, I don't like it!

MIKE: He's just playing with you, Kenny.

JELLY: Yeah, boy. You know I'm just playing with you.

KENNY: Well, I don't like it when people play with me like that. I got a job now. Ain't that right, Mike?

MIKE: Yeah, Kenny.

KENNY: Me and Mike, we go to work at five o'clock in the morning and work until five, six, sometimes seven o'clock at night.

JELLY: I'm impressed.

KENNY: I'm learning how to build houses, Jelly Belly. See, look.

[*He hands* JELLY *the blueprints.*]

I did these myself, didn't I, Mike?

MIKE: With no help from no one.

JELLY [*pushing the blueprints away*]: Please, boy. I'm not in the mood for this shit.

KENNY: I'm working labor right now, but one day, I'm going to be an apprentice, right, Mike? Mike's teaching me how to do everything. Carpentry work and bricklaying. Me and Mike, we're going to start our own construction company, right, Mike?

MIKE: Yeah, Kenny, now will you please shut up?

KENNY: Mike's not feeling too well.

MIKE: I would feel better if you would stop running off at the mouth.

KENNY: Mike was supposed to get promoted at work but they gave the job to this college boy instead.

MIKE: It's no big deal, Kenny.

JELLY: Is that the reason you're all long in the face?

MIKE: It ain't nothing, Jelly.

JELLY: Sounds to me like you can use a little pick-me-up. A little something to help clear your mind. Help you think.

MIKE: What you got?

JELLY: What you want? I got rock, I got powder, I got dust. I got whatever you need to help ease your troubled soul.

MIKE: You know I don't mess with that rock.

JELLY: As well you shouldn't. Crack is a drug for fools, used by fools to make them even more foolish. Angel dust, on the other hand, is a working man's drug. The thinking man's drug.

[*He offers* MIKE *a small foil.*]

Here you are, Mike. Treat your nose to heaven. This here is some ace, number one, primo, mad-dog dust. Untouched by human feet.

MIKE: No thanks.

KENNY: Mike's been working his job and doing the job of the supervisor for almost a year and they didn't even pay him extra for it, did they, Mike? They didn't pay you one dime extra, did they?

MIKE: No, Kenny, they didn't.

KENNY: And yesterday they bring in this college boy and give him the job they should've gave Mike.

MIKE: The boy is educated for the job.

KENNY: No he ain't, Mike. You got to show him everything. You got to show him how to run a theodolite and how to check foundations. You even got to show him how to read a blueprint.

MIKE: It's no big deal.

KENNY: Then how come I saw you cry?

MIKE: You didn't see me cry.

KENNY: Yes I did, Mike. Right after they introduced you to that boy and told you that he was going to be your boss. I saw you walking away and you had tears in your eyes.

MIKE: You didn't see a goddamn thing.

KENNY: OK, Mike. Don't get pissed at me.

MIKE: It's a job, Kenny. A simple fuckin' job. What the hell I look like crying over some goddamn job?

KENNY: I'm sorry, Mike. I thought I saw a tear in your eye and I felt bad. I felt real bad.

MIKE: Well you didn't see nothing, OK?

KENNY: OK, Mike. Just don't get pissed at me.

JELLY: If I've told you once, I've told you a hundred times, you play by the rules, Mike, you get fucked every time.

MIKE: Yeah, Jelly, I don't need to be lectured, OK? You say you got some dust?

JELLY: Of course I got dust. I always got dust.

MIKE: So what the hell are you waiting for? Break it out.

KENNY: You're not going to toot no dust, are you, Mike?

MIKE: Just leave me alone, Kenny.

KENNY: But what about the morning, Mike? We got to go to work in the morning.

MIKE: I ain't got to do nothing but pay taxes and die.

KENNY: You got to go to work in the morning.

JELLY: Leave him alone, Kenny. Can't you see that the man has a lot on his mind?

[*He hands* MIKE *a small foil.*]

He knows he has to go to work in the morning. And from what I hear, you have to go to work in the morning too, don't you?

KENNY: Yeah, Jelly, me and Mike, we work together.

JELLY: That's good, Kenny. Real good. Bet you work hard too, don't you?

KENNY: Yeah, Jelly, I work real hard, 'cause construction ain't easy. You have to be strong if you want to build something, ain't that right, Mike? You got to know how to take some wood and some nails and bricks and build a whole house. I watch them bricklayers working and you know what they do? They'll start with one brick, Jelly. Just one little red brick. And I'll ask myself, I'll say, "Now what are they going to do with one brick?" And I watch them lay it down on the ground, put a little cement on it, and then they go get another brick and lay it right next to the first one. Next thing you know, you're not looking at one or two bricks laying on the ground. You're looking at a brick wall, Jelly Belly. A whole brick wall. And that's how they do it. Using one brick at a time. Did you know that?

JELLY: No, Kenny, I didn't.

KENNY: I didn't either. But I just learned it. Ain't that right, Mike?

MIKE: That's right.

KENNY: You see, Jelly Belly, it takes patience to build something like that. And that's what Mike's teaching me right now. Patience. And I'm learning too, ain't I, Mike?

[MIKE, *who has been concentrating on the foil, has it open, and with one finger covering one nostril, he places the other nostril to the foil and makes a long, distinct snorting sound. This sound arouses* BRUCE, *who, with his eyes closed, slowly sits up as if being drawn by some unseen force. The sound stops,* BRUCE *freezes.* MIKE *switches nostrils and makes another long, distinct snorting sound. Following suit,* BRUCE *starts to lean in the direction of the sound. The sound stops,* BRUCE *freezes, smiles, and lapses back into a stupor.*]

JELLY: Look at that boy. Got built-in radar. Could sniff out a bag of dope a mile away. Hey, Bruce!

[*Beat.*]

Bruce!

[*Beat.*]

Bruce!

BRUCE [*coming out of his stupor*]: Yo, Brother Jelly, brother man.

JELLY: Where are you, Bruce? Do you know where you're at?

[BRUCE *looks around and contemplates his answer.*]

BRUCE: I'm right here, Jelly Belly.

JELLY: No, you're not.

BRUCE: I'm not?

JELLY: Nah, boy. You're lost. That's where you're at.

BRUCE: Lost!

[BRUCE *panics for a second, then slips back into his stupor.*]

JELLY: Sorry son of a bitch. Don't give a shit about how he looks or what people think about him. Got no pride at all. But he's happy. If there's one thing that Bruce is, it's happy. Ain't that right, Bruce? Bruce!

BRUCE: What!

JELLY: Ain't that right?

BRUCE: Ain't what right, Jelly?

JELLY: Ain't you happy?

BRUCE: Yeah, Jelly, I'm real happy. 'Cause I got a strong mind.

JELLY: Why don't you take you and your strong mind for a walk out on the highway somewhere.

MIKE: Man, Jelly, it just don't make no sense. I've been working that job for eight years now. I ain't missed a day of work in five of those eight years. Now

I don't plan on being there all my life, it's no secret, I'll tell anybody who wants to know, one day I plan to move on. But goddamn, man. They should at least give me what I deserve, what's rightfully mine. But what do they do? They bring in this college boy, give him the job they should've gave me, and if that ain't bad enough, they've got the nerve to ask me to train him.

JELLY: Don't do it. Quit.

MIKE: Can't quit. Not now.

JELLY: Money ain't no problem, Mike, if that's what you're concerned about. You and me can hook up and make so much cash that our only problem will be how to spend it without the feds finding out.

MIKE: Nah, Jelly. This one I'm going to do according to the rules 'cause I'm going to make it. You can bet on that. I'm going to end up on top. And when I do, you can bet, I will have no trouble sleeping 'cause I'll know I did it right. By the book. No tricks, no shortcuts, just good hard work.

JELLY: And patience, right, Mike?

MIKE: That's right. Good hard work and patience.

JELLY: So what the fuck are you crying about? If you didn't like the goddamn job, you'd quit. Money ain't no problem. But apparently you like getting fucked over so shut your goddamn mouth and quit your complaining 'cause you ain't getting no sympathy here.

KENNY: Let's go in the house, Mike. We ain't got to stay out here.

JELLY: And you, shut up. Go drink a beer or something.

KENNY: Ain't no beer.

JELLY: I'll get you some beer if that's what you want. You want some beer, I'll get you some beer.

MIKE: I'll go to the store. I could use the walk.

JELLY: Bruce can go to the store. Hey, Bruce! You sorry motherfucker, you! Bruce!

BRUCE: Brother Jelly, brother man.

JELLY: It's party time.

BRUCE: That's what I'm talking about.

JELLY: Go to the store and get some beer.

BRUCE: I ain't got no money, Jelly Belly.

JELLY: I know you ain't got no money, boy. Here. Go down on the boulevard and get some beer.

BRUCE: What kind?

JELLY: Whatever Kenny wants. And Bruce? Bruce! Look at what I'm giving you, Bruce. You see it?

BRUCE: Yeah, Jelly, I see it.

JELLY: What is it?

BRUCE: It's a twenty-dollar bill.

JELLY: Now put it in your pocket so you don't lose it. Bruce! Put the money in your pocket, Bruce. What kind of beer you want, Kenny?

KENNY: I don't want any beer.

BRUCE: I'll get a case.

JELLY: And bring back my change, Bruce. Bruce! You hear me, Bruce!

BRUCE: I hear you, Jelly.

JELLY: What did I say?

BRUCE: You said bring back my change.

JELLY: Not your change, motherfucker! My change! Bring back my change!

MIKE: Hold it down.

BRUCE: I can hear you, Jelly Belly. Goddamn, man. You ain't got to shout.

JELLY: Don't forget, Bruce. You forget my change, I'll have your ass. You understand me?

BRUCE: Brother Jelly, brother man. Cool out. Don't you realize who you're talking to? This is Bruce. I'm your boy. Remember?

[BRUCE *exits.*]

JELLY: That's the very thing that's got me worried.

MIKE: He's getting better. He's not as bad as he was.

JELLY: The boy is like God, Mike. Always was and always will be the same. I have to admit that I was happy to see him. But after six months, I was happy to see a dog walk down the street.

MIKE: I can imagine.

JELLY: I saw the little Patterson boy out, still fucking with them cars. And seeing you and Kenny . . . I'll tell you, Mike. It's just like old times. Just like nothing's ever happened. You want another toot of this dust?

MIKE: Not now. Maybe later.

JELLY: Kenny?

KENNY: No thanks, Jelly.

JELLY: Where's Barbara? She ought to be out here.

MIKE: She probably asleep.

JELLY: It's still early. Liquor store ain't even closed yet.

MIKE: You know Barbara.

JELLY: How about my sister, Mike? You seen my sister?

MIKE: No.

JELLY: Come on, Mike. I know my sister and your ol' lady's tight. I know she had to come by here sometime or another.

MIKE: I ain't seen her.

KENNY: She probably left town, huh, Jelly Belly?

JELLY: What?

KENNY: She probably didn't want to stick around. She probably packed up and left.

JELLY: Let me tell you one motherfuckin' thing. Blood is thicker than mud, you understand that? Me and my sister been together since day one.

KENNY: OK, Jelly. I was just talking.

JELLY: You ought keep your fuckin' mouth shut if you don't know what the hell you talking about. You dim-witted son of a bitch, you.

MIKE: Leave him alone, Jelly. He said he was sorry.

JELLY: He's talking about shit he knows absolutely nothing about, Mike.

MIKE: You was asking if anybody has seen your sister. All he did was answer.

JELLY: I wasn't asking for no speculation as to where she was. I asked you if she had been by here. Hell, I know where she is.

MIKE: Is that right?

JELLY: We're tight, Mike. She don't go nowhere without letting me know.

MIKE: So where is she?

JELLY: She's in Detroit.

MIKE: Detroit?

JELLY: She's visiting relatives, Mike. I know that. I was just trying to figure out when she left.

MIKE: What relatives?

JELLY: What's it to you? You the FBI or something?

MIKE: I thought it was just you and your sister. I never knew you had other relatives.

JELLY: It's just me and my sister here. We've got other relatives. What? You think she would just take off and leave without letting me know where she was at?

MIKE: I don't know, Jelly. I don't know what to think.

JELLY: She's in Detroit, Mike. I know that. Everything's OK.

MIKE: All right.

JELLY: So why don't you go inside and tell Barbara to come out here.

MIKE: Barbara hasn't seen your sister either.

JELLY: Why don't you let me ask Barbara that.

MIKE: I'm not waking her up.

KENNY: She's sleeping, Jelly Belly. You don't want to wake her up if she's sleeping.

JELLY: Mike? Guess who was the first person I saw this morning after I got my walking papers?

MIKE: Who?

JELLY: Bruce.

MIKE: Nah.

JELLY: I'm telling you, man. I walk out of the courthouse and there he is, standing right outside of the door, right in the middle of the sidewalk, nodded out, dead to the world.

MIKE: I didn't even know you was getting out. How he know?

JELLY: Hell if I know. Junkie radar or something. And that motherfucker was the last person I wanted to see this morning. So check what I did. I told him, I said, "Bruce, I got to go to the West Side to score some dust. You want to ride along?" And you know Bruce. "Yeah, Brother Jelly, you and me, we're partners." I figured that I'd put his ass on a train, and by the time he discovered that I wasn't on there with him, I'd be gone. We get to the station, the train comes, doors open, and I say, "This is it, Bruce." Bruce gets on the train. Now, Mike, I'm thinking that this is a local train, and he'll be able to get off at the next stop. But I look up and see that this motherfucker is an express train. It don't stop until it gets out past West Hell someplace.

MIKE: You bullshitting.

JELLY: I'm telling you, Mike. So I figure, I can't do this, not even to Bruce. I start knocking on the window and shit. And what does Bruce do? Bruce finds him a seat, sits down, gets comfortable, turns and looks at me through the window, and starts to wave.

MIKE [*laughing*]: Nah, Jelly.

JELLY: Yeah, man. I'm hollering, jumping up and down, knocking on the window, and this silly motherfucker is sitting there waving. So I said, what the hell? I waved back. The train pulled out of the station and he was gone.

MIKE: So how he find his way back?

JELLY: Junkie radar.

MIKE: He made it here before you did.

JELLY: They ought to get rid of dope-sniffing dogs and use Bruce. Motherfucker'll do a better job.

MIKE: And probably won't eat as much.

[MIKE *and* JELLY *laugh.*]

KENNY: I'm sorry I said that about your sister, Jelly Belly.

JELLY: It ain't nothing, Kenny. Forget about it. You and me, we're still partners.

KENNY: Thanks, Jelly.

JELLY: Now what's this drawing that you got here? What's this all about?

KENNY [*handing* JELLY *the drawing*]: These are blueprints, Jelly Belly. Blueprints to the house I'm going to build.

JELLY: So Kenny's going to build a house.

KENNY: I already know plumbing. I know about electricity. The electricians let me wire some of the breaker boxes when the foreman's not around. Mike's teaching me carpentry work and bricklaying.

JELLY: You been a busy little son of a bitch, ain't you?

KENNY: Me and Mike, we're going to start our own construction company. Ain't that right, Mike?

MIKE: That's right. We going to build ourselves an empire.

KENNY: And when we do, I'm going to build a house for my mother. New stove, refrigerator. New everything, Jelly Belly.

JELLY: That's a nice thought, Kenny. That's very American of you.

KENNY: You got them upside down.

JELLY: What?

KENNY: The blueprints.

JELLY: I knew that. I just wanted to look at them from a different perspective.

KENNY: From upside down?

JELLY: Look, Kenny, it don't matter how I look at the damn things.

KENNY: Yes it do, Jelly Belly. That's stupid thinking you can look at them from upside down. You see that, Mike? He thinks he can read blueprints from upside down.

JELLY: You can turn them upside down, sideways, or catercorner to the moon, it's all going to end up to equal the same nothing.

KENNY: What you mean nothing?

JELLY: You don't actually believe this shit, do you?

KENNY: Believe what?

JELLY: This shit about you and Mike starting a construction company.

KENNY: Yeah, I believe it.

JELLY: You're dumber than I thought.

MIKE: Then that makes us both dumb, Kenny.

JELLY: You don't surprise me, Mike. You always was a sucker for hard work and impossible dreams. But why the hell do you have to pull Kenny into this shit? He don't need this sort of heartache.

MIKE: Ain't no heartache, Brother Jelly.

KENNY: Yeah. We going to build ourselves an empire.

JELLY: You going to get your feelings hurt, that's what's going to happen.

MIKE: Why don't you just give him the blueprints back and let's leave it at that.

JELLY: I can't let Kenny start believing in no shit like this.

MIKE: It ain't up to you what the boy believes in.

JELLY: As long as I got breath in this body and strength to take it, I'm going to look out for this boy.

MIKE: So give him a chance, Jelly. It might surprise you. It just might work.

JELLY: You been taking some new type of drug or some shit? If so, you better leave it alone 'cause it's done fucked up all of your thinking. You know good and goddamn well that the world don't work like that, Mike. For some people, maybe, but for this boy, no.

MIKE: You selling him short, Jelly Belly. You don't know what the boy's capable of.

JELLY: There are three types of people in this world, Mike. Sheep, shepherds, and lamb chops. Now the shepherds are the gods. They tend to the flock. They make sure the sheep stay out of trouble. While the sheep, being the dumb critters that they are, follow the shepherds wherever they go. They take the orders, do as they're told, and tend to stick together. Now this boy right here is a sheep. He was born a sheep, been a sheep all of his life, and will remain a sheep until the day when he is transformed into a lamb chop.

MIKE: You ain't changed one bit, have you?

JELLY: And never will. Now you take somebody like Bruce. He ain't a sheep. He ain't even a lamb chop. That motherfucker is a pork chop. And you got to treat him like a pork chop, smothered in gravy with a little rice on the side.

MIKE: I really don't feel like hearing this shit, Jelly Belly.

JELLY: I speak the truth, Mike, and you know it. Take you and your job for example.

MIKE: Don't you worry about me and my job.

JELLY: They got you, Mike. They know you ain't going nowhere 'cause they know you're a sheep. Just a sheep who will one day be led to the slaughterhouse and butchered for meat.

MIKE: Give him his money, Kenny, and let's get this over with. I've got to go in the house and get some sleep.

JELLY: I didn't mean to hurt your feelings, Mike, but you know I speak the truth.

MIKE: I said give him his money, Kenny. I got to go to bed. Got to go to work in the morning.

JELLY: That's right, Kenny. Give me my money. I done hurt Mike's feelings. Now he wants to go in the house and go to bed.

[KENNY *hands* JELLY *a large roll of bills.*]

KENNY: It's all there, Jelly. You can count it if you want, but it's all there.

JELLY [*counting the money*]: I ain't got to count it, Kenny. I trust you. You're my boy.

KENNY: Thanks, Jelly.

JELLY: You have any trouble?

KENNY: No trouble at all. People come to my house, just like you said.

JELLY: You like that dust you just tooted, Mike?

MIKE: It was all right.

JELLY: I got a whole pound of that coming in in a couple of days. It ought to sell like Popsicles on a hot summer day. Any of those construction dudes like to toot dust?

KENNY: I don't know.

JELLY: Find out.

KENNY: I'll find out for you, Jelly, but I can't sell none.

JELLY: Why not?

KENNY: Too dangerous.

JELLY: Ain't nothing dangerous about it. Just keep your cool, keep your mouth shut, don't let too many people find out what you're doing, you'll be all right.

KENNY: Nah, Jelly. Too dangerous.

JELLY: All right. You scared to make a little cash, I'll find somebody else.

KENNY: I ain't scared, Jelly. I ain't scared of nothing.

JELLY: Then what's your problem?

MIKE: He doesn't have a problem. He just doesn't want to sell for you no more. That's all.

JELLY: Why don't you let the boy speak for himself, Mike?

MIKE: 'Cause I don't want you taking advantage of him.

JELLY: Now I realize that your little feelings are hurt, but that ain't no reason to get sassy. In fact, if I didn't know you as I do, I'd take that as an insult. Kenny's my boy. Ain't that right, Kenny?

KENNY: Right, Jelly.

JELLY: If something's bothering him, I want to know what it is. Now tell me, Kenny. Why are you afraid to sell my dope for me?

KENNY: I told you. I ain't afraid of nothing.

JELLY: So what the fuck's your problem!

KENNY: I got robbed! That white boy that hangs out in front of the liquor store with them Puerto Ricans came into my mama's house one night with a gun and robbed me. Took all the money and the dope. I ain't scared. I just don't want to do it no more. Too dangerous.

JELLY: So what the hell is this if you got robbed?

KENNY: That's money, Jelly. Your money. The money I owe you for the dust. I got a job. I'm working.

JELLY: OK, Kenny. You don't want to peddle no more, I'm not going to ask you to peddle no more.

KENNY: Too dangerous.

JELLY: But what I am concerned about is the welfare of that white boy. What're you going to do about him?

KENNY: What should I do? I can kick his ass if you want.

JELLY: Kick his ass? Ain't you learned nothing, you dim-witted son of a bitch?

MIKE: You got your money, Jelly. Now what's your problem?

JELLY: The problem is, I ain't got my money. This is Kenny's money. Here, Kenny.

[*He hands the money back to* KENNY.]

I don't want this shit. I want my money.

MIKE: I thought it didn't matter to you as long as you were able to spend it.

JELLY: That's where you're wrong, Mike. See, I got pride. A lot more pride than a ditchdigger like yourself. You don't hear me crying about how I got fucked over at work and you don't see dirt under my nails or callouses on my hands. My hands are smooth and clean.

MIKE: That's because you've been in jail for the past six months.

JELLY: My hands were clean before I went to jail. I keep myself clean, Mike. My hands, my nose, my mind, all stay clean. I keep it that way by handling only crisp and new money. Money that crackles when you fold it. Not that limp shit, damp money, money that you get after a hard day's work. Clean money, Mike. Money from the bank. New money. Money from the pockets of Buick-driving, blue suit–wearing, fat, bald white men with a taste for black women and white dope. That's the money I spend and the only money I spend. Not that bullshit you done sweated over.

KENNY: But this is your money, Jelly Belly. I owe you this.

JELLY: You don't owe me nothing. Forget about it.

KENNY: But what about the dope?

MIKE: He said forget about it, Kenny.

JELLY: What I want to know is, what are you going to do about that white boy?

KENNY: You think I should kick his ass? I can get Pookey Dee and a couple other dudes and kick his ass if you want.

JELLY: So you get a couple of your walking partners and kick his ass. He gets a couple of his walking partners and kick your ass. You get a couple more of your walking partners and kick him and his walking partners' ass and what do you got? A whole bunch of sore-assed walking partners who are tired of walking.

KENNY: So what should I do, Jelly?

JELLY: Kill him.

MIKE: Wait a minute . . .

JELLY: If he don't, you know what's going to happen? Word's going to get out that he's a pork chop. That he let a white boy burn him. Next thing you know, every sorry motherfucker on the street is going to think that they can burn him too. He's going to have motherfuckers waiting for him when he gets off of work, waiting in the alley to bust him in the head, knocking on the door of his mama's house in disrespect of the woman who had him. Is that what you want, Kenny? People like Bruce busting your mama in the head while laughing in your face?

KENNY: I'll kill Bruce, he try something like that.

JELLY: You're going to have to kill a whole lot of Bruces if you don't kill that white boy first.

MIKE: But we're the only people who even know that it happened.

JELLY: Where the hell do you think you're at, Mike? This ain't Cincinnati or some shit. There is a wire service out on that street that would make Ma Bell look like two tin cans and a string. You got people passing on information, information moving faster than electricity. I'd bet you half the people in this neighborhood knew he was going to get ripped off before it even happened. You would've known too if you would've kept your ear to the ground instead of fucking around, building houses and shit. Disgrace has been laid upon this boy's head. He's going to have to take revenge or live with it for the rest of his life.

MIKE: You mean go to jail for the rest of his life.

JELLY: Bullshit.

MIKE: Five to ten with no chance for parole.

JELLY: He ain't going to get no five to ten for killing no dope-pushing, whore-hustling white boy. If anything they'll give him a carton of cigarettes and a pat on the back. If you doubt my word, try it.

MIKE: Don't listen to this shit, Kenny.

JELLY: Stay out of this, Mike.

MIKE: He wants you to do his dirty work for him.

JELLY: I'm talking to Kenny so stay out of it!

MIKE: You got to be crazy if you think I'm going to stand here and let you talk him into killing a man just to make you feel better.

JELLY: I've never talked Kenny into doing anything he didn't want to do, now have I, Kenny?

KENNY: No.

JELLY: And never will. All I can do is lay out the facts and let him decide. So. Kenny? What's it going to be? Are you going to be a coward and live in disgrace for the rest of your life or are you going to finally stand up and be a man?

KENNY: I can't kill him, Jelly Belly.

JELLY: So you're telling me that you're not going to do it?

KENNY: You're talking five to ten with no chance for parole.

JELLY: OK. Great. Fine. See? Wasn't that hard. You made up your own mind and that's what I like about you, Kenny. You don't let other people influence you.

KENNY: Thanks, Jelly.

JELLY: Now, you want a little toot of this dust?

MIKE: Kenny's getting ready to go home and go to bed.

JELLY: I didn't hear Kenny say that.

MIKE: You heard me say it. That's good enough.

JELLY: Kenny's a grown man, Mike. Let him make his own decisions.

KENNY: Yeah, Mike. I got a mind. I can make it up if I want.

MIKE: Is that right?

KENNY: Yeah, Mike. That's what you said.

MIKE: So you want to toot some dust? Is that what you're saying?

KENNY: You tooted some, Mike. How come I can't toot some?

MIKE: We ain't talking about me, Kenny. We're talking about you. You want some dust? There it is.

KENNY: I'm just like you, Mike. I want to toot some dust.

MIKE: Go right ahead. Do what you like.

JELLY [offering KENNY a foil]: Here you are, Kenny. Treat your nose to heaven.

KENNY: I don't want any.

JELLY: Come on . . .

KENNY: Mike'll get pissed at me.

JELLY: Forget about Mike. That's just his mother instinct coming through.

MIKE: Fuck you, Jelly Belly.

JELLY: I would let you, Mike, but you wouldn't enjoy it. How about splitting this dust with Kenny instead.

MIKE: I've had enough.

JELLY: Kenny?

KENNY: Mike won't let me.

MIKE: I said do what you want to, goddamn it. You want to end up like Bruce, be my guest.

JELLY: Why don't you split it with him, Mike?

MIKE: You got trouble hearing or something? I said I didn't want any more.

JELLY: Well, I never thought I would see the day when Mike turned down a noseful of dust.

MIKE: You've seen it before and you'll see it again.

JELLY: Ol' Mike here used to have one of the biggest noses around. In fact, I've seen Mike toot enough dust to kill a horse. Ain't that right, Mike?

MIKE: I don't know what you're talking about.

JELLY: I understand. I know it's a touchy subject, going to jail and all.

MIKE: Why don't you shut your goddamn mouth!

KENNY: You never told me you was in jail, Mike.

JELLY: He don't like talking about it. You see, there was this little mix-up . . .

MIKE: I said shut up, Jelly Belly!

JELLY: Cool out, Mike!

[*Beat.* JELLY *and* MIKE *stare at each other.*]

All I was going to do was tell the boy how you was a victim of mistaken identity.

[*Beat.*]

You see, Kenny, one night we was all sitting out here on Mike's front porch getting high on some of the baddest dust that ever came across the tubes. Mike went to the store to get some beer and never came back. Found out the next morning that he was in jail.

KENNY: For what?

JELLY: Murder one. Some dude got beat to death in the alley behind the liquor store. Whoever did it used a brick. Bashed the dude's head in, broke most of the bones in his body. Fucked him up really bad. For some reason, they thought Mike did it.

KENNY: You didn't do it, did you, Mike?

JELLY: Of course Mike didn't do it. I even found a witness that testified that he saw Mike sound asleep in the alley right next to that motherfucker that got murdered. That's how Mike got blood all over his clothes. Ain't that right, Mike?

MIKE: Yeah, Jelly, whatever you say.

KENNY: Wow, Mike. You slept through a murder? You slept while somebody got beat to death right next to you?

JELLY: He was pretty high, Kenny. He don't remember much of what happened that night.

MIKE: That's enough, Jelly Belly.

JELLY: You got married right after that, didn't you, Mike?

MIKE: I said that's enough!

JELLY: And ain't missed a day of work since.

BARBARA [*from offstage*]: Mike?

MIKE: Shit.

KENNY: So everybody's been to jail except me.

BARBARA [*from offstage*]: Michael!

MIKE: Sorry. We'll keep it down.

JELLY: And I got seniority when it comes to time, don't forget that. Yes sir, we're all like peas in a pod. Here you are, Kenny. Toot that up your nose. Let the angels bring us closer together.

[*He hands* KENNY *a foil. Pause.*]

KENNY: Sure you don't want some, Mike?

MIKE: Why don't you go home and go to bed, Kenny?

KENNY: But this is good dust, Mike. Didn't you say it was good dust?

MIKE: Sure it's good dust. You see what it's done to Bruce.

JELLY: Will you shut up talking about Bruce! Bruce is a pork chop! Punk-ass, gutless motherfucker. Ain't good for shit but going to the store for you and he can't do that right half the time. Like that motherfucker I killed. Pork chop. Worthless-assed piece of meat with a brain.

[*Beat.*]

You know, they should have given me a carton of cigarettes and a pat on the back for killing that motherfucker instead of putting me in jail for six months. The dude deserved to die. That's how come I'm sitting here and not still in jail. I did society a favor by killing that dude. Nobody likes a gutless motherfucker. Not even the man. In fact, you know what the police said to me? They said, "Thank you, Jelly Belly, you did us a favor."

KENNY: No shit?

JELLY: I'm telling you, man. Motherfucker's body was sitting in the chair next to me, hole in his head, brains spilled out on the floor. I was watching TV. Police came in, let me finish watching my program. Even sat down with me and watched it. Now that's what you call respect. They respect me 'cause they know that Jelly Belly don't mess with nobody. I even told the dude I was going to kill him before I did it. Showed him the gun I was going to kill him with. Even showed him the bullets. Told him, "Motherfucker, don't come back to this house." And what did he do the very next day?

KENNY: He came back?

JELLY: Damn right he came back. After I told him not to. That's the reason he's dead.

MIKE: He had to come back, Jelly. He lived there.

JELLY: My motherfuckin' sister lived in that house, Mike. I know who lived in that house. And I gave the dude fair warning. Apparently he didn't take me seriously. I mean, shit, man, I didn't want to kill the dude. I used to like him. He was my boy. But he never should've threatened to call the police on me. I told him not to come back but he came back anyway so I blew his mother-fuckin' brains out, turned on the television, called the police, and told them to come and get his body. My sister was freaking out and shit. Cussing at me.

KENNY: I don't blame her. You killed the man she was married to.

JELLY: He was a pork chop, Kenny. Much like yourself. Dumb piece of meat with a brain that don't work.

KENNY: Don't call me dumb no more, Jelly.

JELLY: You've lost your pride and you're too dumb to see that when you lose your pride, people start walking on you, pushing you around, telling you what to do. Like Mike here.

KENNY: Me and Mike are friends.

JELLY: Beware, Kenny. First you lose your pride. Next thing you know, you're planted in the ground, just a dead piece of meat, waiting for the maggots to eat out what's left of your brain.

KENNY: I got a job, Jelly. I ain't lost my pride.

JELLY: You let that white boy burn you.

KENNY: He didn't burn me. He just took some money, that's all.

JELLY: Same difference. Toot the dust.

KENNY: I can't kill him, Jelly Belly.

JELLY: Nobody's asking you to. Now toot the dust.

[*Pause.* KENNY *carefully unwraps the foil.*]

MIKE: You know, Kenny, there's a difference between pride and revenge.

JELLY: No difference.

MIKE: Pride comes from building something, then stepping back and admiring what you've built.

JELLY: You talking about using a brick, Mike? Is that what you're talking about?

[KENNY *looks at* MIKE *for a response,* MIKE *looks away. Pause.* KENNY *toots the dust. As he does,* BRUCE *enters. He has a bloody bruise on his face.*]

I knew all we had to do to get this motherfucker back was to toot a little dust.

[BARBARA *looks out through the door.*]

BARBARA: Mike? What's going on out here?

JELLY: Barbara.

BARBARA: Mike?

BRUCE: I got the beer.

JELLY: Come on out and join us. It's party time.

BARBARA: Mike? I asked you a question.

JELLY: Don't be a party poop. Come on out and join us.

BRUCE: I got the beer.

JELLY: So I see, boy. What happened to your face? Somebody kick your ass or something?

BRUCE: I fell.

JELLY: You fell?

BRUCE: I was just walking. And I fell.

KENNY [*taking the beer from* BRUCE]: You didn't shake up the beer, did you?

BRUCE: I fell before I got the beer. Can I have a little bit of that dust?

JELLY: What dust, boy? What you talking about?

BARBARA: You got dust, Jelly Belly?

JELLY: No, ma'am. Ain't nobody got any dust.

BRUCE: Kenny had some dust. He just got through tooting some.

BARBARA: Kenny?

JELLY: Kenny didn't have no dust, did you, Kenny?

KENNY: Nope.

JELLY: That fall must've fucked up the boy's brain.

BRUCE: Come on, Jelly. Why don't you let me get high?

JELLY: You already high.

BRUCE: Nah, Jelly.

JELLY: You get any higher, you going to touch the moon.

BRUCE: My high went away when that concrete hit me in the head.

KENNY: Why don't you sit down and shut up, Bruce.

BRUCE: Fuck you, Kenny. Suck my dick.

JELLY: Hey, boy, goddamn it! Can't you see that lady standing there! Come here, Bruce! What the hell's the matter with you! Come here!

[BRUCE *moves to* JELLY.]

You want me to rip your motherfuckin' face off?

BRUCE: No, Jelly. That would hurt like hell.

MIKE: Cool out, Jelly Belly.

JELLY: You got a mouth like a goddamn garbage can.

BRUCE: I'm sorry, Jelly Belly. Don't rip my face off.

BARBARA: You all got mouths like garbage cans if you ask me. Out here keeping up a racket like you was in a bar somewhere.

JELLY: I'm sorry, Miss Mike, but the boy is a fool. Now apologize to that woman, Bruce. Apologize for your uncouthed behavior.

BRUCE: I'm sorry, Miss Mike. I didn't see you standing there.

BARBARA: And what's your excuse, Jelly Belly?

JELLY: Excuse me, Miss Mike, but like the idiot here, I did not realize you was standing there, or I would've been more careful with my French. I promise to take more caution in the future.

BARBARA: Kenny? You been tooting dust?

KENNY: No, Barbara, I didn't have any.

BARBARA: Mike?

MIKE: Nah, baby, Bruce is just messed up in the head. That's all.

BRUCE: No I ain't. I saw Kenny . . .

JELLY: Shut up, boy!

BARBARA: Kenny, I find out you been tooting dust and you will never, ever come in this house again. You understand that?

KENNY: Yes, ma'am.

BRUCE: Goddamn. How about a beer? Can I at least have a beer?

JELLY: Nah, you can't have no beer. Take your butt over there and sit down. Everybody here can have a beer except Bruce. Mike, get a beer for your wife. And wipe off the top of it. Kenny, get yourself a beer. Bruce, you go near that beer, I'll kill you. You understand that?

BRUCE: Aw, Jelly Belly.

JELLY: Shut up and sit down before I kick your ass because of general principle. Excuse my French.

BRUCE: I'm sorry, Miss Mike.

MIKE: You want a beer?

BARBARA: I want ya'll to keep the noise down, that's what I want.

JELLY: We'll keep it down, Miss Mike. We was having such a good time, I guess we got carried away. Go on and get yourself a beer there. Mike, get your wife a beer.

BARBARA: I don't want a beer, Jelly Belly. I want ya'll to find someplace else to go.

JELLY: We'll keep it quiet. I promise.

BARBARA: I'll tell you what. You wake up my son and there'll be hell to pay. You understand that?

JELLY: I understand, Miss Mike. Your husband here said my sister came by here. Is that so?

MIKE: I ain't said no such thing.

JELLY: That's not what you said verbatim, but that's what you meant.

BARBARA: I ain't seen your sister, Jelly Belly.

JELLY: Now, Miss Mike, do I look like a fool to you?

BARBARA: It depends on which angle I approach you from.

JELLY: You must be feeling good tonight. Especially good.

BARBARA: I was feeling good until I heard all that noise out here.

JELLY: Why don't you cut out the small talk and you tell me when my sister came by.

BARBARA: I told you. I ain't seen your sister.

JELLY: Now, Miss Mike, both you know and I know that in the history of the world, a week has not gone by without my sister coming by here and jacking off at the jaws with you. Now you trying to tell me that you ain't seen her?

BARBARA: That's exactly what I'm telling you.

MIKE: She's telling you the truth, Jelly Belly. Your sister ain't been by here.

JELLY: I refuse to believe that, Mike.

BARBARA: Then sounds like you got a problem, don't it?

JELLY: Come down off the porch, Miss Mike. You're starting to make me nervous.

BARBARA: I live here, Jelly Belly. I will stand wherever I please. If you don't like it, you can leave.

JELLY: I come here on business. And of course to visit my friends. Now come out from behind me, Barbara.

MIKE: This is her porch and her house, Jelly Belly. She can stand wherever she wants.

JELLY: So everybody's feeling good tonight.

BARBARA: You give him his money, Kenny?

KENNY: I gave it to him.

BARBARA: Then your business here is finished, Jelly Belly.

JELLY: Kenny? You tell this woman what you been doing?

KENNY: I didn't tell her nothing, Jelly Belly.

JELLY: Mike?

BARBARA: What difference does it make who told me what and why? You got no secrets around here just like you got no friends.

JELLY: Look, Barbara. I apologize for any distress I might have caused you . . .

BRUCE: I'm sorry too, Miss Mike.

JELLY: So why don't you just sit down, cool out, have a beer, and we'll discuss the situation at hand.

BARBARA: You got what you came for, there's nothing to discuss. Your business here is finished, I am going to bed. I would appreciate it if everybody cleared off the porch.

[BARBARA *exits.*]

MIKE: You heard the word. Time to clear the porch.

JELLY: Tell me something, Mike. You tell your woman everything or only the things which concern me?

MIKE: I don't think my relationship with my wife is any of your business.

JELLY: I'm disappointed in you, Mike. I'm disappointed in you in a major way.

MIKE: Come on, Kenny. Time to clear the porch.

JELLY: You've bought lock, stock, and barrel into an American pipe dream which will never work for you, brother. The only thing that pipe dream is going to do for you is crack your skull.

MIKE: Time to go, Kenny.

JELLY: Let me tell you something, Mike. When I was in jail, I met this dude named Frosty. Frosty the Snowman. He was in for one hundred and ninety-nine years. Killed his wife, killed his mother-in-law, and killed two of his neighbors when they knocked on the door trying to figure out what was going on. He said that killing his wife was cheaper than getting a divorce.

MIKE: So what's that supposed to mean?

JELLY: Frosty was the coolest white boy I ever met in my life. You'd see Frosty in the chow line and say, "Frosty, what's happening, man?" And Frosty would say, "Just got back from Paris." Or he would say, "Spent the weekend in Las Vegas and lost all my money." At first I thought the motherfucker was crazy. So did everybody else until Frosty killed a guard when the guard pushed him and didn't have five other guards to back him up. They added another ninety-nine years to Frosty's sentence, which didn't bother him none, so they put his ass into solitary confinement. In solitary, there's no light, no people, no voices, there's nothing but darkness. Thirty days passed, they didn't let Frosty out. Forty-five days, fifty-five days, sixty days passed, and they still got Frosty down in solitary confinement. Everybody knew he was going to be crazier than a jailhouse ho when they finally let him out, if he wasn't crazy already. Ninety-one days after they locked him down, here comes Frosty, walking into the yard. Finally somebody said, "Frosty, what's happening, man?" Frosty stopped, looked around, and said, "Just spent three of the most beautiful months of my life in the Bahamas and, baby, it was nice." But that's not the kicker. You know what the kicker is? The motherfucker had a suntan.

KENNY: Nah.

JELLY: I'm telling you. Motherfucker was blacker than me. Had a beautiful tan. Tan all over his body except his butt.

KENNY: I don't believe that, Jelly Belly. You believe that, Mike?

MIKE: Of course not.

JELLY: It's the honest-to-God truth, I swear on my mother's grave. Motherfucker was smiling, glowing, had sand in his shoes.

KENNY: I don't believe that, Jelly Belly.

JELLY: It don't matter whether you believe it or not. Point is, some people are free even though their bodies might be incarcerated, while some people are slaves to any damn thing that comes along, like that half-assed job you and Mike working.

MIKE: Come on, Kenny. Let's go in.

JELLY: See? Got to go in. Got to go to bed. Can't come and go as you please. Got to do what Mike tells you to do.

MIKE: Come on. We can play some Monopoly.

KENNY: Wait a minute, Mike. What about all the beer?

JELLY: Yeah, Mike. What am I supposed to do with all this beer?

MIKE: You can take it with you. Come on.

KENNY: Not yet, Mike.

BRUCE: Don't worry about the beer. I'll take care of that.

JELLY: That's right, Bruce. Get yourself a beer. You too, Kenny. Get yourself another beer.

KENNY: But Mike wants me to go in the house.

JELLY: Mike ain't dictating your drinking habits. Go on, get yourself another beer.

MIKE: Leave the beer where it is, Kenny.

JELLY: Give the boy a break, Mike. I ain't seen him in what . . . six months? I
 know that little job he got don't demand all his time.
MIKE: Let's go, Kenny.
KENNY: Not yet, Mike.
BRUCE: Take your ass to bed, bitch. Now, Jelly, how about a toot of that dust?
KENNY: Bitch?
JELLY: You want another toot of dust, Mike?
KENNY: Where's the change from the beer, Bruce?
MIKE: Come on, Kenny.
KENNY: Bruce!
BRUCE: Come on, Jelly. Just a little bit and I'll go away.
MIKE: Kenny?
KENNY: *Bruce!*
BRUCE: What the fuck do you want now?
KENNY: Where's the change?

[*Pause.* BRUCE *thinks.*]

BRUCE: What change?
KENNY: Call me a bitch.
JELLY: The change from my motherfuckin' twenty, that's what change.
BRUCE: There wasn't no change, Jelly Belly. Now how about letting me toot a
 little bit of that dust.
JELLY: You ain't getting shit until I get my change.
BRUCE: I told you. There wasn't none.
JELLY: You cough up my change, motherfucker, or I'm going to have Kenny
 kick off in your ass.
BRUCE: Kenny ain't going to do shit.
KENNY: What! What you say, punk! You punk-ass motherfucker, you! I ain't
 going to do what!
MIKE: Leave him alone, Kenny!
KENNY: I'll stomp a mudhole in your ass, boy!
BRUCE: Go ahead. I don't give a good goddamn.
JELLY: Don't let him talk to you like that, Kenny.
MIKE: I said leave him alone, Kenny!
JELLY: Hit him!

[KENNY *hits* BRUCE, *knocks him down.* MIKE *intercepts* KENNY.]

KENNY: Punk-ass motherfucker!

MIKE: Take it easy, Kenny.

KENNY: I'm all right, man.

JELLY: Don't let him push you around, Kenny!

KENNY: Get away from me, Mike.

MIKE: I'm not going to let you fight out here!

JELLY: Hit him, Kenny! Don't let him push you around! Hit him.

KENNY: Leave me alone, Mike!

[KENNY *pushes* MIKE *in the chest.* MIKE *comes back at* KENNY *to retaliate but stops short.* MIKE *and* KENNY *square off to fight.* JELLY *watches with enjoyment.*]

JELLY: Get him, Kenny. Fuck him up. Hit him.

[MIKE *and* KENNY *prepare for battle. Pause.*]

BRUCE: Goddamn, Kenny, man. You didn't have to do that. I already fell once.

[MIKE *and* KENNY *relax on each other as* BRUCE *attempts to pick himself up without success.*]

JELLY: Where's my change, Bruce?

BRUCE: Wasn't no change, Jelly Belly.

JELLY: Kenny?

[*He tosses a set of keys to* KENNY.]

Go get my gun out of my car.

BRUCE: Aww, Jelly Belly, wait a minute . . .

MIKE: Don't bring no guns out here, Jelly Belly!

JELLY: Where's my change, Bruce?

BRUCE: I told you, there wasn't none.

MIKE: No guns, Jelly! I don't want no guns in front of my house!

JELLY: Go get my gun, Kenny.

MIKE: Don't do it, Kenny. I'm warning you. Don't go get that gun.

JELLY: What you going to do, Mike? Make Kenny lose his job?

KENNY: Yeah, Mike. What you going to do?

JELLY: We're just playing around, that's all.

KENNY: Yeah, Mike, just a little fun and games.

MIKE: You go get that gun, Kenny, you can forget about going to work in the morning.

JELLY: Aww, he's just bullshitting, Kenny. Go ahead.

MIKE: I'm not bullshitting.

KENNY: Why you taking everything so serious, Mike? We're just playing around, that's all. You know, like we used to. I mean, hell, give me a break, Mike. I'm a grown man. I do what I want to do.

[KENNY *exits.*]

MIKE: You're fucking up, Jelly Belly. I don't play around like this.

JELLY: You mean not anymore.

MIKE: Why don't you get out of here! Why don't you just leave! Why don't you take your goddamn guns and your drugs and leave!

JELLY: I come to visit my friends.

MIKE: You don't have any friends around here. Leave!

JELLY: I thought you and me was partners.

MIKE: You get your ass off of my porch and out of this neighborhood right this minute or I'm going to call the police on you, Jelly Belly. I'll have your ass arrested.

JELLY: You wouldn't do that, would you, Mike?

MIKE: I'll have your ass put under the jail.

JELLY: How old did you say that little boy of yours was?

MIKE: Don't threaten me, Jelly Belly.

JELLY: You threatened me.

MIKE: Get off of my porch.

JELLY: Five, six years old?

MIKE: I don't play that shit.

JELLY: And what's his name? Michael Junior, ain't it?

MIKE: Somebody needs to off you, Jelly. Somebody needs to blow your goddamn brains out.

JELLY: It ain't going to be you, is it, Mike? I'm safe around you. That is, as long as there ain't no bricks around.

MIKE: Maybe I ought to start looking for one.

JELLY: If you do, I hope you find it before Kenny gets back with that gun.

MIKE: Bruce! Hey, Bruce! Bruce!

BRUCE: What?

MIKE: Go on! Get out of here! Run! Leave before Kenny gets back!

BRUCE: I'll pay you back, Jelly Belly. I'll get your money for you.

MIKE: Why don't you just leave, you stupid ass!

BRUCE: I know I owe you a lot of money, but I'll pay you back. I'll get a job or something.

JELLY: Motherfucker, you could work from now until doomsday and never pay me back the money you owe me. I've supported your habits since you were in diapers, Bruce. I own you. You understand that? I own everything about you, Bruce.

BRUCE: I know, Jelly.

JELLY: I own your body, I own your soul, I own your dreams, Bruce. You're just like a piece of property to me. Just like my car.

BRUCE: I know, Jelly Belly, and I'll get your change for you.

MIKE: Why don't you just leave!

JELLY: He ain't going nowhere until I tell him to.

BRUCE: I went to the store, just like you told me. I got the case of beer and gave the man a twenty-dollar bill and he didn't give me no change back. So I left. There wasn't no change.

[KENNY *enters with a sawed-off shotgun and hands it to* JELLY.]

JELLY: You forgot, that's what happened.

BRUCE [*seeing the gun*]: I can go back! I can go back and get your change for you, Jelly! I'll make that dude give me your change!

JELLY: Too late, Bruce. I don't want it now. You are in debt beyond repair, and like a loan company, I am about to repossess what's rightfully mine.

BRUCE: What?

JELLY: Get on your knees, motherfucker.

BRUCE: Aww, Jelly, man . . .

JELLY: Don't make me have to say it again, Bruce.

BRUCE: Nah, Jelly Belly.

JELLY: Bruce! You hear me talking to you? Bruce! Did you hear what I said?

BRUCE: I heard you.

JELLY: What did I say?

BRUCE: You said get on my knees.

JELLY: So what are you waiting for?

BRUCE [*as he goes to his knees*]: Please, Jelly Belly. I thought I was your boy. I thought me and you was partners.

JELLY: Say good-bye to Mike.

BRUCE: Nah, Jelly.

JELLY: I don't want to have to tell you again, Bruce.

BRUCE: I'll get your money for you.

JELLY: Bruce! Say good-bye to Mike!

[*Pause.* BRUCE *whimpers.*]

BRUCE: Good-bye, Mike.

JELLY: Say good-bye to Kenny.

BRUCE: Good-bye, Kenny.

KENNY: Bye, Bruce. Been nice knowing you.

JELLY: Now close your eyes.

BRUCE: Nah, Jelly Belly! Please, man! Don't kill me!

JELLY: Shut up!

BRUCE: I ain't worth killing, Jelly Belly! I ain't shit! You ought to let me live!

JELLY: I said shut up!

[JELLY *kicks* BRUCE. BRUCE *tumbles backward.*]

Close your eyes. Die like a man, motherfucker.

[BRUCE *whimpers, collects himself, crawls back to the foot of the stairs, and closes his eyes.* JELLY *lowers the barrel of the gun to* BRUCE's *forehead, laughs, and pulls the trigger. The gun clicks empty.* BRUCE *falls over, holding his head, screaming.* JELLY *and* KENNY *laugh.*]

Get up, motherfucker!

KENNY: Shut up all of that screaming!

BRUCE: I'm dead!

KENNY: Shut up, Bruce!

BRUCE: My sweet Lord!

JELLY: The gun wasn't loaded, Bruce.

BRUCE: The whole back of my head is gone! I'm dead!

JELLY [*nudging* KENNY]: Well, that takes care of ol' Bruce, huh?

KENNY: Yep. Poor ol' Bruce.

JELLY: Shame he had to die like that.

KENNY: Yeah, what a shame. I'm going to miss the ol' dude.

JELLY: I'm not going to miss him. The motherfucker owed me a lot of money.

[JELLY *and* KENNY *laugh.* BRUCE *hears this and starts to listen.*]

Hey, hey, hold it. Hold it. How did you like the funeral?

KENNY: Oh, sad funeral. Real sad.

JELLY: Too bad nobody came.

KENNY: Yeah, too bad.

JELLY: But then again, who would want to see scum put into the ground?

[JELLY *and* KENNY *laugh.*]

BRUCE: Hey, man. I ain't no scum.

JELLY: You're scum, boy. Dead scum.

BRUCE: If I'm dead, then how come I can hear you talking to me?

JELLY: 'Cause you're a ghost, Bruce. You're dead, your body is burning in hell, but your spirit is right here on earth. You are doomed to walk the streets of the city for all eternity looking to get high, but you know what? Ghosts can't get high.

BRUCE: They can't?

JELLY: Nope.

BRUCE: Oh, Jesus Lord.

MIKE: You're not a ghost, Bruce. Get up off the ground!

JELLY: Don't spoil it for him, Mike.

MIKE: The gun wasn't loaded, Bruce.

BRUCE: You mean I'm alive?

JELLY [*holding up two shotgun shells*]: He didn't say you was alive. He said the gun wasn't loaded.

MIKE: He didn't shoot you, Bruce.

JELLY: I should have, though. Walking off from the liquor store and leaving my change like that. I ought to blow your ass away!

BRUCE: Nah, wait, Jelly Belly! I'll go back to the store and get your change.

JELLY: Forget about it.

BRUCE: I'll go back right now.

JELLY: Bruce! Listen to me, Bruce! Forget about the change. You see that white boy that ripped off Kenny?

BRUCE: Yeah, I saw him.

JELLY: See? Even Bruce knows you got ripped off.

BRUCE: He's down at the liquor store, Kenny.

JELLY: So. What you going to do, Kenny?

[*He offers* KENNY *the gun.*]

KENNY: I'm going to kick his ass.

JELLY: You ain't shit, you know that! You, your whoring mama, your drunken daddy, the whole lot of you ain't shit. I don't know how I got hooked up with you in the first place. You ain't my partner, Kenny. You ain't even my friend. You ain't shit. Go home and go to bed. I don't want you around me.

BRUCE: I told you, Jelly Belly. I tried to tell you about Kenny a long time ago. Now if you would've listened to me—

JELLY: Shut up, Bruce!

MIKE: I'm going in the house.

JELLY: Well go ahead, goddamn it! Don't nobody need you out here anyway.

MIKE: You're sitting on my porch.

JELLY: And will continue to sit on your porch until I get ready to leave. I don't know what's happened to you motherfuckers. I go away for a couple of months and Mike's done got pussy whipped and Kenny's done lost all of his nerve.

MIKE: Kenny hasn't lost anything. And me, I don't care what you say about me. Now I'm going in the house and going to bed.

JELLY: And I ain't leaving, Mike. All of that dust you and me snorted on this porch? Every night we sat out here and snorted enough dust to pay my rent, your rent, and everybody's rent for months. You ever think about how much that cost, Mike? Did you ever, for one minute, think about where it came from? Who was paying for it? I never asked you for a dime, Mike. Not one thin dime. I always gave you everything you asked for 'cause you was my friend. And now you want to throw me off your porch. Call the police on me and shit.

KENNY: You calling the police on Jelly Belly? Why you want to do something like that, Mike? Jelly Belly don't mess with nobody.

JELLY: You even tried to turn Kenny against me. Kenny! This boy has been like a son to me.

KENNY: I ain't turned against you, Jelly. I'm still your boy.

JELLY: Then give me one of those beers. Bruce, open this.

[JELLY *hands* BRUCE *a foil.* BRUCE *attempts to open it.*]

We were friends, Mike. You and your wife needed money, I gave you money, no questions asked. You asked me not to tell her where it came from, I never said a fuckin' word. You got yourself in trouble and I went out of my way to help you. If it wasn't for me, you would be in jail right now. I've always gone out of my way to give you everything you asked for, Mike. And now you want to act as if we're strangers? Act as if you don't know me? It ain't that easy, Mike. It just ain't that easy.

[JELLY *looks at* BRUCE, *who is having trouble opening the foil.*]

What the hell you doing with that dust, Bruce!

BRUCE: Trying to open it.

JELLY: You spill it, I'm going to kick your ass.

BRUCE: Open this for me, Kenny.

MIKE: You figure out what I owe you, Jelly. I'll pay you back.

JELLY: I don't want your money, Mike. What you owe me can't be repaid in dollars.

MIKE: So you're going to hold this over my head for the rest of my life?

JELLY: I ain't holding nothing over your head. I just don't want you to forget who your friends are.

KENNY: Got it open, Jelly.

BRUCE: Can I have a little bit?

JELLY: You got any money?

BRUCE: No.

JELLY: Then how do you expect to pay for it? That shit don't grow on trees, you know.

BRUCE: I know. But I figured that you'd let me have a little bit. You know, like you always do.

JELLY: See what I mean? You boys are living in a dream world, but let me tell you something. You get nothing for free in this world. Absolutely nothing. I own you, Bruce. You know that?

BRUCE: I know, Jelly.

JELLY: And Mike, you owe me a lot. A hell of a lot.

MIKE: You tell me what you think I owe you and I will pay you back.

JELLY: And you, Kenny, you hurt me most of all. You let Mike turn you against me, let him strip you of all your pride. You've turned into a punk, Kenny. A gutless motherfucker.

BRUCE: Since you already own me, mind if I have a little toot of that dust?

JELLY: Go ahead, boy. Toot the whole thing. I hope you get sick and die.

BRUCE: Thanks, Jelly.

KENNY: What about me? Can I have a little toot too?

JELLY: Hell no.

KENNY: I can pay for it if you want.

JELLY: There ain't enough money in the world to make me sell to somebody I don't want to sell to.

KENNY: Then can I buy a beer from you?

MIKE: You don't need a beer, Kenny. You need to go home and go to bed.

KENNY: I need a beer, Mike. Why can't I have a beer?

JELLY: Go on and get a beer and shut up. Keep your money. Just get the beer and get away from me. You make me sick.

MIKE: I'm going in the house and going to bed. You ought to do the same, Kenny. If they want to sit out here all night, let them.

KENNY: After this beer, Mike. My throat is dry. You know how that dust is, Mike. I need something to wet my throat.

JELLY: No pride, Kenny. No pride, no dignity. Working a slave's job for slave wages.

MIKE: Honest work, Jelly Belly. Honest work with plenty of pride. The money we spend doesn't come from the pockets of people who were stepped on and kicked aside. The money I spend is mine. Money I worked for.

JELLY: And where does that leave you, Mike? Sitting on the porch of your cracker-box house crying about how you got fucked over at work, talking about how you got to go to bed so you can get up the next morning to go back to work so you can get fucked over again. You're building houses that you'll never see the insides of, in neighborhoods with streets that they won't let you drive down. Why don't you build a house for yourself if you got pride, instead of living in this cardboard cutout? Why don't you build a house for your friends, the people you know, the people down the street, and spread your pride around? 'Cause they won't let you, that's why. You're a slave, Mike. You spend your life breaking your back, building things for people who would rather spit on you than look at you. If that's what you call honest, you can have it. I'd rather have my pride. I'd rather be a man. Men don't bend their backs at the feet of other men, only slaves do that. Men don't take orders from other men, only slaves do that. Men don't sell their pride for two dollars an hour or a bag of dope and men don't allow other men to walk into their houses without just retribution. Only slaves do that.

[BRUCE, *who has tooted the last foil, comes out of his stupor and speaks in general.*]

BRUCE: That was some damn good shit, Jelly Belly. Damn good. I'm glad I'm your boy.

JELLY: People are laughing at you, Kenny. They're saying what a dumb mother-fucker you are. They're wondering why you're taking the little pride you got and putting it into things you'll never see. If that's the type of life you want to lead, be my guest. But I thought you were a man. I thought you had potential.

KENNY: I am a man.

JELLY: Yeah, sure, Kenny. I just lay out the facts for you and let you decide. You want another toot of this dust before I go?

KENNY: I can pay for it if you want.

JELLY: You ain't got to pay me, Kenny. I like you. You're my boy. Here, take two. They're small.

[*He hands* KENNY *two small foils.*]

I got to piss. Mind if I use your bathroom, Mike? Or you want to try to keep me out of there too?

MIKE: Barbara's asleep.

JELLY: I didn't ask you if I could spend the night. I asked if I could piss in your bathroom. If not, tell me and I'll piss right here.

MIKE: Use the bathroom. But be quiet.

[JELLY *climbs to the top of the stairs and exits.* KENNY *begins to open one of the foils.*]

You shouldn't do that shit, Kenny. It's not good for you.

KENNY: I can handle it, Mike.

MIKE: You see what it's done to Bruce.

KENNY: Why don't you just leave me alone, OK?

MIKE: Be sure you're ready when I come to get you in the morning.

KENNY: I'll be ready, Mike. Ain't I always ready? Don't I always be sitting there waiting for you when you come? Don't I, Mike? Don't I?

MIKE: Yeah, Kenny.

KENNY: Don't I always do what you say? Don't I always do what everybody says? Foreman says, "Kenny, we need a wheelbarrow of sand out back." I take a wheelbarrow of sand out back. "Kenny, we need a flat of bricks on the second floor." I take a flat of bricks to the second floor. "Kenny, dig a hole." I dig a hole. I always do what everybody tells me to do and I'm tired of it, Mike. For once, just this once, I want to do what I want to do and right now I want to toot this dust!

MIKE: OK, Kenny. I'm sorry. Toot the dust.

[*Pause.* KENNY *opens the foil and is about to toot the dust.*]

I know how you feel, Kenny. I feel the same way sometimes. But remember the things we talked about? Remember, Kenny? Remember the business? Kenny and Mike's Construction Company. You and me, Kenny. We're going to have our own business. Then we won't have to put up with that shit anymore. We can come and go as we want. There won't be anybody telling us what to do.

KENNY: But when is that going to be, Mike? When?

MIKE: Soon, Kenny. Soon.

KENNY: That's the same thing you said about your promotion, Mike. You said, "Kenny, I'm going to be a supervisor soon." Same thing you said about me working labor. You said, "Kenny, work labor for now, but soon you're going to be an apprentice." Well, you ain't no supervisor, Mike. And I'm still working labor.

MIKE: We need patience, Kenny. Like the bricklayers. Remember?

KENNY: Yeah, Mike. Sure. Patience.

[KENNY *toots the dust. Aroused by the sound,* BRUCE *comes out of his stupor and stumbles over to* KENNY.]

BRUCE: Heyyyy, Kenny! Can I have a little bit of that dust?

KENNY: Get the fuck away from me, Bruce, before I kick your ass.

BRUCE: You can kick my ass, but you can't hurt me. You know why? 'Cause I got a strong mind. You see, you can be at home in your house, you can be cruising down the street, or you can be in jail. It's all the same, you know what I mean?

MIKE: It's not the same!

BRUCE: I mean, shit, man! You got to be somewhere! Right? Am I right? That is one fact that you cannot deny. . . that you got to be somewhere. And the motherfuckers out there got a lock on your jock no matter where you at. They get you coming and they get you going. The chains are all the same, baby. The only difference is, some of them clink, and some of them clank. But if you got a strong mind like me, it don't matter, clink, clank, coming, going, I could be working your motherfuckin' job. It's all the same. So! Since I made my point, Kenny, you might as well let me have a little bit of that dust.

KENNY: Get the fuck away from me, Bruce!

[KENNY *pushes* BRUCE *in the face.* BRUCE *tumbles backward and lands in the same spot from which he began.*]

JELLY [*entering*]: Bruce giving you a little trouble?

KENNY: Bruce ain't shit. Bruce is scum.

JELLY: You toot that dust, Kenny?

KENNY: Yeah, Jelly. And it was some good dust.

JELLY: Don't you got to piss?

KENNY: Yeah, Jelly. I got to piss. Can I use your bathroom, Mike?

MIKE: Go ahead.

KENNY: Thanks a lot, Jelly. That was some good dust. Some real good dust.

[KENNY *exits.*]

JELLY: Thank you for the use of your facilities, Mike. Pretty wife you got in there. I almost forgot how pretty she was.

MIKE: You son of a bitch, you.

[BARBARA *enters*.]

BARBARA: What the fuck is going on out here? People coming in and out of my house.

JELLY: All I did was look at her.

BARBARA: He stood over my bed, Mike. This motherfucker came into my room and stood over my bed.

JELLY: You shouldn't let your wife sleep in the nude like that. You never know who might walk in your house.

BARBARA: You're sick, Jelly Belly, you know that? You're the sickest son of a bitch I've ever seen in my life.

JELLY: I was looking for my sister.

BARBARA: You are a walking wall of destruction. People try to build something, try to have a little bit, and you come along and tear it down.

JELLY: It was an honest mistake, Miss Mike. I was looking for my sister.

BARBARA: She ain't here, goddamn it. And with God as my witness, you will never see her again. She came by here shaking and crying . . . she wanted to kill herself, Jelly Belly.

JELLY: So you did see her.

BARBARA: Yeah, I saw her. I gave her the money to leave town. Even found a place for her to go. Took her to the bus station myself. She's doing fine, Jelly Belly. She's doing just fine.

JELLY: So where is she?

BARBARA: That, Brother Jelly, is one thing you will never know.

JELLY: This is a damned shame. I don't like to hit a woman. It makes me feel bad afterwards, you know what I mean, Mike?

MIKE: You're not going to hit that woman. That's one thing I know you're not going to do.

JELLY: But if a woman lies to you, what else can you do?

BARBARA: I'll tell you what you can do. You can take that lie for all it's worth. You hold on to it. You can use that lie and believe it. Let that lie be your salvation, 'cause one of these days, you're going to hit a woman, and she's going to have a straight razor under her robe. She's going to take that straight razor and run it across that fat belly of yours. Then you're going to feel rather foolish standing there with your mouth open, your belly split wide, and your intestines laying in the dirt.

JELLY: Where's my sister, Miss Mike?

BARBARA: I ain't got the slightest idea, Brother Jelly. Now get the fuck off my porch.

JELLY: You don't understand, Barbara. She can't live without me. She needs
me. It's always been just me and her. What she going to do without me?

BARBARA: Live a very happy life.

JELLY: You don't understand. I didn't want to kill the dude.

BARBARA: This is the last time I'm going to tell you. Get off my porch.

JELLY: Mike? Talk to your wife for me, OK? For me, Mike. Talk to her.

MIKE: What you want me to tell her?

JELLY: Tell her it's OK, Mike. Tell her, you and me, we're partners. We got to
stick together, Mike.

MIKE: Go to hell, Jelly Belly.

JELLY: Yeah, Mike. My partner. My man. You ain't got to be subtle with me. I
can pick up on the nuances. Hey, Bruce! You sorry son of a bitch. *Bruce!*

BRUCE: Yo, Brother Jelly, brother man.

JELLY: Come on, Bruce. Let's go.

BRUCE: Go? Go where?

JELLY: We're going to hell, Bruce. You want to go to hell with me?

BRUCE: Yeah, Brother Jelly. You know I want to go with you. You and me, we're
partners.

[BRUCE *exits.*]

MIKE: Aren't you forgetting something, Jelly Belly?

JELLY: What's that, Mike?

[MIKE *holds up the shotgun.*]

That ain't mine, Mike. I ain't never seen that before in my life. Jelly Belly
don't mess with guns. Got no reason to mess with guns. Jelly Belly don't
mess with nobody. And Mike? Keep the beer. Consider it a memento.

[JELLY *exits as* KENNY *enters.*]

KENNY: Where's Jelly?

MIKE: He left. Why don't you go home too.

KENNY: He left these shotgun shells in your bathroom, Mike.

BARBARA: What the hell has been going on out here?

MIKE: Give them to me.

KENNY: For what?

MIKE: I'm going to get rid of them.

KENNY: Nah, Mike. These are some good shells. You can blow a punk away
with these. He left the gun too.

MIKE: Give me the shells, Kenny.

KENNY: He left them for me, Mike, didn't he? He left the gun and the shells for me.

MIKE: He didn't leave them for anybody. Now give me the shells.

KENNY: You afraid I'm going to hurt myself or something?

BARBARA: He didn't say that, Kenny.

KENNY: You think I'm stupid, and I'm tired of you thinking I'm stupid. And I'm tired of you telling me what to do.

MIKE: Give me the shells, Kenny.

KENNY: I ain't doing what you say no more, Mike. I'm a man. I got pride. I'm tired of working construction and breaking my back while people laugh at me. I'm tired, Mike.

BARBARA: You're high, Kenny. Go home and sleep it off.

KENNY: Don't tell me what to do!

MIKE: There're going to be people telling you what to do for the rest of your life so you might as well get used to it. It's going to be me or it's going to be Jelly Belly or it's going to be somebody at work. Killing that man who robbed you isn't going to change a thing. There will still be people laughing at you, people thinking you're dumb, people telling you what to do. You can't kill them all, Kenny, so you might as well get used to it.

KENNY: Give me the gun, Mike.

MIKE: Take your silly ass home and go to bed.

[KENNY *knocks* MIKE *to the ground, grabs the gun, and loads it as* MIKE *scrambles to his feet.*]

BARBARA: Oh shit.

MIKE: What you going to do now, Kenny? Shoot me?

KENNY: Just leave me alone, Mike. OK?

MIKE: You going to shoot me, Kenny?

KENNY: Barbara, tell him to leave me alone.

BARBARA: Leave him alone, Mike.

MIKE: You leave here with that gun, you can forget about the morning, Kenny. You can forget about going to work, you can forget about the business, you can forget about everything. You hear me, Kenny?

BARBARA: Just let him go.

MIKE: And that house you was going to build for your mama. You can forget about that too.

KENNY: But it ain't going to happen. None of it. I'm never going to build no house.

MIKE: You can try, goddamn it. If you was a man, you'd try.

BARBARA: Please, Mike. Let go.

MIKE: Give me the gun, Kenny. Come on. Take the blueprints and give me the gun.

KENNY: It ain't going to happen, is it, Mike? The house, the business, none of it's ever going to happen, is it?

MIKE: We can try, Kenny. That's all we can do is try.

KENNY: I've tried every way I know how, Mike, and I can't try no more. I stopped trying. I stopped trying when I saw those tears in your eyes. I felt so helpless, Mike. Well, I'm not going to feel helpless no more.

[KENNY *exits with the gun.* MIKE *moves to go after him.*]

BARBARA: You hear that?

[MIKE *stops.*]

We done woke up Mikie. Come on, Mike. Let's go in the house.

[MIKE *doesn't respond.*]

He's got to go to school in the morning, Mike. Did he tell you? He says he wants to go back again.

[MIKE *doesn't respond.*]

Please, Mike. He says he wants to be like his daddy.

[MIKE *gives one last look in the direction in which* KENNY *exited, then slowly turns, climbs the stairs, and exits into the house.* BARBARA *lets loose a sigh of relief and follows* MIKE *into the house. Lights fade.*]

NORTH STAR

Gloria Bond Clunie

First-Place Winner

1993–1994

To my mother, Mrs. Colley Rakestraw Bond
Thank you for all of your love, wisdom, guidance, and strength;
thank you for being my true North Star!

PLAYWRIGHT'S STATEMENT

The energy sparked by the 1960 Greensboro sit-ins spread through the South like wildfire. Within three or four months, demonstrations sprang up across the South. The courage of four young men ignited kindling that had been laid ready by years of hard work, organization, dedication, and hope.

As a small child growing up in North Carolina in the 1960s, I faintly remember the COLORED signs and vividly recall my mother refusing to eat in a store where blacks had to stand and whites could sit at the counter. I also recall searching the night sky for the North Star with my father. Whether a black rite of passage or a personal idiosyncrasy, I will never know. But I do remember the power of that huge dark sky filled with billions of brilliant stars. Stars that made you look up and wonder, held you in reverence, demanded you see them . . . stars that made you accountable for taking up space under their brightness!

The voices of *North Star* rumbled through my mind, finding their way only on scraps of paper until the Council of Basic Education in 1993 provided a grant, which in essence said, Tell your story! It is not, however, by any means autobiographical. My courage extends only to the filling of a blank page, while the characters I write about represent people who dared to physically face more diabolical enemies—the historical prejudice of a segregated South and the bigotry that still exists in this country. While facing the darkness of ignorance and hate, they fought to maintain self, family, community, and that "universe of light" that stretches across time and exists in all of us.

I am very grateful to the many people who have helped bring *North Star* to life. Many thanks to the National Endowment for the Arts, the Getty Center for Education in the Arts, and the Council for Basic Education for the initial grant; Columbia College Theater Music Center, Chuck Smith, and the Theodore

Ward Prize for African American Playwriting for mounting the first production; and Dennis Zacek, Sandy Shinner, and Victory Gardens Theater for mounting the first professional production.

PRODUCTION HISTORY

North Star, by Gloria Bond Clunie, was first presented by the Columbia College Chicago Theater Department at the New Studio Theater in April 1994. It was directed by Chuck Smith, with set design by John Murbach, costume design by Alicia Turner, lighting design by Leasan Pascoe, and sound design by Chuck Smith. Joel Himelhoch was the stage manager.

Relia Taylor	Tammi Barlow
Uncle Frank	John Blackman
Doc	Da'Non Bolden
Kate Taylor	Tracy Davis
Willie Joe Poole	Wallace Heard
Miss Cooper	Cindi Heimericks
Jake	Joel Himelhoch
Aurelia Taylor	Faith Jaeger
Manson Taylor	Phillip Lee
Reverend Blake	Tracy Livingston
Diane	Nilwona Nowlin
Hawkins	Stefan Prater
Franklin	Chauncey Raglin
Granma	Carla Stillwell and Gina Bacon
Mr. Connell	Jason Tinker

The play was subsequently presented by the Victory Gardens Theater in Chicago in February 1995. It was directed by Sandy Shinner, with set design by Jeff Bauer, costume design by Margaret Moretti, lighting design by Michael Rourke, and sound design by Galen G. Ramsey. Amy A. Field was the production stage manager. In 1995, it won the Joseph Jefferson Award for Best New Work.

Mr. Connell	Don Blair
Willie Joe Poole	Christopher Brown
Relia Taylor	Tomasina Gross
Miss Cooper	Karen Hammer
Aurelia Taylor	Leslie Holland
Franklin	Timothy Jenkins

Reverend Blake . . . . William King
Granma . . . . Audrey Morgan
Jake . . . . Matt Pavich
Manson Taylor . . . . Tim Edward Rhoze
Hawkins . . . . Syd Rushing
Kate Taylor . . . . Jacqueline Williams

CHARACTERS

Aurelia Taylor, African American, adult Relia
Relia Taylor, eleven, Negro, Aurelia as a child
Kate Taylor, Negro, loving but "does not play," Aurelia's mother
Manson Taylor, Negro undertaker, thoughtful and determined, Relia's father
Hawkins, fifties, Negro janitor, big talker but dedicated, Manson's friend
Willie Joe Poole, twelve, Negro, Relia's best friend
Miss Cooper, white, librarian
Granma, Negro, Manson's mother and Aurelia's grandmother
Mr. Connell, white, Woolworth's manager
Franklin, Negro, community college student
Reverend Blake, Negro minister, soft spoken with a slight stutter, clear sighted
    with a quiet will of steel, Manson's friend
Voice of Uncle Frank, Willie's dead uncle, appears in a dream (may be played in
    silhouette by the actor playing Franklin or another male character)
Jake, white, farmer (may be played by the actor playing Mr. Connell)
Woman, white, appears in a crowd (may be played by actor playing Miss Cooper)

STAGING

The play is set in the present and in the summer of 1960 in both a large northern
city and a small town in North Carolina. The set consists of multiple levels that
can transform into a variety of playing spaces. Key areas are Relia's front porch
and house, the library, the church and church basement, Granma's house, a dark
country road, a barn, the eating counter of a southern department store, and a
city beach. Aurelia is constantly onstage. Though ever present, she will need
spaces from which to observe other scenes that don't directly include her. For
convenience, the play is broken up into scenes and acts, but in most cases the
scenes should flow from one into the next, like a story, without pause. Costumes, lighting, and sound should be simple and suggest the fluidity of memory.
The sky, in many forms, is a constant presence.

ACT 1

SCENE 1

[*A summer night in the city. Silhouette of a mother and child is seen. (The actor who plays* RELIA *could play child in silhouette.* AURELIA *is the mother of this child.) Child sings "This Little Light of Mine" joyously. Indistinct whispering voices begin . . . They get meaner. Child sings softly, bravely, but her voice cracks. Whispers end in audible, angry whisper.*]

VOICES: Nigger . . .

[*Child stops singing. In the dark, faint sounds of the late-night city can be heard; traffic almost in slow motion.* AURELIA *rushes to the beach of a modern northern city. She covers her eyes as if looking for something behind her eyelids. She opens her eyes and looks up again at the sky, angry and frustrated.*]

AURELIA: I can't believe . . . I can't believe he called my daughter . . . That cab-driver called my baby girl . . . It was under his breath, but she heard it. A whisper, but in the dark it echoed down the street like cold wind on a mission . . . and she heard it. I saw it in her eyes and she sees in mine . . . She sees in mine . . . I didn't know what to do. I grabbed her hand and walked away . . . ran away.

    I avoid her eyes now. She's frightened because I'm frightened. It rattled something deep. Something I'd put away a long time ago. She's waiting.

    What do I say?

    I don't want her to fear . . .

    I don't want her to hurt . . .

    I don't want her to know . . .

    God, why couldn't I have stopped it!

[AURELIA *has a flashback. She hears/sees* GRANMA *singing "I've Been 'Buked and I've Been Scorned." Then* AURELIA *hears/sees her mother,* KATE, *singing part of "Ain't Gonna Let Nobody Turn Me Round." Song stops when scene begins.*]

RELIA: Ow . . .

KATE: Hold still . . .

RELIA: Ow . . . Mommmmmyyyyy . . .

KATE: Told you a million times . . . Now, you all banged up . . . scarred . . .

AURELIA [*trying to touch memory*]: Mama?

RELIA: You're the one . . . says pretty on the inside . . .

KATE: When it starts to heal . . . we'll put cocoa butter on it. And leave the scab alone!

[*Lights fade on* RELIA *and* KATE. AURELIA *does not want them to fade away.*]

AURELIA: I don't have a bandage for this one, Mama. No cocoa butter. I can't remember how to make it heal . . . I can't remember how you . . . Where do I find . . . ??? They told me a million times . . . in a million ways . . . but what did they say?

[KATE*'s voice is heard singing softly.* AURELIA *watches* RELIA, *the eleven-year-old version of herself, sneak outside to escape bedtime. She sneaks up on* MANSON, *her father, and covers his eyes.*]

RELIA [*to* MANSON]: Shhhhhh . . .

[*They laugh and become quiet conspirators in the night.* RELIA *and her father,* MANSON, *sit on the front porch steps of their two-story home in the Negro section of a small southern town. They live beside the funeral parlor* MANSON *owns. It is a night in 1960. Sometimes* AURELIA *interacts with her memories, at other times she observes. She desperately wants to be a part of these moments in the past.*]

MANSON: Humpty Dumpty back together again?

[RELIA *holds a wound up to be kissed.*]

KATE: Manson, is Relia out there?

RELIA: Shhhhh . . .

MANSON: Be in in a minute . . .

[*He looks up.*]

Do you see it?

RELIA [*shaking her head*]: I can't find it.

MANSON: Shhhhhhh . . . Close your eyes.

[RELIA *closes, then opens, her eyes. Lights dim or go to darkness.*]

RELIA: It's so dark . . .

AURELIA [*with eyes open*]: Daddy . . .

MANSON: Girl big as you, still scared of the dark. Close your eyes. Good. Now, count to a hundred.

RELIA [*opening eyes*]: A hundred?

MANSON: No peeking! Count!

RELIA and AURELIA [*with eyes closed*]: One, two, three . . .

[AURELIA *opens her eyes,* RELIA *continues to count slowly.*]

AURELIA: Daddy, I can't . . . I can't find the stars anymore . . .

MANSON: Slow down . . .

AURELIA: The skies so different now. So small . . . I've lost them. Too much light from buildings, cars . . . Not like before . . .

MANSON: That's better . . . much better . . .

AURELIA: When I was a girl in Carolina,
We had big skies! Huge skies!
With millions and millions of stars.
Brilliant stars in black night skies,
That made you look up and wonder!
Held you in reverence.
Demanded you see them!
Made you accountable for taking up space under their brightness!
Ohhh, to turn off city lights and to see those stars again!

RELIA: . . . ninety-nine, one hundred.

MANSON: Now . . . open!

[*The sky is now a country sky, darker and filled with stars.*]

RELIA [*uncovering eyes*]: Wow! They changed!

AURELIA: So much brighter!

MANSON: No, your eyes just got used to the dark . . .

RELIA [*staring at the sky*]: Where do you think they come from?

MANSON: God blinked and there they were . . .

RELIA: Wouldn't you be scared, sittin' way out there in all that darkness?

MANSON: Not if I was a ball of light.

RELIA: Wonder how many there are?

MANSON: Lord, if questions were money, child . . .

RELIA: How many?

AURELIA: How many, Daddy?

MANSON: Billions!

RELIA AND AURELIA: Billions?

KATE [*calling from inside*]: Relia . . . Relia, why are you still out there? It's past your bedtime.

MANSON: Be in shortly. Is this about stars or stalling?

RELIA: You been out here every night this week.

MANSON: Got a lot to think about.

RELIA: 'Bout the sit-ins? Are you worried about the sit-ins? I'm not worried about the sit-ins. I can't wait to have my turn! Well, maybe a little bit worried. You worried about the sit-ins, Daddy?

[*Pause.*]

MANSON: You know, the stars are a lot like people. Not what they seem at all. Giant balls of energy reduced in our minds to tiny pinpoints of light. All the same, yet all different. All sitting in one sky.

[*Pause.*]

I reckon we'll do all right . . . Just got to remember . . . we're in the company of stars.

RELIA: Mama wouldn't call them all stars. She called some of them redneck—

MANSON: Relia!

RELIA: She said it!

MANSON: Once! And don't you ever repeat—

RELIA: But—

MANSON: End it!

RELIA: Mama says she's not sure I should demonstrate. You wouldn't let her stop me, would you? I've got to be there!

MANSON: White stars, blue stars, new stars, novas . . . I'll talk to her.

[*He points stars out to* RELIA.]

That group is the Kite of Hercules, and over there is the Northern Crown.

[*He pretends to take the crown from the sky and place it on* RELIA's *head.*]

For my lady!

RELIA: Ohhhhhh!

AURELIA: Thank you!

RELIA: What's your favorite?

[*Pause.*]

MANSON: Grandpa favored the North Star.

RELIA: Grandpa was blind.

MANSON: Could still see the stars. Said the North Star was his star, so I guess it's my star, too.

RELIA: Sounds funny. Like you could put it in a will or something.

MANSON: Maybe, not in a will, exactly . . .

RELIA: Never can find it by myself.

MANSON: Right at the end of the Little Dipper.

RELIA [*pointing*]: There?

MANSON: Not enough stars . . .

RELIA: There?

MANSON: If you were Harriet Tubman, we'd all speak Spanish now. First, close your eyes. See it inside. Seven stars . . . a bowl with a handle. Got it?

RELIA: Yes!

MANSON: Now look!

RELIA [*opening eyes*]: There?

MANSON: Close. That's the Big Dipper. The two bright stars on the outside of the bowl? They . . . *point* to the North Star. The faint stars, that's the Little Dipper. Big Dipper, Pointer Stars, Little Dipper . . . North Star . . .

RELIA [*pointing to stars as she finds them*]: Big Dipper, Pointer Stars, Little Dipper . . . North Star! I see it . . . I see it!

MANSON: Now, you're Harriet Tubman, freedom bound.

RELIA: Freedom bound!

MANSON: Tie a string to the North Star. Pull down, just like you're pulling a shade. Now, put your nose right on the string and you're facing due north . . . and this way is . . .

RELIA: South?

MANSON: And this is . . .

RELIA: East . . .

MANSON: And this is . . .

RELIA: West!

MANSON: Now hug the one that you love best!

[RELIA *hugs* MANSON, *who spins her so she sees the North Star.*]

RELIA: I see it! I see it! Gotcha, North Star!

MANSON: Now, find it again.

[*Both* RELIA *and* AURELIA *turn around.* MANSON *spins* RELIA *faster until she is dizzy and laughing. When* RELIA *and* AURELIA *stop, neither can find the North Star.*]

RELIA: It's gone!
MANSON: No, you just got turned around. When you need it, close your eyes, and look here first.

[*He points to* RELIA's *heart.*]

RELIA: I'll never find it on my own!
MANSON: Yes, you will, and then it'll be your star, too.

[KATE *enters, drying a dish.*]

KATE: Manson, that child needs to go to bed.
MANSON: We're moving in that direction now.
KATE: Not unless she's sleeping in the garden!
RELIA [*to her father*]: Ah, come on, it's not like I've got school or nothin'...
KATE: Anything...school or anything. And summer or no, you still have to be up early, young lady. You're suppose to make signs over at the church at nine o'clock.
MANSON: A few more minutes won't hurt her.
KATE: All right, you two. Manson, I'm putting you in the waking-up department tomorrow. Let's see you tangle with Miss Stargazer then.
MANSON: You know something, I think it's time for bed.
KATE: Chicken!
RELIA: Daddy?
MANSON: You heard your mother!

[RELIA *heads upstairs.*]

KATE: Go on. Clean pajamas on your pillow. And let that scab be. Needs time to heal, for goodness' sakes.
MANSON [*hugging* KATE]: You just want to be alone with me on a starlit night.
KATE: Only if you want to be alone with me—and these dishes.
MANSON: Sounds interesting!

[*They kiss.*]

RELIA [*shouting from upstairs window*]: These are too little!
KATE: Then stop growing and get some out of your bottom drawer.

RELIA: I don't see any in the bottom drawer!

KATE: Aurelia Katherine Taylor, find something, say your prayers, and be in that bed before I get upstairs or I will be on you like thunder followin' lightnin'.

MANSON: How about being on me like thunder following lighting.

KATE [*smiling and hugging*]: Man, you are worse than she is. Come on in. You haven't even eaten yet.

MANSON: Can't. Got a few last-minute things to tie up on the Wilson funeral, then I promised to run over and help Ms. Edwards pick out a suit for John. She's taking his death so hard.

KATE: You coming right back?

MANSON: Well, I need to meet with Brother Green and the Rev—

KATE: Another meeting? Morning . . . midnight . . . mass meetings. Meetings before you meet . . .

MANSON: I'll grab something later.

KATE: We haven't sat down to a meal together in I don't know how long.

MANSON: You think we're gonna eat our way to freedom?

KATE: If you drop dead before we get there, it won't mean a whole lot, will it?

MANSON: Well, when you get to heaven, you can tell me about it.

KATE: How? You not going to heaven!

MANSON: I'll see you later.

KATE: At least go up and kiss Relia good night. Before you know it, she'll be at Granny's.

MANSON: Yeah, about Mama's . . . Listen, Kate, it won't kill anybody for her to go at the end of the summer, will it? She and her friends have their hearts set on demonstrating . . .

[RELIA *enters quietly and listens.*]

KATE: That's exactly why I want her at Mama's. These kids think we're playing. Things get serious . . . I'd rather her be down there. That way we can focus on what we've got to do.

RELIA: Ahhh, Mommy.

KATE: Girl, you better get in bed and stop eavesdroppin' on grown-folk conversation.

RELIA: I'll miss everything!

KATE: There'll be plenty to do when you get back.

RELIA: But, Mom . . .

KATE: Girl, we've been fighting for freedom for three hundred years, we won't wrap up the battle in one summer.

RELIA: But Willie, all my friends . . .

KATE: I hope they're good letter writers!

RELIA: Daddy, I promised . . .

MANSON [*to* RELIA]: We'll talk in the morning.

RELIA: But . . .

MANSON: In the morning . . .

[RELIA *exits.*]

Kate . . . I think she should stay.

KATE: She's too young!

MANSON: No, she's not.

KATE [*shouting up to* RELIA *and avoiding* MANSON'*s concern*]: In bed, Aurelia, and turn off those lights. Do you think we have a dynamo in the backyard! An eleven-year-old child, still sleeping with the light on. She'll be in college afraid of the dark.

MANSON: Listen . . .

KATE: Manson . . . I don't know. But right now, let me see if I can get this child in bed before the sun comes up.

MANSON: Kate . . .

KATE: Manson . . . It doesn't always do to see things too early. I'll have to think about it. Aurelia! The light!

[KATE *enters the house while* MANSON *watches the skies for a minute longer.*]

AURELIA: My mother didn't play. There was a right way and a wrong way to everything according to her. It was her job to make sure the way I found was always the right way. If I strayed, she was pretty quick to help me find the path again. Things weren't quite so black-and-white with my dad. He was like reading a good book: you didn't always understand. I watched him watch the skies, standing still as pond water on a hot summer day. Lately, since the sit-ins, he'd been watching the sky a lot. Standing outside for hours, then going off to another midnight meeting.

[MANSON *goes into the house just as* HAWKINS *enters, rushing up to the porch. He is nervous and out of breath.*]

HAWKINS: Manson, Manson . . . glad I caught ya . . . Willie Joe Poole's been arrested.

MANSON: What?

HAWKINS: Four white boys jumped him after the demonstration. I'm not quite sure what started it, but . . .

MANSON: What's he charged with?

HAWKINS: Disturbin' the peace.

KATE [*coming out on the porch*]: Manson?

HAWKINS: Evenin', Kate.

KATE: What's wrong?

MANSON: Willie Joe got beat up and arrested.

KATE: Is he hurt bad?

HAWKINS: Don't know. Nobody's seen him. His mama was too scared to go down to the jail, so she run got the reverend. Reverend called me, say pick up Manson and meet him down there. We got to get that boy out tonight!

MANSON: OK. Calm down . . .

KATE: Lord, Relia would go crazy if anything happened to Willie.

MANSON: Kate, just to be on the safe side, you and Relia sleep downstairs till I get back. But hold off telling her anything till we get more news.

KATE: You think it's that bad?

[MANSON *goes down the steps, then comes back.*]

MANSON: I'll be back when I can.

KATE [*whispering to* MANSON]: Manson. Why do you have to go? Let them handle it.

MANSON: Kate, I've got to. If we don't do something quick . . . you know, they're liable to slip that boy into some creek and we'll never hear of him again. It'll be all right.

KATE: You can't promise me that. You keep going out in the night and I keep wondering are they gonna slip you into some creek.

MANSON: I'll be back. Now, get some sleep.

KATE: Call me!

MANSON: Don't worry. I'll be back when I can.

[MANSON *and* HAWKINS *exit.*]

KATE: Call me!

SCENE 2

[AURELIA *goes to the porch. Lights indicate we have flashed back to another day.* AURELIA *sits on the porch steps and remembers* WILLIE. RELIA *shouts for* WILLIE. RELIA *is not aware* AURELIA *is there.*]

AURELIA: We were all frightened the night Willie Joe was arrested.

RELIA: Willie Joe!

AURELIA: You see, despite his sorry home life, Willie Joe Poole wasn't really a troublemaker . . .

RELIA: Willie! Willie Joe! Come on!

[WILLIE *races up to* RELIA.]

Willie! You've been fighting again!

WILLIE: Some cracker wanted to know why a "little coon" was carrying such a "big book." I just gave him an answer.

RELIA: Willie!?!

AURELIA: Willie just believed in standing his ground!

WILLIE: He started it!

AURELIA: Sometimes I wish I was like Willie, but then again . . .

RELIA: You gonna get yourself killed one day!

WILLIE: Before I do, you wanna take a look at this?

RELIA: You got it!

WILLIE: I got it!

[WILLIE *teases* RELIA *with the book, playing a chase game, and then sits beside her on the porch steps but won't let her see it.*]

AURELIA: He could set a twinkle in your eye, even when you were bound and determined to be mad at him.

[AURELIA'*s presence recedes as* RELIA *and* WILLIE *explore the book.*]

RELIA: Come on . . . Let me see. Stop being so hateful, Willie. You promised to show me if you found it.

WILLIE: All right, all right! [*Getting serious*] Now, I'll show you, but then you got to keep it to yourself. If your daddy found out, he'd kill us both. Spit swear!

RELIA: Nooooo . . . We're too big for that stuff.

[WILLIE *will not give her the book.*]

WILLIE: Spit swear!

RELIA: I hate this, this is so nasty. Spitting is so nasty.

WILLIE: You want to see it or not?

RELIA: You just make me do it because you know I hate spitting in my hands. Ohhhhh. All right.

[WILLIE *and* RELIA *perform a swearing ritual they have done since they were small. Both rub the ground, spit on their hands, rub their palms together, then shake hands.*]

RELIA AND WILLIE: Spit swear! While we both walk the face of the earth, I promise never to tell!

WILLIE: Now wipe your hands real good!

[WILLIE *wipes his hands on* RELIA's *clothes, then shows* RELIA *the book. She is amazed as she turns the pages.* AURELIA *watches.*]

AURELIA: But even as he laughed and joked, you knew Willie's sense of adventure marked him as sure as a cracked egg loses its insides.

RELIA: Where'd you get this?

WILLIE: I hatched it!

AURELIA: His quick mind or his quick mouth would surely lead him into the shadow of death . . . just like his uncle Frank.

WILLIE [*to* RELIA]: Close your mouth and stop eatin' flies, girl!

AURELIA: Maybe he joked so much 'cause he didn't want folks standing around expecting his funeral.

RELIA [*scrutinizing the page*]: You sure it goes like that?

WILLIE: It's plain as day, with pictures and everything!

RELIA: Looks uncomfortable.

WILLIE: According to my brother, you get used to it and it's kinda nice.

RELIA: Has he done it before?

WILLIE: Says he has . . . lots of times.

RELIA: But he's not even married!

WILLIE: You don't have to be married.

RELIA: Mama says . . .

WILLIE: Well, girls do, but boys don't.

RELIA: That doesn't make any sense. Who do they do it with?

WILLIE: Girls who *aren't* gonna get married. Girls like the ones on Green Street. Or the ones boys talk about when they're hanging over car engines and grinning . . .

RELIA: Have you ever done it?

[*Long pause.*]

WILLIE: Never found a girl I really wanted to do it with. One worth holding on to. Like Uncle Frank used to say, don't want myself tied down to some little nobody with small ideas and no sense. You could have a baby doing this. Wouldn't want the mother of my children no less brilliant than me.

RELIA: Swear truth?

[*Long pause.*]

WILLIE: Truth? Scared to ask the girls that would and wouldn't ask the girls I know. They're more just the kissing kind. You ever been kissed before, Relia?

RELIA: You?

WILLIE: I asked first.

RELIA: Not really.

WILLIE: Ever wonder what it's like?

RELIA: Hmmmmmmm.

WILLIE: I could show you?

RELIA: You mean on the lips?

WILLIE: No, on your knee! Yes, on the lips.

RELIA: Does that mean we're going steady?

WILLIE: Heck no. Let's just call it an . . . an experiment.

RELIA: Should I shut my eyes?

WILLIE [looking at the book and then at RELIA]: Don't have to.

RELIA: Uggggh . . . Close your mouth.

WILLIE: But the book . . .

RELIA: The heck with the book. I don't want you spitting all over me!

WILLIE: OK . . . OK . . . At least pucker up!

[WILLIE and RELIA kiss, seriously at first, but then they're not sure how to end it and WILLIE starts laughing.]

RELIA: Stop laughing!

WILLIE: I'm sorry. You want to do it again?

RELIA: No!

WILLIE: Sure?

RELIA [shaking her head]: You play too much.

WILLIE [referring to the book]: I was just . . .

RELIA: Where'd you get this, anyway?

[WILLIE makes a big deal out of showing her the spine of the book.]

WILLIE: The back room [whispering] in the library.

RELIA: That's no big deal. I been to the library before! Haven't seen a book this nice there, though. Why, it's almost new!

WILLIE: I don't mean the colored branch—I mean the big one, with the huge columns out front!

RELIA: You got this from the white library?

WILLIE: Couldn't get books this nice in the colored library!

RELIA: How in the world . . . ?

WILLIE: You wanna go?

RELIA: It's getting late.

WILLIE: Not much past four.

RELIA: Mama would kill me!

WILLIE: Chicken!

RELIA: I can roast your rooster any day!

WILLIE: Then come on . . . and I'll show you the *real* library! Here, hide this!

[WILLIE *hands* RELIA *the book. She hides it under the porch.* AURELIA *takes it out and looks at it.* WILLIE *and* RELIA *head for the library.* RELIA *is awed by the outside of the building.*]

Come on!

[RELIA *hesitates.*]

Come on, will ya!

[WILLIE *enters with confidence,* RELIA *enters reluctantly.* WILLIE *drops his head as he approaches the scrutiny of the pale-faced librarian.* RELIA *drops her head.*]

My daddy's sick, this gal's gonna help me.

MISS COOPER: That's fine, Willie. And, Willie, what I tell you 'bout comin' in the front door?

WILLIE: Just forgot, ma'am.

AURELIA: Granma always said . . .

[GRANMA *appears.*]

GRANMA: Don't want no grandbaby of mine prancin' through no back doors. Can't go in the front—don't go.

AURELIA: Willie grabbed my arm and led me into the storage room. Started handing me dustcloths and a broom.

RELIA: What????

AURELIA: He grabbed a bucket and a pail.

WILLIE: Come on.

RELIA: Willie?

AURELIA: I was so dumbfounded, I didn't know what to do but follow him . . . Granma's voice ringing in my head . . .

[WILLIE *pushes her down on her knees and he starts cleaning.*]

GRANMA: Girl, I don't want you cleaning up behind no white folks. Get your education and don't bring no report cards with mess on 'em. I want As and maybe, just maybe, since the Lord is the only perfect being, on occasion a B . . . with a plus behind it, mind you. You smart. You smart girl. You can do and be anything you want, child. Just get your education. Don't want you end up cleaning in Miss Ann's kitchen.

AURELIA: When I asked her . . .

RELIA: Did you ever clean in Miss Ann's kitchen?

AURELIA: . . . she was silent for a long time.

GRANMA: Only when my children were hungry . . . or needed books. But I done worked too hard to ever see you on your knees, child.

RELIA [*holding the cloth and wondering what to do*]: Willie?

WILLIE [*pulling* RELIA *back onto her knees*]: Shhhhhh . . . start cleaning.

GRANMA: Lord, have mercy!

[GRANMA *exits.*]

AURELIA: Hmmmmmmm. It was quiet as a tomb and almost as empty as we dusted table after table.

MISS COOPER: Willie? When you're done, child, pull the door to, the lock's already on. Hope your father's feeling better soon. See you tomorrow.

WILLIE: Yes, ma'am.

[MISS COOPER *exits.* WILLIE *jumps onto the table and shouts.*]

Welcome to my world! You in high cotton now, girl! What you wanna read?

RELIA: Can we do this?

WILLIE: We're doing it!

RELIA: But are we free to . . .

WILLIE: Free? Free! Heck, Relia, Uncle Frank used to say it's the *little freedoms* we *take* that'll keep us sane till the big freedoms come.

RELIA: I'm scared . . .

WILLIE: Why?

RELIA: I don't know, but it doesn't feel right.

WILLIE: Girl, I used to think so, too! But look around! Why not! It's a public library! Makes me feel like when Uncle Frank used to fly me. Pick me up, hold me over his head, and fly me like I was on top of the world! Come on, Relia, fly! Fly with me? Grab a little freedom and fly!

RELIA: I'm not so sure . . . but . . .

AURELIA: There were wonders there you wouldn't believe!

RELIA: Amazing things! A globe as big as our kitchen table. Along the walls near the ceiling, plaster pictures of Greek and Roman stories. A rack with more magazines than I knew existed.

AURELIA: I couldn't find *Ebony* or *Jet,* but there were . . .

RELIA: *Better Homes and Gardens, Highlights for Children* . . .

AURELIA: . . . and a whole slew of them I'd never seen!

WILLIE: What you want to read about?

RELIA: Gosh, I don't know . . . ahhh . . . the stars . . . I want a book about the stars!

AURELIA: He took me to a place that had row after row of books on . . .

RELIA: . . . the stars . . . the moon . . . the universe!

[RELIA *softly reads from a book about the stars and the constellations as* AURELIA *remembers the library.*]

AURELIA: This became our place. Willie's and mine. We wandered through the aisles, surveying the world . . . mostly the white world, with an occasional volume by . . .

RELIA: Booker T. Washington . . .

AURELIA: . . . or some such passive soul. Willie felt free to "borrow" one, or two, to take home. I don't know what the soft-voiced librarian did if someone else requested the "borrowed" volumes, but she never said anything to Willie or me when we came to "clean."

[*She turns pages from the book the children had earlier.*]

Only occasionally, when Willie's father wasn't too drunk, did he bother to come with us. And when he did, Willie still handled most of the cleaning . . . with his father slowly turning pages and looking very sad. We began to stay later and later. Sometimes Willie would leave a back window open, walk me home, and then come back to finish the cleaning. One day, we were reading this great book about Greek mythology . . .

RELIA: Zeus!

WILLIE: Hera . . .

AURELIA: . . . and matching the stories to the pictures on the wall.

RELIA: Prometheus!

AURELIA: When before we knew it . . .

RELIA: Oh my word, it's an hour and a half past suppertime! My folks are gonna kill me!

[*They run to* RELIA's *porch.* KATE *and* MANSON *are waiting.* KATE *is furious.* MANSON *is quiet.* KATE *fusses at the speed of light. She does not stop to let them explain.*]

KATE: Where in the world have you two been?

RELIA AND WILLIE: We were . . .

KATE: Whatever you've got to say, I don't want to hear it! It's almost two hours past supper! We were half crazy with worry. Where in the world could your head be that you didn't realize it's two hours past supper?

RELIA and WILLIE [*trying to explain*]: We . . .

KATE: Don't even act like you have anything to say that will make good sense! The least you could have done was call instead of having us call all over town, worried sick, worrying the neighborhood . . . Why in God's name didn't you call?

[WILLIE *and* RELIA *try to answer.*]

And don't tell me you didn't have a dime to call! If you don't have a dime in your shoe to call when you leave, then you don't have any business stepping off this front porch! Give you a little freedom and what do you do with it? I've always thought of you as a young lady with good sense . . . We raised you as a young lady with good sense . . . Didn't we raise you with good sense? You better answer me when I ask you a question. Didn't we raise you with good sense?

RELIA [*confused about how much to say*]: Yes, ma'am . . .

KATE: And you, Willie, I know you got good sense!

WILLIE [*quickly*]: Yes, ma'am.

KATE: I depend on your good sense when this child's good sense goes out the window! Where was your good sense tonight?

[WILLIE *tries to answer.*]

Don't even talk to me! Go home, see your mother so she can finish fussing at you. Go on! Now!

[WILLIE *and* RELIA *exchange looks.* WILLIE *exits, running.*]

Your father said, "Kate, she's got good sense," and I was fool enough to believe him. Should I have been fool enough to believe him?

[RELIA *tries to answer.*]

Girl, don't you even talk to me! Don't even talk to me! You better talk to this girl, Manson . . . Talk to your daughter, because I'm so angry if I *listen* to her anymore, I might just go crazy and kill your child!

[*Pause. In the silence,* RELIA *turns to* MANSON.]

MANSON [*quietly*]: I'm disappointed in you, daughter.

AURELIA: For a girl, the disappointment of a father is like reaching to the bottom of a well when you're three days thirsty—and finding sand.

MANSON: Where have you been?

RELIA: At the library with Willie.

AURELIA: He got even quieter.

MANSON: Daughter, you can die and go to heaven or you can die and go to hell. That will be your choice based on the way you live your life, but don't ever lie to me. Library's only open Tuesdays and Thursdays and Saturdays.

RELIA: I wasn't at the *colored* library, I was at the *white* library . . .

MANSON: *You were where???????*

KATE: What????

[*Pause.*]

AURELIA: When my father cooled off . . .

MANSON: What in the world????

AURELIA: . . . and this took a considerable time . . .

MANSON: Where in God's name . . .

AURELIA: . . . after he cooled off . . .

MANSON: What possessed you . . .

AURELIA: . . . he heard all about our voyages.

RELIA: More books than you've ever seen!!!

[RELIA *gives* MANSON *the book from the library.*]

MANSON: Books, huh . . .

RELIA: . . . and a globe . . . a globe . . .

[RELIA *shows him the size of the globe.*]

MANSON: A globe . . . huh . . .

RELIA: . . . bigger than the kitchen! And all along the walls . . . paintings and . . .

MANSON [*to* KATE]: You know, in forty years, I've never seen the inside of that library.

KATE: Foolish and dangerous.

AURELIA: He seemed to regard me with newfound respect.

MANSON [*to* KATE]: Gotta hand it to 'em, Kate. You ever read a book from there? They got spunk, all right!

KATE: Just plain crazy! Both of you are just plain crazy! Relia, go to bed!

RELIA: Mama . . .

[RELIA *exits to the bedroom.* KATE *and* MANSON *argue as they exit.*]

KATE: And you standing there encouraging her . . .

MANSON: They're just children, Kate. Gotta spread their wings! When I
was . . .

AURELIA: Though it took some doing, our library adventures continued. I
guess Daddy understood about taking *little freedoms* . . . till the *big freedom*
comes.

[RELIA *enters and curls up in bed with a blanket and a book.*]

He began to supplement our reading with the likes of Frederick Douglass
and Langston Hughes, Arna Bontemps and Zora Neale Hurston . . . books
he would get when he drove to Detroit to buy a new hearse or went to a
black embalmers convention in some northern city.

[KATE *comes upstairs, turns off* RELIA's *light, and* RELIA *turns on a flashlight.*
MANSON *enters, signals her not to tell, and turns on* RELIA's *light again.* RELIA
turns off the flashlight and falls asleep.]

Years later, after seeing the glories of big city public libraries, I came back to
that place of forbidden fruits with its fading globe and well-thumbed volumes on the universe. It looked like a small room with books in it . . . a small
room with a big sky. God, where did that sky go?

SCENE 3

[*Later, on the evening of* WILLIE's *arrest.* KATE *enters, guiding a sleepy* RELIA *into
the living room.*]

KATE: Come on, Relia.

RELIA: What time is it?

KATE: Late.

RELIA: I smell coffee.

KATE: Your daddy wants you to sleep downstairs tonight.

RELIA: Why?

KATE: Don't worry about why, just come on. You can snuggle up on the sofa
until he gets back.

RELIA: What's wrong? Where's Daddy?

KATE: He went with Hawkins to meet the reverend. Now you know almost as much as I do, so no more questions. Good night.

[KATE *turns off the light.*]

RELIA: Mommy!

[KATE *turns on a small dim light and then exits.*]

AURELIA: The night Willie was arrested, I really needed the light. I used to get so scared sometimes when Daddy was away. It was weird. I felt like I had a hole in my stomach. A dark hole that I couldn't fill up with anything. Like I was homesick, even though I was home. I'd felt it before and Daddy told me . . .

[MANSON *enters and cradles* RELIA *as if she's a small child.*]

MANSON: Oh, that's just the growing-up hole! You have to have a place to store all the stuff you need to learn and feel to grow up. And it's bottomless . . . like a black hole.

RELIA: Is it dark inside? You know I'm scared of the dark. Is it dark?

MANSON: Very dark . . . until you see . . .

RELIA: What? What will I see?

MANSON: Look real carefully, and way near the end that doesn't end, you'll see a light! And staring back in that light is an older person that looks like you.

RELIA: Looks like me?

MANSON: Looking at you! That's why it's called the growing-up hole.

RELIA: But why does it hurt so bad?

MANSON: Sometimes, right about the time you're ready to do a whole lot of growing, you can feel it getting bigger. Stretching. It hurts a little bit, but then you just start filling it up with good growing-up stuff—good thoughts, things you've done well—then you hardly notice it's there.

AURELIA: Does it ever fill up?

MANSON: I hope not!

AURELIA: Not even when you're an old, old lady?

MANSON: Not even then. You just have to know what it is, so you're not afraid when you feel it.

[MANSON *exits.* AURELIA *tries to follow, but he is gone.*]

AURELIA: I can still feel it, Daddy. Daddy? Daddy, I want . . . I want the hole filled up . . . I want . . .

SCENE 4

[*No actual scene break.* AURELIA, *hearing* MR. CONNELL, *turns and is in the library.* MR. CONNELL *is a potbellied, middle-aged store manager.* MR. CONNELL's *"I want" should immediately echo* AURELIA's *"I want."*]

MR. CONNELL: I want the Raleigh paper, if that's not too much trouble.
MISS COOPER: Not at all, Mr. Connell.

[MR. CONNELL *sits to read the paper.* WILLIE *enters.*]

In early, aren't you, Willie?
WILLIE: Records day for colored teachers. Half day at school. Thought I'd finish up before it got late, if that's all right?
MISS COOPER: Not many folks here, I don't think that'll be a problem. Go 'head.
RELIA [*entering and nodding*]: Ma'am.

[RELIA *and* WILLIE *begin to clean the library. They move about* MR. CONNELL, *dusting and sweeping.* MR. CONNELL *moves automatically, without being aware they are there as he reads the paper. It is like a dance between two people who can't acknowledge the other is there.* MR. CONNELL *responds to a news article, without noticing the children.*]

MR. CONNELL: Coons!

[RELIA *and* WILLIE *are offended and angry but must keep cleaning.*]

AURELIA: It's interesting to watch a world when that world isn't aware that you exist. Especially, if being aware of their world is so important to your survival. You appear and disappear when needed and otherwise go unnoticed.

[MR. CONNELL *crosses to* MISS COOPER's *desk with paper in hand.*]

MR. CONNELL: You going to the church supper tonight?
MISS COOPER: I might be. How's your sister feeling?
MR. CONNELL: Oh, she's still pretty poorly. Just can't seem to shake those allergies. Goes outside the house, and you think she was watering the grass the way her eyes tear up.
MISS COOPER: I would go to the church supper tonight, if I had a ride I could count on. My ol' car is trying to act up and sure wouldn't want to be stuck out with it at night. But it seems so late to call anybody.
MR. CONNELL: Oh, now, you know, I wouldn't mind picking you up atall. Wouldn't mind atall. I'll holler at home, then be by 'bout seven if that's OK.

MISS COOPER: Why, that would be mighty kind of you, Mr. Connell.

MR. CONNELL: Then I'll see you 'bout seven. Shoot, I better get outta here and pick up some gas. Wouldn't wanta run out drivin' you home, now, would I?

MISS COOPER: I don't know about that . . . Where you been burning up so much gas?

MR. CONNELL: Oh, here and there. Took a day and ran over to see my cousin in Winston-Salem. Stopped in Greensboro.

[MR. CONNELL *and* MISS COOPER *freeze.* RELIA *and* WILLIE *continue to clean and react to* MR. CONNELL.]

AURELIA: You are aware and don't even realize you are aware of everything they do and say.

MISS COOPER: Greensboro? What's new in Greensboro?

[MR. CONNELL *and* MISS COOPER *freeze.* RELIA *and* WILLIE *continue.*]

AURELIA: You are aware you go unnoticed, and sometimes you begin not to notice how unnoticed you are until something jars you into their conscience.

MR. CONNELL: Lord, they got some mess going on downtown there! Ever since those colored kids started that sit-down mess, don't know whether you can find a decent place to eat or not downtown. Sitting in Woolworth's talking about they want to be served. Shoot, if they were really hungry, there's a stand-up counter not fifteen feet away.

MISS COOPER: I know, I know . . .

MR. CONNELL: Tell ya, some of the businesses just closed up the eating sections. Just took the chairs out rather than have niggers dictate what was gonna happen in a store we done owned longer than they been black! It's not just in Greensboro; seem like every little town and crossin' trying some kind of mess. It's all in the paper here. Spreading like the jitterbug. Only it's the niggerbug. Lord, I hope we don't see that mess over here. Not at my lunch counter. If we're not careful, we're going to have niggers everywhere!

MISS COOPER: Our Negroes aren't that big a fools. It's just those college kids not knowing what to do with themselves come summer.

MR. CONNELL: Maybe so, maybe so. But we got to keep an eye out. Shoot, look at the time. Let me get out of here. Pick you up at seven?

MISS COOPER: See you later!

[*As* MR. CONNELL *exits, he and* RELIA *briefly see each other for the first time.* MISS COOPER *puts away a book and goes to get her purse.* WILLIE *pretends to put up the paper* MR. CONNELL *has left but is really trying to read it.*]

WILLIE [*with his head in the paper*]: Greensboro is still at it! Been demonstrating over four months!

[MISS COOPER *returns.* WILLIE *hides the paper behind him.*]

MISS COOPER: Willie, I'm locking up just a little early today. I doubt anybody's going to drop in this near closing.
WILLIE: Yes, ma'am.
MISS COOPER: Pull the door tight when you finish. Hope your father feels better.

[MISS COOPER *exits.* WILLIE *reads the paper.*]

RELIA: Come on, Willie Joe. Let's get this done first, then we can read.
WILLIE: Seems like every town in the state has had some kind of sit-in . . . Raleigh, Durham, Statesville, even Monroe . . . everywhere 'cept us.
RELIA: As many late-night meetings as Daddy been to, we may be having one soon. Been over to Winston-Salem and Roxboro and to Greensboro twice. There was a big old meeting over in Raleigh where Dr. King spoke and everything. When he's not out of town meeting, he's at a church, or the barbershop, or the funeral parlor with a group of folks. When they're not meeting . . .

SCENE 5

[*No actual scene break.* MANSON'*s home or funeral parlor, 8:00 P.M. Civil rights planning meeting.* RELIA *and* WILLIE *help* KATE, MANSON, HAWKINS, FRANKLIN, *and* REVEREND BLAKE *set up furniture for the meeting, with a burst of loud argument as they enter. They freeze in midargument.*]

RELIA: . . . they're meeting about meeting . . .

[*Another loud burst.*]

    [*To* MANSON, *who is in the midst of the meeting*] Can we stay?
WILLIE: Can we?
MANSON: If I don't hear a peep!
KATE: Manson . . . ?
MANSON: Children got to learn sometimes. Willie, call your mother, tell her you'll be late . . .

[*Burst of argument about future demonstrations. All freeze except* RELIA, MANSON, *and* AURELIA.]

    Real late . . . but I'll bring you home.

RELIA: What are you doing at all these meetings?
MANSON: Organizing!
RELIA: Organizing what?
MANSON: People, baby.
RELIA: How?

[*Burst of very angry sound from the middle of the meeting.* MANSON *stands among frozen people, talking to* RELIA.]

MANSON [*smiling to himself*]: Patiently.
AURELIA: But I have no more patience . . . How . . . ?

[MANSON *moves among and points to frozen people as if naming stars.*]

MANSON: It's like learning the stars . . . Each one is different . . . Each one, a whole solar system with its own peculiar planets. So many ideas of how things could be. It all has to fit into some Grand Design. Organizing people is like trying to figure out what that mysterious Grand Design is . . .	AURELIA: Orion. Ursa Major. Ursa Minor. Big Dipper. Little Dipper. Pointer Stars. Polaris!

[AURELIA *points to her father on* "Polaris." *She becomes a silent player in the meeting. There is a burst of angry sound. Freeze.*]

MANSON: . . . before they kill each other!

[*Meeting continues. All talking.* FRANKLIN *and* HAWKINS *are in the midst of an argument.*]

I can't hear! I can't hear! Franklin has the floor!

[FRANKLIN, *a student from the local community college, has been trying to convince* MANSON, KATE, HAWKINS, *and* REVEREND BLAKE *to begin demonstrations against the downtown merchants. They have been arguing a long time; it is now almost 2:00 A.M. They are tired but still arguing with vigor.* WILLIE *and* RELIA *are in the corner, falling asleep.* FRANKLIN *argues with* HAWKINS.]

FRANKLIN: Now, I don't mean any disrespect, sir, but I don't want to be as old as you before I can sit at a lunch counter downtown and get myself a meal.

Matter of fact, I don't want to be as old as you before I can work in one of those stores that don't seem to have any problem taking my money. For that matter, I don't want to be ancient before I can buy a store on Main Street, so I can take their money!

HAWKINS: You not gonna change things in a day or two that were here long before you knew what a diaper was, boy!

REVEREND BLAKE: Look at Montgomery, man. It took them a year just to get the buses desegregated.

FRANKLIN: But if we don't start . . . We've got students ready now! I say we go ahead.

HAWKINS: I don't see why we're fooling with these kids . . .

KATE: Because nobody needs to go off half-cocked in all different directions.

HAWKINS: We don't have a jackbird's chance your way. I say talk first, then pull out the big guns if they're not listening.

FRANKLIN [*shouting*]: Listening? So, all of a sudden, they're gonna listen? Man, we gotta ride the momentum of Greensboro . . .

[FRANKLIN *takes the newspaper* WILLIE *has brought from the library.*]

HAWKINS: Boy . . .

FRANKLIN: You had fifty years to do it *your* way. Now, it's *our* turn!

HAWKINS: And I'm s'pose to roll over and pretend it doesn't matter if it gets done right?

FRANKLIN: Gets done right? Lord, is that what we've been waiting on all these centuries? To do it right?

HAWKINS: Be careful, boy.

FRANKLIN: I just want to get it done!

HAWKINS: How you get it done is important! If I'm hungry, I can steal a loaf of bread or I can work for it.

FRANKLIN: Ahhhh . . . Massa . . . Massssaaaa. Massa. I so sorry I ain't worked hard enough! Gimme a few crumbs, Massa, pleeeeeeeease.

HAWKINS: Get out of my face, boy!

MANSON: Both of you, that's enough.

FRANKLIN: Everybody else been eating off this lousy loaf of bread, how come we can't get some?

HAWKINS: If you're not careful, bread can lose its flavor!

FRANKLIN: Hell, if I don't get to taste it, the flavor won't matter!

REVEREND BLAKE: All jackasses and mules . . . just . . . hush!

[*Everybody stops, stunned.*]

Stop butting heads and let's see if we can get something c-constructive done. It's getting late, and I don't mean clock time.

KATE: Oh, Lord, it's past two . . .

MANSON: Let's decide something! I've got a funeral first thing in the morning.

KATE: So? What do we do? And don't anybody else raise their voice in my house again!

[*Pause.*]

FRANKLIN: I'm sorry.

[*Pause.*]

Just give us a chance. That's all we're asking.

[*Pause.* RELIA *gets the newspaper and hands it to* MANSON.]

RELIA: Daddy, paper says everybody's demonstrating . . .

[*Pause.*]

MANSON: It couldn't make matters much worse. Kate?

KATE: We got to make a move sometime.

MANSON: Reverend?

REVEREND BLAKE: As I said, it's getting late . . .

MANSON: Hawkins?

HAWKINS: I still don't know . . . but I guess I'll go along with Kate and the reverend.

MANSON [*to* FRANKLIN]: We're talking about only four or five students to begin with . . . with backup in the store, of course. Just test out the situation . . . See what happens . . .

REVEREND BLAKE: Like a trial balloon . . .

MANSON: Then we'll approach the mayor with our demands . . .

KATE: Here's the final list.

MANSON: Good . . . good. Desegregate lunch counters, black clerks . . . include the *public library* in that.

HAWKINS [*taking the list from* KATE]: Yeah. We gonna bust it all out. Lord knows the police and fire department need some color . . . right on down to the garbage workers. Hell, we pay they salaries.

REVEREND BLAKE: So when we gonna run this by folks?

MANSON: Monday?

HAWKINS: Flyers be ready tomorrow!

REVEREND BLAKE: Announcements will be in church bulletins Sunday. We've got to make sure large groups are ready to go when these white folks say no to our demands.

HAWKINS: Ye of little faith!

REVEREND BLAKE: Oh, I have faith, I'm just not a fool!

FRANKLIN: Looks like we're moving.

HAWKINS [*to* FRANKLIN]: We may be creaking, but when we cracking, watch out! Hot damn. It'll be just like the voter registration drive in '48. We turned this county out! You kids weren't even wiping your nose good . . .

MANSON: We weren't even wiping our noses good.

HAWKINS: But it was a hell of a victory, hell of a victory. Went from eight thousand colored voters to forty-four thousand in less than a year. I was janitor over at the old elementary school. Used to go in . . . four in the morning, crank that mimeo up, and, baby, this here arm could pump out two, three thousand flyers 'fore the teachers got in.

FRANKLIN: We got electric ones over at the college now.

HAWKINS: Well, we did it by hand back then.

REVEREND BLAKE: I hear the P-Presbyterians have a new one, too. Lord, those were some days! We must have sat in every little church this side of heaven.

HAWKINS: Scared them crackers to death!

MANSON: Shoot, scared some of us to death.

HAWKINS: And old "meek and mild" here, put the fear of God in 'em!

FRANKLIN: You threatened people?

REVEREND BLAKE: Nah. We'd just go pay 'em a little visit.

HAWKINS: There were some so terrified to register, when we came to the front door . . . they'd be sneaking out the back! Well, the reverend here would ease on round the back and meet 'em. He'd be so gentle like, they were ashamed of themselves. He'd sit down with 'em and explain how he was "once afraid, but with the Lord's help, he found the strength."

REVEREND BLAKE: It's true!

MANSON: They didn't have the heart to say no to his face, and they didn't have the nerve to lie to him! If "meek and mild" Reverend Blake could do it, they sure could! It was perfect!

HAWKINS: Next election, the black vote was so strong, all them crackers were sitting up, paying attention! Mayor Crawford even kissed a black baby!

MANSON: Won the election for him! Asked Mary Phillips would she vote for him and she stuck that baby, dirty diaper and all, right in his face.

HAWKINS: He liked to died, but he kissed it!

[*All laugh.*]

Shoot, one of these days, we gonna get our own man in.

REVEREND BLAKE: Mayor Manson . . . Sounds good to me.

HAWKINS: But till then, that turkey, Mayor Crawford, better cackle in our key, or he knows his ass is out of there—baby kissing or not.

[*All laugh.* HAWKINS *takes out a small flask.*]

To the good old days! Reverend, it ain't gonna hurt you none to have a little sip.

REVEREND BLAKE: It's so late, I think I'll rely on j-just the *holy* spirit for now.

HAWKINS: Suit yourself . . .

[MANSON *subtly signals* HAWKINS *to put up his flask because of the children.*]

KATE: Sounds like we're set!

REVEREND BLAKE: Yes . . .

FRANKLIN: We're ready!

HAWKINS: And if they don't respond, we'll have the whole damn community eatin' chitlins at their precious lunch counter.

REVEREND BLAKE: Yes, got to go the distance.

MANSON: Well, we got more than a notion . . . so come on . . . let's get a motion.

[*All form a circle for the closing prayer. They sing "Oh, Lord, Hold My Hand While I Run This Race" as* REVEREND BLAKE *prays.*]

REVEREND BLAKE: Oh, Lord, show our hearts the way and guide our feet as we move on up to victory.

[*Singing continues as chairs are removed and* WILLIE *and* RELIA *take their places.* RELIA *finishes the song, this scene dissolving into the next.*]

SCENE 6

[*On the street,* RELIA *and* WILLIE *pass out flyers.* RELIA *has just given someone a flyer.*]

RELIA: Come to the meeting. There's going to be a workshop on nonviolence, too . . . OK? It's real important.

WILLIE: Seems like I've passed out a thousand of these.

[FRANKLIN, *holding a stack of flyers, runs to catch them.*]

FRANKLIN: Wait up! Glad I caught you. We just got some more printed up. Can you guys take Chestnut and Rock Spring first thing in the morning?

RELIA: Sure! Sure!

FRANKLIN: Great! Hurry up and finish up here, then head home before your mother gets worried. See you later!

WILLIE [*under his breath*]: I hope not!

RELIA: Come on, Willie!

WILLIE: I got to take a break!

RELIA: A short one! It's almost dark.

[*Pause.*]

WILLIE: So what do you think's gonna happen with all this?

RELIA: I'm not sure. I guess we'll find out at the meeting tomorrow night. You going?

WILLIE: 'Course I'm going. You going?

RELIA: Of course I'm going.

WILLIE: My cousin, over in Nashville, said there are mass meetings there near 'bout every night. Been like that for months. Said that everybody, the college kids, the high school kids, near 'bout the whole town, is taking shifts protesting. They go in, sit at a lunch counter, and ask to be served.

RELIA: Anybody ever get served?

WILLIE: Not yet.

RELIA: Wonder how it is? I mean I've thought about it . . . but to actually do it.

WILLIE: She said things were cool for a little while, then some of those crackers started getting mean—pouring ketchup and eggs on 'em, throwing bottles and bricks, burning 'em with cigarette butts . . .

RELIA: What did they do?

WILLIE: Said they just sat there. That's what you're suppose to do. Can't hit, can't curse, can't do nothing but sit there and take it. Suppose to show you're stronger than evil!

[*Pause.*]

Do you think you're stronger than evil?

RELIA: I don't know.

[*Pause.*]

I don't know if I've ever seen evil real close-up. I mean, we talk about it in church, and I guess I've had some pretty mean thoughts sometime . . . but evil is heavy-duty stuff. Sometimes in the dark, I think maybe it's in my room . . . That's why when I'm by myself at night, I got to have some kind of light on. But I don't know whether it's really there or not anymore.

WILLIE: I've seen it, I've seen it in broad open daylight!

RELIA: I think, if I've come close, my daddy must have stopped it.

WILLIE: But your daddy can't stop this! Not by himself. Yep, they just sit there, stronger than evil.

[*Pause.*]

You think you could sit there if somebody was burnin' you with a cigarette butt?

RELIA: I don't know. Could you?

[WILLIE *takes out matches or a lighter.*]

WILLIE: Give me your hand.

[WILLIE *lights a match or the lighter and pulls* RELIA's *hand toward the flame.*]

RELIA: Are you crazy?

WILLIE: Come on. Try it. Don't pull back.

[*She thinks about trying but changes her mind.*]

RELIA: No!

[WILLIE *strikes a match or flicks the lighter.*]

WILLIE: Let's see if I'm stronger than evil!

[*He holds his hand closer and closer until* RELIA *knocks his hand down.*]

RELIA: That's stupid! Stop it, Willie. Stop it!

[RELIA *grabs and keeps the matches or lighter away from* WILLIE.]

WILLIE [*angrily*]: Yeah, we can stop it now, but what about at the sit-in? You think they'll stop just 'cause you say stop? Stronger than evil. Me, personally, I'd be kicking some behind. Kick evil's behind up one side and down the other . . .

RELIA: We'll just see when the time comes. So stop acting crazy. We'll be in it soon enough.

[*She hesitates.*]

At least, I hope it's soon . . . otherwise I'll be at Granny's.

WILLIE: Granny's? What do you mean, go to Granny's? You can't go to your granny's now! You just can't go . . .

RELIA: I got to go! I go every summer!

WILLIE: You can't go this summer!

RELIA: What am I gonna do?

WILLIE: Talk to your mother! No! Talk to your dad! Have him talk to your mother! You got to be here! You just got to be here!

RELIA: I tried to talk . . .

WILLIE: Nah . . . don't give me that weak-willed, namby-pamby stuff. You're either with me or you're not! I need to know. Are you going to demonstrate when the time comes or not?

RELIA: Are you?

WILLIE: When the time comes, I'll be right there on the front lines.

RELIA: Then I guess I'll be there, too!

WILLIE: Swear! Spit swear!

WILLIE AND RELIA: Spit swear! While we both walk the face of the earth, I promise to be there.

RELIA: If you weren't the closest thing I have to a brother . . . I swear . . .

[*She wipes off her hands.*]

WILLIE: You wanna seal it with a kiss instead?

[RELIA *and* WILLIE *break out laughing.*]

RELIA: Get out of here!

WILLIE: Kick evil's behind. Stronger than evil. Yeah!

[WILLIE *exits with library props*, RELIA *has the pail. Focus shifts to* AURELIA; *bits of memory flood her imagination.*]

AURELIA: Oh, Lord! To be able to kick evil's behind up one side and down the other! To be stronger than evil again! Come on, Willie! Show me how it's done! Show me something stronger than evil, brighter than darkness . . . My daughter's waiting . . .

SCENE 7

[*In the library, after five.* MR. CONNELL *enters the library and speaks to* MISS COOPER.]

MR. CONNELL [*angrily*]: I need to talk with you about something outside.

[MISS COOPER *exits with* MR. CONNELL. RELIA *dusts as she watches for* WILLIE. WILLIE *enters.*]

RELIA: Where have you been? I had to lie like the dickens to get Miss Cooper
   to wait so you could get in.
WILLIE: Thanks.
RELIA: So, where were you?
WILLIE: Demonstrating!
RELIA: What?
WILLIE: Demonstrating!
RELIA: You're lying.
WILLIE: Well, not exactly. But the college kids started today and I watched the
   whole thing.
RELIA: Swear!
WILLIE: I swear.

[*Fast spit ritual.*]

   . . . Walk . . . face . . . earth . . . there!
RELIA: Nasty . . . Huhhhh. Really?

[*Lights fade up on* FRANKLIN *as he enters and begins shopping. They replay the
sit-in, aware of* WILLIE *but not aware of* RELIA'*s presence.*]

WILLIE: I was downtown and saw Franklin and these college guys all dressed
   up—suits, ties, looking right serious-minded—so I followed them. When
   they got to Roses, they all bought something—pencils, paper, toothpaste . . .
   Then, they thanked the clerk, real politelike, and started walking toward the
   lunch counter. Weren't many people there 'cause it was almost two-thirty . . .

[*Pause.*]

RELIA: So . . . what happened?!?
WILLIE: They sat down!

[FRANKLIN *sits as if at the lunch counter. As* WILLIE *and* FRANKLIN *tell the story,
they interrelate with imagined characters at the sit-in.*]

RELIA: At the white counter?
WILLIE [*sarcastically*]: There ain't no black counter! At first I don't think they
   wanted me there.

RELIA: I know old man Connell didn't want you there!

WILLIE: No, I mean the college kids. But when they saw I was a serious-minded fellow, they didn't mind me watching atall.

RELIA: What happened?

WILLIE: Well, when they sat down, the waitress looked like a squirrel eating buckshot. She was screaming, "Oh, my word . . . my word . . . my word . . ." Then Franklin asked for . . .

FRANKLIN: A Coca-Cola and a hamburger, please.

WILLIE: She dropped a whole glass of soda all over her white shoes, then whispered [*as waitress*], "We don't serve colored here . . ." and *took off* like a scared rabbit. She was running so fast . . . almost knocked the manager down. Ms. Patterson—

RELIA: The colored cook?

WILLIE: Yeah. She poked her head out from the kitchen [*as Ms. Patterson*]: "What you doing starting all this mess around here? This ain't Greensboro or Raleigh. Go on away from here and stop this foolishness before there's trouble."

FRANKLIN: We don't mean to cause any trouble. I just want a Coca-Cola and a hamburger . . . please.

WILLIE [*as Ms. Patterson*]: "Well, go on home and tell your mama to cook you one!" Then Ms. Burwell, the other colored cook, whispered [*as Mrs. Burwell*], "Leave those children alone and get on back here and tend to your business!" *By then,* Mr. Connell was out there . . .

MR. CONNELL: I'm sorry, boys, but you know we don't serve colored at this counter.

WILLIE: Connell was as cool as a pig in mud! As if he'd expected us and had practiced what he'd say. Franklin was even cooler . . .

FRANKLIN: Well, sir, you served us at that counter over there, how come you won't serve us over here? Doesn't seem quite right. If we could be served at one counter, we should be served at all counters.

RELIA: Sounds reasonable to me.

MR. CONNELL: Now, I want to be reasonable. I read the paper and know what's going on here, there, and yonder, but like I said, our policy at this point is not to serve coloreds at this counter. To be blunt, we don't serve nig—

WILLIE [*jumping up, ready to fight* MR. CONNELL]: You don't serve who . . . ???

[FRANKLIN *grabs* WILLIE *and tosses him back.*]

FRANKLIN [*under his breath*]: Sit down and shut up!

MR. CONNELL: Now, I'm afraid I'm going to have to just close this here counter right now. You can sit there till hell freezes over if you want to, but the counter is closed. Girls, why don't you just clear up for the day.

FRANKLIN [*leaning toward* MR. CONNELL]: Sir, do you intend to close up every day?

MR. CONNELL [*leaning toward* FRANKLIN]: We'll just have to see about that, won't we?

[FRANKLIN *and* MR. CONNELL *stare at each other.*]

RELIA: Then what happened?

WILLIE: They sat quietly for about an hour or so and then left.

[FRANKLIN *and* MR. CONNELL *exit.*]

RELIA: So where'd they go?

WILLIE: The college kids are meeting someplace with your dad and the reverend, but I had to get over here real quick. Hey, girl, they movin'. So, did you ask your mom and dad? Can you stay?

RELIA: I'll be here. Mom made me promise everything including my soul, but I'll be here. To start with, I've got to clean my room, weed the garden, clean out the garage, and wash down the kitchen walls. When I'm not on the front lines fighting for freedom, I'll be a pure-dee slave for my mother!

[WILLIE *hands* RELIA *the bucket and cloth.*]

WILLIE: That's OK, Beulah, long as you get to fight!

RELIA: Here, I've got my own cleaning to do.

[*She hands the bucket and pail back and exits.*]

SCENE 8

[*No break between scenes. In the library,* MR. CONNELL *exits, and* MISS COOPER *calls* WILLIE *to her desk.*]

MISS COOPER: Oh, Willie.

WILLIE: Yes, ma'am?

MISS COOPER: Ahhhhh. Willie, you've been doing an excellent job when your father's been sick . . .

WILLIE: Thank you.

MISS COOPER: But I don't think that we'll need the library cleaned for a while.

WILLIE: Ma'am?

MISS COOPER: What I mean to say . . . is . . . it's really your father's job and . . . ahhhh . . . since he's not well enough to take care of it . . . and, well, I hear you're so busy . . . demonstrating . . .

WILLIE: I wasn't demonstratin', I was just watchin'. Besides, you said I'm doing an excellent job!

MISS COOPER: I'm sorry, somebody else has been hired to take over. I'm sorry, Willie. If it were up to me . . .

[WILLIE *races out.*]

Willie, Willie?

AURELIA: Willie . . . Oh, Willie. Later that day, Willie was arrested. And that night, we wondered if Daddy would ever come back.

SCENE 9

[*On* RELIA's *front porch, 1:30 A.M. The night* WILLIE *got arrested.* RELIA *is curled up on the sofa, asleep.* KATE *sits on the porch steps watching the dark intently. She occasionally glances at the night sky.* RELIA *wakes and comes to the door. They are both worried about* MANSON.]

RELIA: Daddy back yet?

KATE: No.

RELIA: What time is it?

KATE: Late.

RELIA: What time?

KATE: One-thirty.

RELIA: Is it OK if I sit out here with you?

KATE [*starting to say no but changing her mind*]: For a little bit.

[KATE *moves over as* RELIA *snuggles up to her.* RELIA *realizes her mother has a pistol in her hand.*]

RELIA: I thought this was s'pose to be nonviolent.

KATE: I believe in nonviolence, but until your father gets back, I'll nonviolently sit here with this gun under my apron. When he gets back, I'll put it away and we'll just not tell him.

[*Pause.*]

Smells like rain.

[*Pause.*]

RELIA: The college kids sat in at Woolworth's today. That's three places in one
week!

KATE: I guess it'll be in the paper tomorrow.

RELIA: I wish we could've been there.

KATE: We'll go when the phone tree calls.

RELIA: But we could have gone, just to see . . .

KATE: That's not the plan. We'll go when we're called. Don't need hundreds of
people crowding down there. Besides, we shouldn't even be talking about
this now. Loose lips sink ships.

RELIA: What?

KATE: Just something they used to say when I was a child.

[*Pause.*]

Yep, smells like rain.

RELIA: Why didn't Daddy go? I could see us not being there . . . but how come
Daddy didn't go?

KATE: Wasn't his job. What if everybody got arrested? Who would be around
to bail folks out?

RELIA: So that's what Daddy's suppose to do?

KATE: Some of what he's suppose to do.

RELIA: I don't think I can wait till we're called. History's just marching on
without me! Folks taking a stand! And I'm here just sitting!

KATE: Calm down and lower your voice.

[*Pause.*]

Tomorrow, after we finish painting picket signs at the church, I've got to
help Miss Burton make lunches for the demonstrators. You want to help?

RELIA: I guess that's better than nothing. Seems funny, though. To make lunch
for people who been sitting at a lunch counter all day. Can we take it to
them, too?

KATE: No. They'll go over to Second Baptist to eat.

RELIA [*surprised*]: But they'll lose their seats?

KATE: Another group will slide right in and hold them.

[*The phone rings.*]

KATE and RELIA [*both jumping up*]: I'll get it!

KATE: Hush, and be quiet . . .

[KATE *goes to answer the phone,* RELIA *stays on the steps.*]

Hello ... No ... No ... All right. Thank you.

RELIA: Well ... ?

KATE [*returning to porch*]: That was Hawkins. Wanted to know if your father had gotten back yet. Wanted to know if we wanted him to come by. I told him no, we were just fine, and he didn't need to come over. I told Delia and John we were just fine an hour ago, I told Andrea we were just fine two hours ago, I told Kate and Curtis we were just fine three hours ago, and four hours ago ... who was it that called? The next person who calls better be your father or it won't matter what I've learned about nonviolence.

[*Sound of* MANSON, WILLIE, *and* HAWKINS *coming.* KATE *raises the gun.*]

Who's there?

MANSON: It's us.

KATE [*hugging* MANSON]: Thank goodness ...

[MANSON *and* HAWKINS *help* WILLIE *into the house.* WILLIE *has been brutally beaten. His face is badly bruised and swollen. He is limping and holding ice on his face.*]

RELIA AND KATE: Oh my God.

MANSON: Come on in the house, Willie. Honey, get him some more ice.

[KATE *goes for ice.*]

RELIA: What happened?

WILLIE [*with speech muffled from swollen lips*]: I'm all right ... I'm all right ...

MANSON: Doc says he should be OK when the swelling goes down.

RELIA: What happened?

[KATE *returns with ice in a towel.*]

HAWKINS: A group of hoodlums saw him at the sit-in. They jumped him over by the library.

WILLIE: Four of 'em. I was sitting on the steps. I just wanted to see who got my job.

RELIA: You lost your job?

KATE [*putting ice on face*]: Don't talk, baby.

MANSON: They left him in the street. When he came to, he staggered over to the police station.

[*Pause.*]

He tried to take out a warrant for their arrest.

KATE: He tried to do what?

HAWKINS: Take out a warrant for their arrest.

WILLIE: There were four of them, they beat me up . . . I didn't do anything wrong.

HAWKINS: Not too many grown men would have dared to do what he did. Try to bring a complaint and all, but he was in his rights to do it. Now, there's a whole new pair of pants on this suit!

MANSON: He was very insistent, and when he wouldn't calm down, they arrested him.

KATE: A twelve-year-old boy?

MANSON: They say it was for his own protection until they could get someone to take him home.

WILLIE [*very upset*]: I told them I got rights! They just laughed at me! I got rights. I read it in a book. They can't do this to me! I got rights!

MANSON: And it's true! If we don't make somebody accountable for the violence now, Lord knows what will happen later.

WILLIE: I got . . .

MANSON: Willie, we'll work it out . . . Kate, his mother's scared out of her wits. She thought he'd be safer over here.

KATE: That's fine.

WILLIE: I got rights . . .

HAWKINS: Doc said give him two of these, they'll help him sleep.

[RELIA *gets water*, WILLIE *takes the pills.*]

KATE: Are you hungry?

[WILLIE *shakes his head.*]

MANSON: Then, you all get some rest.

KATE: And you?

MANSON: Folks are meeting at the funeral home. We've got to decide how to handle this thing. We've got to phone . . .

KATE: Phone? It's three o'clock in the morning!

MANSON: It's better for folks to hear about it now . . . from us.

HAWKINS: There're already rumors that he's dead.

MANSON: We need to set up a mass meeting tomorrow so we can give out the details. Any way we look at it, we'll start full-blown demonstrations Monday.

KATE: Manson, I'm not going to get any sleep. Do you want my help?

[*Pause.*]

MANSON: Thanks. Start the blue and the red phone trees. The list is on the night table . . . Oh, call Barb Nash, she's waiting. Tell her to get flyers out for the eleven o'clock services. You kids get some sleep. We'll be right next door if you need us. Kate, if I see the porch light go off . . .

KATE: I know.

[HAWKINS *exits.* MANSON *turns to leave.*]

Manson . . .

[MANSON *stops.*]

I'm driving Relia to her grandmother's first thing in the morning.

RELIA: Mom . . . ?

KATE: Should I take Willie with me?

WILLIE: No!

RELIA: If he's not going, I'm not going!

WILLIE: I can't run away!

KATE [*shouting*]: This is not a game! This is not a game! Look at his face! Boy keep going he'll be just like his uncle Frank, hanging from a tree!

[*All are quiet.*]

MANSON: I'll speak to his mother in the morning. See what she wants him to do. Get some sleep, children.

RELIA: But, Dad, we've got to be here for the demonstration!

MANSON: You heard your mother. Good night and not another word about it!

KATE: Relia, take Willie up to your room. You can sleep in our room tonight.

[RELIA *and* WILLIE *exit.*]

MANSON [*pulling* KATE *outside on the porch*]: Kate . . . I think they should stay.

KATE: Not Relia. Willie's mother can decide for him, but not Relia.

MANSON: Just think about it.

KATE: No.

MANSON: All right, all right, I won't fight you on this, but I want them both at the meeting tomorrow.

KATE: You're using that child, Manson. You are using that child's beat-up face!

MANSON: I want them both at the meeting! If they've got to go, they can go after.

[MANSON *exits.* WILLIE *and* RELIA *enter* RELIA'S *room.*]

KATE [*going to* RELIA]: Relia, I need to run next door to talk to your father about something.

RELIA: Can't you call him?

KATE: No. I'll be right back. Doors locked. You'll be fine, but if you even think something's wrong, blink the porch light.

RELIA: All right, Mama.

[KATE *exits.*]

You want some more ice?

WILLIE: Uhhhh . . . uhhhhh.

RELIA: You sure?

WILLIE: Don't need no ice . . . tired . . . God, I'm tired.

RELIA: It's the medicine. Just let it put you to sleep, Willie.

[WILLIE'S *dream:* WILLIE *hears* UNCLE FRANK. GRANMA *is singing, humming an eerie arrangement of "I've Been 'Buked and I've Been Scorned." They are in silhouette as* WILLIE *dreams. Shadows emerge . . . a tree . . . an ax. (Note: Phrases in parentheses can be said by individuals in shadow or as an offstage chorus.)*]

VOICE OF UNCLE FRANK: Willie . . .

WILLIE [*drifting off from exhaustion*]: Can't go to sleep. He won't let me sleep.

RELIA: Who . . .

VOICE OF UNCLE FRANK: Willie . . .

WILLIE: Can't go to Granny's. He won't let me . . .

RELIA: Who?

WILLIE: Got to . . .

RELIA: Go to sleep . . .

VOICE OF UNCLE FRANK: Willie.

WILLIE: Wasn't gonna be afraid . . .

RELIA: Just go to sleep.

WILLIE: Uncle Frank . . .

RELIA: I'll be here . . .

WHISPERS: Frank Poole . . .

AURELIA: Folks only whisper about Frank Poole . . .

WILLIE: Don't go, Uncle Frank!

AURELIA: When a white man (loved his mama) beat his mama . . .

VOICE OF UNCLE FRANK: She was
lying in a puddle of blood.

AURELIA: He took plumb crazy (Frank
Poole) . . . said he had rights (and
nobody listened) . . .

VOICE OF UNCLE FRANK: Going for
big freedom, boy.
WILLIE: Big freedom!

RELIA: Willie?

VOICE OF UNCLE FRANK: Swear! Spit
swear!

WILLIE: I swear!?!

WHISPERS: Frank Poole . . .

AURELIA: Took an ax and . . .

WILLIE: Uncle Frank?

AURELIA: Cut that man's head . . .
clean off.

WILLIE: Why?

AURELIA: Wanted justice.

VOICE OF UNCLE FRANK: Wanted
big freedom.

AURELIA: Walked through town, with
a bloody head . . .

VOICE OF UNCLE FRANK: Justice!
WHISPERS: Frank Poole . . .

AURELIA: Sat in Willie's yard, under
the sycamore tree . . .

WHISPERS: Waiting . . .
VOICE OF UNCLE FRANK: It hurts so
bad to hate this way . . . Don't hate
this way, Willie.

AURELIA: Strung him up (set him on
fire) . . .

WILLIE: Uncle Frank!

AURELIA: . . . in the sycamore tree . . .

WILLIE: I hid under the bed . . .

AURELIA: . . . listening to him pop and
crackle.

[WILLIE *screams. Dream fades.* WILLIE *wakes, hysterical.*]

WILLIE: Mama screamed no, but Daddy dragged me from under the bed and out to the sycamore tree. He made me look. Said, "Boy got to know, or he'll end up just like his uncle Frank!" He was all burnt up, swinging in the sycamore tree, meat fallin' off and skin smokin'... He keeps coming back... Daddy wouldn't listen, nobody would... so he keeps coming back to me.

VOICE OF UNCLE FRANK: Don't hate this way, Willie.

RELIA: It's all right, Willie. You just dreaming.

WILLIE: They kept hitting me and hitting me, I thought I would die like Uncle Frank. Relia, I peed on myself I was so scared.

RELIA: It's all right to be scared...

WILLIE: Not this kinda scared. It's not drunk scared, like Daddy. I'm scared 'cause I wanted to kill 'em. I wanted to kill 'em dead! Every time they hit me, I wanted them to die. If I had the strength... I would have killed them. If I had an ax or a gun or... I would have killed them all! God help me... I would have killed them. For me and for Uncle Frank, too. And it hurts so much to hate this way. Relia... it hurts... and I'm so scared.

RELIA: It's all right... it's all right to be scared... Granny used to say...

[GRANMA *enters or appears behind scrim.*]

GRANMA: The only way to beat death is to die... and the only way to beat fear... is to be afraid. Once you've tasted it, you'll know how to chew it... and you can learn how to spit it out.

[GRANMA *exits.*]

WILLIE: Relia. I'm not going to your granny's. And you can't go, either! You promised, Relia.

RELIA: But my mother...

WILLIE: I could do it with you there. Do it the right way.

RELIA: But I can't...

WILLIE: You swore!

RELIA: But...

WILLIE: It's the big freedom, Relia. You swore. Spit swore.

RELIA: All right, somehow I'll be there.

WILLIE: Spit swear!

[WILLIE *spits on his hand and holds it up to* RELIA *to take.*]

WILLIE AND RELIA: ... while we both walk the face of the earth... Spit swear.

AURELIA: I step off the curb with my daughter. We get in quickly. The cabdriver is surprised. I give him the address. He says "Sorry, I don't know where it is. Get out!" I start to explain . . . argue . . . plead . . . "It's late, my little girl . . ." but then he called her . . . I wanted to kill him! And it hurts so bad to hate this way! Show me how to spit it out!

RELIA: My . . .

AURELIA: . . . daughter's . . .

KATE: . . . waiting . . .

[KATE, RELIA, *and* AURELIA *echo words from the phrase "My daughter's waiting," creating a brief sound chorus. End echo.* KATE *and* GRANMA *may be seen or may be only voices.*]

GRANMA: Pick the scab of an unhealed wound, and blood's bound to run red. You can learn how to chew it . . . and you can learn how to spit it out!

ACT 2

SCENE 1

[AURELIA *on the beach; bits of memory flood her imagination.*]

AURELIA: We sit for minutes that feel like hours in the dark. My daughter can feel my anger grow. "Let's walk, Mommy . . . Let's walk," she pleads. I breathe deeply. Then quietly, I take her hand. We get out and start to walk. The cabdriver slowly pulls up beside us and rolls down his window. We turn . . . And then he looks straight in my daughter's eyes and says . . . "Nigger." It's not the first time she's heard the word . . . but it's the first time she *really* hears it. And her eyes shock wide. I throw my hands in the air . . . grabbing shattered silence I cannot catch. She's heard it. Now what do I do before he is gone like a thief in the night with her innocence. He slowly pulls away. I begin to . . . Then she says, "He's just a stupid cabdriver, Mommy!" We stand under very faint stars, and in each star I see her tear-filled eyes asking, "What can we do?"

[*Evening. Church basement. Faint voices singing civil rights songs like "We Shall Not Be Moved" come from the sanctuary above.* FRANKLIN *is conducting a nonviolence workshop.* HAWKINS *pushes* KATE *from a chair and* FRANKLIN *instructs her how to fall.* REVEREND BLAKE, MANSON, RELIA, *and* WILLIE *are watching. The audience members are addressed as if they are in the workshop.*]

FRANKLIN [*pulling* KATE *to the floor*]: That's better, Kate. But you're still too stiff. Loosen up!

KATE: I'm trying . . .

FRANKLIN [*to workshop*]: When you're knocked down to the floor, don't tense up . . . go limp. You'll break less. If they start hitting, cover your head first. Then try to get close to someone else . . . That gives them two people to hit instead of one, which will help distribute the blows a little more.

KATE [*as* FRANKLIN *helps her up*]: God knows we want to distribute those blows!

FRANKLIN: Good! Now, we have time for one more short round. [*To the workshop*] Who's ready?

[WILLIE *rises.*]

You don't have to do this today, Willie.

WILLIE: I want to.

KATE: Willie? Manson?

[MANSON *nods.* KATE *sits.*]

FRANKLIN: OK, it's your turn, Willie.

[WILLIE *limps up.*]

So where's your book, unless you knit? Be prepared, people. Freedom might take a while, so bring something to do. And a book is good head protection.

WILLIE: In case of arrest, my cousin in Nashville says girls should have candy bars and clean underwear in their purse.

MANSON: What? Boys don't need clean drawers to be free?

[*Laughter breaks the tension.*]

RELIA: Daddy ...

FRANKLIN: All right, all right, come on. Now, remember ... no matter what we say or do to you, keep your cool. Go ahead, Hawkins.

HAWKINS [*as a white store manager*]: What you doing here, boy?

WILLIE: I'd liked to be served.

HAWKINS: Oh, would you. And what would you like?

WILLIE [*uncertain and surprised*]: He's not going to ask me that?

FRANKLIN: Who knows? You might be the first!

WILLIE: A hamburger, fries ... and a glass of ice water ... please.

HAWKINS: Here's your ice water.

[*He dumps a glass of ice water on* WILLIE'*s head.*]

WILLIE [*jumping from his chair, ready to fight*]: You sorry son of a ...

FRANKLIN [*pulling* WILLIE *back*]: That's what you don't do! People have been cursed, beaten, and burned ... without cracking. And you just let a little glass of ice water defeat you. I think you're stronger than that. Are you stronger than ice water?

WILLIE: But he ...

FRANKLIN: Are you stronger than ice water?

WILLIE: I guess so ...

[*Pause.*]

Yes.

FRANKLIN: Good. Go ahead ... And don't pull any punches. He needs to do this.

HAWKINS [*directly in* WILLIE's *face*]: You wanted ice water . . . You got it! What makes you think I want to serve your nigger baboon ass at my counter. Huhhh . . . huh! You better go back to Africa and swing in the trees to show you got some sense. Nigger ain't been nothin', nigger ain't gonna be nothin'!

[HAWKINS, *in one ear, continues to bait* WILLIE *while* FRANKLIN *encourages* WILLIE *(next speech). While* WILLIE *struggles between them, voices in the sanctuary sing "Ain't Gonna Let Nobody Turn Me Round."*]

FRANKLIN: You're tensing up, Willie. Relax, breathe . . . Blank out everything else. Get some image in your mind and hold on to it. Look, look at this picture. See that little girl . . . Little Rock. All those crackers behind her . . . She was scared, but she didn't crack. Kept on walking, kept on going . . . You got that kind of courage in you? You got to love that son of a gun into seeing how ignorant he is. Never stoop to his level. Climb on up to higher ground . . . That's what non-violence is about. You can do it! Climb on up to higher ground. 'Cause if you're not on higher ground, there's no need fighting for the dirt!

HAWKINS: Buck-faced niggerrrrrr! Better not go out in the dark . . . thou preparest a dark nigger. You think we can't see you? You heard of night vision, well, we got us some nigger vision. We gonna lynch your black ass tonight!	WILLIE: . . . green pastures. Yea, though walk through the valley of . . . the shadow of death . . . I will fear no evil . . . comfort me . . . comfort me . . . Thou preparest a table . . . the presence of mine enemies . . . I shall fear no evil. I shall fear no evil. I shall fear no . . . no . . . no . . . no!

[WILLIE *cracks and attacks* HAWKINS.]

RELIA: Mama!
KATE [*standing*]: Stop it! He's a child!

[MANSON *pulls* WILLIE *off* HAWKINS. *Pause.*]

WILLIE: It don't make sense. If somebody's coming to lynch me, I don't need to pray, I need a gun or an ax or something to stop them. If they're gonna kill me, why can't I kill them?
FRANKLIN: You gonna kill them all, boy?
MANSON: And even if you do, will it make you right?
REVEREND BLAKE: Higher ground, boy! Got to work that hate out of you or it'll get you before they do.

MANSON [*watching from the door*]: You OK, Willie?

[WILLIE *nods.*]

We'd better break it up now and join them upstairs.

FRANKLIN [*softly, with his arm around* WILLIE'*s shoulder*]: It's not easy. That's why we're doing this. You OK?

WILLIE: Yeah . . . Yeah . . .

HAWKINS: Sorry, kid. You just start to saying those things and . . .

FRANKLIN [*to* HAWKINS]: No, you were fine, just fine.

SCENE 2

[*Sanctuary of the church. All join in "Ain't Gonna Let Nobody Turn Me Round." Music fades out as* REVEREND BLAKE *speaks. The audience members are addressed as if they are part of the congregation.*]

REVEREND BLAKE: "Ain't gonna let nobody turn me round." How easily we get turned around sometimes. When we face a Red Sea of d-doubt and despair, oh, to find the strength of ages past. From Exodus we learn nobody could hold God's people when God demanded of Pharaoh, "Let my people go!" Now I don't have the eloquence of a Martin K-King or an Adam Clayton P-Powell. I just have to put it in plain speech. From the d-depths of degradation and segregation, we're going to move on up to higher ground and claim freedom's soil. Gonna say, "Let my people go!" And to make it to higher ground, we must find the strength to go forward in a loving, nonviolent, Christian way. We may not win every battle, but as long as we don't lose ourselves in the mire of hatred and anger, the war cannot be lost! Now, Brother Manson will review a plan we feel will help us in our e-efforts. Go 'head, Brother Manson.

MANSON: Thank you, Reverend. While watching our sister cities across the state battle segregation, we have *talked* for a long time about what are we going to do here. Now it's time for action. The Granville College students have tested the waters and found the river of segregation running deep. They demonstrated nonviolently, but the beating of one of our children indicates things have become more serious. On Monday, mass demonstrations and boycotts begin. The phone tree will call and let you know what time you're assigned. Now, I know you have been reading the paper and watching the news, but this sit-in thing can be even harder than it looks. If you're going to demonstrate, sign up for one of the workshops. Saying you're nonviolent is

one thing, but being nonviolent is a whole different ball game when somebody's beating you over the head with a baseball bat. Now . . .

HAWKINS: Brother Manson . . . I know we've been here for a while, but may I
have the floor for just a minute or two? I'll be brief!

REVEREND BLAKE: That'll be a miracle!

HAWKINS: There's just one little point that's important we all understand before we leave.

MANSON: Go 'head, brother.

HAWKINS: Now people, let me just lay it on the line like laundry in the breeze!
See those doors back there? They closed for a reason. And before it's all over,
our mouths need to be as closed as those doors. So, if there are any questions,
discussions, or *objections,* bring it forth tonight! Open up, speak out, and air
your grievances now, behind the closed doors of the Lord, because when we
pass through 'em later on tonight, we got to walk as a unified front.

[*Pause. No interruptions.*]

Do I hear anybody? Sure? Good! Just so we are clear . . . Gonna break it
down for you one more time. Now I'm not talking about anybody special . . .
but don't want any loose-lipped Uncle Toms tellin' Massa what we doin'
down in the slave quarters. I tell you like Harriet Tubman told her passen-
gers, she raised that shotgun of hers when they got scared, or wanted to run
back, or didn't know what to do . . . She said, "Dead folks can't jaybird
talk . . . you keep on going now or die!"

We can't have no jaybirds singing like a canary, killing our movement.
So if you are Polly parrot, better fly the coop now! In other words, we have
agreed . . .

MANSON: Yes, brother . . . Stand together and keep our mouths shut!

HAWKINS: That's it! Can't have no backbiting . . . No backsliding . . . No contrary walking or two-faced talking! We have agreed . . .

REVEREND BLAKE: Stand together and keep our mouths shut! Break it down,
brother, break it down!

HAWKINS: Get it clear and straight, or it's got to wait . . . till we're back together behind the closed doors of the Lord's house! We have agreed . . . Let
me hear you say it now . . .

ALL: Stand together and keep our mouths shut!

[*Amens.*]

HAWKINS: Again! Louder!

ALL: Stand together and keep our mouths shut!

HAWKINS: After you leave this place, you can take it to the Lord in prayer . . . but just make sure he's the only one there! In other words, we have agreed, so . . .

ALL: Stand together and keep our mouths shut!

HAWKINS: Keep your ears open all you want, especially at your place of work . . . but—

ALL: Stand together and *keep our mouths shut*!

HAWKINS: Thank you.

[HAWKINS *sits.*]

MANSON: And you know if Hawkins can keep his mouth shut, there ain't no excuse for anybody else!

[HAWKINS *and others laugh.*]

Any more questions? Good. Sign-up sheets for shopping car pools, phone tree calling, lunch making, and others are in the back.

REVEREND BLAKE: Praise God. Let us stand. We ask, Lord, that you be with us in our struggles "so can't nobody turn us around." We ask for the strength to overcome nonviolently and we thank you in advance as we claim our victory in your name. Amen.

[*The congregation breaks up.* WILLIE *is staring at* RELIA.]

KATE: Come on, Aurelia, we've got to get going.

RELIA: Just a minute, Mama . . .

[KATE *leaves* WILLIE *and* RELIA *to talk.*]

WILLIE: Relia, you promised.

RELIA: I know . . . but . . .

WILLIE: Relia, big freedom's coming and you promised.

KATE: Relia, come on!

[RELIA *and* KATE *exit.*]

AURELIA [*watching the beach sky*]: Oh, Lord, deliver us from everything that's evil, and all the days of our lives, may we walk in the light of billions and billions of stars as we move on up to higher ground . . . forever and ever. Amen.

The cab moves slowly down the street and we stand in silence under a starless sky. "Mama, Mama . . . I think it's going to rain." It's gonna rain . . .

SCENE 3

[*Light change to* GRANMA'*s farm, late morning.* GRANMA *sits, meticulously balling yarn. She smells the air.*]

GRANMA: Gonna rain.

[KATE *and a sullen* RELIA *enter.*]

Willie didn't come?

KATE: No. [*To* RELIA] Why don't you take your bags in the house.

RELIA: Please . . . I'm going to miss everything!

[RELIA *exits into the house with the suitcase. Pause.*]

GRANMA: Smells like rain.

KATE: She's really bent out of shape about not being there, but under the circumstances . . .

GRANMA: What did you expect? Since the day she was born you been preparing her for something like this. Pretended like it was teaching her history . . . Wasn't history, it was future you were teaching her. So why are you surprised? If you plant a pear tree you better not go looking for plums in the spring.

KATE: I'll call you.

GRANMA: We'll be fine.

[KATE *exits.* GRANMA *rolls yarn.* RELIA *enters.*]

So, you're going to mope?

RELIA: It's not fair! Willie didn't have to come.

GRANMA: You're not Willie, are you?

RELIA: You have no idea how I feel!

[GRANMA *offers yarn to* RELIA. RELIA *hesitates, then accepts the job.*]

GRANMA: No idea? Humphhh! No idea . . . Listen, child, when I was a youngster, to get to school, me and my cousins had to pass by this white school. Now, their school was a nice big brick building, had green grass growing out front with ivy on the walls, and ours was in an old tobacco barn. Our school bus was made of worn brown shoe leather, if we were lucky, and was at the bottom of our legs. So when their school bus passed, they spit out the window at us.

RELIA: Ahhh . . . nasty!

GRANMA: What was worse, every day, at this one place, the same group of white kids locked arms. Forced us to walk in the ditch while they walked on the sidewalk. Wet or dry, we were in the ditch. There was this one boy, Connell Willis, and his cousin Avery who was the ringleaders of it all. Foul-mouthed little buggers. Well, this happened day after day, month after month, until Reesee, who was a pretty thing, but tall as a boy and twice as strong, got new shoes. New shoes in the middle of the school year! That day, when Connell blocked our path, Reesee jumped him and all we saw was legs and dust. [*Laughs.*] When that dust settled, she was the only one getting up. She beat the tar out of that boy. We were jubilee!

RELIA: Wow.

GRANMA: Well, then, this old white lady, lived on the corner, came out. Everybody stood dead still. She said, "I been watching you from that window since September and that boy you just beat the tar out of . . . is my great-nephew." We were so scared, we could have all peed in unison, right there. Then she said, "I'm so glad you did it, I don't know what to do. He deserved every bit of it. Now get up, boy, go wash your face, and if you breathe a word of this to your parents, I'll make this whippin' seem like the first course to the main meal." There is a God! From that day on, we didn't have no trouble walking on the sidewalk! Now spit from the bus was another matter . . . that was a battle of another sort, for another day. But we didn't have no problems with the sidewalk.

RELIA: Wow!

[*Pause.*]

GRANMA: Baby girl, you don't know how badly I wanted to be Reesee that day . . . but I wasn't. I guess there were plenty of battles I missed, but plenty I fought, too.

[*She gets up and spits on the ground.*]

RELIA: Tomorrow's my battle. I just know it!

GRANMA: Maybe so . . . maybe no. Just be ready when the lighting strikes, and your day will come!

RELIA: I've got to be there, I promised Willie!

GRANMA: Well, baby girl, unless you plan to *walk* all the way to the next county, you're gonna be fighting another day.

[GRANMA *exits.*]

AURELIA: The mind of a child can seize upon an unintended idea like dust balls gathering beneath a bed . . . until, one day, it seems perfectly rational to justify their actions by saying . . . "But Granma said . . . I should *walk*!"

RELIA: I could do it! I could walk! I know the way by heart!

AURELIA [*trying to warn* RELIA]: By car . . . We've only been by car . . . [*Remembering*] In the old black Oldsmobile, my feet barely touching the floor . . .

RELIA: Won't take much more than an hour . . .

AURELIA: In a car!

[RELIA *hears* AURELIA *for the first time. She is shocked and then feels a growing pain.*]

RELIA: Owww . . . my stomach . . .

AURELIA: I had fallen, headfirst, in a growing-up hole.

RELIA: One deeper and wider than I've ever felt!

[RELIA *and* AURELIA *circle each other.* AURELIA *begins to cover her face.*]

AURELIA: I don't want you to see . . .

[RELIA *takes her hand down, gently.* AURELIA *and* RELIA *look at each other.*]

For the first time . . . when I peeked into the growing-up hole . . .

RELIA [*quietly amazed, trying to recognize this strange, older image of herself*]: I see her . . .

AURELIA [*quietly amazed*]: Like looking in a clouded mirror, there was . . .

RELIA: . . . an older me staring back . . .

AURELIA: Where did this child go?

[RELIA *accepts* AURELIA *but realizes she must convince this older, more practical* AURELIA *to go.*]

RELIA: I could do it . . . It's only three towns away! I could go when Granma's sleeping . . . I could make it for the demonstration tomorrow.

AURELIA: No!

RELIA: I promised Willie.

AURELIA: I know . . . but . . .

RELIA: I'm going!

AURELIA: You don't have to do this . . .

RELIA: I promised Willie . . . You coming?

AURELIA [*reluctantly following*]: I left a note on my pillow, grabbed a flashlight, and quietly crept downstairs. When I opened the front door . . . it was . . .

RELIA: . . . dark!

AURELIA: Country dark!

[RELIA *leads,* AURELIA *follows as they begin "the journey."*]

Bathed in moonlight, the windows of Granma's room stared down at me . . . like two dark eyes. I half expected her to call me back.

RELIA: She would shake me good for doing something so foolish!

AURELIA: But all was quiet . . . A deep breath and I was headed to Faison's. Every summer, when Granma said, "Run down to Faison's and get a loaf of bread," like a flash, I was down this road and back. But now . . .

RELIA: It seemed to take forever . . .

AURELIA: And even in the moonlight . . . it was . . .

RELIA: . . . so dark!

AURELIA: I passed the church graveyard . . .

RELIA [whispering in fear]: There's no such thing as ghosts . . . There's no such thing as . . .

[AURELIA and RELIA back into each other. Both are scared. RELIA screams and runs.]

AURELIA: Faster and faster I ran . . .

[Headlights shine. Sound of motor and wheels on pavement indicate car passing.]

RELIA: Car!

AURELIA: Duck!

RELIA: Down!

[She gets up after the car has passed.]

Let's go!

[She starts to run.]

[Breathlessly] Made it!

AURELIA: Faison's was closed.

RELIA [looking in the store window]: Must be after ten . . .

AURELIA: Main Street . . . a ghost town . . .

RELIA [whispering]: I don't believe in ghosts . . . I don't believe in . . .

AURELIA: A fork in the road . . .

RELIA [reading sign]: Forty miles to . . . Turn left . . .

AURELIA [taking flashlight and reading the crossroads sign]: Are you sure?

[Sound of another car on the highway. AURELIA and RELIA duck.]

RELIA: The flashlight!

[She turns the flashlight off. Both crouch in the dark.]

It's gone . . .

[*She turns on the flashlight and notices the railroad tracks.*]

Look! The railroad tracks! We could follow the tracks, that way we won't
have to worry about cars passing.

AURELIA: But you don't know which way . . .

RELIA: As long as we can see the main road, we're fine!

[*She dashes for the tracks.*]

AURELIA: Wait!

[*She runs to catch up.*]

By flashlight and moonlight, I hopped from tie to tie . . . There were shapes
in the trees . . . shadowy figures moving in the mist . . . My stomach felt like
a giant hole.

[*Train whistle sounds and train lights shine.*]

RELIA: Oh, God!

AURELIA: Huge cars almost sucked me back onto the tracks.

[*Train sound and lights end.*]

Squatting in the bushes in the after silence . . . there were all kinds of sounds . . .

RELIA [*whispering*]: A cricket . . . an owl . . .

AURELIA: A cabdriver's voice in the night . . . a child crying softly . . .

RELIA: What?

AURELIA: Nothing.

RELIA [*jumping up as a mouse runs across her feet*]: *Ahhhhhhhhhhh!*

AURELIA: Get back on the tracks!

[*Frightened, both try to figure out what to do.*]

What did they say in the workshop?

RELIA: Clear your mind.

AURELIA: Find something that gives you strength . . .

RELIA: That gives you courage . . .

AURELIA: For a while, I was Harriet Tubman, leading slaves to freedom. I
knew from Dad . . .

RELIA: Home was north, and a little bit west. Big Dipper, Pointer Stars, Little
Dipper . . .

AURELIA: I would have checked for moss on the north side of a tree, but I didn't want to leave the tracks again.

RELIA AND AURELIA: Big Dipper, Pointer Stars, Little Dipper . . .

RELIA: There! It's mine . . . Now it's my star, too!

[AURELIA *is momentarily out of the moment, watching the moment. She is sad. She walks a few steps ahead of* RELIA *and is very quiet.* RELIA *does not notice the change.*]

AURELIA: So why can't I find it?

RELIA: The tracks are going the right way. Come on. We've got a long way to go.

AURELIA: To crowd out dark thoughts and dark skies . . .

RELIA: "By the shore of Gitche Gumee, by the shining Big-Sea-Water . . ."

AURELIA: I recited all the poems and songs and stories I learned in school.

RELIA: I used to wonder why they taught us all that stuff. Now, I know it's to fill odd moments, like this, when you don't have anything important to think about.

AURELIA: I recited multiplication tables.

RELIA: Six times twelve equals seventy-two . . .

[*She looks at* AURELIA *to answer.*]

AURELIA: I tried to figure out how many Bible verses I knew.

RELIA: One. "Jesus wept." Two. "In the beginning, God created the heaven and the earth . . ." Three. [*Whispering softly with* AURELIA] "Suffer the little children to come . . ."

[*Sound of faint rumble of thunder in the distance.*]

AURELIA: I was glad I was not a stupid person and had studied well in school, otherwise, I would have been . . .

[*Pause.*]

RELIA [*with frightened realization*]: Lost?

AURELIA: No matter how I strained, I couldn't see the main road.

RELIA: Oh, God! I know the road goes home . . .

AURELIA: But I only *guessed* about the *tracks*. I had planned to follow them only as long as I could see the road. If I hadn't been playing stupid games . . .

RELIA: Oh, Lord! The North Star is gone! What do I do?

AURELIA: Go back!

RELIA: How far? If I lose too much time, I won't make it.

[*Pause. She shines the flashlight about.*]

I'll cut cross the field and see if I can find the road.

AURELIA: No!

RELIA: It can't be too far.

[*She begins to run.*]

AURELIA: No!

[RELIA *does not stop.*]

The field was muddy from last night's rain. The further I got from the track, the muddier it became.

RELIA [*panicking*]: Where's the road?

AURELIA: The more I walked, the more I believed . . .

RELIA [*as if slogging through mud*]: Just a few more steps . . . I'll find it.

AURELIA: My heart pounded . . . My mouth went dry . . . It was harder and harder to move in the sticky field. Red mud was past my ankles.

RELIA: A swamp! I'm in a swamp!

AURELIA: Stop! It's mud!

[*Loud clap of thunder and flash of lightning at the same time.* RELIA *and* AURELIA *scream. They both run. Rain pours . . . They must shout to be heard. (Note: While running,* AURELIA *can slip the flashlight in her bag.)*]

RELIA [*running aimlessly*]: The flashlight! I've lost the flashlight. Where's the flashlight? Where's the road!

AURELIA [*trying unsuccessfully to grab* RELIA]: Stop! Stop . . .

RELIA [*hysterically*]: The North Star! Look for the . . . oh, God . . . oh, God. It's raining so hard! Where is it? Daddy, where is . . .

AURELIA [*grabbing* RELIA *and shaking her hysterically*]: There is no stupid North Star! What the hell was I thinking . . . Could your precious North Star stop that stupid cabdriver . . . stop my daughter from hearing those words . . . stop her tears . . .

[RELIA *and* AURELIA *drop down in mud and cry in the rain.*]

RELIA [*crying hysterically*]: I found it, Daddy . . . I found it . . . I just couldn't hold on to it!

AURELIA: There is no North Star! It's just dark!

RELIA: Dark!

[*Lights fade out.*]

SCENE 4

[GRANMA's *house.* GRANMA *notices* RELIA's *light is still on.*]

GRANMA: Relia, Relia . . . Turn off that light in there, girl! You too big to sleep with a light on! Waste of electricity. Relia? Relia!

[*She picks up a note.*]

Oh my God!

SCENE 5

[RELIA's *house. The same night, around midnight.* HAWKINS *is banging on the door, frantically.* MANSON *and* KATE *have been asleep.* MANSON *goes to the door.*]

HAWKINS: Manson! Katie! Open up!

[MANSON *opens the door.*]

MANSON: What's wrong?
HAWKINS: Your mother's been trying to get you for over an hour.

[KATE *enters.*]

KATE: What's wrong?
HAWKINS: The phone must have been off the hook.
KATE: We had to get some sleep.
MANSON: Man, what's wrong?
HAWKINS: It's Relia! She's run off!
KATE: What?
HAWKINS: Your mother said she left a note. She's trying to get here for the demonstration tomorrow.
KATE: What kind of crazy . . .
MANSON: Doesn't matter. Kate, call Mama, try to find out what time she thinks Relia left. I'll get dressed . . . Kate!

[KATE *tries to dial but is confused.* MANSON *exits to the bedroom, returns with pants and shirt, and begins to dress as he listens.*]

HAWKINS: Your mother had a neighbor drive up the main route to Warren. She figured she couldn't have gotten much further than that. They didn't see her. She must not be on the main road. You think we should call the police?

MANSON: Oh, God. Ahhhhh. No . . . not yet. Not with what's happened to Willie. I don't want too many of them knowing she's out there. Oh, God!

HAWKINS: That's a smart little girl you got, Manson. She'll be fine. She's got a lot of good sense.

KATE: It's been raining most all night . . .

MANSON: I'm going to drive straight out there. Go to the reverend. Have him get some men together and four or five cars. Have one start a slow search from here, another about halfway, and have at least Doc and whoever's with him come straight to my mother's and start there.

HAWKINS: You got it!

MANSON: Oh, tell them, no matter what—call here or my mama's every half hour or so. I don't care if they have to wake up every farmer in the county, just get to a phone.

HAWKINS: Right . . . What about Kate?

MANSON: Willie's here.

HAWKINS: I'm gone.

[HAWKINS *exits.*]

KATE: Mama . . . Mama . . .

MANSON: Katie, let me speak . . .

[MANSON *gently takes the phone from* KATE.]

SCENE 6

[*Muddy field.* RELIA *and* AURELIA *sit side by side. They are wet and covered with mud. They are lost and in quiet shock.*]

AURELIA: The rain was cold, but I stopped feeling it.

RELIA: How long have I been sitting in the mud?

RELIA AND AURELIA: It's so dark . . .

AURELIA: I look at the sky and curse every star, every planet, every solar system that exists.

RELIA: I can't go back 'cause I don't know which way to go . . .

AURELIA: And I can't go forward 'cause I don't know which way to go . . .

RELIA AND AURELIA: All I could think of was Daddy said . . .

RELIA: "When I needed it, I would find it."

AURELIA: But there is no North Star in the rain. No North Star . . . I don't know what to do?

[*Pause.*]

RELIA: We'll do what Daddy said. We'll close our eyes and count to a hundred. Our eyes will get used to the dark.

AURELIA: We've been out here for hours. Our eyes are already used to the dark . . .

RELIA: Then why are we so afraid?

AURELIA: It's not this dark. It's not this dark we're trying to fight. You'll close your eyes and they won't ever get used to . . . to . . . the . . . The dark we're trying to fight is hiding behind this night.

RELIA: What is it? You're frightening me. Is there something out there, something out there that will hurt me?

AURELIA: There's another kind of dark . . . You don't know about it yet . . .

RELIA: Let's count. Daddy says . . .

AURELIA: In this dark . . . there isn't any daddy . . . There's a frightened little girl but there isn't any daddy . . . There's nobody else . . . It's so vast . . . and there are no stars . . .

RELIA: Close your eyes. Close your eyes and count . . . You'll see . . . Count!

AURELIA: Why?

RELIA: What else is there to do? We must do something. We must do something 'cause we've got to go on. So count.

[*Pause.*]

We'll count, and then at a hundred, we go on. No matter what, pick a direction and go. Close your eyes. One, two . . . three . . . Count!

AURELIA: It won't . . .

RELIA [*shouting angrily*]: *Count!*

AURELIA [*closing her eyes*]: One, two, three . . .

SCENE 7

[GRANMA's *house, an hour later.* GRANMA *is on the phone.*]

GRANMA: Manson, most everybody's checked in. The sheriff came by and got some of her clothes and a pair of shoes for the dogs. He's talked to all the police between here and there. A bunch of folks, white and black, have volunteered and are out looking. They're going house to house in each town.

Manson. Go home. There are a lot of people out looking, somebody's going to find her. I talked to Kate. Just go home. Help with the phone calls. That's where you'll do the best good. Go home to Kate.

SCENE 8

RELIA AND AURELIA: Eighty-nine, ninety, ninety-one . . .

AURELIA: At first my eyes were closed so tightly, my head hurt.

RELIA: Find it here . . .

AURELIA: I watched the dark behind my eyelids . . . it was as infinite as the night sky. The more I counted, the more I relaxed. At about ninety-seven . . . I began to see . . .

RELIA: Dots?

AURELIA: Yeah, dots . . . dancing behind my lids . . . dots.

RELIA: Or maybe . . .

[*They stand, eyes closed but as if they can see something in front of them . . . Slowly they begin to laugh.* AURELIA *and* RELIA *take each other's hands.*]

RELIA AND AURELIA: Stars . . . ?

AURELIA: Stars! Find it here!

RELIA: Stars in a night sky . . .

AURELIA: They stopped dancing and I could make out patterns.

RELIA: Just like the ones in the book.

AURELIA: Patterns like Daddy had pointed out . . .

RELIA: There's Orion . . . and the Bear . . .

AURELIA: And the Pointer Stars . . . and . . . and . . . In the center of all those stars . . .

RELIA: Not the brightest . . .

AURELIA: But bright enough . . .

RELIA: I can see it! I can see it!

RELIA AND AURELIA: The North Star!

RELIA: Now, all I have to do is open my eyes!

AURELIA: No!

[*Pause.*]

RELIA: Once you've found it . . . you can find it again . . .

[RELIA *takes* AURELIA'S *hand. They open their eyes.*]

AURELIA: I remember now. When I opened my eyes, it was still dark . . .

RELIA: Not as dark . . .

AURELIA: I remember. When I opened my eyes . . . the rain came down gently.

[*Pause.*]

RELIA: There was no light in the sky . . .

AURELIA: But when I opened my eyes . . . I still could see my North Star!

[*Pause. Thunder.*]

RELIA: Tomorrow's the demonstration!

[*Thunder.*]

　　We've got to get out of here!

[*Lightning flashes.*]

AURELIA: Somebody's got to own this field.

[*Lightning.*]

RELIA: Look, look over there!

AURELIA: I can't make anything out!

[*In the next flash of light,* RELIA *sees a shape.*]

RELIA: Keep looking. Wait for the lightning flash . . .

[*Flash.*]

AURELIA: Look! There! A barn!

RELIA: There's a barn over there . . .

AURELIA: I see it! I see it! It's gone.

RELIA: Come on!

[AURELIA *and* RELIA *struggle, make it to the barn, and collapse in the dark.*]

AURELIA: Thank God!

[RELIA *laughs as she realizes she is covered with mud.*]

RELIA: Lord, I look like Granma's pig.

[*They laugh until they hear a dog barking in the dark.* JAKE, *a big white man with a lantern and a shotgun, enters. He has a blanket around his shoulders.*]

JAKE: Shut up! . . . Shut up, dog. Git! Who's there? . . . Who's there?

AURELIA: I couldn't speak. The bottom of my stomach lurched. A black girl in the dark with a white man. If anything happened to me, my father would surely kill this man and then my father would be killed. The huge shape filled the barn door. I could see no way round him . . .

JAKE: What in the world . . . What you doing here? Can you speak, gal? What you doing here?

[RELIA *tries to run past* JAKE. *He grabs her.*]

Hold on. Hold on.

[RELIA *bites* JAKE'S *hand.* JAKE *slings her across the barn.*]

Oww . . . Damn you! You little . . . what you do that for? Ain't tryin' to hurt ya . . . awww . . . you got teeth like Clara's old mule . . . Awww . . . Just sit there!

[JAKE *tosses* RELIA *the blanket he has over his shoulders.*]

Throw this round you 'fore you die of cold. Now listen, I'm not gonna hurt you. I got girls myself . . . But you can't go wanderin' round here in the dark in a storm like this. You running away?

[RELIA *shakes her head no.*]

Then what you doin'? Answer me, girl.

RELIA: Got lost.

JAKE: Live far?

RELIA: Next county.

JAKE: You got folks?

[RELIA *nods.*]

They must be worried sick. Lord . . . Well, come on. Ain't got no phone, but get in the pickup. I'll take you home. Come on . . . I'm not gonna eat ya. Come on.

[RELIA *and* AURELIA *hold each other without moving.*]

Now listen, you're cold and wet and shivering. I wouldn't leave a dog out like this. I'm not gonna hurt you, but if you don't come with me, I'll have to go fetch the sheriff. I can't just leave you out here.

AURELIA: It was the sheriff that did nothing about Willie getting beat up.

RELIA: You take me straight home?

JAKE: Yeah. I take you straight home. Truck's outside. Come on . . .

[*Dog begins to bark.*]

Shut up, dog! Shut up! Won't hurt you. Just sounds mean. Go on.

AURELIA: I must have fallen asleep as soon as the truck started. The next thing I knew, I was home.

[RELIA's *house and porch.* KATE *and* MANSON *sit holding each other. They follow* AURELIA's *description of the moment.* WILLIE *waits on the steps.*]

As we walked up to the front porch, it seemed like everything was in slow motion. I saw the hazy forms of my mother and father, suspended, through the screen. Mommy was sitting so still. Daddy was on one knee in front of her, with his arms around her. My mother's face looked like a frightened child, and his was so sad that I thought it might break. When they heard us, their heads turned at the same instant. They seemed like startled deer caught in somebody's headlights. I think that was the first time I ever saw them as people. He moved to open the screen. Her body was perfectly still, then she moved with the swiftness of a doe. My mother held me for a very long time and didn't say anything. After he saw to it I was all right, I could hear my father thanking the man over and over again. My mother just held on like she would never let me go. When she did, the man was gone.

KATE [*whispering*]: Thank God . . . Praise his name. Lord, have mercy . . . You could have been killed out there. Half the world was out looking for you. Are you all right . . . are you all right?

[RELIA *nods.*]

Why?

[MANSON *shakes his head, as if this is not the time.*]

AURELIA: My father held me. He let go and she took my hand as if I was a little child, a child which I knew I was not anymore, or at least not in the same way. Then I saw . . .

[*They look at each other.*]

RELIA: Willie . . .

WILLIE: It's big freedom tomorrow.

MANSON: Come on, Willie.

[WILLIE *exits with* MANSON.]

AURELIA: My mother took me in and bathed me. I was too tired to protest. She put me in the bed, kissed me, and I fell asleep before she turned off the lights.

[MANSON *enters, talks on the phone, then sits, yawning on the sofa.* KATE *returns to* MANSON.]

MANSON: Is she all right?
KATE: Sound asleep.

[*Pause.*]

It's past five o'clock.
MANSON: Oh, God. I'm so tired. I got Willie home and called everybody I know to call and told them. I've got to get some sleep.

[*He yawns, then starts to rise.*]

In exactly four hours we'll be at the demonstration.
KATE: You're not still . . .
MANSON: What do you mean?
KATE: It's just been . . . first Willie, now Relia . . .
MANSON: How does that change things?
KATE: I guess I didn't expect all those people, especially the whites, and even the sheriff . . .
MANSON: What are you saying?
KATE: It would be like a slap in the face to . . .

[*Pause.*]

MANSON: Wait a minute, Kate . . . Let's not get confused about all this. They're not animals. They're human just like us. And if one of their children was lost, I'd search just like I searched for Relia. But that doesn't change the fact that tomorrow, if I want a hamburger at Woolworth's, they're not going to see me as a father, or a husband, or a mortician, they're going to see one thing. This!

[*He holds up his black hand.*]

KATE: I know . . . but . . .
MANSON: When Relia goes to sit at that lunch counter tomorrow, she'll know nothing has changed. Nothing will change, unless we change it.
KATE: Fine! Then let *us* change it. So far, it seems like only our children . . . Relia doesn't need to be there.

MANSON: How can you say that after what she went through tonight.

KATE: Just postpone it!

MANSON: Postpone it and then what? The sun comes up, and the sun goes down, and I'm suppose to thank God I made it through one more day!

KATE: Yes! . . . With all your family living and breathing! Yes!

[*Pause.*]

MANSON: Living and breathing . . . You know, sometimes, when I'm working late over there, I stare at the bodies. If you stare hard enough, long enough, your mind plays tricks on you. You imagine they're breathing. Sometimes I wonder which group I belong to. My chest goes up and down, but there's . . . like a weight I've got to get off. I've got to get it off or I'll suffocate and die. Do you hear me, die.

KATE: Just hold off for a day or two . . .

MANSON: Hold off? Kate, all my years, I done had him standing on my chest. I can't take you standing there, too. We're going to do this thing. We're going to do it tomorrow.

KATE: Then, I don't want Relia there.

MANSON: You've got to understand . . .

KATE: No, understand me! This "thing" is swallowing you up! I can see it! The meetings, the planning, living on the edge . . . but it's different for me.

MANSON: Kate . . .

KATE: You're fighting for the fight. I'm fighting for the end. And it will end . . . it has to. Afterwards, I plan to have a life! I don't want "race" to be my life!

MANSON: Whether you want it to be or not, it is your life.

KATE: No, it can't be! Not all of it!

MANSON: Listen . . .

KATE: No, you listen! Do you realize how much time we spend talking about . . . thinking about . . . dreaming about . . . race! Not about culture or our history . . . but race! We sit down at the table for a meal, go for a drive in the country, have people over for cards . . . before the evening is over, it's "What da white folks done done now" or "What black folks ought to do" . . . it sucks up so much of us . . . so much of you, there's not much left for me anymore . . .

MANSON: It's not going to last forever, but right now . . .

KATE: There must be a point when we finally arrive, when we get there! Someday we have got to be free or I'll go crazy. There's got to be a day when I can sit in a garden by my child or even my grandchildren and touch their hair and smile and breathe deep and there is nobody standing on my chest, either! That's what I'm working for. Getting there so we can get on with life. God, I keep dreaming, we may be the first generation in this country to do that! To get on with life!

MANSON: I want that, too . . .

KATE: Manson, I'm so tired . . .

MANSON: I know, baby . . .

KATE: So tired . . . but I can make the phone calls, cook the lunches, go to the meetings, I can do it as long as I know that someday we'll arrive. And when we get there . . . I want Aurelia to be a whole person . . . I don't want her to have all the scares and the hurts that we've had. I don't want her bloodied and mangled and piecemealed . . . She has a chance to be a whole person . . . She and the children after her have a chance.

MANSON: Not if they don't know . . . not if they don't remember.

KATE: I don't want her to go, Manson. I don't want her to see . . . I don't . . .

[MANSON and KATE *look up.* RELIA *is standing there. They don't know how long she has been listening.*]

AURELIA: Don't want her to . . . to hear . . .

RELIA [*quietly*]: I've got to go, Mama.

KATE: I think you did enough going for one night.

RELIA: Mama . . .

KATE: Are you going to defy me, girl?

MANSON: Kate, don't make it any harder than it is for her.

KATE: Did you see that boy's face? Do you want Relia to come home looking like that? Or worse? It's one thing for us to be out there . . . but I only have one little girl, and as much as I love you, I'm not ready to sacrifice her.

MANSON: Sacrifice her to what? We're sacrificing her now . . . to lies! Trying to protect her with lies that everything's all right. In one breath we tell her she's as good as everybody and in the next breath we tell her she has to be twice as good to make it. But we both know that one day, all those lies and that intricate tunnel we build to get through one more day, one more week, one more year, one more lifetime . . . at one point or another, that tunnel will collapse in on us, bury us! Crush us. [*Pointing to his chest*] Crushes us here! Could anything worse happen out there? Even if they killed her, she would at least die in the truth. I don't want my daughter pretending to be a cleaning woman just to sit in a damn library!

[*Pause.*]

RELIA: Mama...

MANSON: Sweetheart, I want you to have your time in the garden. And someday, I want to stand all night, all night and watch the stars without having to
run to a meeting. But life just isn't like that now, baby.

RELIA: Mama, I'm sorry about tonight. I know you were worried. I didn't mean
to hurt you. I wouldn't hurt you for the world... I love you, Mama, but I got
to go.

[*Pause.*]

MANSON: Kate, she's saying she's got to do this. Give the girl credit, Kate, and
give her her due.

KATE: I couldn't stop you if I wanted to, could I?

[*Lights fade out.*]

SCENE 9

[AURELIA *sits looking at the sky. She begins "Ain't Gonna Let Nobody Turn Me
Round" in the dark as the lights fade up on a shadowed tableau of a lunch counter the
next day. We see fragments of a demonstration as the scene progresses. Some KKK hoods
are visible.* FRANKLIN, WILLIE, KATE, RELIA, *and* MANSON *enter. All other characters become the crowd voices that jeer and spit.*]

AURELIA: Next day, we slipped into our seats at Woolworth's.

[RELIA *and* AURELIA *sit with* MANSON.]

MANSON: Keep your eyes straight ahead.

FRANKLIN: We'd like to be served.

MR. CONNELL: Not at my lunch counter!

AURELIA: In a seventeen-month boycott, my mother lasted one day. All agreed
her temperament more suited driving people to shop in Raleigh during the
boycott. But on that day, she was there... So was Willie...

RELIA: Face bruised...

WILLIE: Book [*pats pocket*], candy bar [*pats another pocket and whispers*], underwear! In case of arrest!

FRANKLIN: We sat for a while. Nothing happened.

AURELIA: One white woman I didn't know smiled and whispered...

WOMAN [*in the crowd*]: You had quite a trip last night, didn't you, young lady?

AURELIA [*embarrassed*]: Eyes down, I nodded. Then I heard Willie whisper...

WILLIE: It's them!

AURELIA: I wanted to turn around . . .

MANSON: Look straight ahead.

AURELIA: I heard them . . .

CROWD VOICES: Hey! You!

AURELIA: It got louder . . .

CROWD VOICES: Hey, you! Jigaboo!

AURELIA: I blanked out my mind and tried to think of something to fill it . . . Number facts—

RELIA: Seven times four equals twenty-eight . . .

AURELIA: —states—

RELIA: Alabama, North Caroli . . .

AURELIA: —countries—

RELIA: Egypt, England . . .

AURELIA: —continents—

RELIA: Africa . . .

AURELIA: —Bible verses—

RELIA: Jesus wept.

AURELIA: I closed my eyes and tried to see the stars just like I saw them last night . . .

RELIA: Big Dipper, Pointer Stars, Little Dipper, North Star . . .

AURELIA: I screamed them in my head to drown out what the crowd was saying . . .

RELIA: Big Dipper, Pointer Stars, Little Dipper, North Star . . .

CROWD VOICES: Hey, you, nigger!

KATE: We need to go.

RELIA: Big Dipper . . . Little Dipper . . .

KATE: Manson, we need to go . . . I don't want her to hear . . .

AURELIA: I don't want her to hear . . .

MANSON: No.

RELIA: Big Dipper, Pointer Stars, Little Dipper, North Star . . .

CROWD VOICES: Nigger!

AURELIA: I tried to block it out . . . but then someone screamed . . .

CROWD VOICES: Hey, you! I'm talking to you, *NIGGER*!!!!!

KATE: Manson!

MANSON: Kate!

RELIA: North . . . North . . .

AURELIA: North . . . North . . . People had said the word before . . . I had heard . . .

CROWD VOICES: Nigger . . .

AURELIA: I knew they were talking about my race . . . but no one had ever called me . . .

CROWD VOICES [*whispering*]: *Nigger!*

AURELIA: I tried to block it out . . .

RELIA: Big . . . Dip . . . Point Stars, Little . . . North . . .

AURELIA: I tried, Big Dipper, Pointer Stars . . . North Star . . . I tried, but the word slipped by . . . It passed my ears and for the first time in my life . . . I *heard* . . . it!

CROWD VOICES: *Nigger!*

[*Darkness except for* AURELIA's *upper body and* RELIA.]

AURELIA: I couldn't see the face, but I could feel his thin, knife-sharp lips carve away at the years my mother had protected me. The rasping, crazed edge in his voice did not cut cleanly but made a flesh-ripping, jagged tear.

CROWD VOICES: Nigger . . .

AURELIA: I grabbed my heart and began to cry. I saw my mother's eyes and knew she knew.

CROWD VOICES: Nigger . . .

AURELIA: I was naked and wanted to cover my shame.

CROWD VOICES: Nigger . . .

AURELIA: I didn't want her to know. Because it would hurt her so. Because she could not patch the ragged flesh . . .

CROWD VOICES: Nigger!

AURELIA: So the wound became her wound and when the blood ran down from her heart, I could do nothing to stop her pain . . . She was naked before me as Eve before God.

RELIA: Mama . . .

[*Sound of spitting is heard as* FRANKLIN, MANSON, KATE, *and* RELIA *take turns wiping spit off the back of their necks.*]

AURELIA: This was different from yesterday's fear of being lost . . . fear of the night . . . It was the darker dark . . . Last night I was a little girl growing up. Today I was a black girl growing up.

RELIA: I want to die.

AURELIA: There was a searing, knowing pain, but I could not die. I could only sit there, hand on my heart, hurting more with each breath. My mother knew . . . and then my father. There was no "I told you so" between them . . .

Just their hands on my shoulder, squeezing as if they, together, they could keep me from breaking. I must keep my child from breaking . . .

MANSON: Do you want to go?

RELIA AND AURELIA: No.

RELIA: It hurt so badly.

AURELIA: I now understand the breach between my parents. My father felt the wound would heal and I would be stronger for it. My mother felt no wound at all best, and I would be freer for it. It was not an issue now. The wound was there and would not go away.

RELIA: We would never talk about it.

AURELIA: But I must tell my daughter.

[*Long pause.*]

When I turned around, I saw the man who brought me home in the storm.

[JAKE *is surprised to see* RELIA. JAKE *almost waves but stops when he hears the crowd.*]

RELIA AND AURELIA: He was with the group spitting on us and yelling "nigger this" and "nigger that." When he saw me, he froze, our eyes met, he almost smiled. The spit dribbled down his chin. When he wiped it away, he must have felt the eyes of his friends.

CROWD VOICES: Do you know her?

RELIA AND AURELIA: He took a deep breath, called me "nigger". . . it sounded hollow, with no conviction. I almost felt sorry for him when he grabbed his heart.

[*Pause.*]

Then he spit right in my face . . .

WILLIE: Noooooo . . .

[WILLIE *jumps up to attack* JAKE. RELIA *stops him.*]

RELIA: "Ice water!"

AURELIA: Willie wanted to kill him but I gritted my teeth and whispered . . .

RELIA: "Ice water!"

[WILLIE *lunges again.*]

"Ice water!" . . . Remember, Willie. Don't let a glass of ice water defeat you, Willie.

[WILLIE *doesn't back off.*]

That's a little freedom, Willie. We're working for the big freedom, now ...

[WILLIE *begins to pull back.*]

WILLIE: The big freedom ...
RELIA: Shines like a star!

[*Voice begins singing softly* "Ain't Gonna Let Nobody Turn Me Round."]

RELIA AND AURELIA: I shall not want ...

WILLIE: To kill ...

[*Pause.* WILLIE *sits.*]

He maketh me lie down in ...
KATE: Green gardens ...

RELIA: The big freedom.

WILLIE AND VOICES: He restoreth my soul ...

RELIA: Stronger than evil.
KATE: How deep the scar ...
AURELIA: But the wound begins to heal ... I must tell my daughter ...

WILLIE AND VOICES: Though I walk through the valley of the shadow of death ...

RELIA: Love overcomes hate ...

WILLIE AND VOICES: I shall fear no evil.

AURELIA: Climb on up to higher ground ...

WILLIE: For thou art with me.

RELIA: Spit swear!

WILLIE AND VOICES: In the presence of my enemies ...
WILLIE AND VOICES: Restoreth my soul ...

RELIA AND AURELIA: Find it here!
RELIA AND AURELIA: See millions and millions of stars ...

[*Pause.*]

AURELIA: I never saw the man there again.

[*All sing "Ain't Gonna Let Nobody Turn Me Round."* KATE *holds* RELIA. *All take a moment to look at the sky before exiting. The song continues softly as they each leave while looking up at the stars.* AURELIA, RELIA, *and* MANSON *are left onstage.*]

Demonstrations and boycotts continued for months. After things cooled off a bit, Willie quietly got his job back at the *integrated* library. Mama was right. It wasn't all over in a day or a month or a summer...

[*Dark sky with brilliant stars fades up as* AURELIA *speaks.*]

I would fight again and again, until I lost the glimmer of a star in my heart among all those tall, brightly lit buildings. The stars are faint in the sky above—but they are there. And I don't walk in the dark very much anymore, unless forced to. It's too dangerous here. But I know tonight, before I turn out the lamp, I must tell my daughter... "There will be no school tomorrow." Our school will be at the Grand Cab Company and I will be the teacher. And tonight, before I turn out the lamp, I will hold my daughter close ... and show her my scars. I will weep with her and let my tears wash her wounds. I will pray for her children and her children's children, then dry her face and tell her to close her eyes. "Look up. There's a whole universe of light inside us! We just have to find it."

[RELIA *and* MANSON *watch the stars.*]

RELIA: Look up! See!

MANSON: A whole universe of stars!

AURELIA: There really is a North Star ...

MANSON: And if you find it once, you can find it again.

AURELIA: Turn off the lights ...

RELIA and AURELIA [*slowly begin counting as lights fade*]: One, two, three ...

[*Lights fade to darkness except for stars and a very bright light on* AURELIA *as if she is a star. She touches her heart, as if pained, looks up, and smiles when she sees the North Star.*]

RELIA [*pointing to the sky*]: There!!!

AURELIA [*pointing to her heart*]: Here!

HAMBONE

Javon Johnson
First-Place Winner
1999–2000

For Mr. August Wilson
The Struggle Will Continue

PLAYWRIGHT'S STATEMENT

Having no formal education in playwriting and a writing history of only two years, one may suspect that my biggest challenge would be based on the technicalities of script construction—plot, structure, character development, through line, and so forth. Such, however, has not been the case. What has proven to be most challenging is fighting the very person I consider to be my most prominent inspiration, that is, theater great August Wilson. There have been countless times that I have crossed out and rearranged my writing in order to strip away what seems to me to be too Wilsonish. Nonetheless, I met with Mr. Wilson for the second time in Valdez, Alaska, in the summer of 1998. After I discussed with him my dilemma, his advice to me was to write whatever comes out, however it comes, and then let the critics decide what they will. Taking this advice in stride, I then sat down to write *Hambone*, creating only from the idea that I was relieved from this burden of fighting against the Wilson influence. As a result, I have developed this piece to pay homage to Mr. Wilson and as a way of thanking him for the inspiration and support. I hope that I have allowed all Wilson influences to surface in *Hambone* and that God may use me as his instrument to inspire others as he has used Mr. Wilson to inspire me.

"This grown-folk business" is a phrase I often heard in my childhood. As the years passed, I understood for myself what that business was, but my interpretation was what I made of it. Some things I accepted, others may have been too painful. I was often uncertain of which topics were taboo. If things had been explained to me early on, who knows? Thus, what interests me most about *Hambone* is the idea of the suppression of the truth. "The truth gotta come however it's gonna come." In every dark corner lies a secret with immeasurable patience. It is the moment when this secret is unleashed that I find most intriguing. "The truth come out and ain't nothing the same no more." Many of us are shackled by some suppressed truth that perhaps if revealed would bring more comfort than pain. After knowing a classmate for two years, he revealed to me that he was

HIV positive. Maybe I didn't notice anything missing before, but I know now when I look at him I see a whole person. No longer does the truth have to be a burden between him and me. It is instead freedom. *Hambone* is an exploration of this idea and how painful it must be to live life under one truth only to discover later that it never was the truth at all.

Special thanks to Shirley Jo Finney, Marion McClinton, Dennis Zacek, Jill Morris, Robert Blacker, Chuck Smith and Columbia College, Ron O. J. Parson, Ian McGloin and Underwood Theater, Stacey Waring, Eileen Morris, Benjamin Cane, and the Sundance Lab.

PRODUCTION HISTORY

Hambone, by Javon Johnson, was first presented by the Columbia College Chicago Theater Department at the New Studio Theater in February 2000. It was directed by Shirley Jo Finney, with set design by Lily Xie, costume design by Nancy El Rassi and Clare McMahon, lighting design by Victor Mahler, sound design by Steven Mezger, and fight choreography by David Woolley. Jacob Snodgress was the stage manager, and Tabitha Faith Cross was the production stage manager.

Bobbilee	Lance Barnes Jr.
Bishop	Tory Davis
Henry	Wallace Heard Jr.
Tyrone	Omar Muhammad
Harrison	Joe Vonderhaar

The play was subsequently presented by the Victory Gardens Theater in Chicago in January 2001. It was directed by Ron O. J. Parson, with set design by Mary Griswold, costume design by Christine Pascual, lighting design by Geoffrey Bushor, and sound design by Chris J. Johnson. Ellyn Costello was the production stage manager.

Bobbilee	Francois Battiste
Bishop	Freeman Coffey
Tyrone	Anthony Fleming III
Harrison	Tom Roland
Henry	A. C. Smith

CHARACTERS

Bishop, forty-eight-year-old African American store owner with a commanding presence and an unsettled spirit

Henry, stout African American ex-football player in his fifties, griot of the diner

Tyrone, African American teenager just looking to get by, acutely aware of what he sees as the disadvantages of being black

Harrison, vulnerable elderly white railroad employee in search of a lost salvation

Bobbilee, African American teenager, a gentle soul with rough edges and inner struggles, admires James Brown and always wears a do-rag

STAGING

The setting is a sandwich diner in Anderson, South Carolina, in 1988. A large wall-size window sits upstage. Actors can be seen through this window when working in the garden. Three or four booths run alongside this window. A counter with stools sits stage left. Across from the counter are the grill, refrigerator, sandwich meat, and related props. There are two hallways. One, with double doors, leads to the stockroom and back door. The other leads to Bishop's bedroom. Another door leads to the bathroom. Photos of Jesse Jackson, Bishop in chef attire, Walter Payton, Jim Brown, Martin Luther King, James Brown, Malcolm X, and Sugar Ray Leonard may hang throughout the diner. There's a large menu sign. Somewhere there is a clock. The front door is downstage right with a reversible WE'RE OPEN/WE'RE CLOSED sign hanging from it. A bench and steps leading to the front door are outside.

ACT 1

SCENE 1

[*The diner is dim. A toolbox sits under the counter. The sound of feet stomping and hand rhythms against the body can be heard. Several men are "hamboning." Beneath the hand rhythms, a voice chants, "Choo-choo, hear the train a-roaring. Choo-choo, hear the train a-coming. Choo-choo-chugalug, train ride high. Choo-choo-chugalug, train never die." From a distance a train sounds. The hamboning, humming, and foot stomping increase in volume and intensity as the train approaches. The chant remains steady. The train whistles several times. Finally, when the hamboning is at its peak, the train arrives in full force. Waking up from a dream,* BISHOP *enters from the back room. The hamboning stops. The train passes and fades off into the distance as the last sound is heard: "Choo-choo-chugalug, train never die." Hand to forehead, he turns on the light and calls for* TYRONE.]

BISHOP: Tyrone?

[*Pause.*]

Tyrone!

[*He crosses to the front door, opens it, looks out for a moment, and then closes the door.*]

Tyrone!

[*Pause. He pours himself a cup of coffee and takes a sip.*]

Damn coffee cold. Tyrone!

[BISHOP *exits through the double doors.* HENRY *enters through the front door carrying a newspaper and a football. He walks with a homemade cane and wears a Kofi hat. He is eager to share some good news with* BISHOP.]

HENRY: Bishop? Hey, Bishop?

[*He opens the door leading to* BISHOP'*s bedroom.*]

Bishop!

[*He pours himself a cup of coffee.*]

Damn coffee cold.

[*He yells through the double doors.*]

Bishop! Hey, Bishop!

BISHOP [*reentering from back*]: Man, what you doing all that hollerin' for?

HENRY: Man, when you gone fix that coffeepot? Ain't nobody wanna drink no cold coffee.

BISHOP: Ain't you drinking it?

HENRY: That don't mean I like it. I just drink it 'cause I know you need the business! [*Laughs.*] Hey, Tyrone! C'mon in here, Tyrone!

BISHOP: Stop all that hollerin'!

HENRY: I ain't hollerin'! I was warming up my vocals! Don't you know nothing about vocal training?

BISHOP: What you know about it?

HENRY: What I know about it? What you talking what I know about it?

[*He slams the football on the counter.*]

That's what I know about it! My boy sent me his game ball! Yeah, he over there breaking records, Bishop! Look where he signed to Pop on there! [*Pointing*] "To my pop." And the boy sent me a card, Bishop. Ain't that something? The boy ain't never sent me nothing but he sent me a card.

[*He puts on his eyeglasses.*]

"Thanks, Pops, for sitting in and not sitting out. Thanks for the inspiration. Love, Son." See that? He talking about them sit-ins we was a part of back in our day. My boy taking that spirit and putting it into his feet and running with that ball. Gonna be just like his daddy. The best there ever was! Now c'mon and hambone with me! The spirit telling us we gotta celebrate!

[HENRY *beats on the counter.* BISHOP *takes chairs down from tables.*]

BISHOP: Don't you start that, Henry . . .

HENRY [*beating his thigh and chest*]: C'mon, old man! Hambone waiting on you!

BISHOP: Go on with that, Henry! I gotta get the shop opened up for business.

HENRY: I told you don't nobody wanna drink no cold coffee! C'mon!

BISHOP: I ain't in the mood for that right now!

HENRY: Your ancestors worked them plantations so you can sit here and hambone with me and you don't wanna do it?

BISHOP: I gotta open up this shop.

HENRY: You wouldn't have this shop if it wasn't for hambone. Now, c'mon! [*Singing and patting his thigh*] Hambone hambone have you heard? Bishop don't wanna sing no words. Hambone get him and let him go. He can't sing 'cause he too old . . .

BISHOP: Too old? Who old?

HENRY: You old!

BISHOP: Get out my way!

[*He takes* HENRY's *stool.*]

HENRY: Hold on now! Watch that leg!

BISHOP: I'm gonna take this to the next level! You gonna feel like you back on them plantations after I show you what I know about the hambone! [*With one foot on the stool, singing and beating away at his thigh*] Hambone hambone have you heard? Daddy's gonna buy you a Thunderbird.

[HENRY *beats his cane on the floor.*]

If that Thunderbird don't shine, Daddy's gonna buy you a bottle of wine. If that bottle of wine ain't sweet, Henry gonna mash some grapes with his feet.

HENRY [*stopping abruptly*]: Nigga, I ain't mashing no grapes with my feet!

BISHOP: It's the song, Henry! I'm just making it up!

HENRY: Well, make up something else! Don't be singing about my feet! You know how I am about my feet!

BISHOP: C'mon, man! You done got me started up now! [*Singing*] Hambone hambone have you heard? . . .

HENRY [*grabbing his leg*]: That's enough, Bishop!

BISHOP: What's the matter with you? Your ancestors ain't leave you enough to hang with the hambone?

HENRY: I can hang. I gotta rest my thigh. You just have to give me a minute.

BISHOP: Come in here doing all that hollerin' then you wanna ask for some time off.

[*He watches* HENRY *rub his thigh.*]

When you going to that clinic?

HENRY: What clinic?

BISHOP [*handing* HENRY *a small piece of paper*]: You know what I'm talking about.

HENRY: I ain't going down there.

BISHOP: You need to go down there.

HENRY: Too many white folks at that clinic.

BISHOP: They the ones know what they doing.

HENRY: That's what you say. You can be feeling fine. It ain't until you go to that clinic you got health problems. The last time I was at that clinic them people talking about cutting off my leg. I ain't having that.

BISHOP: Let 'em cut it off. Hell, you can't do nothing with it nohow.

HENRY: Them people ain't cutting up on me!

[*Pause.*]

They get to digging around in my body with that knife there ain't no telling what else they might come out with. They do that, you know. Cut something out of you and pass it on to somebody else. Don't even tell you they took it, it's just gone. You walking around feeling all lopsided and not knowing it's 'cause you ain't got but two ribs and half your stomach missing. Nah, I ain't going down there. I'm going down to Ms. Thomasina Francis. Let her fix me up.

BISHOP: Ms. Francis? What that woman gonna do?

HENRY: All she needs is some garlic salt, some chicken bones, and a piece of my hair and she'll fix me up just fine.

BISHOP: Yeah, you and the devil both. Negroes always talking about white folks. There ain't one better than the other. People gotta look past what they see to see what's really there. They get so hung up on black and white till that gray sitting there. That gray run deeper than you know.

HENRY: I don't know about all that. All I know is I ain't going to them white folks. I'd rather somebody black work on me.

BISHOP: You make sure you put that ten dollars you owe me in your will before you go see Ms. Francis.

HENRY: It's gonna cost me ten dollars to see her.

BISHOP [*playfully pointing the knife at* HENRY]: Man, if you don't give me my money . . .

HENRY [*laughing but backing away*]: Fix me a club, Bishop! Turkey with no mayo and pickles on the side!

BISHOP [*fixing a sandwich*]: You crazy, Henry. You ignorant with no purpose.

HENRY: See, that's where you wrong. Only smart people go see them white folks. I'd rather be ignorant and let Ms. Francis fix me up. Besides, you the one crazy. You the only Negro I know in Anderson County serve a club sandwich with no bacon.

BISHOP: You know I don't serve no pork.

HENRY: And you know I ain't going to that clinic.

BISHOP [*holding the knife up to* HENRY]: Man, just say you scared of that knife!

HENRY: I ain't scared of that knife!

[*The knife issue is obviously too sensitive for* HENRY. BISHOP *pulls the knife back and continues to cut sandwich meat. Pause.*]

BISHOP: You see Tyrone out there?

HENRY [*in obvious pain*]: Nah, I ain't seen him. He ain't in the back?

BISHOP: If he was in the back I wouldn't be asking you if you seen him out there.

[*Pause.*]

That boy ain't open up this shop this morning, Henry. He ain't count the money, he ain't swept the floor, the coffee ain't heat up, he ain't done nothing. It ain't like him not to be here to open up.

HENRY: You know Tyrone ain't going too far without letting you know something. He'll be back in time enough to open up this shop.

BISHOP: That just ain't like him.

HENRY: Tyrone growing up. There's gonna be a whole lot of things that ain't like him.

[*Pause.*]

You hear about Bobbilee? Heard he got thirty days.

BISHOP: Thirty days? What that boy do now?

HENRY: Say he wasn't doing nothing. Say he was just standing on the corner and they gave him thirty days.

BISHOP: He had to do something. They ain't gonna give you thirty days for just standing on the corner.

HENRY: Well now, that's what Bobbilee was doing. He was standing there in that white neighborhood and they locked him up. He ain't even do nothing.

BISHOP: C'mon now, Henry, that boy had to do something. The boy always doing something.

HENRY: You don't always have to be doing something for them to do something to you, Bishop. That's what they doing to these young boys. They letting these youngbloods kill each other off and then they selling their body parts. Getting a hundred percent profit.

BISHOP: Say what?

HENRY [*with an air of secrecy*]: Black man kill a black man ain't nobody getting locked up. If they do lock up somebody it ain't but for a month or so. You ever wonder why everybody just getting thirty days? See, they need them back out there on the streets so they can kill another black man. They take the body parts, sell them, and don't nobody know nothing. Mamas and uncles crying over the casket and the casket weighing more than the body. I'm telling you, Bishop, they making big money off these young boys. That's why I'm glad my boy at that school. He can do something I ain't do. Get himself a degree. Something that say he got what it takes to make it in this world.

BISHOP: Your boy's a Morehouse man.

HENRY [*throwing the football to* BISHOP]: Good football player, too.

BISHOP: I said the boy a Morehouse man. That mean more than football. You trying to force yourself on that boy. Lummie majoring in criminal justice, he ain't going to the NFL.

HENRY: You don't know what Lummie gonna do. Might go to the Hall of Fame for all you know.

BISHOP: You put your whole life into that football. Now, you sitting up in here leaning on a cane waiting on Lummie to live life for you. Something happen to Lummie and he can't run that ball then what you gonna do?

HENRY: You sounding like Martha. Always second-guessing what I'm doing with my boy. If Lummie wanna play ball then that's what Lummie wanna do. Ain't my fault I played ball, too. You telling me that if I wash my hands after I piss, he can't do that 'cause I done already done it?

BISHOP: It ain't the fifties no more, Henry, the boy's got options.

HENRY: I thought we was talking about Pattie's boy. I was saying something about Bobbilee and you done got all into my business about what Lummie doing. When I wanted to talk about Lummie you wanted to talk about the damn clinic. Now, I ain't getting into how you raising Tyrone, I was talking about Bobbilee . . .

BISHOP: What about Bobbilee?

HENRY: Well!

[*Pause.*]

Say they got him for disturbing the peace. He wasn't doing nothing. He was just singing that James Brown song and they got him.

BISHOP: He know better than to go down there in that white neighborhood yellin' about James Brown.

HENRY: But they gave him thirty days, Bishop. He ain't cut nobody. He ain't steal nothing. He ain't do nothing but tell them white folks, "Papa don't take no mess," and they locked him up for a whole month. That ain't disturbing the peace. That's them white folks tampering with our constitutional rights.

BISHOP: Now you being a racist.

HENRY: I bet if there wasn't no white folks there wouldn't be no colored folks either.

BISHOP: You want provolone, American, or Swiss?

HENRY: See, if there were no white folks you wouldn't know you was black. You can go wherever you want in this world and just be who you are and that's it. It's when you come across somebody white you remember you a black man. I look at my wife, I see I'm a good husband. I look at my boy, I see I'm a good father. I look at a white man, he looking at me, I see that I'm colored. He ain't even gotta open his mouth. He just standing there telling me I'm a black man.

BISHOP: Henry, you don't know nothing.

HENRY: I know you better not put that pickle on my sandwich, and give me some honey brown mustard . . . on the side.

[BISHOP *starts to hand him the sandwich.*]

How's my tab looking?

BISHOP [*pulling the sandwich back*]: Now if you ain't got no money you ain't got no sandwich.

HENRY: I got the two dollars for the sandwich. Just put the pickles on the side.

[BISHOP *hands him the sandwich.*]

I need me a soft drink. You got that strawberry flavor soft drink?

BISHOP: Here, drink that grape. That's all I got.

HENRY: I don't want no grape.

BISHOP: Well, give it back then.

HENRY: Nah, grape all right.

[*Excited,* TYRONE *enters through the front door and turns the* WE'RE CLOSED *sign around.*]

TYRONE: Y'all hear about Bobbilee?

BISHOP: Boy, where you been?

TYRONE [*putting on an apron*]: Downtown.

BISHOP: You don't know how to tell nobody where you going?

TYRONE: You was sleep. You don't like for me to mess with you when you sleep.

BISHOP: You let me know where you going, boy. Something happen around here I need to know where you at!

TYRONE [*unsure why* BISHOP *is so upset*]: Sorry, Mr. Bishop, but I wasn't gone that long.

HENRY [*interrupting*]: What you doing downtown?

TYRONE: Unemployment office. Y'all hear about Bobbilee?

BISHOP [*grabbing the toolbox*]: I've been hearing about Bobbilee all morning.

TYRONE: Thirty days, Mr. Henry. Can you believe that?

[TYRONE *gets a broom from the back.* HENRY *burps.*]

BISHOP: Man, don't you know how to say "Excuse me"?

HENRY: I don't know why they call it soft drink when it's so damn hard on you.

TYRONE [*while sweeping*]: This the second time they did Bobbilee like that. I think they got his number or something. Ain't nobody got that kinda bad luck.

[BISHOP *removes new gardening tools from the toolbox.*]

BISHOP: Bobbilee gotta learn how to keep his mouth shut.

HENRY: They got your number, Bishop's number, they got everybody's number.

TYRONE: He wasn't even doing nothing, Mr. Henry.

BISHOP: The boy was disturbing the peace like they say.

TYRONE: That ain't how it was, Mr. Bishop. He was just waiting on the corner for the bus.

BISHOP: There's over a hundred places for that boy to catch the city bus. What he down there in that white neighborhood for?

TYRONE: Bobbilee say he catch the bus wherever he want. They always try to keep you on your side, but Bobbilee say it ain't nobody's side. Say they ain't got the right to say where he can or can't catch the bus. He wasn't doing nothing but standing there. He started singing and that's when they grabbed him and started beating on him. He started fighting back and that's how he got them thirty days. That's the same way they did him the first time when he was trying to get away from them white boys.

BISHOP: I know the circumstances of the situation, boy. I was down there when Bobbilee got into it with them boys. Had I not come down there to get you outta that mess you and Bobbilee both would've been getting thirty days.

TYRONE: But they jumped on him, Mr. Bishop. I was just telling the police Bobbilee ain't do nothing.

BISHOP: Boy, Bobbilee was the one started the whole thing. He down there hollerin', "Free James Brown! *Owww!* Free the Godfather!" He ain't even been to a James Brown concert and he down there hollerin' for the man.

TYRONE: You ain't gotta go to a James Brown concert to holler for him. All you gotta do is listen to his tape. That's the same as being at the concert.

BISHOP: If you at the concert you can see the man. That's what it's about. You can put your eyes on him. Bobbilee ain't never seen the man or nothing.

TYRONE: Bobbilee got his cassette tape.

BISHOP: That don't mean nothing.

TYRONE: They got his picture on the cassette tape. That's how Bobbilee seen him.

BISHOP: So what that mean, boy? That tape don't shake your hand! Henry, you ever shake hands with a cassette tape?

HENRY: Nah, I ain't never done nothing like that.

BISHOP: That's what I'm saying. Why he gonna go down there screaming for the man when he ain't never seen him? You tell me.

TYRONE [*imitating James Brown*]: "Owww! 'Cause he the Soul Man!" You ain't gotta see him to feel that. You ever seen Jesus? You always shouting for Jesus, Mr. Bishop, but you ain't never seen him.

BISHOP: That's different. They got books on Jesus.

HENRY: Ain't nobody got him on tape.

[TYRONE *and* HENRY *laugh.*]

BISHOP: Shut up, Henry! Ain't nobody ask you nothing about it.

TYRONE [*checking a stack of letters*]: Mr. Bishop, I didn't get no mail?

BISHOP [*setting the box and tools behind the double doors*]: That's yesterday's mail.

TYRONE: You didn't check the box?

BISHOP: Mailman ain't run yet. It's too early. What you worried about the mail for?

TYRONE: I got my papers coming, Mr. Henry.

HENRY: What papers?

TYRONE: Gettin' my name changed.

[*Pause.* BISHOP *and* HENRY *look at each other.*]

BISHOP: Gettin' your name changed?

TYRONE: Yeah.

BISHOP: Why you wanna change your name?

TYRONE: So I can work.

BISHOP: What you mean so you can work? You don't like what you doing here?

TYRONE: Nah, Mr. Bishop, it's all right but I need me a big job and a white name. There ain't no white people name Tyrone.

BISHOP: What that gotta do with you working?

TYRONE: 'Cause I can't never get no interview if my name Tyrone. Everybody hiring is white. They look at my application and they see Tyrone Jackson on there and they know right offhand I'm black. Then they wanna put me in the kitchen somewhere. I'm better than that. My mama said I'm better than that.

HENRY: Your mama was right. You do what you have to. Change your name, hell, change your birth date, I don't care. Do whatever it takes to keep them from pulling your number.

TYRONE: I'm thinking about Timothy. That's a good name, ain't it? That's in the Bible, too. Right, Mr. Bishop? Ain't that a Bible name? [*To himself*] Timothy Jackson . . . Jackson.

[*Pause.*]

Nah, I better change my last name, too.

BISHOP: You ain't changing nothing. You hear me? You keeping everything your mama gave you.

TYRONE: But how I'm gonna work if I don't change my name?

BISHOP: Work ain't no good if you don't know what you working for. You black, I know you black. Henry know you black, hell, anybody look at you know you black. You talking about changing your name 'cause you don't like how it sound. A man don't know who he is ain't a man at all. He ain't got nothing to fall back on. You keep your name. That way when something goes wrong out there in the world you got something to come back to. Start over if you have to, but start somewhere.

[TYRONE *is a bit confused by* BISHOP's *reaction.*]

TYRONE: I just wanna work, that's all.

BISHOP [*almost to himself*]: Yeah.

[TYRONE *takes some chips from* HENRY's *plate and then starts to exit.*]

Where you going?

TYRONE: Almost nine-thirty. I told Mr. Banks I'd be by to pick that shit up by ten.

BISHOP: Fertilizer, boy. It's fertilizer.

TYRONE: Mr. Banks say it ain't nothing but shit.

BISHOP: It may be shit to Mr. Banks, but in here it's fertilizer.

HENRY: It is shit, Bishop. It's good shit, too. Anytime you can put shit in the ground and make more shit grow, that's some good shit.

BISHOP: I don't care what it is, I don't want him saying "shit" in my shop!

HENRY: Now, Bishop, you just said it! Tyrone, didn't you just hear Bishop here say "shit"?

TYRONE: That's what it sound like he said!

BISHOP: That's because it's my shop!

[*Pause.*]

TYRONE: I'm gonna pick up the ... doo-doo.

[*They all laugh.* BISHOP *gets flyers from behind the counter.*]

BISHOP: Here, boy, put these flyers up while you out there.
TYRONE: Flyers?
BISHOP: I gotta get me some customers in here somehow.
TYRONE [*taking the flyers*]: This nice here, Mr. Bishop. This picture make you look like you almost know how to cook.
BISHOP: Boy, get on out of here and make sure you back here in time enough to open up this kitchen.
TYRONE: All right ... If some mail come for me just put it in the basket on the counter.
BISHOP: Ain't that where I always put it?
TYRONE: Talk to you later, Mr. Henry.

[TYRONE *exits through the front door.*]

BISHOP: Put his mail in the basket. Henry, ain't that where I always put the mail? You ever see me put the mail anyplace else?
HENRY: I don't care what you say, Bishop. It is shit. All you gotta do is smell it and that tell you it's shit.

[*Pause.*]

BISHOP: I had this dream last night, Henry. I ain't had a dream in years I can re-member but I had one last night. There was this train. This train was on fire and it was coming straight at me. It felt like the whole ground was shaking. [*Almost to himself*] This train was coming at me and ... I could see Tyrone. All I can remember is seeing Tyrone running. I'm reaching out for him and the more I'd reach, the further he'd run, and the louder that train got. Then all of a sudden, the train whistled and Tyrone was gone. Just like that ... he was gone. [*At the front door*] Then I wake up this morning, the shop ain't open, and Ty-rone out there somewhere. Now he talking about changing his name.
HENRY: You know, if you had've set things right with Greta you wouldn't be having these problems outta Tyrone.
BISHOP: Tighten it up, Henry.
HENRY: If you had've listened to Greta you wouldn't—

BISHOP: I don't wanna hear nothing about Greta.

HENRY: I'm just saying Greta told you—

BISHOP: Stay out of my business!

HENRY: Forty-two years now you want me to stay out of your business. You ain't ask me to stay out of your business when you was trying to get this place started. You ain't ask me to stay out of your business when them white folks wouldn't give you no license. Had me out there sitting on the steps of the courthouse. It's raining you mad and wanna protest. You ain't ask me to stay out of your business when you wanted to marry Greta. Come talking about, "I'm scared, Henry. What I'm gonna do, Henry?" Now you telling me to stay out of your business!

BISHOP: I ain't said nothing about you killing that white man from Hartsville! Now why you bringing up that boy's mama?

HENRY: Wait a minute now.

[*Pause.*]

You know I ain't kill that man.

BISHOP: He dead ain't he?

HENRY: I ain't kill him! I was just defending myself!

BISHOP: That ain't what them records say!

HENRY: I don't give a damn about what them records say! You see what that man did to me! I was gonna be the best there ever was and he took a knife to my leg! Now, I ain't no killer, Bishop, you know that!

BISHOP: People be who they are. You say you ain't no killer, the police say you shot a man. Hell, I done shot at three people come in here trying to rob this joint! Ain't nobody die, so I ain't no killer. Still I shot at 'em. It all depends on who's looking at it to see how you come out. All I know is that white man from Hartsville dead.

HENRY: You saying I can't defend myself?

BISHOP: I'm saying if you ain't no killer, then stop bringing up Greta!

HENRY: Man, I come over here to hambone with you and celebrate my boy and you making me wanna go back home!

[*He starts to exit.*]

I think I'll call you next time!

BISHOP: Look, Henry, I'm . . . I'm just worried about Tyrone.

HENRY: Tyrone just trying to find his way.

BISHOP: Well, he can find it some other way.

HENRY: Now, Bishop, you found your way through Grandma Ida. If she hadn't have baptized you Bishop you'd be out there just like Tyrone.

BISHOP: The point is I was out there, Henry. I was out there and I didn't have nothing to turn back to.

HENRY: You turned to me and Grandma Ida. You saying me and Grandma Ida wasn't enough for you?

BISHOP: I ain't saying nothing bad about you and Grandma Ida. All them hot meals she put into my belly. That's one of the best things I remember about that woman. Smelling her golden brown buttermilk biscuits a mile away.

HENRY: Her sweet potato pie.

BISHOP: Green onions and collard greens.

HENRY: Mash potatoes and corn bread.

BISHOP: Fried fish and cheese grits.

HENRY: Neck bones and black-eyed peas.

BISHOP: Country fried chicken and buttered lima beans.

HENRY: Polk salad and fatback. Ham hock and gravy.

BISHOP: Ham hock and . . . ham hock? Fool, Grandma Ida ain't serve us no pork!

HENRY: No, but that's what Martha's cooking this evening. Ham hock and gravy!

[HENRY *and* BISHOP *laugh.*]

BISHOP: I told you you ignorant.

HENRY: Yeah, Grandma Ida sure fed us right. You gotta feed Tyrone like that.

BISHOP: What that supposed to mean, Henry?

HENRY: That mean you need to do what Greta told you and . . .

BISHOP: I said I didn't wanna hear nothing else about Greta! Now, give me that plate and go grab that broom from the back!

HENRY: Broom? What the hell I'm gonna grab the broom for?

BISHOP: Take care of your tab.

HENRY: I told you I got the two dollars!

BISHOP: That don't make up for the ten dollars you already owe me!

HENRY: I'm gonna give you that, Bishop! Why you all upset about it?

BISHOP: I just need my money! I'm already low on my customers!

HENRY [*getting the broom*]: That's because you got that cold-ass coffee!

[HARRISON *enters through the front door.* HENRY *looks at him with a sense of dis-belief.*]

Damn.

[HARRISON *remains by the door. There's a long uneasy silence as both* HENRY, *as he sweeps, and* BISHOP *stare.*]

HARRISON: Coffee.

[BISHOP *places a cup of coffee on the counter.* BISHOP *and* HENRY *stare at* HARRISON *as he crosses to the counter.* HENRY *looks out the front door to make sure* HARRISON *is alone. He continues to stare at* HARRISON *as he sweeps.*]

BISHOP: You from around here?
HARRISON [*sipping coffee and coughing*]: Coffee's cold.

[HENRY *laughs.* BISHOP *looks at him, he stops. Pause.*]

HENRY: You the law?
HARRISON: I work railways.
HENRY: Yeah? Where 'bout?
HARRISON: Charleston.
HENRY: Yeah? Where 'bout?

[*Sensing he's unwelcome,* HARRISON *places a few coins on the counter and starts to exit.* HENRY *steps between* HARRISON *and the front door.* HARRISON *stops.*]

BISHOP: What brings you to Anderson County?

[HARRISON *walks around* HENRY, *then stops at the door. He turns back to* BISHOP.]

HARRISON: Thanks for the coffee.

[HARRISON *exits.*]

HENRY: What you think that white man want, Bishop?
BISHOP: Man just wanted some coffee.
HENRY: That's what he told you. He don't look like no railroad man to me. You see how he was looking around here? That's suspect.
BISHOP: Come off all that crazy talk, Henry. I'm going to the stockroom. You watch out front while I check the inventory.

[BISHOP *exits into the back room.* HENRY *ponders with a look of serious concern.*]

HENRY: That white man come up in here. Ms. Francis gotta hear about this.

[*He takes powder from his pocket and sprinkles it throughout the shop, retracing* HARRISON'S *steps.*]

Shoo, devil! Shoo! Get on off from around here!

[*He opens the front door and blows powder.*]

Shoo!

[*Suggested song: "Voodoo Woman."*]

SCENE 2

[*The following morning.* BISHOP *is cleaning the grill.* HENRY's *football now sits on a tee somewhere in the diner.* TYRONE *enters, dragging a bag of fertilizer.*]

BISHOP: How many that make, boy?

TYRONE: That's seven bags. You think seven bags enough?

BISHOP: Seven bags good.

TYRONE: Man, I ain't never had my own garden before. I ain't sure I know how to take care of it.

BISHOP: Ain't nothing to it. Just check on it every other day. Make sure you got soft dirt.

TYRONE: I guess that's what this shit for, huh?

[BISHOP *glares at him sharply.*]

Sorry.

BISHOP: Why don't you take that to the back.

TYRONE: How you know so much about gardens, Mr. Bishop?

[*Pause.*]

BISHOP: You go ahead and take that to the back. I want you to finish cleaning this grill.

TYRONE [*taking letters from his back pocket*]: All right . . . well, here's the mail.

BISHOP: What you handing it to me for? Put it in the basket.

[TYRONE *puts the mail in the basket and exits into the back room.* HENRY *enters through the front door. He has a newspaper and sniffs the air.*]

HENRY: Wheew! Bishop, what the hell is that smell? You cooking chitterlings?

BISHOP: You know I don't serve no pork.

[HENRY *opens the front door. He swings it back and forth.*]

Man, what you doing? Close my door! I can't have them flies in here!

HENRY: Man, this place smells like shit!

BISHOP: I got that fertilizer in the back!

HENRY: Well damn, Bishop, sit it outside! Ain't nobody gonna come in here with this place smelling like this!

TYRONE [*reentering from back*]: Hey, Mr. Henry.

HENRY: Hey, Tyrone. Tyrone, you smell that shit?

[TYRONE *laughs.*]

BISHOP: All right, the both of you shut the hell up! Tyrone, do like I told you!

[TYRONE *cleans the grill.* HENRY *closes the front door and covers his face with a handkerchief.*]

HENRY: You bringing all that shit in here and it ain't gonna do nothing for you.

BISHOP: It's gonna save me some money, that's what it's gonna do.

HENRY: It ain't gonna do nothing but run off your customers.

BISHOP: I ain't getting enough customers as it is. I start up that garden out there and I can cut back on my inventory.

HENRY: Oh, so you just gonna grow your own food and sell that?

BISHOP: That's right.

HENRY: What about the meat? You can't grow the meat. You gonna get you a bunch of cows and graze them, too?

[TYRONE *laughs.* BISHOP *looks at him sharply.* TYRONE *stops and returns to cleaning the grill.*]

BISHOP: I'm gonna grow my vegetables. Vegetables costing me just as much as the meat these days.

HENRY: You seen that white man?

BISHOP: A man is a man don't matter what color he is.

HENRY: People say he been hanging around the black neighborhoods. I saw him going into the Earl Homes yesterday. Ain't but two reasons a white man goes into the Earl Homes. He buying or he locking somebody up. I think that white man looking for Bobbilee.

[*The phone rings.* HENRY *answers it.*]

Who this?

BISHOP: Man, I told you about answering my phone like that. This ain't no private line. You greet the people the way they supposed to be greeted.

HENRY [*into the phone*]: I said, who the hell is this?

BISHOP [*taking the phone from* HENRY]: Get on out the way! That's the main reason I ain't got no customers now!

HENRY [*picking up the newspaper*]: Ah, nigga, I know how to take the order. Ain't nothing to doing that. I just wanna know who I'm talking to. White man come around here drinking your cold coffee, shit, I gotta be careful.

BISHOP [*into the phone*]: Fifteen thirty-one East River Street. Yeah, this Bishop's Sandwich Shop.

[*Pause.*]

Who? Who you wanna speak to?

[*Pause.*]

Who? Nah, there ain't no Timothy here. You got the wrong number.

TYRONE [*rushing to the phone*]: That's me! I got it!

[*He takes the phone from* BISHOP.]

Yeah, this Ty . . . [*proper and "white"*] Timothy Snyder here. Hey, Mr. Kramer. Yeah, everything here is . . . going swell.

[HENRY *and* BISHOP *look at each other.*]

You say my application looks OK? Monday morning? Well, don't you want me to come in for an interview? No interview? No, that is no problem, I will be there by nine. Thank you, sir. Yes sir, I am looking forward to it myself.

[*He hangs up the phone and breaks into a James Brown frenzy.*]

"Yeah! I feel good! Get up off of that thing! Dance till you feel better!"

BISHOP: Boy, what's wrong with you?

TYRONE: Got me a job, Mr. Bishop! Working downtown!

HENRY: Where you working at?

TYRONE: At the courthouse! Sortin' out papers and stuff! [*Singing*] "Gotta get on the good foot! Ugh! Gotta stay on the scene!"

BISHOP: You ain't working down there.

[TYRONE *stops dancing.*]

TYRONE: Say what?

BISHOP: I say you ain't working down there.

TYRONE: But Mr. Kramer just told me I got the job. Say I start Monday morning.

BISHOP: I don't care what Mr. Kramer just told you, you ain't working down there.

TYRONE: Why can't I? That's a good job. Tell him, Mr. Henry. Tell him that's a good job!

HENRY: Now, that is a good job, Bishop. Boy be the first nigga in the court-house who ain't getting locked up.

BISHOP: What you talking about, Henry? There blacks all around that court-house.

HENRY: But the proportion's off. Half them Negroes on community service or in low-class positions and the other half don't count. They just what they call quota Negroes. Them niggas ain't nothing but numbers walking around that place.

BISHOP: Well, Tyrone ain't gonna be one of them.

HENRY: Tyrone might be able to change things up.

[*He holds up the newspaper.*]

Look at what Reverend Jackson doing. Born fifteen minutes up the road, now he a black man running for president. He ain't gonna win but at least he running. All that ambition Tyrone got in him, he might be able to do something like that. Might even pull up the rear on Jackson.

BISHOP: I said he ain't working down there!

HENRY: This ain't the fifties no more, Bishop. The boy's got options.

BISHOP: Tyrone ain't tell that man he black!

TYRONE: I ain't gotta tell him!

BISHOP: What you think he gonna do when he see you walk through that door? What he gonna say when he find out your name Tyrone?

TYRONE: I don't care what he say as long as I get me a chance to do something! He see how good I am, he gonna forget my name Tyrone and let me stay on! Full-time, maybe!

BISHOP: You got a hard head, boy, but you gonna learn.

TYRONE: Why you won't let me do nothing? Why you always . . .

BISHOP: You go on down there and see! I'm tired of telling you! You go down there and you see for yourself!

[*He exits through the double doors and is seen through the upstage window taking a bag of fertilizer into the garden.*]

TYRONE: What he getting mad at me for? He ought to be glad I'm working!

HENRY: He just looking out for you, son. Just like he promised your mama, he just trying to look out for you.

TYRONE [*cleaning the grill*]: I don't care what he promised my mama. I'm gonna leave here soon as I start my job. Save up enough money to where I can't see the top of it and I'm gone. I'm tired of cleaning this old grill.

HENRY: You got someplace you can go?

TYRONE: I'm gonna get me something. Everything the world owe me I'm gonna take back.

HENRY: What the world owe you, youngblood?

TYRONE: The world owe me twenty years!

HENRY: Boy, you standing there barely filling your britches. Now how the world gonna owe you twenty years when you ain't even seen twenty years?

TYRONE: Then how come I feel like I'm thirtysomething? That ain't right, Mr. Henry. I ain't even twenty years old and I feel like I done lived already. Between Mr. Bishop hollerin' at me and everything else, I'm gonna rot solid for trying to make it. Now, you know that ain't right.

HENRY: Boy, there ain't nothing wrong with that. That's what black is. We the first people. That make us the oldest. Hell, you come out of the womb on borrowed time. You carrying around the years your mama gave you, your daddy gave you, your great-grandpappy, your great-great-grandmammy . . .

TYRONE: Then why everybody adding onto it? What give them that right? I feel like I'm running out of time and time ain't even started for me yet.

HENRY: That's how it is for colored folks. What you got is regular growing pains.

TYRONE: What I got is this black skin and that's making me old. I bet Bobbilee feel old too and he one year younger than me. And what I got these big old hands for? What I'm gonna do with that? I don't wanna lift nothing. I wanna be able to think things through. All I do is lift sacks of fertilizer.

HENRY: Boy, you know where them hands come from? Them hands come all the way from Africa. Them your ancestor's hands. They used those hands to create life. To shape and mold Mother Nature. Those hands could cut diamonds. Crush gold into copper. Take the ocean by the neck and squeeze pearls out of her. The African king could raise that hand and put jungles to sleep.

[*He grabs* TYRONE's *hand.*]

Your people built pyramids and tombs with these hands. Boy, you don't know what you got there, do you?

TYRONE [*pulling his hand away*]: Mr. Henry, those days are gone. Don't nobody build pyramids no more. People figuring stuff out with their heads now, but I'm stuck with these big old hands. Feet big, too.

[*He grabs the football.*]

I guess that's for football and jumping.

HENRY [*grabbing the football, offended*]: My boy got a scholarship to run this football. Now he breaking records setting new grounds for everybody else to reach up to. If it takes you running a football to use your head, then you do that. But don't you dare knock it.

[*He replaces the football.*]

TYRONE: Can't use my head if all I do is clean the grill.

HENRY: Yeah . . . I can see where they got your number.

[BOBBILEE *enters through the front door, singing and dancing.*]

BOBBILEE: "Papa don't take no mess! C'mon now! Papa don't, Papa don't, Papa don't! Papa don't take no mess!"

TYRONE: Bobbilee!

BOBBILEE: "Say it loud! I'm black and I'm proud!"

HENRY: Look at youngblood cuttin' the rug!

TYRONE: Man, I thought you got thirty days. When they let you out?

BOBBILEE: Just got out about thirty minutes ago. Hey, Mr. Henry!

HENRY: You go by and see your mama?

BOBBILEE: She say hey to everybody.

[*He stops dancing.*]

Whoa . . . what's that smell?

HENRY: Oh, that's that shit Bishop got in the back!

TYRONE: Mr. Bishop growing a garden. Got fertilizer, tools, and everything.

BOBBILEE: Smells like dirty work to me.

[*He removes a sheet of paper from his pocket.*]

Hey, Mr. Henry, take a look at that!

HENRY: What you got me reading here, boy?

BOBBILEE: Lyrics! That's a song I was working on in the pen.

TYRONE: You singing now?

BOBBILEE: I ain't just singing. I'm writing songs for the Godfather.

HENRY: You doing what?

BOBBILEE: That's who they had me in jail with.

TYRONE: You was in jail with James Brown?

BOBBILEE: Nah, I was in jail with C70517. That's what they do, Mr. Henry.

They give you them numbers and a bar of soap. Tell you not to bend over in the shower and to forget about the life you had out there and try to hold on to the one you got in here.

[*He points to his head.*]

HENRY: Boy, you ain't telling me nothing. They got numbers for all of us.

TYRONE: How you gonna be in jail with James Brown when he locked up in Georgia and you here in South Carolina?

BOBBILEE [*crossing behind the counter for a soda*]: 'Cause he in South Carolina, too.

HENRY: Yeah? Where 'bout?

BOBBILEE: State Park Correctional Facility in Columbia.

TYRONE: That's still two hours away from where you at. How you see him?

BOBBILEE: That's 'cause they took us over there. Stayed over there three days while they tried to figure out whether or not they was gonna keep me in jail. You just have to sit there in jail, Mr. Henry, and wait until they decide what they gonna do with you. Then they try to scare you by letting them Columbia pigs beat you around and make faces at you. Hell, the bus ride over was worse than the stay. Yeah, I was over there three days before the riot broke out and they brought us back over here.

HENRY: Riot?

BOBBILEE: Yeah, I told everybody James Brown was from South Carolina and everybody in there from Georgia got mad.

HENRY: James Brown tell you he from South Carolina?

BOBBILEE: Nah, I just wanted to see everybody fight.

TYRONE: Three days with the Soul Man. Man, I ought to kiss you!

BOBBILEE [*pushing* TYRONE *away*]: Hey! I saw enough of that in prison. Men kissing on each other. Talking all soft like they can't see that neither one of them a woman. Made me sick. One of them Georgia men standing there with a razor blade asked me to do something for him.

TYRONE: Ask you to do what for him?

BOBBILEE: He say, "Get down on your knees and lick my balls." Told me if I didn't do it, he'd cut my tongue out and do it hisself.

TYRONE: You do it?

BOBBILEE: Hell no I ain't do it! I got down on my knees, grabbed his balls, and twisted them right out the sack!

[HENRY *and* TYRONE *grimace.*]

He laying there bleeding and crying like a baby. Grown man like that screaming for his mama, but he can't get it out. It took a lot for me to do that. But I figured that was the only way I was gonna get out of there with my tongue 'cause there was no way in hell I was gonna lick his nuts. I tell you what though, ain't nobody else gonna be licking his nuts, either.

[BOBBILEE *laughs as* TYRONE *and* HENRY *stare at him with a hint of repulsion. In midlaughter,* BOBBILEE *holds out his hand to* TYRONE *for a high five.* TYRONE *ignores it and stares at* BOBBILEE.]

TYRONE: That didn't scare you?

BOBBILEE: Man, prison ain't nothing to be scared of. You go there to be a man. That's all it do. Shape you up into a man so when you get out, there ain't nothing in the world you can't get past. You done seen everything. Ain't that right, Mr. Henry?

HENRY: Depends on what kinda man you wanna be.

BOBBILEE: You know, Mr. Henry, I didn't believe you the first time when you was telling me about them numbers. But when I got locked up and they put us in those lines and started herding us around like sheep, I said Mr. Henry was right. I'd be walking around that courtyard and all I see is numbers and black people. Did you know that's all that's in there? Black people? Mexicans, too. Everybody got them numbers planted across their chest and they all blind, too. I mean, they can see, but they walking around like they can't. Some of them just be looking into space at nothing. Walking around in circles until one of them sheepherders come by and hit them in the right direction. Some of them got their eyes open, but you can't look at them. You try to look into their eyes and it feel like they trying to suck the life out of you. Like they ain't got no life of their own.

HENRY: Once they got your number that opens you up. They can reach inside you and take your spirit.

BOBBILEE: That's why me and the Godfather writing this song. We ain't finished it, but I know where to go with it. Soon as the Godfather get out we going on tour!

TYRONE: You going on tour with the Soul Man?

BOBBILEE: Soon as he get out!

HENRY: What this song called?

BOBBILEE: "Sleepwalking"! The Godfather told me black folks in prison ain't doing nothing but sleepwalking. They walking around in their sleep like zombies. They get out, they go back, 'cause all they know to do is sleep. The brothers that ain't been to jail yet on their way 'cause half of them sleepwalking, too.

HENRY: Sleep the only time we get a break.

BOBBILEE [*playing a drumbeat on a stool*]: But me and the Godfather gonna wake everybody up!

[*He holds up* HENRY's *newspaper.*]

Me and him gonna wake up the whole nation! Check out this new step we been working on!

[*He points to* TYRONE *as he sings and crosses to center stage.*]

"Baby, baby, baaaaby! Baby, baby, baaaaby!"

[BOBBILEE *kneels to the floor.* TYRONE *takes off his apron and drapes it around* BOBBILEE's *shoulders.* BOBBILEE *suddenly jumps to his feet and performs his new step.*]

"I got that feeling! Ugh, baby, baaaby, I got that feeling! Owww!"

[*He spins, stops, then points to* TYRONE *and* HENRY.]

You black?

TYRONE AND HENRY: Yeah . . . I'm . . . I'm black.

BOBBILEE: Nah, man! You black?

TYRONE AND HENRY: Yeah . . . yeah . . . sure, we black.

BOBBILEE: Nah, nah! Say it like you mean it! [*To* TYRONE] You black?

TYRONE: I'm black!

BOBBILEE [*to* HENRY]: You black?

HENRY: I'm black!

BOBBILEE: Then say it loud!

TYRONE AND HENRY: I'm black and I'm proud!

BOBBILEE: Nah, say it like you mean it! Say it loud!

TYRONE AND HENRY: I'm black and I'm proud!

[HENRY *bangs his cane on the floor. They all sing and dance.* BISHOP *enters from the back.* HENRY *stops banging his cane.* TYRONE *stops.* BOBBILEE *spins and notices* BISHOP.]

BOBBILEE: How you doing, Mr. Bishop?

BISHOP: You making all that noise in my shop?

TYRONE: They just let him out.

BISHOP: What you doing here? Shouldn't you be with your mama?

TYRONE: He came by to see us.

BOBBILEE: My mama said hey to everybody.

[BISHOP *goes to the phone and dials.*]

BISHOP: Hello, Pattie? This Bishop over here at the shop.

[*Pause.*]

I'm well. How you?

[*Pause.*]

That's good. Listen, Pattie . . . how much time they give little Bobbilee? When the last time you seen him?

[BOBBILEE *sneaks and hangs up the phone.*]

Where's your papers, boy?
BOBBILEE: What papers?
BISHOP: Your release forms.
HENRY: Bishop.
BOBBILEE: I ain't got them.
BISHOP: You get out of here.
HENRY: C'mon now, Bishop.
BISHOP: The boy run away from jail, Henry!
HENRY: Now, you don't know that!
BISHOP: He ain't got no papers that say he free!
BOBBILEE: I don't need no papers! I ain't no slave!
BISHOP: Are you free?
HENRY: Now, damn it, Bishop!
BISHOP: The boy done run away from prison, now he done come up in here! I don't want that pressure on me! I'm fighting for my customers as it is! The last thing I need is some jailbird hiding out at my shop!
BOBBILEE: I ain't no jailbird!
BISHOP: Go on back to jail, boy!
BOBBILEE: That ain't where I'm supposed to be! Tell him, Mr. Henry! Tell him how they got our number! Tell him how they marking us up like sheep!
BISHOP: Get out of my shop with all that!
BOBBILEE: They want you to forget who you are! They put that number across your chest and you ain't you no more! All you got is those six numbers! They cut off your nuts and give you six numbers!
BISHOP [*starting for* BOBBILEE]: Boy, you get the hell out of my shop!

HENRY: Pull back, Bishop!

BOBBILEE: You been letting me come in here all this time now you wanna kick me out?

BISHOP: I don't want no jailbirds in here!

BOBBILEE [*sincerely*]: So what I went to jail? I ain't done nothing to you! I ain't hurt nobody in this shop and now you trying to hurt me?

[*Pause.*]

Man, you sleepwalking, Mr. Bishop! I see you ain't nobody! [*Exiting through the front door, shouting*] Free James Brown! Free James Brown! Free the Godfather . . .

[*Pause.*]

BISHOP: Boy come in here talking about numbers! Henry, you need to stop filling these young boys' heads up with all that voodoo crap. You got them all paranoid.

HENRY: I ain't have to tell that boy nothing. He figured it all out for himself.

[TYRONE *takes off his apron and starts to exit.*]

BISHOP: Where you going?

TYRONE: I'm gonna talk to Bobbilee.

BISHOP: Finish cleaning that grill.

TYRONE: I'm done with the grill.

HENRY: Let him go on, Bishop.

BISHOP: What? So he can get himself locked up, too?

TYRONE: Why you always bossing people around?

BISHOP: Boy, who feeding you?

TYRONE: That don't mean you can boss me around. Telling me I can't work. My daddy in New York City working for the state!

BISHOP: What that man ever do for you? You tell me what he do, huh?

HENRY: Let it go, Bishop!

BISHOP: Nah, Henry! I want this boy to tell me! He proclaiming about who his daddy is! I want him to tell me what he done for him!

TYRONE: Just 'cause you raised me don't make you nothing! J.P. my daddy and he working for the state of New York!

BISHOP: That man in prison, boy! He working for Long Island State Penitentiary!

HENRY: Pull back, Bishop! I said for you to pull back!

TYRONE: Nah, he ain't! He working law enforcement!

BISHOP: Yeah, he working law enforcement! The damn law enforcing him!

TYRONE: You lying!

BISHOP: Why the hell you think you ain't seen him? You got an address on him?

TYRONE: You ain't doing nothing but lying! You just mad 'cause J.P. my daddy and you ain't nothing!

BISHOP: Give him a call! You proclaiming about J.P.! You pick up that damn phone and you dial him up! Ask him where he been all your life! Ask him why you ain't seen him for the past thirteen years!

[TYRONE *stares at* BISHOP. *He then throws his apron to the floor and exits through the front door. Pause.*]

HENRY: You went too far this time, Bishop.

BISHOP: I raised that boy, Henry! I went through hell to see him through! Now he talking to me about J.P. like J.P. done something for him? Gonna stand up here and tell me I ain't nothing?

HENRY: Ain't no way you can blame him for that.

BISHOP: Every time he get around that badass Bobbilee he start acting up! I'm gonna have to put a stop to that!

HENRY: You can't stop that boy. Unless you planning on living in his back pocket, Tyrone's gonna see who he wanna see.

[*He grabs his leg in pain.*]

Ahhh, shit!

BISHOP: Man, go to that clinic!

HENRY: I done told you them people ain't cutting up on me! Now give me some gin!

BISHOP: I told you about my stash.

HENRY: I'm just asking for a nip.

BISHOP: Just 'cause you ask I'm supposed to give it to you?

HENRY: C'mon now, Bishop, my leg hurt.

BISHOP [*exploding*]: Then go to the damn clinic!

[*Pause.*]

HENRY: You want me to go to that damn clinic? That's what you want, Mr. Bishop? For them crackers to cut up on me? All right, I'm gonna give you and Martha both what y'all want!

[*He goes to the phone and dials.*]

This the damn clinic? Well, I need an appointment! I'm Henry Tisdale! I used to be Bishop's big brother, but he told me to come down here and let y'all cut me up! I'm gonna bring my leg down there and I want y'all to take it off! You hear that? I want an appointment to turn in my body parts! You take anything you want, you white bastards! Take my liver! Take my balls! Take my dick if you want that! Just give me my appointment, you sons of bitches! Give me my a-point-ment!

[*He hangs up the phone.*]

Now . . . Mr. Bishop . . . can I have the goddamn gin?

[*Pause.*]

BISHOP: You know where it's at.

[HENRY *and* BISHOP *stare at each other.* HENRY *exits into the back room.* BISHOP *picks up* TYRONE's *apron. He thinks, then exits through the front door. Suggested song: James Brown's "I'm Black and I'm Proud."*]

SCENE 3

[*Lights are dim to indicate a passage of time.* TYRONE *enters. He realizes the front door is locked. He uses his key and enters. He turns on light.*]

TYRONE: Mr. Bishop?

[*Pause.*]

Mr. Bishop?

[TYRONE *exits into the back room.* BOBBILEE *enters and taps at the front door.* TYRONE *reenters.*]

Who is it?
BOBBILEE [*from outside*]: It's me, Tyrone! Open up!

[TYRONE *opens the door.* BOBBILEE *enters.*]

What you doing, man?
TYRONE: Getting ready to go to bed. Why you ain't at home?
BOBBILEE: I'll go home in a minute. Where's Mr. Bishop?

TYRONE: I dunno.

BOBBILEE: He ain't here?

TYRONE: I don't know where he at.

[BOBBILEE *crosses into the kitchen.*]

What you doing?

BOBBILEE: Fixin' me a sandwich. Man, I'm hungrier than shit.

TYRONE: Your mama ain't fix you nothing?

BOBBILEE: Nah . . . she ain't fix me nothing.

[*He devours the sandwich as* TYRONE *looks on.*]

TYRONE: That true what you said about that man's balls?

BOBBILEE: This hand right here. Twisted them right off.

TYRONE: Man, I couldn't do that.

BOBBILEE: I guess you would've licked them.

TYRONE: Nah, I wouldn't have done that, either.

BOBBILEE [*getting a soda from the refrigerator*]: Then you better not ever go to prison.

TYRONE: Well, I gotta get outta here. Mr. Bishop getting on my nerves. You know he told me my daddy in prison?

BOBBILEE: Say what?

TYRONE: He say my daddy locked up in New York.

BOBBILEE: So.

TYRONE: So, I been thinking he been working for the state.

BOBBILEE: So.

TYRONE: What you mean so? My daddy in prison, Bobbilee.

BOBBILEE: So. Why you whining about it? Talking about you gotta go see him. You don't need no daddy. Hell, I ain't need my daddy for nothing just like he ain't need me.

TYRONE: I just thought he was working, that's all.

BOBBILEE: If he was working you still ain't heard from him, so what's the difference? Look here, Tyrone. There ain't no such thing as daddies. That's just something they made up 'cause we got mamas. The only reason we have daddies is 'cause we gotta do something they didn't do. My daddy got shot, now I can't do that. I gotta go out there and do something different. Something better than what he did.

TYRONE: Well, if my daddy in jail I ain't gonna do that. I'll go see him 'cause he gotta explain stuff to me, but I'm gonna be better than that.

BOBBILEE: You already got a job.

TYRONE: This ain't no job. I been doing this all my life. Mr. Bishop just decided to pay me for it and make it seem like a job, but that's just 'cause he thinking I'm gonna take over.

BOBBILEE: Take over what?

[TYRONE *picks up the phone and mimics* BISHOP.]

TYRONE: Fifteen thirty-one East River Street.

[BOBBILEE *laughs.*]

He think I'm gonna run this shop when he get old but I ain't gonna be here for that.

BOBBILEE: I don't like Mr. Bishop, either.

TYRONE: I didn't say I didn't like him.

BOBBILEE: Not right out, but you said it.

TYRONE: Mr. Bishop all right. I just wonder why he wait until now to tell me my daddy in jail.

BOBBILEE: 'Cause Mr. Henry got a son and Mr. Bishop don't. Old people get jealous like that. Mr. Bishop trying to claim you so he can feel good about who he is 'cause he done spent all this time raising you.

TYRONE: Well, he oughtta just go on and make a baby and leave me alone.

BOBBILEE: Tyrone, why I gotta explain everything to you? You older than me, you should be telling me stuff.

TYRONE: 'Cause all I see is this grill and sandwich meat all the time. You go out there and you come back with something new every day.

BOBBILEE: That's 'cause I'm living life and you stuck in this box. Prison done taught me. I done seen everything I need to see to live the rest of my life.

TYRONE: Yeah, but you done changed, Bobbilee.

BOBBILEE: What you mean I done changed?

TYRONE: I mean, you talking about prison and stuff. Me and you was raised together, but I don't know nothing about all that. You used to come in here all the time and Mr. Bishop wouldn't say nothing. That used to be our table right over there. We used to sit there and arm wrestle and see who could drink their soda the fastest. Now we don't even sit over there no more.

BOBBILEE: What that mean? You wanna arm wrestle?

TYRONE: Nah, I just want us back, man. What happened to us talking about what we was gonna do when we grow up? All you do now is get into trouble, but that ain't what we talked about. And man . . . I . . . I love you, Bobbilee, but I ain't gonna be able to keep loving you if you keep living the way you do 'cause Mr. Bishop say you dangerous.

BOBBILEE: Why he saying I'm dangerous? Because I know how to use my head and think for myself?

TYRONE: Nah, 'cause you keep getting into trouble.

BOBBILEE: Let me tell you something, Tyrone. You know I ain't got no daddy. We was arm wrestling right over there at that table when my mama called over here to tell Mr. Bishop to send me home 'cause something bad done happened. My mama, she just wants me to go to church all the time. Mr. Henry always talking about Lummie this and Lummie that. Ain't nobody listening to me and what I wanna do! Me and you talked about being free and making our own way, but you done let Mr. Bishop tie you up.

TYRONE: You went to jail, though, Bobbilee. I ain't like coming to see you in reform school, but you went to jail. What am I supposed to do?

BOBBILEE: Stick with me, man! Mr. Bishop ain't gonna do for you what me and you can do for each other. Him and Mr. Henry always hamboning and doing that old man stuff. That ain't for us. We gotta find our own way 'cause they ain't gonna give it to us.

TYRONE: They all I got, Bobbilee.

BOBBILEE: You got me.

TYRONE: Until they find out you done run away from prison.

BOBBILEE: I ain't run away!

[*Pause.* BOBBILEE *takes some papers from his pocket and hands them to* TYRONE.]

Them my release forms. I just gotta check in with my probation officer every week.

TYRONE: But they gave you thirty days.

BOBBILEE: Yeah, they gave me thirty days, but my probation officer talked them out of it. Said he'd take responsibility for me 'cause I had po-tential . . . or something.

TYRONE: Why you ain't show Mr. Bishop?

BOBBILEE: 'Cause Mr. Bishop can't hear me. He'd look at them papers and say it don't mean nothing 'cause I shouldn't have went to jail in the first place. I ain't got time for Mr. Bishop to be telling me I can't do nothing right. Soon as I get me some money I'm gonna show him what I can do.

TYRONE: What you gonna do?

BOBBILEE: I'm gonna get me a tape recorder. Finish my song. Soon as I get me some money. That way he know what I can do.

TYRONE: I dunno, Bobbilee. Things just ain't the same no more.

BOBBILEE: Look, I might be getting into trouble, Tyrone, 'cause I ain't figured everything out yet, but when you think I ain't the same Bobbilee who used to sit at that table, then you look at them papers. Then you think about who I am.

TYRONE: But this paper don't say you won't go back. The way you say you grabbed that man's balls and how you got into it with them white boys, I didn't expect all that. How I know you won't get into something else?

[*Awkward silence.* BOBBILEE *crosses to the refrigerator and gets two bottles of soda. He crosses to "their" table and sits. He waits for* TYRONE, *who finally sits across from him.* BOBBILEE *holds up the two bottles.*]

BOBBILEE: You beat me, then you right about everything you say about me. But if I beat you, then you gotta back me up like you used to. You gotta believe I ain't going back to jail for doing nothing bad and that if I do go back it's 'cause I chose to think for myself. And if you can't roll with me on that, then we ain't supposed to sit at this table together.

[TYRONE *takes a bottle.* BOBBILEE *grabs the other. They perform a brief ritual of preparing for competition and with a nod of agreement they drink. However,* BOBBILEE *watches* TYRONE *struggle for a moment. He then turns his drink up and with ease finishes before* TYRONE, *who continues to struggle.* TYRONE *finally slams his bottle on the table and falls to the floor in agony.*]

TYRONE: You finish?

BOBBILEE: You finish?

[*They laugh and burp.* BISHOP *enters. He stares at the two as they gather themselves.*]

BISHOP: I been looking for you all night.

TYRONE: I just got back.

BOBBILEE: See you later, Tyrone.

[BOBBILEE *exits and stands outside the front door, eavesdropping.*]

BISHOP: I told you I don't want you hanging around Bobbilee.

TYRONE: Bobbilee my friend. He ain't done nothing wrong.

BISHOP: Bobbilee don't have to do wrong to be wrong. He set himself up for that. You keep hanging with that boy you gonna run into something I ain't gonna be able to get you out of.

[TYRONE *hands* BISHOP BOBBILEE'*s release forms.*]

What's this?

TYRONE: Bobbilee's release forms.

[BISHOP *reads, then hands the papers back to* TYRONE.]

BISHOP: Yeah, well . . . he shouldn't have went in the first place.

[BISHOP *starts to exit into his bedroom. His feelings hurt,* BOBBILEE *kicks the door in frustration.* BISHOP *and* TYRONE *turn to the door.*]

SCENE 4

[*The following morning. The radio is playing.* BISHOP *enters from the back room and turns the radio dial to gospel music (suggest Mahalia Jackson). He takes a moment to enjoy the tune before putting on an apron.* TYRONE *enters, unnoticed. He puts on a jacket and ball cap and heads for the front door. He then stops.*]

TYRONE: Hey, Mr. Bishop?

[BISHOP *is still caught up in the song.*]

Mr. Bishop.

BISHOP: Yeah, boy, what is it?

TYRONE: I'm going out.

BISHOP: Where you going?

[TYRONE *hesitates to respond.*]

Tyrone?

TYRONE: I gotta get some clothes for work.

BISHOP: Well . . . go on.

TYRONE: You told me to let you know if . . .

BISHOP: I know what I told you.

[TYRONE *does not move.*]

Go on.

[TYRONE *exits.* BISHOP *returns to the song and opening up the diner.* HARRISON *enters through the front door. Pause.*]

HARRISON: Thought I'd try some more of that coffee. Would get some up the street but they had a sign say be back in twenty minutes. You only have

about five minutes before you lose your taste for something and they ain't
gonna be back for twenty.

BISHOP [*eyeing* HARRISON *for a moment*]: Come on in. Have a seat. It's gonna
take a minute to heat it up. If you can wait that long. I gotta get me a new
pot. You want something to eat?

HARRISON: No, thank you.

[*The phone rings.* BISHOP *answers it as he turns on the coffeepot.* HARRISON *mills
about the diner.*]

BISHOP: Fifteen thirty-one East River . . . Oh hey, Martha, how you doing?
No, I ain't seen Henry this morning. Not since last night.

[*Pause.*]

Hold on, I'll check.

[*He goes to the door to the back room.*]

Henry! Henry, you back there?

[*He returns to the phone.*]

I didn't get no answer. If I hear from him I'll give you a call . . .

[HENRY *enters from the back room. It is obvious he has been drinking.*]

HENRY: What's wrong with you, hambone?

BISHOP: Hold on, Martha.

HENRY: Fix me some coffee, Bishop.

BISHOP: You been in my stash?

HENRY: No, I ain't been in your stash.

[*He is startled as he notices* HARRISON.]

What the hell that white man doing here?

BISHOP: Look, man, your wife on the phone. Now I suggest you pull yourself
together and get over here and talk to her. She been looking for you all night.

HENRY: No cream. [*To* HARRISON] I don't want no damn cream in my coffee.

[*He crosses to the phone.*]

Hey, baby . . . no, I ain't been drinking!

BISHOP: You want cream and sugar in your coffee?

[HARRISON *signals no.*]

HENRY: Woman, I told you I ain't been drinking nothing!

HARRISON: Not too many people come around this place.

HENRY: Martha, I'm coming home. I gotta help Bishop here at the shop!

[*Pause.*]

What you talking about he don't need no help? There thirty people waiting in line to get their food right now!

[*He bangs the dishes and beats the phone on the counter.*]

Hey, y'all, stop all that pushing! We ain't got no insurance coverage in here! You get your food in a minute! [*Into the phone*] Ah, baby, don't you hear that? People can't wait to eat! They all pushing and carrying on!

[HARRISON *sits at the counter.* BISHOP *sets a sandwich in front of him.*]

BISHOP: Try that. Let me know what you think.

HENRY: Martha, I'll spend time with you tomorrow! I . . . woman, I said . . . that was last week! I spent all night with you the other night!

[*Pause.*]

If you'd just . . .

[*Pause.*]

She hung up on me.

BISHOP [*laughing*]: You know you ain't supposed to be drinking nohow.

HENRY: Thirty years was all it took to get that woman to hang up on me.

HARRISON: You give a woman what she wants, you won't have any trouble.

HENRY [*glaring at* HARRISON]: Is that right?

[*Pause.*]

What you know about it, Mr. Railroad Man?

BISHOP: Henry, go on back there to the back and get yourself cleaned up!

[*Pause.*]

HENRY: I want my coffee black! You hear that, Mr. Railroad Man? Black!

[*He shows off his hand to* HARRISON.]

Like the hands of Africa!

[*He exits into the back room.*]

BISHOP: I don't know what's wrong with people. Man body falling apart and he speeding up the process with all that drinking.

HARRISON: Must have a demon.

BISHOP: A what?

HARRISON: Some folks get demons in their lives and they can't move on. Maybe he's drinking to kill those demons.

BISHOP: I don't know if he got demons. He lost the use of that leg playing football. If he got a demon, I guess that's it 'cause that's when he started drinking.

[*Pause.*]

You sure you ain't the law? My partner said he seen you wandering around the Earl Homes the other day. Not a place you'd wanna be if you ain't the law.

[*Pause.*]

HARRISON: You from Anderson County?

BISHOP: By way of Georgia.

HARRISON: By way of Georgia?

[*Pause.*]

I think I would've stayed in Georgia.

BISHOP: Wasn't nothing to stay in Georgia for. I got my shop. All my business here.

HARRISON: How long you been in Anderson County?

BISHOP [*suspiciously*]: Not long.

HARRISON: You ever think about going back to Georgia?

BISHOP: About as much as Negroes think about going back to slavery.

HARRISON: Something back there keeping you in Anderson County?

[BISHOP *simply stares at* HARRISON. *After a moment,* HENRY *reenters from the back room, tucking in his shirt and wiping his face with a towel.*]

HENRY: Uh . . . Bishop . . . look . . . I sat that shit outside. Now . . . if you wanna go out there and bring it back in here that's up to you. But I can't breathe with that shit clogging up the air. All hot and sticky.

BISHOP: You leave my fertilizer where I put it. Drink that coffee. Get that monkey off your back.

HENRY [*getting a beer from the refrigerator*]: I don't want none of that cold coffee.

HARRISON: Actually, it's pretty hot.

HENRY [*mockingly*]: "Actually, it's pretty hot." You hear that, Bishop? Railroad Man here says he likes your cold coffee. [*Laughs.*] What's your name, Railroad Man? You walking around here in black neighborhoods. What's your name?

HARRISON [*offering* HENRY *his hand*]: Harrison.

[BISHOP *looks at* HARRISON. HENRY *does not shake* HARRISON'*s hand.*]

HENRY: Well . . . I'm Henry. Henry Tisdale. That there is my partner, Bishop. He a Tisdale, too. By way of butcher knife.

[*He shows off his thumb, then looks to* BISHOP.]

Show this man your thumb, Bishop.

[BISHOP *unwillingly holds up his thumb.*]

HARRISON: Blood brothers.

HENRY: Till the gates of heaven open up!

[*He presses his thumb against* BISHOP'*s.*]

Now, me and my brother don't like you hunting around here for Bobbilee. Bobbilee ain't done nothing to nobody . . .

BISHOP: Henry . . .

HENRY: Bobbilee a good boy . . . he ain't done nothing wrong . . .

BISHOP: Henry . . .

HENRY: He don't belong in that place! That place for criminals! Bobbilee ain't no criminal . . .

BISHOP: Henry, the man ain't looking for Bobbilee!

HENRY: Well, who in the hell he looking for then? He probably looking for body parts!

[HARRISON *suddenly grabs his side and moans in pain.* BISHOP *and* HENRY *stare at him. After a moment,* BISHOP *speaks.*]

BISHOP: You all right?

HARRISON [*in obvious pain*]: Yeah . . . yeah, I'm all right.

[HARRISON *takes a moment to breathe through the pain as* BISHOP *and* HENRY *look on. The pain ceases.* HARRISON *sighs in relief, then turns to* BISHOP *and* HENRY.]

I'm a diabetic. Diagnosed about a year ago. I lost my kidney . . . It won't be long before I lose the other one.

HENRY: See? See, what I tell you, Bishop? They after the body parts! They probably gonna experiment on poor little Bobbilee!

BISHOP: Henry, please! Sit your drunk ass down!

[HENRY *unwillingly sits.* BISHOP *turns to* HARRISON.]

What happens if you lose the other one?

HARRISON: They got a machine waiting for me. I'll live my life tied to that for as long as I can live it.

HENRY: What makes him think Bobbilee gonna give him his body parts?

BISHOP: Henry, goddamn it, the man ain't looking for Bobbilee!

HENRY: Well, whoever in the hell he looking for! What make him think he gonna get the man's kidney? He might have something he wanna do with them!

BISHOP: Then let that man deal with that!

HENRY: I ain't giving up my kidneys for nobody.

BISHOP: Ain't nobody asked you to give up your kidneys!

HENRY: I'm just saying I ain't giving up my body parts. Ask the man down the street for his, don't come to me. When I die I'm taking everything with me.

BISHOP: You gonna be laying there dead, Henry. They cut you open there ain't nothing you gonna be able to do about it.

[BOBBILEE *is seen outside the shop looking in.*]

HENRY: You wrong there, Bishop. Railroad Man here knows you ain't supposed to mess with the spirit. They teach that in them white churches, too. Ain't that right, Railroad Man?

HARRISON: I'd imagine if you're dead it wouldn't make much difference.

HENRY: How you know? You been dead before?

HARRISON: Reincarnation.

HENRY: See? See . . . now you being a racist! That's some kinda overseas thinking! Them people over in Europe done brought that kinda thinking over here. Black people don't believe in that! Elvis dead! You hear that, Railroad Man! That fat bastard's dead!

[HENRY *notices* BOBBILEE *peeping through the front door window. He waves for* BOBBILEE *to come in.* BOBBILEE *enters.*]

Bobbilee, come here! Come on in here, youngblood!

[HENRY *puts his arm around* BOBBILEE'S *shoulder.*]

Did you see Nat Turner out there when you come in?

[BOBBILEE *shakes his head.*]

How about Harriet Tubman? Martin Luther "the" King?

[BOBBILEE *shakes his head again.*]

You sure?

[BOBBILEE *nods.*]

You see that, Mr. Racist? Black folks don't believe in that shit! Dead people die where we come from! They ain't walking around shopping in stores, pumping gas at the Texaco stations, 'cause they dead! We might get the holy ghost, but we ain't partying with them! You best believe that, Railroad Man! 'Cause when they dead . . . they gone . . . deceased . . .

[HENRY *bangs his cane on the floor and falls.* BOBBILEE *tries to help him up, but* HENRY *pushes him away. Embarrassed,* HENRY *exits into the bathroom.* BISHOP *looks to* BOBBILEE.]

BISHOP: What I tell you about coming into my shop?
BOBBILEE: Where Tyrone?
BISHOP: Tyrone ain't here.
BOBBILEE: Well, then I'll wait for him.
BISHOP: You ain't waiting in here.
BOBBILEE: You can't kick me out. I got money to buy something.
BISHOP: Where you get money? You ain't been seeing your mama.

[*Pause.*]

BOBBILEE: I cut grass. Five dollars a yard.
HENRY [*reentering*]: I'm so damn mad I can't even piss!
BISHOP: Well, I don't want your money. You take your money someplace else.
BOBBILEE: I ain't gotta. The law say I can take my money wherever I want.
HENRY [*sitting*]: Fix the boy a sandwich, Bishop. You see he hungry.
BISHOP [*crossing to* BOBBILEE]: Bobbilee? I ain't got nothing against you, but I got Tyrone to tend to. You run them streets and do all you want, but I'll be damned if I'm gonna let you mess up that boy's life. [*To* HENRY] He got five minutes, Henry . . . and he's on your time.

[BISHOP *prepares a sandwich.* BOBBILEE *stares at* HARRISON *as he crosses to sit with* HENRY.]

BOBBILEE: Hey, Mr. Henry? You here about the prophecy?

HENRY: What prophecy?

BOBBILEE: We ain't gonna be around much longer. They trying to wipe us out.

HENRY: Who?

BOBBILEE [*continuing to stare at* HARRISON]: White people.

[HENRY *looks at* HARRISON, *then turns back to* BOBBILEE.]

HENRY: Who they trying to wipe out?

BOBBILEE: Us. You and me. Everybody black. See, I figured it out while I was in prison. Me and this blind man named Willy. Blind Man Willy the only sleep-walker in prison that ain't sleeping. I mean, he see things people can't see who got two good eyes. We came up with 2301.

HENRY: Twenty-three hundred and one what?

BOBBILEE: Future time. That's the year there ain't gonna be no more black people.

HENRY: Wait a minute, now. How they gonna wipe out a whole race of people? We making more babies than anybody. It take a thousand years to do something like that.

BOBBILEE: A thousand years done passed already. They could be in the middle of the process and we don't even know it!

HENRY: Damn boy, I think you done tapped into something. They started this process a long time ago. They started when Lincoln signed the Emancipation Proclamation. He said we was free . . . [*Looking at* HARRISON] White folks started wiping us out.

[BISHOP *drops the sandwich and the bill on the table in front of* BOBBILEE.]

BOBBILEE: What you gonna do, Mr. Bishop, when they lock you up? What my friend Tyrone gonna do if you ain't here to help him make these sandwiches? They lock you up you ain't gonna have no job and when they do let you out you ain't gonna be able to vote. So, you still ain't nobody! I ain't got what it takes to be no doctor or no lawyer! So, why they taking away from what little I got? I gotta do what I feel gonna make me into something! You making these sandwiches 'cause that make you feel good, but what if you ain't have that? What if they take away your citizenship?

HENRY: You hear him, Bishop? That damn Confederate flag tell you the boy done tapped into something. That damn flag been flying over Columbia telling us we don't belong here for over a hundred years.

BOBBILEE [*looking at* HARRISON]: The only way we gonna feel like we somebody is if we behind bars somewhere!

HENRY: Once they lock you up, that throws everything else off! Boy ain't got no daddy, woman ain't got no man, mama ain't got no son! Hell, man, we operate on a family basis! The process tearing up the family!

HARRISON: Washroom?

[*They suddenly look at* HARRISON. *Pause as they stare at him.* BISHOP *points.* HARRISON *exits into the bathroom. They all watch him as he exits.*]

BOBBILEE: That's why the police all the time come around here and not up there on the North Side! They know we gotta break the rules to get by sometimes.

BISHOP: Them boys stop selling them drugs, the police wouldn't come around here! We got old people around here!

HENRY: Ah, man, white folks selling drugs, too. They just got a different technique to how they sell it.

BISHOP: There ain't no technique to selling drugs! Selling drugs ain't no craft!

HENRY: White folks got that "in-house" technique. Black folks got that "outhouse" technique. That's where we messing up. We put all our business out there in the streets for everybody else to see. See, white folks write shit down, we always talking about it. And because we come from an oral tradition, we don't know how to shut the hell up. Just be talking and talking until we talk ourselves into a bad situation.

BOBBILEE: You wait and see what happens, Mr. Bishop. Twenty-three hundred and one come around, things gonna change for black people.

BISHOP: Now, how am I gonna wait and see what happens? That's over three hundred years from now. I ain't gonna be around to see none of that.

BOBBILEE: That's because they wiping us out!

HARRISON [*reentering from bathroom*]: You're out of towels.

[HARRISON *stands with his hands wet.* BISHOP *exits into the back room.* HARRISON *sits at the counter.* BOBBILEE *crosses to* HARRISON.]

BOBBILEE: Where you from?

HARRISON: Charleston.

BOBBILEE: Charleston where?

HARRISON [*obviously*]: South Carolina.

BOBBILEE: They got prisons in Charleston?

HARRISON: Sure, we have prisons in Charleston.

BOBBILEE: Ain't no white people in there?

HARRISON: Well, I try to stay on the other side of the fence, son, but I'd imagine there're some.

BOBBILEE: You ain't hear about the prophecy?

HARRISON: Can't say that I have.

[BISHOP *reenters from the back room with a roll of paper towels. He hands* HARRISON *a piece, then exits into the bathroom.* BOBBILEE *watches.*]

BOBBILEE: You trying to wipe me out, mister?

HARRISON: Son, I'm just a little old railroad man. I don't have enough life in me to wipe out anyone.

BOBBILEE: Why you trying to wipe me out, mister?

HARRISON: I'm sorry, son, but I don't know anything about this prophecy.

BOBBILEE [*approaching* HARRISON]: Blindman Willie say you know! I say you know, too!

HENRY [*standing*]: Bobbilee?

BOBBILEE: I ain't done nothing to you! Why I can't grow up and have babies, too? Why you gotta look at me funny all the time? Say, mister?

HENRY: C'mon now, Bobbilee . . .

BOBBILEE [*backing* HARRISON *into a corner*]: You ain't gonna wipe me out! I'm writing my song with the Godfather!

[BISHOP *reenters and pulls* BOBBILEE *away, throwing him to the floor.* TYRONE *enters through the front door carrying a shopping bag.* BOBBILEE *gets up.*]

Time to wake up, Mr. Bishop! Time to wake up the whole nation!

[BISHOP *grabs* BOBBILEE *and forces him out the front door.*]

TYRONE: Why you kick Bobbilee out?

[BISHOP *ignores him.*]

I said why you kick Bobbilee out?

BISHOP: How much money you got in your pocket?

TYRONE: Why?

BISHOP: You get you a hundred and fifty dollars, start paying half the mortgage, then you can ask me why I kicked Bobbilee out!

[*Angered,* TYRONE *exits into the back room.*]

You all right?

HARRISON: Oh, that doesn't bother me. I'm a white man from Charleston. That doesn't bother me at all.

[*He takes out his wallet.*]

What I owe you for the sandwich?
BISHOP: Consider it on the house.

[HENRY *bangs his cane on the floor.* BISHOP *looks to* HENRY.]

Next one's full price.
HARRISON: Thanks for the hospitality.

[HARRISON *offers* BISHOP *his hand. They shake hands. The moment is awkward and long. Lights shift as the sound of a roaring train passing by is heard that seems to affect only* BISHOP. *He tries to pull away from* HARRISON'S *tight grip. Finally,* HARRISON *releases* BISHOP'S *hand.*]

HENRY: Mmmm uhhh. Yeah, I'm gonna have to tell Ms. Francis about this.

[HARRISON *exits. The foot stomping, hand rhythms, and humming sounds are heard in the distance as* BISHOP *grabs his forehead.* HENRY *takes powder from his pocket and sprinkles it throughout the shop.*]

Shoo, devil! Shoo! Get on off from around here!

[BISHOP *massages his temples as he finds a place to sit.*]

Bishop, you all right?

[BISHOP *does not respond.*]

Bishop?

[BISHOP *finally looks to* HENRY. *The chanting stops.*]

BISHOP: Henry?

[*Pause.*]

I ain't never asked you to leave this shop before. I know you put your work into it, too. But as my brother ... and as my partner ... I'm asking you right now ... to just go home.
HENRY: Man, if you wanna talk ...
BISHOP: Henry, please.

[*Pause.*]

Go home.

[*After a moment,* HENRY *gets his hat. Though his feelings are hurt, he honors* BISHOP'*s request and exits through the front door.* BISHOP *turns the sign around to* WE'RE

CLOSED. *He heads for the back room when he hears a voice faintly chanting, "Choo-choo-chugalug, train ride high. Choo-choo-chugalug, train never die." The sound of a roaring train quickly whistles by.* BISHOP *suddenly looks up as if to see the passing train.* TYRONE *enters from the back room. He looks to* BISHOP. *After a moment,* TYRONE *speaks.*]

TYRONE: You hear that?

[*Suggested song: "I Feel Good" by James Brown. Blackout.*]

ACT 2

SCENE 1

[*Late evening.* HENRY *enters from the back room carrying a jar. He goes to the refrigerator and gets a carton of milk, a spoon, a cup, a knife, and a lemon. The phone rings. He answers it.*]

HENRY: Who this?

[*Pause.*]

   Who?

[*Pause.*]

   Who? Hold on a minute. [*Away from the phone*] Y'all stop all that pushing! [*Into the phone*] Martha?

[*He bangs the phone on the counter.*]

   I said stop all that pushing! Y'all gonna eat! [*Into the phone*] Martha, what you want? We are really really busy.

[BISHOP *enters from the back room. He gets a cup from the kitchen and takes aspirin.*]

   I'm coming home!

[*Pause.*]

   I need something to drink, but I ain't had nothing! [*Pleadingly*] I'll be there in a minute, OK?

[*Pause.*]

   Martha . . . Martha . . . one minute.

[*He hangs up the phone.*]

   Had to hang up on her before she hung up on me. I don't appreciate that kinda acting.
BISHOP: Tyrone back yet?
HENRY: Nah, he ain't back yet.
BISHOP: He ain't call?
HENRY [*pouring milk into the cup*]: Nah, he ain't call.

BISHOP: He should've called he was gonna be working late.

[*Pause. He notices* HENRY.]

What you doing with my milk?

HENRY: I gotta take my medicine.

BISHOP: What kinda medicine you gotta take with milk?

[*The phone rings.*]

HENRY: If that's Martha, you tell her I ain't here.

BISHOP: She already know you here.

HENRY: Just tell her I walked out!

BISHOP: My head hurting, Henry.

HENRY: Well, tell Martha I ain't here then go lay back down. I'm watching the
  shop.

BISHOP: I ain't lying for you.

HENRY: Ah c'mon, Bishop. Tell her I'm down to Ms. Francis or something.

[BISHOP *answers the phone.*]

BISHOP: Fifteen thirty-one East River Street.

[*Pause.*]

Who?

[*Pause.*]

Nah, ain't nobody by that name here.

HENRY: Who they asking for?

BISHOP: I don't care what number you got, ain't nobody here by that name!

[*He hangs up the phone.*]

HENRY: That somebody for Tyrone?

BISHOP: I don't believe in what that boy's doing, Henry, but he proved his
  point. I can't even count how many people done called here asking for Timothy Snyder.

HENRY: The boy know how it is. Him and Bobbilee both know what's going on.

BISHOP: Ah, don't you start, Henry.

[HENRY *carefully pours the contents of the jar into the cup.*]

Man, what are you mixing in my cup?

HENRY: My medicine!

BISHOP: You been to that clinic?

HENRY: I told you I was going to see Ms. Francis. She gimme this juice for five dollars.

BISHOP: I don't want none of that cat blood in my cup.

HENRY: Why you always talking about some cat blood? Somebody say something about some natural treatment and all you know to talk about is cat blood!

BISHOP: What natural treatment you talking about? Ms. Francis into voodoo. Everybody but you know what that woman about.

HENRY: Well, this ain't no cat blood!

[*He observes the cup like a scientist.*]

Possum extract don't look nothing like cat blood. Possum extract got a green tint to it.

BISHOP: Possum what?

HENRY: Extract, nigga! Extract!

BISHOP: Get that shit out of my shop!

HENRY: This for my thigh, Bishop! Ms. Francis say this relax that pain out of my thigh! Now go on and let me do what I gotta do!

BISHOP: Don't you spill none of that mess on my counter! I'm liable to come in here and find shit growing! Shit I ain't even planted yet!

[HENRY *stirs the drink with the spoon, then drinks as* BISHOP *looks on. The mix is extremely potent.*]

You are one nasty Negro.

[HENRY *slams the cup on the table, cuts the lemon in half, sucks on it, then takes a deep breath and shakes it off.*]

HENRY: Wheew! You ought to try some of this. Test your nuts. See if you a real Bishop.

[*Pause.*]

That white man come by here looking for you.

BISHOP: What you tell him?

HENRY: Told him you was in Mississippi on vacation.

BISHOP: He say what he wanted?

HENRY: Say he wanted to talk to you.

[*Pause.* HENRY *stares at* BISHOP.]

BISHOP: What, Henry?

HENRY: I wanna know what's going on, Bishop. That white man come by here grabbing his side talking about he wanna talk to you. I wanna know what he wanna talk to you about.

BISHOP: I don't know, Henry. Go track the man down if you wanna know what he wanna talk about.

HENRY: I think he got your number figured out.

BISHOP: I told you about them numbers.

HENRY: I just don't like how he look at you. The way y'all was holding hands didn't . . . feel right.

[HENRY *almost spills the juice as he tries to muscle down another swallow.* BISHOP *grabs the knife* HENRY *used to cut the lemon.*]

BISHOP: Go on and waste that shit, Henry. I got something for you.

HENRY: I'm trying to tell you something about that white man, and you standing here threatening me! He the one got your number, nigga! Cut him! Don't be pulling no knife out on me! Shoot! Can't nobody tell you nothing!

[BISHOP *puts the knife away. Pause.*]

BISHOP: I just got a lot on my mind, Henry. My register come up short fifteen dollars this morning.

[*Pause.*]

HENRY: What you looking at me for?

[*Pause.*]

Bishop, you know I ain't gonna take your money. We brothers, man, I ain't about that. You getting old. Maybe you ain't counting right.

BISHOP: Over twenty years I ain't never miscounted. Last week I thought I miscounted. I come up short four dollars then. Two or three dollars since that. Now fifteen. Somebody been picking off the top hoping I wouldn't see nothing missing at the bottom.

HENRY: Man, I cut my finger for you! Why you questioning me?

BISHOP: I ain't saying you the one who took it. I think it might've been Bobbilee.

HENRY: Bobbilee?

BISHOP: That boy ain't nothing but trouble, Henry.

HENRY: What you talking about, Bishop? Bobbilee ain't gonna steal from you.

BISHOP: I don't know what Bobbilee gonna do. The boy sat right there and ate my sandwiches for most of his life, now the boy a jailbird.

HENRY: That's 'cause he ain't got no daddy.

BISHOP: He got Pattie. Women been raising children by themselves long enough to be getting it right by now. Bobbilee ain't no excuse. Pattie just as good as any two men.

HENRY: Bobbilee might be doing wrong but I don't think he gonna do no wrong to you. You miscount that money!

[TYRONE *enters through the front door. He wears a shirt and tie. Visibly upset, he stands by the door.* BISHOP *and* HENRY *stare at him.* TYRONE *slams the door shut.* BISHOP *and* HENRY *watch as he exits into the back room.*]

BISHOP: That dream come back to me, Henry. I done prayed over it forty times over but I was back there laying down and I see Tyrone again. This time there was this burning house and Tyrone was running straight for it. I started running after him but he disappeared into that fire.

[*Pause.*]

Then, damn it, here comes that train again. I couldn't see it, but it felt like it was right there in front of where I was standing. Then Tyrone come out of that house except now he's on fire and his face was burn off. He started running straight at me, and the closer he'd come, the louder that train got, and then he jumped at me. It felt like he and the train both hit me at the same time. Then I see Greta. She was trying to say something to me, but as soon as she opened her mouth . . . I woke up.

[*Pause.*]

Now, I don't know what to make of that, Henry, but I think Greta trying to tell me something about Tyrone. I think God using her to tell me what I need to do with him.

[*Pause.*]

HENRY [*whispering*]: Let me take you down there to see Ms. Thomasina Francis.

BISHOP: I ain't going down there to see that woman.

HENRY: Ms. Francis know how to find things out like that. She know how to talk to people who done crossed over. It ain't gonna cost you but thirty dollars.

BISHOP: Say what?

HENRY: C'mon and let me take you down there. It don't work, hell, I'll give you the thirty dollars back myself. Might do you some good to talk to Greta. Maybe she'll tell you to serve some pork. Get you some customers up in here.

[*Pause.*]

Look, man, I'm your brother. I ain't gonna let nothing happen to you.

[*Pause.*]

BISHOP: All right . . . I'll go down there and I'm gonna give her the thirty dollars. Now if she let me talk to Greta, me and you straight. If she don't let me talk to Greta, me and you ain't straight. That means you gotta go to that clinic and let them people fix you up.

HENRY: I'm going home. I'll be back here to get you tonight by midnight.

BISHOP [*using a napkin to pick up* HENRY'S *cup*]: Tonight by midnight? Why we gotta wait until midnight? Man, let's get this over with! I don't wanna walk around all day with this voodoo crap on my mind!

[*He tosses the cup into the garbage.*]

HENRY: That's the only time Ms. Francis can talk to the dead.

BISHOP: She can't talk to them no earlier than that?

HENRY: That's how it work, Bishop. Now I'm going home. Would stay but Martha's been acting funny lately. Stopped cooking and now she talking to her mama all the time. Woman starts talking to her mama every day you know something ain't right.

BISHOP: Well, take that possum juice outta here and put my milk back.

HENRY [*replacing the milk*]: I'm gonna put some of this juice in your coffee. Heat that shit up.

BISHOP: You late, I ain't going.

HENRY: I'm gonna wrap myself around Martha for the rest of the day, then I'm gonna eat me some pork! After that, I'll be back here to get you by midnight.

[*He holds up his thumb.*]

All right, my brother?

[*They press thumbs.*]

BISHOP: Till the gates of heaven open up.

HENRY: Well, all right.

[TYRONE *reenters from the back room. He somberly crosses into the kitchen and puts on his apron.*]

See ya, youngblood.

[*He exits through the front door.*]

BISHOP: Where you been?

[TYRONE *does not respond.*]

Where you been? They close the courthouse at six.

TYRONE: I ain't working down there.

BISHOP: You mean to tell me Timothy ain't working at the courthouse? Timothy ain't been down there a day yet. I thought Timothy had himself a good job.

TYRONE: Tyrone ain't working at the courthouse. I got down there and they questioning me at the door. Asking me for identification. I went in there and they sent me straight to the probation officer. I kept telling them I was there to work and they kept trying to direct me everywhere but Mr. Kramer's office. Said he don't take unscheduled appointments. I had to call in or come back later to see the secretary. I told them to eat . . . fertilizer. I been out looking for another job . . . that's why I'm late.

BISHOP: Well . . . as long as I can keep shop you always got work here.

TYRONE: What you mean keep shop?

BISHOP: I may have to shut down, Tyrone. Thought hard on it, but maybe it's time I do something else.

TYRONE: But this all you got, Mr. Bishop.

[*Pause.*]

I ain't gotta get paid . . . I mean, I'll take a cut if . . .

BISHOP: No, you ain't taking no cuts. I'm gonna pay you for the work you do around here.

[*Pause.*]

I'm going for a walk.

[*He starts to exit.*]

TYRONE: Mr. Bishop?

[*Pause.*]

What you know about my daddy?

BISHOP: I told you what I know.

TYRONE: He ain't in jail, is he? I mean, you just said that 'cause you got mad, right?

BISHOP: You asking questions you might not want an answer to.

[*Pause.*]

TYRONE: I guess I'll clean the grill.

[TYRONE *prepares to clean the grill. After a moment,* BISHOP *speaks.*]

BISHOP: Your daddy beat your mama.

[TYRONE *turns back to* BISHOP.]

You asking me so I'm gonna give it to you straight.

[TYRONE *sits.*]

J.P. was drafted to fight the Vietnam War in '67. That's when I first met your mama. She'd come in here all the time and sit over there in that corner. She'd have two cups of coffee thumbing through the newspaper trying to find out whether or not that war had killed J.P. They promised to marry when he got back, but since Greta had been reading how they was putting all them blacks on the front line she didn't think J.P. was ever gonna make it.

[*Pause.*]

Few years later he come back and . . . just like that . . . they got married. Greta still came by to have her two cups of coffee, but all of a sudden she stop showing up. Come to find out J.P. had been beating on her. People say it must've been the war that did it to him. He took a hot iron to her one night. Burnt her up pretty good. Greta almost didn't make it. That put J.P. in a tight spot. He ran upstate and the last I heard he was in jail.

[*Pause.*]

TYRONE: You ain't tell me. You raising me. Why you ain't say nothing?

BISHOP: I ain't supposed to tell you unless you ask. You old enough to ask, you old enough to know. You ain't never asked.

TYRONE: Why you taking care of me?

BISHOP: I owe it to your mama.

TYRONE: But I ain't your son.

BISHOP: People do things 'cause they have to be done. Your mama ain't have nobody else to look after you. I put that on my shoulders. Ain't enough people out there willing to put that weight on their shoulders. Didn't matter who you were. It mattered if you got taken care of.

[*Pause.*]

TYRONE: Well . . . I guess I'll close up the shop.

[*Long silence as* BISHOP *watches* TYRONE *clean the grill.*]

BISHOP: Tyrone?

[TYRONE *turns to* BISHOP, *who seems to change his thought.*]

My register come up short fifteen dollars this morning.

TYRONE: You saying I took it?

BISHOP: I ain't saying you took it. I'm just asking 'cause I thought you might know something.

TYRONE: I don't know nothing.

BISHOP: I ain't saying you took it. Make sure you lock up good. I'll be back in a minute.

[BISHOP *exits through the front door. The phone rings.* TYRONE *answers it.*]

TYRONE: Fifteen thirty-one East River Street.

[*Pause.*]

Nah, we about to close.

[*Pause.*]

Nah, I can't run it right now 'cause we about to close.

[*Pause.*]

Well, you gonna have to wait while I shut everything else down.

[*Pause. He gets pen and pad.* BOBBILEE *is seen outside the front door of the diner.*]

All right, what you want?

[*Pause.*]

Nah, you can't have steak, that take too long to cook. Get something else.

[*Pause.*]

Two Reuben sandwiches?

[BOBBILEE *taps on the window.*]

I ain't taking no more customers! [*Into the phone*] Nah, that come on rye bread.

[*Tapping continues.*]

I say we about to close! [*Into the phone*] What you say you want?

[*Pause.*]

Well, it's gonna have to be cold 'cause I done shut the grill down.

[*Pause.*]

Nah, I done shut the toaster down, too.
BOBBILEE [*tapping again*]: Tyrone, open the door!
TYRONE: Bobbilee?
BOBBILEE: Yeah, man, open up!
TYRONE [*into the phone*]: Hold on.

[TYRONE *opens the door.* BOBBILEE *enters.*]

BOBBILEE: "I ain't taking no more customers." [*Laughs.*] Man, you crazy!
TYRONE: Shoot, man, I'm tired. Been looking for a job all day.

[*He crosses back to the phone.*]

You know what you want yet 'cause we closing.

[*Pause.*]

All right, that's gonna be about fifteen, twenty minutes.

[*Pause.*]

Yeah, I know where that's at.

[*He hangs up the phone.*]

BOBBILEE: Where's Mr. Bishop?
TYRONE: I dunno, but we closing, Bobbilee.
BOBBILEE: So! Open back up!
TYRONE: I can't open back up. Mr. Bishop catch you in here, I'm gonna get into trouble.

BOBBILEE: Mr. Bishop ain't here. He ain't gonna know.

TYRONE: I'm just saying, you might not wanna be here when he comes back.

BOBBILEE: Mr. Bishop don't scare me. I done seen worse than him in prison. C'mon, man, I want you to help me finish this song. I got writer's block or something.

[BOBBILEE *takes a handheld tape recorder from his pocket. He sets it on the table.* TYRONE *stares.*]

What?

TYRONE: Where you get that?

[*Pause.*]

BOBBILEE: I just got it.

[TYRONE *looks at the register, then back to* BOBBILEE.]

What, Tyrone?

TYRONE: Mr. Bishop thinking about closing down his shop.

BOBBILEE: Well, let him close it down, then! What that gotta do with me? I told you I was gonna get a tape recorder. You know I cut grass!

[TYRONE *continues to stare.*]

Tyrone! I ain't got nothing to do with it! Now c'mon, man, and help me with this song! The Godfather depending on me!

[BOBBILEE *takes out a pencil and paper. He sits at a table and writes as he plays a James Brown or James Brown–like tune on the tape recorder.* TYRONE *finally resolves within himself not to discuss the obvious. He crosses behind the counter and prepares the order.*]

TYRONE: Who you think better? Michael Jackson or James Brown?

BOBBILEE: Man, you crazy? Michael Jackson got all his moves from James Brown. He ain't doing nothing new. Ain't nobody doing nothing new. MC Hammer, Heavy D, everybody singing and dancing got their moves from the Godfather. That's why he's the hardest-working man in show business and that's why I don't listen to all that rap and stuff, 'cause it ain't nothing but James Brown all over again.

TYRONE: When they gonna let him out?

BOBBILEE: Supposed to be next year sometime. He been doing concerts for the warden and stuff, so they talking about letting him out early.

TYRONE: Is he cool like he is on TV?

BOBBILEE: Without all that dancin' stuff. I mean, he don't go around dancin' and hollerin' all the time, but he still James Brown. I thought he'd be taller... but he ain't.

TYRONE: If I knew they was gonna lock me up with the Soul Man, I'd go straight to jail. Get me a number and everything.

[BOBBILEE *stares at* TYRONE, *then turns off the tape recorder.*]

BOBBILEE: You don't want them numbers, Tyrone. They don't do nothing but take away from you. You sitting there with them numbers across your chest thinking about how you got to this point, but you can't think back to what point you started from. Like you was born yesterday or something. Them brothers in prison look like they ain't never had no childhood. Some of them don't even talk no more. They just be hummin' songs or mumblin' to where you can't understand what they saying. Rockin' back and forth, pissin' on themselves, and just mumblin'.

[*Pause.*]

People always looking at me like I don't believe in nothing good. I believe in God, too. I just can't act like he want me to act all the time. That's why I gotta finish this song, Tyrone. I gotta prove to people I got some good in me and maybe people wake up and see they got some good in them, too. Godfather say ... the only way to speak to the soul is through rhythm and blues. They ain't gonna listen to nothing else, but they gotta listen to our song, 'cause if you sleep too long ... you might not wake up. Then that prophecy come true.

[*After a moment,* TYRONE *grabs the broom.*]

TYRONE: Let's finish the song.

BOBBILEE: All right ... now the chorus go like this.

[BOBBILEE *plays the tape recorder and sings.* TYRONE *uses the broom as a guitar.*]

Don't want no sleepwalking! C'mon, brothers, wake up! Don't need no sleepwalking! C'mon, brothers ...

[TYRONE *sings along but gets carried away.* BOBBILEE *stops him.*]

Hey, hey, hey!

[TYRONE *stops.*]

That's as far as I got on the chorus part. Now, somewhere in there I gotta say something about Maceo. Ain't no James Brown song unless I say, "Talkin' 'bout Maceo!"

TYRONE: Yeah! And "Good Gawd!"

BOBBILEE: And "Can I take it to the bridge?"

TYRONE: "Look out now, ugh! Gotta get on the good foot!"

BOBBILEE [*dancing and singing*]: "C'mon witcha come on!"

TYRONE: "Gotta stay on the scene, ugh!"

BOBBILEE: "Alika sex machine!"

BOBBILEE AND TYRONE: "Popcorn!"

BOBBILEE: "Owwww, watch me now!"

TYRONE: "Make me jump back and kiss myself!"

[BISHOP *enters through the front door.* TYRONE *and* BOBBILEE *stop dancing.*]

BOBBILEE [*under his breath*]: Ahhh, shit.

[TYRONE *quickly hands the tape recorder to* BOBBILEE, *who slyly puts it away.*]

TYRONE: Bobbilee leaving! Go on, Bobbilee!

BOBBILEE: I came to borrow some . . . some mayo for mama. She making potato salad for dinner. She told me to tell everybody she said . . . hey.

BISHOP: I look like a fool to you?

BOBBILEE: I just came from by there. She say she need some mayonnaise.

BISHOP: Pattie call here about some mayonnaise, Tyrone?

TYRONE: Uh . . . yeah . . . yes sir.

[*There's an awkward silence, which rattles* BOBBILEE's *and* TYRONE's *nerves.*]

BISHOP: Get Bobbilee the mayonnaise.

[TYRONE *gets a jar of mayonnaise and hands it to* BOBBILEE.]

BOBBILEE: I'll bring it back soon as . . .

BISHOP: I'll send Tyrone by there to pick it up. You tell your mama to call me. I don't want you back in my shop.

[BOBBILEE *exits through the front door.* BISHOP *confronts* TYRONE.]

You so grown you can lie to me?

[*Pause. The phone rings.*]

Take that order.

[TYRONE *does not move.*]

Boy, didn't you hear me say take that order?

TYRONE: We closed.

BISHOP: I say when we closed.

TYRONE: Well, I gotta run this dinner.

BISHOP: You take that damn order!

TYRONE [*answering the phone, with attitude*]: Fifteen thirty-one East River Street! Yeah, this the sandwich shop! [*Calming*] Hey, Mrs. Johnson.

[TYRONE *looks at* BISHOP.]

Nah, I'm fine.

[*Pause.*]

You want cheese on it? No onions . . . extra ketchup. All right . . . about fifteen minutes.

[*Pause.*]

Oh no, I'm sorry, Mrs. Johnson, but you can't come pick it up.

[*Pause.*]

No ma'am, I don't mind, but Mr. Bishop don't want nobody in his shop no more!

[BISHOP *goes after* TYRONE, *who drops the phone and exits with the dinner.* BISHOP *hangs up the phone, then locks the front door. He turns out the light and starts to exit into the back room when he hears a knock. He turns the light back on and takes off his belt as he goes to open the front door.*]

BISHOP: What I tell you, boy?

[*He notices that it is* HARRISON. *They stare at each other for a moment.*]

We closed.

[HARRISON *continues to stare.*]

I say we closed, Harrison.

HARRISON: That scar. You got a scar right there on the back of your arm. I noticed it when I was shaking your hand.

[BISHOP *looks at his arm.*]

Two people can stand alike but can't no two people stand the same.

BISHOP: I told you . . . we closed.

[*He tries to close the door, but* HARRISON *blocks it with his foot.*]

HARRISON: You got a mark. You can run but you can't run from that. That mark make it so you can't hide.

BISHOP: You stay away from my shop.

[BISHOP *slams the door shut. He locks it, then peeps out the window and watches as* HARRISON *walks away.*]

SCENE 2

[*It is after midnight.* BOBBILEE *is seen peeping through the window from the garden. Obviously breaking and entering, he enters the diner from the back, then through the double doors. He peeps through the door that leads to* BISHOP*'s bedroom. He then goes into the kitchen. He takes a soda from the refrigerator and fixes himself a sandwich, which he devours. As he eats, he glances at the register. He takes several glances at it before finally opening it. He takes some money and stares at it. He then hears* BISHOP *laughing outside the front door.* BOBBILEE *pulls his do-rag over his face and hides.* BISHOP *unlocks the door and enters. He turns on the light and suspiciously looks about the shop. He then crosses into the kitchen.*]

BISHOP: Damn boy make a mess in the kitchen.

[*He picks up the phone and dials.*]

Martha? Hey there, this Bishop.

[BOBBILEE *sneaks to grab his soda off the counter.* BISHOP *turns and again* BOBBILEE *hides.*]

Sorry to call you so late, but is Henry there yet?

[*Pause.*]

Put him on the phone.

[*Pause.*]

Henry . . . you owe me thirty dollars! I told you that shit wasn't real! [*Laughs.*] Uh-huh . . . yeah? Well, hold on . . . Henry, one minute.

[*He hangs up the phone and laughs. He then replaces the sandwich meat in the refrigerator.*]

Talking about Ms. Francis know how to talk to the dead. Henry, if you ain't a fool, then I don't know what a fool is!

[BISHOP *starts to exit, then suddenly stops laughing. He turns back to the counter and senses that something is not right. He looks around for a moment, then turns out the light and exits into the bedroom. After a moment,* BOBBILEE *emerges from his hiding place. He starts to exit, then stops and looks at the money still in his hand. He crosses back to the register. Unwillingly, he starts to replace the now crumpled dollar bills when* BISHOP *suddenly reenters from his bedroom carrying a pistol.*]

You put that money back.

[*There's a scuffle. The gun accidentally fires.* BOBBILEE *falls.* BISHOP *turns on the light and pulls the do-rag from* BOBBILEE'*s face.*]

Bobbilee.

[TYRONE *quickly enters in sleep attire and turns on the light.*]

TYRONE: Mr. Bishop, you all right?

[*He notices* BOBBILEE.]

Bobbilee?

[BISHOP *goes to the phone and dials.*]

BISHOP: I caught him sneaking in my register.
TYRONE: What you do to Bobbilee . . . you shot him?
BISHOP: I didn't mean to shoot him, Tyrone. The boy was stealing, I ain't know who he was! [*Into the phone*] I got a boy here been shot! Fifteen thirty-one East River Street!
TYRONE: You shot Bobbilee!

[*He lunges at* BISHOP, *who quickly restrains him.*]

How you gonna shoot my friend?
BISHOP: Boy, we can fight this thing out until kingdom come, but that means little Bobbilee ain't gonna make it!
BOBBILEE: Tyrone?

[TYRONE *rushes to cradle* BOBBILEE. BISHOP *goes back to the phone.*]

TYRONE: Bobbilee?

BOBBILEE: I ain't get my chance. I ain't do better than my daddy! [*Coughs.*] They sleepwalking, Tyrone. We gotta . . . we gotta wake up the . . . the whole nation.

[*He sings as he hands* TYRONE *his unfinished song.*]

Don't want no sleepwalking . . . don't need no sleepwalking . . . stop all that sleepwalking . . .

[*He dies.* TYRONE *looks at the paper, then removes* BOBBILEE's *do-rag. He stands eye to eye to* BISHOP.]

BISHOP: I'm sorry, Tyrone, I . . .

[TYRONE *exits through the front door. Brokenhearted,* BISHOP *drops the phone and crosses to* BOBBILEE.]

Damn, Bobbilee.

[*A James Brown tune plays as the lights fade to black. Suggested song: "Public Enemy Number One: Part 1." The intro dialogue of song should play through the fade to black.*]

SCENE 3

[*Lights rise on the diner.* TYRONE *sits at "their" table. Two bottles of soda and* BOB-BILEE's *tape recorder sit on the table. He opens both bottles, then stares. He taps the bottles together as if* BOBBILEE *were sitting across from him. He then drinks his soda empty, showing very little sign of pain. He puts on* BOBBILEE's *do-rag. He wipes away the tears and takes out* BOBBILEE's *piece of paper and pencil. He plays the tape recorder.* BOBBILEE's *voice is heard. In his quiet rage,* TYRONE *writes.*]

TYRONE [*singing as he writes*]: C'mon and get up! 'Cause we gotta get down! You running out of time, brother. Stop foolin' around. Stop that sleepwalk-ing! We gotta get on up! You can either start talking or you can either shut up! Don't want no sleepwalking! C'mon, brothers, wake up! Don't need no sleepwalking! C'mon, brothers . . .

[*Pause.*]

C'mon, brothers . . . Shit!

[*He stops the tape recorder and thinks.*]

C'mon, brothers, and . . . ? C'mon and . . . !

[*Pause.*]

What would the Soul Man say?

[*He looks at James Brown's picture.*]

C'mon and . . . shake . . . something up. [*Writing*] Yeah . . . shake something up.

[BISHOP *enters through the front door with* HENRY. *They both are in black suits.* HENRY *carries a plate wrapped in aluminum foil. They pause as they notice* TYRONE.]

BISHOP: Pattie was disappointed not to see you at the funeral.
HENRY: A good service that was. Best one I've seen yet. Pastor Brown didn't do that good of a job when he preached over Grandma Ida. You should've been there, youngblood. They cooked up a storm.
BISHOP: Tyrone, you hear Henry talking to you?
TYRONE [*continuing to ignore them, he sings*]: C'mon and get up. 'Cause we gotta get down.
BISHOP: Tyrone.
TYRONE: You running out of time, brother. Stop foolin' around.
BISHOP: Tyrone! I said did you hear Henry here talking to you?
HENRY: Let me talk to him, Bishop.

[*Pause.*]

BISHOP: Yeah . . . you talk to him.

[*He exits into the back room.*]

HENRY: I see you ain't changed your clothes. It's been four days, Tyrone.

[TYRONE *hums. Pause.*]

Pattie sent this plate by for you. Got some greens, barbecue ribs . . . beef ribs. You know Bishop wouldn't let me bring you no pork. Got some sweet corn . . . some yams . . .
TYRONE [*playing the tape recorder and singing*]: Don't want no sleepwalking. C'mon, brothers, wake up. Don't need no sleepwalking. C'mon shake somethin' up.
HENRY: That's Bobbilee's song, ain't it? You writing Bobbilee's song?
TYRONE [*writing*]: When you 'bout to fall down. Owww! Gotta get on the good foot. Ooooh, brother.

HENRY: Tyrone, this hard for everybody. You and Bobbilee was close, I know that. As much as you may want him to come back, shutting the world out ain't gonna help it none.

[*Pause.* HENRY *turns off the tape recorder.*]

Bishop ain't mean to kill that boy, but he was stealing. Bishop feel real bad about it. I had to pull him off that casket he got so carried away.

TYRONE [*threateningly*]: Don't want no sleepwalking! We gotta get on up! Stop all that sleepwalking! C'mon, brothers, wake up!

HENRY: I'll put this plate in the fridge.

[BISHOP *reenters in a T-shirt and his black dress pants and stares at* TYRONE. HENRY *crosses to the refrigerator as he takes a rib from the plate and eats. He tries to lighten the mood.*]

Boy, I tell you what. That Smith girl was looking good, wasn't she? Her mama feeding her right. And what black boy Eddieran doing at the funeral? I thought that nigga was incarcerated.

BISHOP: Tyrone?

HENRY: Man got twenty-eight babies by six different women. Ain't no sense in that. He know he can't take care of all them children. Twenty-eight babies.

[*Pause.*]

You think them women know each other?

BISHOP [*crossing to* TYRONE]: Tyrone? You don't see me standing here?

HENRY: Bishop, I'm gonna . . .

BISHOP: Tyrone!

HENRY [*giving up*]: I'll give y'all a minute.

[*He exits through the front door and sits on the bench outside the diner. He takes a stick from his pocket and sucks on it.*]

BISHOP: I told you I ain't mean to kill Bobbilee.

TYRONE [*singing and writing*]: You sleepwalking, brother. Goin' nowhere fast.

BISHOP [*sitting across from* TYRONE]: Ty . . .

TYRONE: Don't get caught sleepwalking! Stop foolin' around!

BISHOP: I'm trying to talk to you, Tyrone!

[*He reaches for* TYRONE'*s arm.* TYRONE *quickly pulls away and stands glaring at* BISHOP.]

You standing there looking at me like that. You thinking about hitting me? [*Rising*] That's all right, I'm gonna give you your shot. I owe you that. Go on . . . take your shot.

[*Pause.*]

Go ahead.

[*Pause.*]

Take your shot, Tyrone.

[*Pause.* TYRONE *crosses to* BISHOP. *He looks him over as if sizing him up. He might even sniff him. After a long moment,* TYRONE *speaks.*]

TYRONE: You my daddy?

[BISHOP *does not respond.*]

Say, Mr. Bishop? You my daddy?

[*Pause.*]

Bobbilee said I'm a lot like you. So, I looked at myself and I thought about J.P. and how you been raising me. I thought about how you don't never want me to do nothing. How you want me to run this shop when you get old like you passing it down to me. Then I see where I got your hands and your eyes and how my face looks like you. [*Fighting the tears*] So, you tell me, Mr. Bishop. You my daddy?

BISHOP [*reaching for* TYRONE]: Tyrone . . .

TYRONE [*pulling away*]: Get your hands off me!

[*He crosses to the counter and writes.*]

BISHOP: Tyrone, I'm trying to explain this thing to you!

[*Pause.*]

Greta wanted me to tell you about this, but when we found out she was pregnant she was already married to J.P.! He started beating on her when he found out me and Greta had been seeing each other while he was over there fighting the war and . . .

TYRONE: I said are you my daddy! I ain't asked you nothing about my mama! I ain't asked you nothing about J.P.! I asked if you my daddy!

BISHOP: Tyrone . . .

TYRONE: Man, are you my daddy or not!

[*Silence as they stare at each other.*]

BISHOP: You're my son, Tyrone.

TYRONE [*fighting back tears*]: You lying. You ain't doing nothing but lying.

BISHOP: I ain't lying to you. I'm trying to set this thing straight.

TYRONE: If you ain't lying, then why my mama ain't marry you?

BISHOP: 'Cause we didn't know for sure who you belonged to! So, I thought it best to just deal with the circumstances! I told Greta to go ahead and be with J.P. 'cause that's what I thought was best for you . . .

TYRONE: You lying!

BISHOP: After J.P. went upstate Greta came back to me . . .

TYRONE: Tighten it up, Mr. Bishop . . .

BISHOP: We found out you belonged to me after J.P. run off! We tried to get married, but J.P. wouldn't sign the papers . . .

TYRONE: Tighten it up, Mr. Bishop! I said for you to tighten it up!

BISHOP: Greta said for me to go ahead and tell you the truth, but, damn it, I wasn't gonna let them point their fingers at you! I wasn't gonna let them talk about you like you wasn't nothing! I wasn't gonna let them call you no bastard saying you didn't come from somewhere!

[*Pause.*]

After Greta died God knows I wanted to tell you, Tyrone, but as soon as I'd fix my lips to spit it out you'd call out for J.P.! You been missing J.P. so much that I was scared to tell you. All I could see was me reaching out for you and you running away from me. I thought I'd wake up one morning and you'd be gone.

TYRONE: What you want me to do, huh? I ain't gonna hug you! You done robbed me of my time, now I'm feeling old! I think about me and you and now everything different! Everything makes sense and ain't nothing ever made sense to me!

[*Pause.*]

Why you ain't tell me before I got big, huh? Why you wait until I get old to tell me I ain't who I am?

[*He crosses to the kitchen and paces.*]

I've been lied to all this time! Thinking my daddy got a big-time job in New York, thinking you just raised me!

[*Enraged, he grabs a knife and crosses to* BISHOP.]

Nah . . . nah, fuck you, Mr. Bishop!

[*He holds the knife to* BISHOP'S *throat.*]

I don't know whether to shoot J.P. or to kill you for lying to me . . . but I gotta kill somebody . . . at least it feels like I do!

BISHOP [*not resisting*]: The truth gotta come however it's gonna come.

TYRONE: You ain't my daddy, man, you ain't!

BISHOP [*after a moment*]: If I wasn't your daddy . . . I'd be dead by now.

[TYRONE *drops the knife to the floor.*]

Tyrone . . .

TYRONE: Don't you touch me! I gotta write this song! Bobbilee's song!

BISHOP: Me and you got some fixing to do.

TYRONE [*crossing to the counter*]: I gotta write this song! Don't you bother me! You stay away from me while I'm writing! [*Singing as he writes*] Stop that sleepwalking. Gotta get on up . . .

BISHOP: Me and you gotta talk this thing through . . .

TYRONE: You can either start talking or you can either shut up . . .

BISHOP: Let's set this thing straight, Tyrone. I let your mama go, but I gotta hold on to you . . .

TYRONE: You running out of time, brother! Stop foolin' around . . .

BISHOP: Tyrone, damn it, I'm trying to talk to you, now, tighten it up . . .

TYRONE: C'mon and get up! 'Cause we gotta get down! Don't want no sleep-walking! Don't need no sleepwalking!

BISHOP [*grabbing* TYRONE]: Goddamn it, boy, you listen to me!

HENRY [*entering through the front door*]: Bishop!

TYRONE: Stop all that sleepwalking . . .

HENRY [*crossing to* BISHOP]: Hey, Bishop!

BISHOP: This my son, Henry! Stay out of it!

HENRY: Your son, my nephew!

[*He pulls* BISHOP *off* TYRONE.]

Let it go!

TYRONE: There ain't but one thing I like about you, Mr. Bishop! You got this shop! You put all this together by using your head! What I don't like about you is that you just might be my daddy!

[*Pause. Obviously hurt,* BISHOP *looks to* HENRY, *then back to* TYRONE. *After a moment,* BISHOP *exits into the back room.*]

Bobbilee was my friend.

HENRY: Bobbilee's number come up.

TYRONE: I gotta write his song.

[*Pause.*]

HENRY [*sighing*]: You got a lot of your daddy in you.

TYRONE: He ain't my daddy!

HENRY [*sitting next to* TYRONE]: You know how he got that name? Bishop?

TYRONE: I gotta finish this song, Mr. Henry.

HENRY: I found him in a box. He had been hiding out in that box on a train for I don't know how long when—

TYRONE: He's your brother. How you find your own brother in a box?

HENRY: He wasn't my brother until we cut our thumbs. Now, he was hiding out on that train when—

TYRONE: He ain't your real brother?

HENRY: We got the same blood. That's all we need.

TYRONE: But you ain't got the same mama? You ain't got the same daddy?

HENRY: I say we got the same blood.

TYRONE: I'm leaving this place! Everybody got secrets! Telling stories half backwards!

HENRY: People gotta do that sometimes. The truth come out when the time is right.

TYRONE: Well, the time ain't never right! Not around here it ain't!

HENRY: Truth hurts, but it gotta come out.

TYRONE: There ain't no truth! From this point on I'm gonna make my own truth!

HENRY: Your daddy got that name 'cause he came out of that box calling the shots—

TYRONE: I don't wanna hear this, Mr. Henry.

HENRY: Six years old and he telling the world which way to turn—

TYRONE: I said I don't wanna hear this!

HENRY: I'm standing in the middle of the warehouse . . . waiting on the clock. My mama and daddy dead in their graves. Twelve years old I'm working . . . packing and unpacking. The last crate come off the train and I'm one foot out the door when . . .

[*He taps his cane on the steps several times. Pause.*]

Who there?

[*He taps again. Pause.*]

I turn back to that crate and something tells me this ain't no coal and this ain't no pipes. There's something else in there. I pick up a crowbar and crack that lid open and there he is . . . folded up Indian style and crying.

[*Pause.*]

"I'm Henry. What's your name?" He just looked up at me like if he said it he'd die on the spot. I knew he was running from something and I didn't think it right to help him, but it was just me and my Grandma Ida and . . . I needed me a partner.

[*Pause.*]

I took him home and Grandma Ida ain't said a word. She just laid a hand on him and gave him some food. Three days go by and we ain't done nothing more than look at each other. Then Grandma Ida took him to the church. That night I hear him . . . outside my window shoveling dirt. "Psst! Hey, what you doing?" "I'm planting me a seed." First words come out of his mouth after three days and he planting him a seed. I shut the window and run out onto the porch and there was Grandma Ida . . . staring at him. We stood there watching him dig and cry over dirt half the night before he finally dropped that shovel. He raised his head and fell to his knees. In the middle of that garden he bowed down . . . and he prayed. From that point on Grandma Ida started calling him Baby Bishop. She say whatever it was he was running from he was putting it into the ground for God to step on. I knew then I had me a partner who don't let nothing stand in his way.

[*Pause.*]

You got that in you.

[*Pause.*]

TYRONE: You and Mr. Bishop did this to me! Lying to me! That ain't right! How I know he ain't lying about being my daddy? How I know you ain't lying about who you are?

HENRY [*a bit nervously*]: Now I ain't gonna lie to you! I tell the truth when I'm supposed to tell it! It wasn't my place to say nothing! Bishop had to do that!

[BISHOP *reenters. Realizing* BISHOP *has overheard and that he may have over-stepped his boundaries,* HENRY *exits into the back room.* BISHOP *looks to* TYRONE.]

BISHOP: You only got one, Tyrone. There ain't no other like me. Without me you always gonna be trying to find you. Without me you ain't never gonna have anything to measure yourself against. I might not be what you want me to be, but I'm all you got to be who you are. That's what a father is. Everything my father never was.

[TYRONE *stares at* BISHOP, *then starts to exit through the front.*]

Where you going?

TYRONE [*stopping*]: How much money you got in your pocket?

[TYRONE *exits and sits on the bench outside the diner. He hums as he writes. Lights go down on* BISHOP, *who sits and lowers his head on the counter inside.* HARRISON *enters outside the diner and notices* TYRONE. *Pause.*]

HARRISON: How about a cup of coffee?

[TYRONE *glares at* HARRISON, *then continues to hum. After a moment,* HARRISON *continues.*]

You're an entertainer?

[TYRONE *still ignores him as he hums.*]

That's a nice tune. What's it called?

[*Again,* TYRONE *does not respond.* HARRISON *looks into the diner and sees* BISHOP *folded over the counter. Pause.*]

Well . . . since you're closed I . . . I guess I'll move on.

[*He starts to exit.*]

TYRONE: "Sleepwalking."

[*Pause.* HARRISON *turns back.*]

It's called "Sleepwalking."

[*Pause.*]

HARRISON: Sounds pretty good.

TYRONE: It's a song for my friend.

HARRISON: Your friend having trouble sleeping?

TYRONE: All he can do is sleep.

[*Pause.*]

I'm just writing this song 'cause I miss him.

[*Pause.*]

Now, I don't feel like talking, mister.
HARRISON: Maybe you can write my song.
TYRONE: What you need a song for? You ain't sleeping.

[HARRISON *suddenly grabs his side and moans in pain. Each attack is worse than the one before.*]

HARRISON: No, but I'm barely walking.
TYRONE [*staring at him*]: You all right?
HARRISON: Yeah . . . yeah, I'm all right.

[HARRISON *takes a moment to breathe through the pain as he struggles to remove his jacket.* TYRONE *finally helps him. Pause.*]

It's my kidney.
TYRONE: What's wrong with your kidney?
HARRISON: Doesn't work anymore. I'm running on a spare. Won't be long I'll be . . . [*Smiles.*] It would be nice to have someone remember me like you remember your friend.
TYRONE: I'm writing this song but I don't even know why I'm writing it. I ain't never gonna see him again. All I got is a piece of paper with words on it.
HARRISON: I been working railroads forever, but I don't have a song like your friend. No one's dancing or writing words to say I meant something to them or to this world. That paper there says that your friend had a life . . . and that he left his mark on it. He left it with you.
TYRONE: You don't understand, mister.
HARRISON: I had a song I used to sing to my boy. I used to take him up to the tracks and we'd stand on the edge of the Savannah Bridge and watch the trains roll by. That song would move us inside one another and it seemed like couldn't nothing in this world come between us.

[*He stands on the bench holding on to a rail, if available.*]

TYRONE: Hey, you gotta get down, mister.

[HARRISON *marches in place, making train sounds as he warms up his engine.*]

HARRISON: Chugachuga-chugachuga-chugachuga...

TYRONE: Hey, man, you can't climb up there. Mr. Bishop don't like that.

HARRISON [*singing*]: Choo-choo! Hear the train a-roaring! Choo-choo! See the train a-coming!

[*Lights go up on* BISHOP, *who suddenly raises his head from the counter. He walks toward the front door as he listens.*]

Chugachuga-chugachuga-chugachuga! Choo-choo-chugalug, train ride high! Choo-choo-chugalug...

BISHOP [*opening the front door and joining in*]: Train never die.

HARRISON [*turning to* BISHOP]: That's right! Train never die.

[*Pause.*]

BISHOP: Tyrone...go on inside.

TYRONE: How you know that song, Mr. Bishop?

BISHOP: I said for you to go inside!

[TYRONE *starts to enter the diner.*]

HARRISON: Tyrone?

[TYRONE *stops.* HARRISON *crosses to him and shakes his hand. He then suddenly hugs* TYRONE. BISHOP *pulls* TYRONE *away. Confused,* TYRONE *stares at them both as he enters the diner. He listens from inside the front door.*]

That was our song. I used to sing it to you on the Savannah Bridge. You're a long way from home, son.

BISHOP: You got the wrong man, Harrison. Now, I told you to stay away from my shop.

HARRISON: I was half the way back to Charleston. Thought I'd give you more time, but I don't have any time left.

BISHOP: Tighten it up.

HARRISON: Forty-two years. I never thought the train would take you this far.

BISHOP: Tighten it up, old man! I said tighten it up!

HARRISON: If I could go back forty-two years I'd take that train and I'd shut it down... 'cause you're my son.

BISHOP: Nah, Harrison, you got the wrong man!

[BISHOP *exits into the diner and heads for the back room.* TYRONE *is hidden by the door as* BISHOP *enters.* HARRISON *follows.* TYRONE *looks on.* HARRISON *takes one of* BISHOP'S *flyers from his pocket, then places his jacket and hat on the back of a chair.*]

HARRISON: No . . . no, you're my son. You was born right there on Harper Road, Savannah, Georgia. September 30, 1941. Your mother died when you was six and then you run off.

[*Pause.* BISHOP *stops and turns back.*]

BISHOP: You telling me that I'm your son? That you're my daddy? You ain't nothing to me! You making babies that ain't supposed to be made!

[*Pause.*]

Six years old you'd think you'd forget, but I remember! I remember my mama . . . down on her hands and knees . . . putting seeds into the ground telling me how precious life is! How I got the power to create life where there is none! How sometimes life come out in a way that people don't want to accept it! She laying there with death on her face telling me how I belong to somebody! "Somebody planted a seed inside her and can't nobody accept it!" So what I do? I go looking for my daddy! Six years old and I go looking for my daddy just so I know I come from somewhere! Somewhere man, goddamn it, somewhere!

HARRISON: Son . . .

BISHOP: Everywhere I'd go people was staring at me! "That's him! That's the half-Negro boy who they raped his mama! He belong to that white man on Harper Road! Run, zebra, run! You belong to the devil!" Nah! That ain't me! I don't belong to the devil!

HARRISON: I never raped your mother! I loved your mother more than any man could ever love a woman!

BISHOP [*tearfully*]: Then why you ain't come after me, huh? You sneaking me up to that bridge! I'm always wondering why it was at night! Why my mama got this white man bringing me all them clothes! Why we gotta grow our own food and eat out the ground 'cause somehow my mama ain't got nobody to turn to! Something done happened! Something that had to do with her being darker than me and me not quite as light as you! So I go out there and I see the world the way the world see me!

HARRISON: You run away from something you never understood!

BISHOP: I come up on Harper Road and I knock on your door. The door open and I say, "I'm looking for my daddy." And you shut that door on me. You ain't say nothing! You just stood there looking down on me like I ain't come from somewhere!

HARRISON: Son . . .

BISHOP: I got on that train and I said to hell with you and everybody else who said I was a nobody! I come up here and I got me a new life, but I still gotta fight! I gotta fight 'cause I'm a little lighter than everybody else! I open up this shop now I'm fighting 'cause I'm better than everybody else! I gotta hold up picket signs and walk a thousand miles just to prove how black I am! I gotta sit in just to sit with my own people! All the while I'm sitting there thinking I got a part of me on the other side. On the other side I'm a piece of the very thing I'm fighting against! Now, don't you come in here trying to lay claims on Bishop! Not after what you did to me!

HARRISON: People didn't like the idea of mixing bloods! I shut that door because I had to! My whole life was standing there and I couldn't reach out for it because of the life I had inside that house! The life that could never accept that you belonged to me! I did as much as this world would allow me to do for you. That bridge was the only place where I could be your father. At night was the only guarantee I had that I could live to be your father for at least one more day.

[*Pause.*]

I love you, son. But I couldn't come after you. 'Cause had I loved you then . . . the way a father should be allowed to love his son . . . I would've lost all I had.

[TYRONE *steps aside as* BISHOP *opens the front door.*]

BISHOP: Get out.

[*Pause.*]

You get the hell out of my shop! Go back to where I left you!

HARRISON: I'm dying, son.

BISHOP: You think I give a damn about you dying? You expecting me to hug and comfort you 'cause you dying? Then I gotta go on and live my life after all this shit you done brought back on me? Nah! You go on, Harrison! I ain't got no sympathy for you! You been dead forty-two years!

[HARRISON *takes an envelope from his pocket. He offers it to* BISHOP. HENRY *can be seen peeping through the double doors.*]

HARRISON: This is all I have.

BISHOP: Ain't nothing you got to give can set straight what you did to me. Now, I want you to get out of my shop. This time don't you look back.

HARRISON: I'm running out of time, son.

BISHOP [*pacing the kitchen area*]: I'm tired, Harrison! I ain't got no more energy for you! Now you go on before you make me . . . go on, now!

HARRISON: I don't think I can get back on that train . . .

BISHOP [*grabbing a knife from the kitchen*]: Goddamn it, Harrison, you go on! Don't make me tell you again!

[HENRY *enters from the back room carrying a bottle of gin. He looks on.*]

HARRISON: I never stopped loving you. Every day I waited for you.

HENRY: Cut him, Bishop! Cut him and get your hundred percent profit!

HARRISON: You are my son! This is my life! The only thing I have left to give to you.

HENRY: What the hell you waiting for, Bishop? Cut this white motherfucker's body parts out!

BISHOP: That's my daddy, Henry! That's my blood standing there!

HENRY: He got your number figured out, Bishop, now you gotta cut him!

BISHOP: I'm looking at my flesh and blood, man! There it is right there in front of me!

HENRY: Nigga, I'm your flesh and blood! I cut my finger for you, now you cut this white bastard for me!

HARRISON [*singing*]: Chugachuga-chugachuga-chugachuga . . .

HENRY: You see what they did to my leg!

HARRISON: Choo-choo, hear the train a-roaring . . .

HENRY: They took away my dream, Bishop . . .

HARRISON: Chugachuga-chugachuga-chugachuga . . .

HENRY: Bishop!

HARRISON: Choo-choo, see the train a-coming . . .

HENRY: If you my brother, man, you cut him!

HARRISON: Choo-choo-chugalug, train ride high. Choo-choo-chugalug . . .

HENRY: Goddamn you, Bishop! Cut him! You cut him clean or you cut me loose!

[HENRY *shoves* BISHOP *into* HARRISON. BISHOP *now holds the knife to* HARRISON'S *throat.* HARRISON *holds out his arms as if offering himself in sacrifice.*]

HARRISON: Train never die.

[*Pause.* TYRONE *crosses between* BISHOP *and* HARRISON. *After a moment,* TYRONE *speaks.*]

TYRONE: If he wasn't your daddy... he'd be dead by now.

[BISHOP *looks at* TYRONE, *then back to* HARRISON. *He drops the knife and collapses in grief.* HARRISON *wants to comfort him but holds back.*]

HARRISON: I'm sorry you hate me, son. Sorry I didn't come after you.

[*He starts to exit, then turns back to* TYRONE.]

I'll be waiting for that song.
BISHOP [*to* HARRISON]: What's my name?

[HARRISON *looks to* BISHOP, *then drops the envelope on a table. He exits, leaving behind his jacket and hat.*]

I can't remember my own name.

[TYRONE *stares at* BISHOP, *then exits after* HARRISON. BISHOP *sits in silence.* HENRY *notices the envelope* HARRISON *left on the table. He opens it and removes two sheets of paper. He reads, then turns to* BISHOP.]

HENRY: Bishop, you... you might wanna take a look at this. That white man left you all his money.

[*Pause.*]

Guess you ain't gotta close up shop.

[HENRY *hands the letter to* BISHOP. BISHOP *reads. After a moment,* BISHOP *speaks.*]

BISHOP: I wish I never got on that train.
HENRY [*holding up the other letter*]: Bishop... I'm standing here holding your history in my hand and I don't even know you.

[*He reads from the second paper.*]

"Born September 30, 1941. Savannah in the state of Georgia under the name of..." [*Exploding*] Man, I cut my finger for you! You got on that train 'cause you was supposed to! You here 'cause me and you supposed to keep each other straight! Now, why in the hell you ain't tell me about that white man!
BISHOP: Tell you I was a mistake? Tell you I ain't supposed to be here? I had've told you where I come from you would've shut the lid on that crate just as fast as you'd opened it.
HENRY: After all these years... I don't know who you are.

BISHOP: I can't remember my own birth name, Henry. I don't even know who I am.

[TYRONE *reenters.* HENRY *looks to him, then puts the letter back into the envelope, places it on the counter, and exits into the back room.*]

Tyrone, I . . .

TYRONE [*stopping*]: My name ain't Tyrone. I changed my name.

[*Pause.*]

I'm leaving here. I'm gonna catch me a train.

BISHOP: Where to?

TYRONE: To wherever I need to go to get back what the world owe me.

BISHOP: Tyrone . . .

TYRONE: My name ain't Tyrone.

BISHOP: Son . . . that train ain't nothing but hollow grounds.

TYRONE: It took you where you wanted to go.

BISHOP: I got on that train looking for salvation. I ended up with this lie, now I ain't got nothing to turn back to. I wanted you to keep your name because I didn't have one of my own.

[TYRONE *starts to exit.*]

I love you, Tyrone.

[*Pause.*]

TYRONE [*turning back*]: You can't love me . . . 'cause I don't love you. Even if you are my daddy, I don't feel nothing for you. I wouldn't go if I felt something . . . but I don't feel nothing. Nothing at all.

[HENRY *reenters from the back room. Pause.*]

I'm going to Charleston. I don't know who this man is . . . but I don't know who you are, either. Ain't none of this my fault. Ain't his fault he's gonna die . . . but he my blood, though. And if I got a kidney for him . . . I'm gonna give it to him. After that I don't know what I'm gonna do. Might just stay on the train until I die, but I'm gonna finish this song for Bobbilee. I'm gonna finish it for me. You can't cut me off from everything, Mr. Bishop.

[*He exits into the back room.*]

HENRY: Youngblood say he gonna give that white man his body parts. They got his number, Bishop.

BISHOP: The truth come out and ain't nothing the same no more.

[*Pause.*]

HENRY: Well . . . I'll be damned if I'm gonna stand here and let them pull my number.

[*He grabs the football.*]

Bishop? You can have this gin. I'm going home to Martha. Might even go and see my boy.

[*Pause.*]

I'll try to stop by in the morning. You get you some sleep, I'll . . . I'll see you tomorrow.

[*He starts to exit.*]

BISHOP: Henry?

[HENRY *stops.*]

Hambone with me.

[BISHOP *can no longer fight the tears. It is hard for* HENRY *to look at him.*]

C'mon and hambone with me.

[*Pause.*]

HENRY: I . . . I gotta go home, Bishop. I'll give you a call tomorrow.
BISHOP [*pleadingly*]: I cut my finger for you. Now, you come and hambone with me.

[HENRY *does not respond.* BISHOP *begins to hambone.*]

Hambone hambone have you heard? Henry don't wanna sing no words . . .
HENRY: Bishop, I gotta go, but I'm gonna call you. Soon as I . . . I'm gonna give you a call.
BISHOP [*still singing*]: If that bottle of wine ain't sweet, Henry gonna mash some grapes with his feet . . .
HENRY: Bishop, I'm gonna . . .
BISHOP: Hambone hambone have you heard? Henry don't wanna sing no words. Hambone get him and let him go. He can't sing 'cause he too old . . .

[HENRY *starts to exit.* BISHOP *desperately holds out his thumb.*]

You my brother, Henry!

[HENRY *stops. Pause.*]

HENRY: Till the gates . . . till the . . . don't do this to me, Bishop! Now I done done all I can do for you, but you lied to me! I shed my blood for you and now you got that white man's blood running around inside me!

[*Pause.*]

Now I'm going home and I'm gonna try to get over this shit! I'm gonna call you just like I say . . . but I can't . . . I'm . . . gonna call you, Bishop. First thing.

[*As painful as it is,* HENRY *exits.* BISHOP *notices the envelope left on the counter. He takes the paper from it and reads. He is brought to tears. After a moment,* TYRONE *reenters from the back room carrying a duffel bag. He looks to* BISHOP, *then grabs* HARRISON's *coat and hat. He starts to exit through the front door.* BISHOP *beats his thigh and chest as he sings.*]

BISHOP: Hambone hambone have you heard . . .

[*Pause.*]

Hambone hambone have you heard . . .

[*Pause.* TYRONE *stops.*]

Hambone ham . . . bone . . .

[BISHOP *finally gives up. After a moment,* TYRONE *turns back to* BISHOP. *He sets his bag down, then crosses to the counter and pulls out a stool. He waits for* BISHOP, *who finally crosses to him and places one foot on the other side of the stool.* BISHOP *teaches* TYRONE.]

Hand-eye coordination.

[TYRONE *holds out his hand.* BISHOP *hambones as* TYRONE *tries to follow.*]

No, now . . . you gotta slow down. Take your time and feel the rhythm out.

[HARRISON *enters the diner. He shuts the door behind him.* BISHOP *and* TYRONE *stop. They all stare at each other.* BISHOP *then turns back to* TYRONE.]

It's like a drum. You gotta listen.

[HARRISON *watches as they hambone. The lights fade as a roaring train passes. Suggested song: a recording of* BOBBILEE's *song.*]

THE GIFT HORSE

Lydia R. Diamond

First-Place Winner

2000–2001

For David

PLAYWRIGHT'S STATEMENT

I'm proud of the play that follows and I'm pretty sure it says, more eloquently than I can right now, something about life and love and tragedy and passion and perseverance. This publishing thing, unquestionably a wonderful progression in any writer's career, is a leap of faith for me because the play was written to live on a stage. I had never thought of a play as complete until the contributions of fellow theater artists lift it from the page and let it walk and breathe in front of an audience. Jordan says, "I mean the art happens here, right here in between you and me is where the art happens. It's not music without you . . ." She's speaking to her audience. And so I will trust that I'm speaking to mine. Thank you for making that space with me. And thanks to all of the audiences and artists who have and will continue to make this story breathe.

PRODUCTION HISTORY

The Gift Horse, by Lydia R. Diamond, was first presented by the Columbia College Chicago Theater Department at the New Studio Theater in February 2001. It was directed by Shirley Jo Finney, with set design by Victor Mahler, costume design by Kristine Roof, lighting design by Kevin Freese, and fight choreography by David Woolley. Sarah Lueptow was the stage manager.

Noah . . . . Maximino Arciniega Jr.
Ernesto . . . . Daniel Bernardo
Brian . . . . Tory O. Davis
Ruth . . . . RaShawn Fitzgerald
Jordan . . . . Elizabeth Isibue
Bill . . . . Michael Quinn

The play was subsequently presented at the Goodman's Owen Theatre in February 2002. It was directed by Chuck Smith, with set design by Felix E.

Cochren, costume design by Birgit Rattenborg Wise, lighting design by Robert Christen, and sound design by Ray Nardelli. Ellen Hay was the stage manager, and Kimberly Osgood was the production stage manager.

Ruth	Lynn M. House
Jordan	Yvonne Huff
Noah	Alfred Kemp
Bill	Christian Kohn
Ernesto	Andrew Navarro
Brian	Tim Edward Rose

CHARACTERS

Jordan, twenty-three to twenty-seven, African American or biracial; pretty and engaging and somewhat more centered than Ruth; relates to the audience with ease and warmth; plays the cello

Ruth, twenty-six to thirty, African American; personable and charming if somewhat neurotic; has a great sense of humor and laughs easily

Ernesto, twenty-seven to thirty, Latino with a barely detectable accent, if one at all; intelligent, warm, charismatic, sexy

Brian, forty to fifty, African American; handsome, serious, warm, caring

Bill, thirty to forty-five, white; dangerously attractive and engaging

Noah, twenty-seven to thirty, Latino; gentle, warm, loving, intelligent; Ernesto's soul mate

STAGING

The set should be very minimal and rely on the use of levels and lighting changes to communicate scene and time shifts. Jordan usually occupies an area that is raised and somewhat set apart from the rest of the action. She shares only the main playing spaces with the other actors when the script specifically makes reference to doing so. Stage directions will often make reference to "areas" (for example, college, therapy, bedroom, and so on); these areas should remain relatively consistent and can be established with a minimum of movable furniture. Often actors speak to the audience and each other across time and space; again, this interaction should be handled with subtleties of light and movement.

ACT 1

SCENE 1

[*Stage is black. Cello is heard. A special rises on* JORDAN *playing. She acknowledges the audience and continues.* RUTH *enters.* JORDAN *stops. They share a brief look.* JORDAN *resumes.*]

RUTH [*making a list*]: Holy Mary, Mother of Jesus. Mother Courage, Mother Teresa, Mother Goose . . . There must be some rap star with "mother" . . . Little Ma Ma Boodie Boodie or something . . . Mother, mother . . . I'm a bad motha—

JORDAN: Shut yo' mouth . . .

RUTH: I'm talkin' 'bout Shaft.

JORDAN: I got it.

[*Beat.*]

Go on, please. You were listing mothers?

RUTH: Right. Mother Goose, Mother Hubbard, Ma Kettle, Ma Rainey.

[*Pause.*]

JORDAN: Don't forget the Greek ones. Gaea, mother of Uranus; Rhea, mother of Zeus; Leto, mother of Apollo and Artemis; Maia, mother of Hermes; Dione, mother of Aphrodite; Thetis . . .

RUTH: OK, OK. Thank you. So, this is my list. Of mothers. Famous mothers. Someday I will join their ranks. Foggy as pieces of my childhood are, the parts I do remember are dreamlike sepia-toned or Kodachromed romps through dandelion-covered fields and across pebbled streams. I was Laura Ingalls, from the book, not the TV. Jo, from the book, not the movie. And, at the height of my ongoing identity issues, Anne of Green Gables. So my mom was hard pressed to find young black literary heroines. She made up for it by supplying me with a steady stream of caramel- to cocoa-colored dolls. I only remember one blue-eyed baby. The Christmas Black Baby Alive was on back order. She had the prettiest curly hair, and all the white moms bought her . . . which is truly amazing, considering the toy companies hadn't even started making black Kens . . . I think they were afraid Barbie would start dating Kenjufu . . . or Ken-dall Jackson—get it? Anyway, dolls were little people to be treated with care and respect. At least until that great day when I'd have to put aside the things of childhood and reign as kick-ass numero uno mother supreme of the century.

[*Beat.*]

[*To* JORDAN] So. I really was trying to say something.
JORDAN: I'm sure.
RUTH: I always knew I'd be a great mom.

[JORDAN *begins to play.*]

I don't know what happened, but I think I know where. Somewhere around the edges of a pre-midlife crisis. Really it started years before that, in my first week of college, where I met the only man I've ever really trusted with my heart and soul.

[*Establish the college area.* RUTH *and* ERNESTO *are college age.* ERNESTO *enters.*]

ERNESTO: *Buenas noches.*
RUTH: *Bien, merci, et vous?*
ERNESTO: That's not Spanish.
RUTH: I know.

[*Pause.*]

I don't speak Spanish.
ERNESTO: *Oui, um, bonjour, Mademoiselle, comment allez-vous?*
RUTH: All right then. I don't speak French either. But I'm single.
ERNESTO: Is that what you thought? That I was picking you up?
RUTH: Would that be impossible?
ERNESTO: Well, yeah.
RUTH: So what's with this coming up to a strange woman and speaking in Spanish, if not to ingratiate yourself?
ERNESTO: *Lo decía sólo por educación.* Um . . . I was trying to ingratiate myself. I might even have been flirting. Maybe, but to no end.
RUTH: OK.

[*Beat.*]

Well, I'll be seeing you around.
ERNESTO: Probably, we're neighbors.
RUTH: All right then.
ERNESTO: All right.

RUTH [*to the audience*]: Thank God for coed.

[ERNESTO *fades into the background as* RUTH *steps downstage and into her light.*]

We saw each other, coming and going, and our conversations got longer and longer... but never as long as I'd have liked.

ERNESTO [*to the audience*]: I really wanted to make friends, but I was so careful then. What with all the WASPs and frat boys, and frat-boy WASPs, I'd learned to be private as a means of self-preservation.

[*Previous lighting resumes.*]

RUTH: Hey.
ERNESTO: Hey.
RUTH: Ready for finals?
ERNESTO: About as ready as I'm gonna be.
RUTH: Do you want to get coffee or something?
ERNESTO: Well, I really should get back to my—
RUTH: Studying.
ERNESTO: Yeah.
RUTH: What happened to "I know as much as I'm going to"?
ERNESTO: But I'm in denial. I keep thinking that if I study harder I'll get smarter.
RUTH: You're psych, right?
ERNESTO: Yeah.

[*Pause.*]

I can tell from the way you dress that you're something artistic.

RUTH: Mom said to do something more practical than painting, so I majored in theater. But she said she'd cut me off if I didn't reconsider the word "practical." So I'm an education major, art minor.

[*Long moment of silence, turning into awkwardness.*]

You should join me. Interfacing with real people can only help you in your psychological pursuits, I mean you want to be a good psychiatrist—

ERNESTO: Psychologist.
RUTH: Sorry, my dad's a psychiatrist. Fine, psychologist. Same beast, no drugs. Let's get coffee.
ERNESTO: No really.
RUTH: Lunch? You have to eat.
ERNESTO: *Niña, déjama quieto!!!* Please.

RUTH: OK, look. We've been speaking to each other like this for a while now. It's like you don't find me attractive, and I just . . . I can't wrap my mind around that.

ERNESTO: Is it your humility that turns men on so?

RUTH: Ow.

[RUTH *begins to walk away.* ERNESTO *stops her.*]

ERNESTO: Ruth.

[*Beat.*]

   I'm gay.

RUTH: Oh. Yeah, and I'm thirsty.

[*Beat.*]

   Oh, were you thinking coffee was like an invitation to sex?

ERNESTO: You come on a little hard.

RUTH: Only because I knew you were gay.

[*Beat.*]

   I did.

ERNESTO: Here, let me help you with those bags. So, the world is your testosterone oyster, eh?

[*Light fades on* ERNESTO *and* RUTH *and comes up on* JORDAN, *playing scales on her cello.*]

JORDAN [*to the audience*]: I never liked practicing.

[*Beat.*]

   I hate practicing! I was made for an audience, and without one it just seemed pointless. I mean the art happens here [*indicating space between the audience and the stage with her bow*], right here in between you and me is where the art happens. It's not music without you. When it's just me and my instrument, it's not making love, it's more like brushing and flossing before making love. Maybe putting goo on the diaphragm . . . But when you join the mix—that's where I live. That's the only place where I know how to . . . That's where it all happens.

[*She plays.*]

   Now see, this is music.

[JORDAN'S *music continues; light rises on* RUTH. JORDAN'S *music and light fade gradually through* RUTH's *monologue.* JORDAN *plays a Mozart minuet that becomes more stylized and jazzy, fading during* RUTH's *monologue.*]

RUTH: Understand, Ernesto was not my first love. He is not the only man I have loved; just the only one who does not make me feel . . . off balance. But what we share is special, and if you think that's hard to understand, try explaining it to your husband.

[*Many years after college. The phone rings in the living room area, where* BRIAN *lounges with a morning newspaper and coffee. He answers the phone as* RUTH *snuggles in.*]

BRIAN: Morning, Brennans.

[*Beat.* BRIAN *displays thinly veiled annoyance.*]

Oh. Hey. Yeah, she's right here. No, she can talk, hold on.

[BRIAN *hands* RUTH *the phone as light comes up on* ERNESTO.]

ERNESTO: Jane Fonda. *Klute.*
RUTH: You're right. [*To* BRIAN] Ernie's helping me with my list.
BRIAN: Stupid Bush quotes or rappers turned actors?
RUTH: No, those got too long. Hollywood hoes. [*To* ERNESTO] So, that gives us
     Pretty Woman, Leaving Las Vegas, Irma La Deuce, The Owl and the Pussycat . . .
ERNESTO: Double ho for Barbra . . . crazy ho in *Nuts.*

[*Beat.*]

     Breakfast at Tiffany's.

[BRIAN *makes a big fuss, searching for some unseen newspaper section.*]

BRIAN: *Breakfast at Tiffany's.*
RUTH: I know, Ernie said it. [*To* ERNESTO] Holly Golightly wasn't a prostitute.
BRIAN AND ERNESTO: She was.
BRIAN: Baby . . . can you count hoes later?

[*He reaches for the phone.*]

RUTH: Oh, honey, I have to go. Brian needs some stroking.
ERNESTO: Yeah, well when duty calls . . .

[RUTH *hangs up.*]

RUTH: You're mad.

BRIAN: I'm hungry.
RUTH: Ernesto says hi.
BRIAN: Um.

[RUTH *gropes to make it better. Pause.*]

RUTH: I was thinking I'd make you dinner.
BRIAN: Really?
RUTH: You pick. Steak, potatoes, and a nice salad. Or eggs and a blow job.
BRIAN: You know you're only half as cute as you think you are.

[*Beat.*]

Scrambled?

[*Early stages of* RUTH *and* BRIAN's *relationship.* BRIAN *nuzzles her neck while* RUTH *narrates.* JORDAN's *music plays softly in the background.*]

RUTH: I really thought I was—
BRIAN: Cute . . .
RUTH: Youth's wonderful. That time when you still smell young—

[BRIAN *stands behind her, running his hands down her sides.*]

BRIAN: —and taste young—
RUTH: —and your breasts are—
BRIAN: —perky—
RUTH: —firm. And you feel the power, or maybe it's not power, it's a little more spiritual than that, I don't know what it is—oh, that's nice . . .

[*This is a very stylized love scene; while* RUTH *continues to narrate,* BRIAN *picks her up, still she maintains her concentration and speaks to the audience.*]

Heady stuff. I don't think the downstairs neighbors liked us much. They couldn't believe that a mattress could make that much noise—
BRIAN: —for that long—
RUTH: —at any time of day.
BRIAN: Several times a day.
RUTH: It was powerful. A spiritual, intellectual, and sensual gift from Brian. He taught me to enjoy my body and his, helped me not be ashamed, made the bad thoughts go away, and replaced them with . . . Now it's not power so much as it's, oh, I don't know what it is, but I've never been one to look a gift horse in the mouth.

[*Lights fade as* RUTH *kneels in front of* BRIAN. *Lights come up on* JORDAN, *still playing—she notices* RUTH *and* BRIAN.]

JORDAN: Oh my. Over here. Hi.

[*Beat. She smiles.*]

> I started playing when I was six. They make little cellos, but I always had a big one. I was tall. I almost stopped taking lessons because I thought I'd die if I had to play any more variations on "Twinkle, Twinkle, Little Star."

[BRIAN *exits.*]

RUTH [*to the audience*]: You know those stories where the woman wanders around, hopeless and sad and pathetic until the prince comes and rescues her and then she's happy.

JORDAN: But just when I'm about to quit Uncle Noah gives me this book of Mozart pieces and explains that Mozart was just a kid too when he wrote them. Didn't matter that cello wasn't his instrument. His mistake. It was on! Mozart became not my ally or inspiration, but the competition.

RUTH: Well, they never show the princess being happy, you just know that she is, because the prince is kissing her, or carrying her, or kissing and carrying her off on a big white horse. Actually, usually they're all white, but somehow that doesn't keep little girls like me from identifying with the princess. You have to identify with somebody, right? Clearly I didn't think I looked like Cinderella or Snow White, but who else did I have?

[RUTH *moves downstage where a college-age* ERNESTO *is drawing figures on a notepad.* RUTH *completes her monologue to* ERNESTO *as she settles.* ERNESTO *folds a piece of the paper and hands it to* RUTH, *who holds it to her head, Carnak the Magnificent style.*]

ERNESTO: That's awful. Last one.

RUTH: You said that fifteen minutes ago. Do you want me to graduate or not?

[*Beat.*]

> It's a house.

ERNESTO: How are you doing that?

RUTH: Insomnia-induced clairvoyance.

ERNESTO: But you didn't even see it.

[*Beat.*]

> I'm sorry. You're still not sleeping?

RUTH: It's worse than not sleeping. It's like not being able to breathe. As soon as I get in the bed I just, I just . . . I don't know, I feel . . . for as long as I can remember. And now it follows me around all day this feeling. It lurks. So I watch television for women all night.

ERNESTO: That can't be good.

RUTH: I can't help it. I can't stop. It's like one Middle American housewife getting her ass whipped after another. And I'm crying and telling myself I'll turn it off and go to sleep right after the next commercial . . . but all I can do is lay there and wait for Meredith Baxter Birney to fight for her child or Connie Sellecca to get her head bashed in.

ERNESTO: OK, night owl, bet you can't do this one.

RUTH: The point isn't to mess me up.

[ERNESTO *closes his eyes again, concentrating.*]

I can't play, I have to study or I'll flunk psych.

ERNESTO: I'll take it for you if you'll write my English lit.

RUTH: Not Fuentes again? And how can they call that English?

ERNESTO: It's translated. They're diversifying.

RUTH: That's cheating. Hey, how can you have such a devious mind and go to mass every Sunday?

ERNESTO: We can sin, we just have to feel guilty about it. Now shut up and concentrate.

RUTH: I can't do this one.

ERNESTO: Sure you can. *Estoy pensando, estoy pensando.*

RUTH: Clearly, if you think about it in Spanish, I won't get it.

ERNESTO: Sorry. Hey, what's this with the "clearly" thing? You've been saying that a lot lately. Clearly, i.e., ya big dumb fuck . . .

RUTH: Is this animosity?

ERNESTO: No, I'm just trying to save you from the many people you will alienate later in life if you begin every sentence with "clearly."

RUTH: Thank you. Clearly, I'm indebted.

ERNESTO [*laughing and drawing furiously*]: Try this one.

RUTH [*laughing*]: Ernesto, you have a filthy mind, and the one before that was a *triángulo.*

ERNESTO: You were meant to have my baby one day.

RUTH: It's possible. How 'bout we graduate from college, get settled, find husbands, and see what happens. Oh, and the test is at three, in the pavilion. And please don't forget to put my name on the blue book this time.

ERNESTO: And, honey, it's not Fuentes, it's Gabriel García Márquez.

RUTH: Oh God, a hundred years of writing that paper, in solitude. Thanks.

[RUTH *exits the college area and lands on the couch she most recently inhabited with* BRIAN. *She is now in postcollege/pre-*BRIAN *time.*]

[*To the audience*] The only thing that changed after college was Brian's income and my hair. So, two weaves, one extension, a texturizer, and one relaxer later . . .

[ERNESTO *enters.*]

ERNESTO: Sorry I'm late, prelims are a bitch.

[*He stops and assesses* RUTH's *mood.*]

Good day or bad day . . .
RUTH: It matters?
ERNESTO: If you're having a bad day we're going to the movies.
RUTH: So you don't have to talk to me.
ERNESTO: Fair enough.
RUTH: Good day?
ERNESTO: Well, then I would have two words for you.
RUTH: OK. I'm intrigued.
ERNESTO: Ice cream. But still, you'll have to take a shower and comb your hair.
RUTH: Sounds good, but I'd really like something a little more . . .
ERNESTO: Substantive . . .
RUTH: Spirited . . .
ERNESTO: I'll see what I can do.
RUTH: If it's your treat we could do dinner too. [*To the audience*] It's fun when your roommate has money. It's funny too, 'cause it's never caused tension. I pay when I can and Ernesto pays the rest of the time.
ERNESTO [*to the audience*]: Most of the time. [*To* RUTH] My treat . . . dinner, beverages, and a movie.
RUTH: I feel better already, you'll be a great uncle one day.
ERNESTO: Oh my God . . . Are you . . . ?
RUTH: No. Have you seen me anywhere in the vicinity of a penis?
ERNESTO: Uugghh. The picture, flashing before my eyes. Lighten up on the crudeness and you'd be a great mom.
RUTH: So would we both.
ERNESTO: I'd be the doddering Uncle Ernie. *Tío.* They'd call me Tío.
RUTH: Well, Tío, dinner and ice cream it is.

SCENE 2

[*Lights indicate a shift forward in time.* RUTH *and* ERNESTO *are in the same living space as previous scene—postcollege.*]

RUTH [*to the audience*]: OK, so I think I get why people like romance stories. It's not because we want that thing. That whatever it is that Meg Ryan, Halle Berry, Sandra Bullock, and Julia seem to find over and over again with handsome, too old male leads. OK, so not Halle Berry as much. Really, I don't think we'd know what to do with it if we got it. I think it's just that we have to long for something. That's the most I can make of it. Because even when it looks like a movie, especially when it looks like a movie, it feels like crap.

[*Beat.*]

ERNESTO: You're becoming more and more morbid.

RUTH: Is that your clinical opinion? [*To the audience*] All right, I don't mind sharing. Ernesto, I think, got tired of being my shoulder. [*To* ERNESTO] I've always been morbid, I'm just becoming more poetic in my morbidity.

ERNESTO: Honey, I'm starting to feel like one of those gay guys in the movies, you know, the one whose sole purpose in life is to comfort the female protagonist.

RUTH [*clearly upset*]: But, Ernesto, you're not that pretty.

ERNESTO: OK, the *Will and Grace* bitchy thing—not so cute either.

RUTH: I'm sorry. I just, feel so, like, like shit. All the time. [*To the audience*] I just felt awful. Things were going all right. I really enjoyed teaching. The kids were cute. But I was so lonely, and just kind of hurt, through my heart and into my bones all the time. And I think I was starting to scare Ernesto.

ERNESTO [*to the audience*]: I wasn't afraid, but being the best shrink in the world just didn't give me license to mess with my best friend's head. That would be like incest. But Ruth hadn't really slept in a year and was turning into this nervous, bitter, lethargic, depressed person. [*To* RUTH] Here, take this number. He's good. Most of his clients are therapists. You need that, what with your overly analytical, self-deprecating ass. You're depressed. That's a sickness, go to the doctor.

RUTH: Is he . . .

ERNESTO: Expensive?

RUTH: Black.

ERNESTO: How long have we known each other?

RUTH [*to the audience*]: Depression is this weird thing. It's like being stuck in quicksand with the flu. And even though nothing is really wrong with you, you just kind of hurt all of the time, and in places that are hard to locate. And you don't ever properly nurse it yourself, because you don't know how, and your friends can't do much about it because they can't see it. And if you do make it known to them, they just kind of want to help, but they don't know how, and then, I think no matter how much they love you, eventually they just want you to buck up and be strong. I didn't know how to be that strong. How was I supposed to figure it out, I was too busy being depressed.

[RUTH *crosses and establishes the therapy area, where all scenes in* BRIAN's *office will take place.*]

It was a real head trip. I stood him up twice. I just couldn't bring myself to go. I couldn't. When I finally went, I was, like, ten minutes late, for no reason.

BRIAN: It's OK, it happens, the first time. Now you know how long it takes.

RUTH: Takes?

BRIAN: To get here.

RUTH: Yeah. [*To the audience*] His office was comfortable. A lot like my place, but with, um, nicer stuff. More expensive stuff. It smelled expensive. It looked more expensive, like the difference between a white Kmart T-shirt and a white Ann Taylor T-shirt. Still white, but just sort of nicer around the edges. The thing I noticed most of all, though, was how comfortable he looked in the middle of it all. Like he'd been sitting there all day, just waiting for you, me, to complete the picture.

BRIAN: You like it?

RUTH: It's comfortable. What should I call you?

BRIAN: What would you feel most comfortable calling me?

RUTH [*to* ERNESTO]: My little kumquat. [*To* BRIAN] I'm sorry, you were saying...?

BRIAN: Why don't you call me Brian.

RUTH: OK.

[*Beat.*]

Brian.

BRIAN: You know, you can sit wherever you feel most comfortable, you don't have to take the couch if you don't want to.

RUTH [*to the audience*]: That's what he said to me my first day there, which made me laugh because—here let me show you ... OK, there was a chair behind his desk, which sat in a corner of the room, and two chairs kind of next to each other facing the couch, which was this amazingly beautiful beige chambray thing with dark green and burgundy and rust pillows and a cashmere throw, all sort of saying, Come sit your crazy ass on me. [*Laughs.*]

BRIAN: "Sit anywhere you want" is funny?

RUTH: Yeah. But you probably realize also that that was a, uh, nervous reaction. I'm feeling, maybe a little, vulnerable, and have a tendency to be, or seem, no, be, flip.

BRIAN [*smiling*]: So, you've had therapy before?

RUTH: Briefly, right after college, but it was with this white woman to whom I kept having to explain the emotional ramifications of racism.

BRIAN [*amused*]: So, you haven't had therapy. Good, we'll cut to the chase then. Why are you here?

RUTH: I don't know.

[*She sits on the couch and immediately begins to sob. Lights fade on office.*]

SCENE 3

[*Lights come up on* JORDAN's *area, where the cello rests next to her chair.* JORDAN *enters from the opposite side, crossing downstage.*]

JORDAN [*to the audience*]: What would you most like to be called? It's not a trick question, really. Would you most rather be called beautiful or really great at whatever it is that you do? It's not a fair question and I'll tell you why. It's impossible to answer honestly. First, to be *called* beautiful and to *be* beautiful are two such entirely different things. And we all think we have a bead on where we fall. [*To an audience member*] Try it. Tell me I'm really beautiful. I mean it. Say "Jordan, you're really beautiful."

[*She finds someone willing and continues.*]

There now. Yeah, oh yeah, thank you, but I told you to say that, you don't really mean it. Now listen to this.

[JORDAN *crosses to the cello and plays a few bars of something beautiful.*]

Now say "Jordan, you're a really, really wonderful cellist." Say it.

[*Beat.*]

Thank you. And you all know she meant it, because you heard it, right? But now, what if I'm a model.

[JORDAN *strikes a pose.*]

No, no, don't say anything, don't speak . . . I wouldn't be flattered even if my whole identity was wrapped up in my looks, because I'm either going to think that what's on the outside is all you see, or I'm gonna think you want to sleep with me. So, you know, I really am trying to say something here.

[JORDAN *puts the cello down and walks off. Lights rise on* ERNESTO, *outside, holding a big bag of groceries, waiting.* BILL *enters.*]

BILL: You look burdened.
ERNESTO: I'm OK, thanks.
BILL: I'm in the lot if you need a ride.
ERNESTO: Thanks, I'm waiting for my . . .
BILL: Roommate?
ERNESTO: So I've heard them called.

[*Beat.*]

BILL: It's looking more and more like rain, huh?
ERNESTO: You don't get out much, do you?

[*Pause.*]

I'm sorry, that was a little bitchy. He knows that they're coming at eight. I told him to be here at six. Princess had to go to the vet, and he has this macho thing where he has to drive me everywhere. So here I stand and there's a soufflé in the oven about to turn into—
BILL: You're being theatrical.
ERNESTO: Beg your pardon?
BILL: Yeah, I was with you right up until the soufflé part, when I figured out you were full of shit.

[*Beat, beat.*]

Or you're a pathological liar. No one leaves a soufflé in the oven.
ERNESTO: Are you a chef?
BILL: I'm a Renaissance man. And in addition to being a consummate musician, an excellent carpenter, and an all-around nice guy, I can whip up a mean truffle soufflé. Wha-da-ya say I join you all for dinner? I'll cook and you can make up with what's his name. What is his name?
ERNESTO: Ruth.

[*Pause.*]

BILL: Jordan better have a fifteen-inch dick, or you're more pathological than I thought. Do you have saffron at home?

[*Lights fade on* BILL *and* ERNESTO. *Special up on* RUTH, *standing in the doorway of* BRIAN'S *office in the therapy area.*]

BRIAN: I'm glad you're back, Ruth.
RUTH [*standing nervously in front of stool*]: I don't know why I'm here?
BRIAN: Why don't you have a seat and I can make us a cup of tea. Do you like tea?
RUTH: If I say yes will that mean something about me?
BRIAN: Probably.
RUTH: Yes.
BRIAN: Sugar or honey?
RUTH: Straight up.

[*Light up on* ERNESTO.]

　　[*To* ERNESTO] I thought this transference thing or whatever you call it was supposed to happen later.
ERNESTO: What are you talking about?
RUTH: That thing where you fall in love with your shrink. Isn't it a phenome-non or something? He's cute—he got me tea.

[BILL *hands* ERNESTO *a mug while* BRIAN *hands* RUTH *a mug.*]

RUTH AND ERNESTO: Thank you.
ERNESTO: I think it's only transference when he falls in love back. Which he won't.
BRIAN: So, I say again, what brings you here?
RUTH: A friend of mine suggested it. [*To* ERNESTO] Yes, "cute" is the word.
ERNESTO: How cute?
RUTH: Very.
BRIAN: Do you want to be here?
RUTH AND ERNESTO: Very. I want to be here very much. I think.

[*Lights fade on* BRIAN *and* RUTH, *lights up on* BILL *and* ERNESTO.]

BILL: You think?
ERNESTO: I'm a thinker.

[*He takes a sip of tea.*]

This is great. What is this?

BILL: It was in your kitchen. Orange and lemon juice, cinnamon, cloves, brown sugar, and one peppercorn. A little something I picked up on a *National Geographic* gig in Kathmandu.

ERNESTO: Why are you still here?

BILL: Come again?

ERNESTO: Don't take this the wrong way, but you don't strike me as the stick-around kind.

BILL: Do you always live in such a bleak future?

ERNESTO: It's the influence of my other boyfriend. Ruth.

[RUTH *and* ERNESTO *sit at a café table.*]

OK. Five minutes for something other than Dr. Brian's eyes.

RUTH: What else is there?

ERNESTO: Me.

RUTH: Fair enough.

ERNESTO: Bill's eyes are so beautiful. They're like the color of a silver cloud . . .

RUTH [*to the audience*]: It was exciting seeing Ernesto in love.

ERNESTO: . . . dancing in the reflection of a shimmering moon, and his lips are so beautiful . . .

RUTH: Mostly nice . . . sometimes just corny.

ERNESTO: . . . like the softest petal of the dew-covered morning rosebud.

RUTH: So yes, it was exciting seeing my best friend in love.

ERNESTO [*to the audience*]: Pretty damned exciting being in love.

RUTH [*to the audience*]: For so long we'd only had each other . . .

ERNESTO: And Princess . . .

RUTH: Yes, there is Princess . . . one part Pekingese . . .

ERNESTO: . . . three parts adorable ball of fur.

RUTH: Anyway, I suspect it was the closeness of this triumvirate that made it so hard to find others. I'm convinced that you put out a kind of "manless woman scent," and I just know the men could smell Ernesto on me. I smelled and looked taken care of, because I was, spiritually. I was loved and nurtured and made to feel special. There was someone around who really knew how to do those guy things that I'm completely competent at, but it's so damn nice to have someone around who can fix that towel rack or replace that washer or say . . .

ERNESTO and BILL [ERNESTO *to* RUTH, BILL *to* ERNESTO]: Let me put that doorknob back on for you.

RUTH: The only thing our little domestic situation didn't offer me was sex. For Ernesto I think it was harder . . .

ERNESTO: Lonelier.

RUTH: . . . and there I was, reminding him of just how lonely he was. What he could almost be for me I couldn't come close to being for him. Enter Bill. Exit Ernie.

[ERNESTO *is moving into* BILL'*s place. There are very subtle cross-fades when scenes overlap, less subtle when a huge change of time is denoted.*]

ERNESTO: So what haven't you done?

BILL: I haven't been a rocket scientist.

ERNESTO: But you probably had to study about them when you wrote for *Encyclopaedia Britannica.*

BILL: OK, OK. And your point, Doctor?

[*Lights come up on* BRIAN *in his office.*]

BRIAN: You like Ernesto's new boyfriend . . .

RUTH: Bill.

BRIAN: You like Bill?

RUTH: I think so. I guess so.

[*The phone rings.*]

BILL: Hello.

RUTH: Oh, Bill. Hi.

BILL: Hey.

RUTH: Ernie there?

BILL: Sure.

[*Long pause.* BILL *makes no effort to get* ERNESTO.]

RUTH: I thought that if you and Ernesto wanted we could skip the movie and just hang out at my place.

BILL: That sounds good. Yeah, I could whip up a little dinner and we could catch a movie at my place.

RUTH: Could you put Ernie on.

BILL: Ernie's indisposed at the moment. Can I have him call you back?

RUTH: Sure.

BRIAN: So what do you think of him?

RUTH: He's OK. He takes good care of Ernie.

[*The following interactions between* ERNESTO *and* BILL *take place in different places at different times. Lights remain up on both playing areas.*]

ERNESTO [*on the phone*]: Hey, honey, I have to stay late tonight. I have a client that needs to come late, and I, I can't refuse her. I'm sorry to ruin our plans, I'm just not going to be any good for a date. I'm exhausted right now.

BILL: Well, what time are you done?

ERNESTO: I have some assessments to do after, probably 10:30.

BILL: How about I pick you up then, and we come to my place. I'll put in *Aida* and draw a bath, a hot dinner, you'll be good as new.

RUTH: He's maybe a little too good.

BRIAN: And what's too good?

BILL: Oh shit, I'm late for my class. Have you seen my keys?

ERNESTO: Right here. [*Tossing* BILL *the keys*] Honey, do you like teaching TaeBo or step aerobics better?

RUTH: He has looks, and money, and talent, and wit . . . it's just not right.

ERNESTO [*working crossword puzzle*]: Um . . . honey, um, starts with *a*, fifteen letters down, people centered . . . ?

RUTH: Narcissistic?

ERNESTO: That's an *n*.

BILL: Anthropocentric.

ERNESTO: It fits . . . You're truly amazing.

RUTH: And it's not like he's a show-off, and I guess I'm not jealous. Well, not very jealous. Something's just not right. I've been wanting to say something, but I wouldn't know what to say. You can't just say, "Ernesto, your boyfriend's perfect and I don't trust that."

BRIAN: And why don't you?

RUTH: I just don't believe that anyone gets to have it all. It doesn't work that way. We all come with compromises. Like me for instance. I'm a lot of things that a lot of men would, at first glance, think they'd want. What? You look amused.

BRIAN: Do I?

RUTH: Yeah, in a kind of condescending way. Like I'm a kitten or something.

BRIAN: You think I look amused?

RUTH: Anyway, I'm just saying that a man would have no way of knowing who I am, what baggage I come with, how difficult I can be to love.

BILL: I'm falling in love with you, Ernesto.

ERNESTO: I think it's mutual, but I always tell my clients to enjoy it, but be careful.

BILL [*embracing* ERNESTO]: We're always careful.

ERNESTO: You know what I mean.

BILL: Look, I, uh, I have been all over the world, met all kinds of people, climbed mountains, crossed deserts. So, maybe I'm guilty of using this, this great life I've been so lucky to have as a social crutch. But listen, and you have to hear this. I look into your eyes and I see myself so much more clearly. I like the way I reflect back. I am so much better than I am, with you, and for the first time in a long time, I don't want to be anywhere else. Don't get weirded out, I know we're moving fast, and I've never been a fan of boy-boy commitment ceremonies. I think they're queer. But I'm reconsidering. I want people to know. I want a little fidelity insurance. And I want gifts.

[*They kiss.*]

RUTH: When things are too good it just scares me.

BRIAN: Let's talk about that next week.

RUTH: Why is it always next week just when we're getting somewhere?

BRIAN: Where are we trying to go?

RUTH: I thought the purpose of this whole thing was for me to—

BRIAN: Let's save that for next week. You think about that.

SCENE 4

[*Lights shift,* BRIAN *exits, and* RUTH *remains standing in what was the therapy area.* RUTH *advances downstage, where* ERNESTO *joins her, midmonologue.*]

RUTH [*to the audience*]: When I told my grandma that I was in therapy, her response was, "Well, baby, have you thought about going to church?" Which I have to admit did make me take pause. I've just never been able to reconcile my personal dislike of most religious institutions with my desire to be a part of something that feeds and nurtures my soul.

ERNESTO: Why reconcile? Why not just accept?

RUTH: I'm not an atheist. I'm even a little more than an agnostic. I don't go to church every Sunday, but I'm a little more religious than people who say . . .

BILL [*appearing in a jogging suit*]: I'm a very spiritual person, but I don't go to church. God is in the trees and I commune with the trees when I'm jogging.

RUTH: And not nearly as religious as . . .

ERNESTO: What would it hurt for you to come to mass with me just every other Sunday?

RUTH: I don't have time.

ERNESTO: Ruth, they have like four different times . . .

RUTH: I know.

[RUTH *crosses herself, backward, and kneels downstage . . .* ERNESTO *joins her, genuflecting correctly.* ERNESTO *recites the Lord's Prayer in Spanish, beginning alone and continuing under* RUTH'*s monologue.*]

ERNESTO: *Padre nuestro, que estás en el cielo, santificado sea tu nombre, venga tu reino, hágase Señor tu voluntad en la tierra como en el cielo, dános hoy nuestro pan de cada día, perdona nuestras ofensas como también nosotros perdonamos a los que nos ofenden, no nos dejes caer en tentación y líbranos del mal, amén.*

[ERNESTO *repeats the prayer until his next line. Upstage* BILL *begins to warm up for a jog. His light will eventually fade out.*]

RUTH [*to the audience*]: You know, when I was a kid I just knew that if God was going to be anywhere he would be in a Catholic church. If I were God I would really groove on the pomp and circumstance of the whole thing. The smoke, and wine, and gilded statues. Those old city Catholic churches are built to make you feel insignificant . . .

ERNESTO: And you have a problem with being insignificant next to God?

RUTH: When you say it like that it makes me feel so . . .

BILL: Yeah, I think I'm a pretty spiritual person. God is definitely in me.

RUTH: There's something so off-putting about the whole Catholic thing. Besides the obvious ones that creep out most non-Catholics, like the no-sex thing, there are also the in-club things. Like what to do with the water on your way in, and what are you supposed to do if you aren't Catholic, and when to kneel, and what to say back to the priest and when you're supposed to say it . . .

ERNESTO [*saying it*]: And also with you.

RUTH: . . . and when you're supposed to sing it . . .

ERNESTO [*singing it*]: And also with you-ooo.

RUTH: My biggest fear is that if I take communion I'll be struck with lightening, but if I don't [*pause*] I'll be struck with lightening. It's a club. It's a big ol' religious frat, with noble intentions. I want to think that God and his Son are bigger and better than all that and are in some little old lady's kitchen, lighting the pilot light so she doesn't gas herself.

[RUTH *gets up and crosses to* BRIAN'*s office, where they have been in session.*]

Brian, do you believe in God?

BRIAN: Is it important to you that I do?

RUTH: No.

BRIAN: Um.

RUTH: I *do* think that what you do is not so different from what they do.

BRIAN: They?

RUTH: The priests. You take care of other people at the expense of yourself.

BRIAN: I'm not sure that that's what I do.

RUTH: I am.

BRIAN: We're here to talk about you.

RUTH: Exactly. What a perfect job for someone who can't confront his own stuff.

BRIAN: I tell my clients that I am vulnerable in this relationship too.

RUTH: Brian, this isn't a relationship. I pay you.

BRIAN: And I provide a service. We've been through this.

RUTH: Not through why you devote your life to listening to people like me bitch about their shit.

BRIAN: I like to think that I'm helping people like you help themselves.

RUTH: Yes, but the priests own that they get off on helping others. That's all they have. You don't even get doughnuts and brownies and the affection of little old ladies. You just get the problems, and maybe a family and a life, sex.

[*Beat.*]

Is your significant other person "of color," Brian?

BRIAN: Well, I see we're out of time. We'll start with this next week.

RUTH: No we won't.

BRIAN: I'll tell you a trick. I don't want to talk about this, but it is the end of your session, so I'm going to write down where we stopped. If it's really important to you, you'll bring it up next week, and if you don't, I won't.

[*Light begins to fade on* BRIAN, *up on* BILL *and* ERNESTO *at a restaurant table, where* RUTH *joins them.*]

RUTH: But isn't there a conflict of interest?

BILL AND ERNESTO: No.

RUTH: No?

ERNESTO: No. Because I believe in the Body of Christ.

RUTH: I don't understand.

ERNESTO: And so you're not Catholic. I really, really could use my beer.

BILL: Isn't that your third?

ERNESTO: Yeah, and?

RUTH: But you're gay.

ERNESTO [*jokingly*]: Shhhh ... someone will hear you.

RUTH: You know what I'm saying, don't you, Bill?

ERNESTO: We don't talk about this. [*To* RUTH] Pass me your beer.

RUTH: I do respect it. Here.

[RUTH *pushes her beer toward* ERNESTO. BILL *intercepts it and hands the glass back to* RUTH.]

I just don't understand how you can be so devoted, how you can say you belong to an institution that says you don't count.

ERNESTO: The same way you can call yourself an American.

[*Lights rise on* JORDAN, *who plays a couple of bars of something snappy and patriotic.*]

JORDAN: I've never been good at relationships. Not just the romantic ones, but
across the board. I don't know how to sustain them. Once it's serious enough
for me to care if a person's in or out of my life, they're out. I could say it's my
profession, keeps me on the road, hard to sustain a relationship that way, but
my father wouldn't have let me get away with that.

[*Lights rise on* BRIAN *and* RUTH, *in session.*]

BRIAN: I'm raising the bar today, Ruth. I don't want you to perform for me . . . I
want you to talk to me.

RUTH: Fine. Then ask me a question.

BRIAN: Are you dating?

RUTH: Isn't that a little forward?

BRIAN: If we were in a bar, possibly. Since you pay me to ask you these things,
you should consider answering the question.

RUTH: Oh . . . look at that. Time's up.

[*She hands* BRIAN *a check.*]

Could you hold my check until Friday?

BRIAN: Does something scare you?

RUTH: Brian, everything scares me.

SCENE 5

[RUTH *is in* BRIAN's *office. Light and blocking have shifted to indicate a time change.
We are seeing a later session.* RUTH *addresses the audience, changing her focus to* BRIAN
toward the end of the monologue.]

RUTH: The school I teach at is this kind of, well, it's a school for rich, urban, mostly white kids. It's not even a magnet school, it's just shamelessly placed in the richest neighborhood in Chicago and caters to a, like, ten-block radius of richness. I just landed there, and the first year I was like, This is bullshit, I've got to get out of here and into a real neighborhood and around some real black kids or I'm gonna lose my mind. Then I started to know them and they stopped being fucked-up little white kids with blue hair, and black and Hispanic kids with white-kid friends with blue hair. They actually turned into real people, and somewhere along the way they became my kids.

[*Pause.*]

I'm always amazed. I mean, when I was a kid I never wanted for anything in a real way, but these kids have things like beepers and cell phones and sex.

BRIAN: Do you enjoy sex, Ruth?

RUTH: Not that kids weren't having sex ten years ago, it's just that I wasn't.

BRIAN: Do you like sex, Ruth?

RUTH: These girls carry pills and condoms around in their purses like I carried Bonne Bell lip gloss and Pop Rocks. It's just that they seem like such kids to me.

BRIAN: Do you like sex?

RUTH: Is this really what we're talking about?

BRIAN: Is this making you uncomfortable?

RUTH: No, not really. Yeah.

BRIAN: OK. Well we can, um, start here next week.

[*Blackout, then lights up.*]

So your first sexual experience was when?

RUTH: Huh?

BRIAN: Does this make you uncomfortable, Ruth?

RUTH: Yeah, I guess.

[*Lights down and back up.*]

BRIAN: Does this make you uncomfortable?

RUTH: Yeah.

BILL AND ERNESTO: Why?

[*Lights rise on* BILL *and* ERNESTO *in a café.* RUTH *remains in therapy but communicates with them as though she were right there.*]

BILL: You're about the most unprudish person I've ever met.

ERNESTO: Yeah.

RUTH: But that's in a different context.

ERNESTO: Sitting across from a sexy guy is the wrong context?

RUTH [*to* BRIAN]: So sex is what we're talking about.

BRIAN: Some schools of thought suggest that it's all we're talking about. I don't
necessarily agree with that.

[*Pause.*]

Have you ever been raped?

RUTH [*to* ERNESTO]: It's like it came out of nowhere.

ERNESTO: He's good.

RUTH: He's difficult.

ERNESTO: That's his job sometimes, honey.

RUTH [*to* BRIAN]: I'm sorry, you caught me off guard.

[*Beat.*]

They say that one out of every three women has been sexually assaulted,
right?

BRIAN: Give or take, depending on definition.

RUTH: Well, my two closest girlfriends have not, ever, been, um, you know. So
the odds are in my favor.

BRIAN: That's not very direct, Ruth.

RUTH: Because it's not why I'm here. It was a date thing. I was stupid. He was
young. I've worked through all that.

BRIAN: OK.

RUTH: When I thought about going into therapy I got stuck on whether I
wanted a woman or a man, and a woman seemed better. I just trust them
more. And then I thought, Well, the only person you can really trust is your
therapist, right? You're paying him to be trustworthy, right?

[*Pause. She waits for an answer but doesn't get one.*]

So, anyway I just, I just thought, Maybe a male, a man psychologist would
help me get over my fear of them.

[*Beat.*]

You.

[*Beat.*]

Men.

BRIAN: Are you afraid of me?

RUTH: No, because I don't care about you.

[*Pause.*]

Yet.

[RUTH *crosses and ends up in the café with* BILL *and* ERNESTO.]

ERNESTO: I think it's totally normal.

BILL: No, it's very movie-of-the-week.

ERNESTO: Everyone falls in love with their therapist. It's part of the process.

BILL: Maybe it's only movie-of-the-week if he falls in love back.

RUTH: That's not movie-of-the-week; that's illegal.

BILL: I had sex with a therapist once.

RUTH: Cool.

ERNESTO: A psychologist? No you didn't.

BILL: I didn't say he was my therapist.

RUTH: How cute do you think you are?

BILL: He was my therapist, but it was only our first session, and I was talking about, oh, I don't know, something my mother did wrong or something and he was sitting there with his leg crossed looking so damned . . . invested. And I said, "Look, you know, there are so many psychiatrists in this city and so few good lays, so, seeing as it's a conflict of interest, how about I quit and you fuck me." And he did, right there on the couch. And it was the best . . .

ERNESTO: Careful.

BILL: It was just about the best sex I've ever had.

RUTH: What happened?

BILL: What do you mean?

RUTH: Did you date him or something?

BILL: I would have, just to have sex on that couch again, but he freaked out on me. I mean, he got off of me and turned like a dozen shades of red and then white and was like, "That has never happened." And then he started to cry and said, "Please leave, just go. Don't come back." I think he moved away from town and changed his name. I never found him.

[*Beat.*]

Could I get some more foam on this latte?

[RUTH *and* ERNESTO *exchange a glance and* RUTH *crosses downstage to* BRIAN'S *office. Light fades up gradually.*]

RUTH: Fine, OK. Sex.

[*Beat.*]

Louis Gates. He was the first.

BRIAN: OK.

RUTH: Not Henry the famous intellectual, he's got a white wife. Oooo, that sounded bitter, oh well, it was. 'Course I wouldn't kick Peter Jennings or Tom Selleck out of my bed for eating crackers. I even had a profound adolescent crush on Itzhak Perlman. OK, anyway, my Louis was a football player with a red sports car and I wanted him. And when you're a girl you're not supposed to have sex with people you just want, you're supposed to love them, so I loved him. And he was so . . . you know . . . [*beat*] huge . . . that it took forever just for him to get it . . . in.

[*Long pause.* RUTH *is embarrassed; she looks at* BRIAN, *who matches her with a steady, professional gaze.*]

[*To* ERNESTO, *still at the café table with* BILL] I can't believe he got me to talk about this.

ERNESTO: I can't either.

RUTH: First we're talking about how stupid *Titanic* was.

ERNESTO: The film or the musical?

BILL: That's so gay.

RUTH: Whichever . . . [*To* BILL] Don't you ever have somewhere to be? [*Back to* ERNESTO] And then I'm talking about my boyfriend's hard-ons, like Brian's my best gal pal.

ERNESTO: Damn, he's good.

RUTH [*to* BRIAN]: So Louis was fast. Like, clinically premature.

BRIAN: How long did the relationship last?

RUTH: Too long. The second guy, Thor, was real pretty and [*beat*] white. Which lends a certain irony to my Henry Louis Gates white wife thing I was having. But I have issues. [*Laughs.*] I mean, that's why I'm here, right? So, he was very very rich and took me to the most expensive restaurants. Oh, and he was gay.

BRIAN: You knew this?

RUTH: No.

BRIAN: Did you . . .

RUTH: Of course, all the time. It was nice because unlike with, uh, Louis, I didn't feel impaled . . . [*To* ERNESTO] He's completely unflustered by it.

ERNESTO: He's supposed to be.

BRIAN: Anyway, we were talking about your relationships–slash–sexual history.

RUTH: Oh, yeah. [*To* ERNESTO] Shouldn't he get like a . . .

[RUTH *indicates she is speaking of an erection but does not say the word.* BRIAN *crosses his legs, still the picture of professionalism.*]

ERNESTO: Your issues aren't sexy, honey.

RUTH: But sometimes?

ERNESTO: Usually we don't. It's amazing how well your dick will behave if you know your career's on the line.

RUTH: There are some relatively tangible and recent examples to the contrary.

ERNESTO: We have our tricks.

BRIAN [*placing his notebook in his lap*]: You were saying.

RUTH: Well, it lasted for a year, and then I had a problem with that he was . . .

BRIAN AND ERNESTO: Gay?

RUTH: An alcoholic.

[*Beat.*]

Oh, and finally, Professor Keys, my art teacher. Very sexy, very long locks, shiny dark brown arms, and paint splatters. Always did like older men, and he said I was talented, so what could I do but put out? It was great until I walked in on him on top of some freshman, right there, on his desk, and he just looks up and says, "Oh, Ruthy, office hours don't start until three."

BRIAN: Do you like sex?

RUTH: Oh God, not that again.

BRIAN: Ruth, have you ever had an orga—

RUTH: You were going to tell me what strange thing about you makes you enjoy being a psychologist.

BRIAN: I'm not that easily manipulated, and our time is up.

ERNESTO: You probably should be having orgasms.

RUTH: But I'm not even having sex.

ERNESTO AND BILL: So?

RUTH: For women it's not absolutely necessary. We can still enjoy it without having, you know . . .

ERNESTO AND BILL: Right.

BRIAN: What about your dad?

RUTH: I don't remember much about him. What are you asking me?

BRIAN: I'm asking you what your relationship with your dad was.

RUTH: Nonexistent. He left when I was eight. I guess I missed him, but somehow the idea of seeing him just made me sick.

[*Pause.*]

I see where this is going. I know all about Freud.

BRIAN: Oh.

RUTH: Is that what it's about? Trying to find a daddy? That's too easy. I'll be damned if I'm paying hundreds of dollars to figure that out.

BRIAN: Have you even read Freud?

RUTH: No.

BRIAN: So what are you talking about?

RUTH: I'm just saying . . . Hey, wait. Your job isn't to make me feel stupid.

BRIAN: I can't make you feel anything.

RUTH: You're right, you can't. I don't feel a thing.

[*Long pause.* BRIAN *dims the light and changes his tone . . . soothing, casual, and conversational.*]

BRIAN: OK. Change of subject. Where did you eat breakfast?

RUTH: What?

BRIAN: At home, when you were a girl. Where did you eat breakfast?

RUTH: This morning?

BRIAN: Before. When you were little.

RUTH: At the breakfast table. What are you doing?

[*Light rises on* ERNESTO, *standing alone in an upstage area.*]

ERNESTO: Hey, Ruth. I need you.

RUTH [*to* ERNESTO]: I'm in the middle of something.

ERNESTO: Can I call you later?

RUTH: Sure . . . but I have that thing after work and then a—

BRIAN: Stay with me. Where?

[*Light out abruptly on* ERNESTO.]

RUTH: In the nook. Beside the refrigerator.

BRIAN: Where?

RUTH: In the kitchen.

BRIAN: Where did you watch TV?

RUTH: The couch.

BRIAN: What color was it?

RUTH: Brown.
BRIAN: Tell me more.

[*Light rises on* ERNESTO, *standing alone center stage. He addresses the audience.*]

ERNESTO: Ruth, you're supposed to call me.
RUTH: I'm so busy. This weekend . . . or maybe next week—
BRIAN: Ruth. The couch.

[*Light out abruptly on* ERNESTO.]

RUTH: Brown with little flecks on it and a dark spot in the corner where I
spilled some orange juice when I was six. And it smelled old, but comfort-
able, you know. And a little tuft of lint or stuffing or something popping up
out from where there was a button, like a little indentation where there was
an upholstered button. And when you would fall asleep on it, it was com-
fortable, like you were supposed to be there, you know?
BRIAN: Is that where you slept?
RUTH: Yes. No. I guess not?
BRIAN: Then where else?
RUTH: Did I sleep?
BRIAN: Where?
RUTH: Upstairs.
BRIAN: Where?
RUTH: Up the stairs, at the end of the hallway, no. No. No, to the right.
BRIAN: Where?
RUTH: My room was to the right.
BRIAN: Where you slept?
RUTH: Where I played.
BRIAN: And . . .
RUTH: And painted.
BRIAN: And at the end.
RUTH: Of the hall.
BRIAN: Where you slept?
RUTH: Of course not, I slept in my room, on the couch.
BRIAN: On the couch in your room?
RUTH: Downstairs, in my room. I'm confused. What . . .
BRIAN: And at the end of the hall . . .
RUTH: His room.
BRIAN: Whose?

RUTH: Mom's.

BRIAN: You said "his" . . .

RUTH: His. But I didn't sleep there. That's where . . . At the end of the . . . no . . . I slept on the second floor, to the right, at the end of the hallway. I . . .

[*Her voice drops off and she stares straight ahead, almost catatonic.*]

BRIAN: Where are you, Ruth?

RUTH: Clearly, I'm right here. I was just . . . thinking . . . you know, I really need to call Ernesto . . . he's been calling and—

BRIAN: We've never talked about your . . .

RUTH: Father?

BRIAN: Rape.

RUTH: I told you, I don't want to.

BRIAN: You don't have to. You have a lot of control here, Ruth.

RUTH: It really annoys me when you do the "therapist speak."

[*Long pause.*]

BRIAN: I'm just saying that you set the agenda. It's your money.

RUTH: Well, I guess I'm wasting it, because I don't have anything else to say to you.

[*She gets up to leave.*]

BRIAN: We have fifteen more minutes.

RUTH: Fuck you.

BRIAN: I wish you'd stay with me.

RUTH: Shut up for a second, will you.

[*She fights to gather her thoughts, then crosses to a far side of the office.*]

I was so happy when I got my first teaching paycheck. I thought it was a lot of money. The first thing I did was go to the Pottery Barn outlet and buy this magnificent bed. Brian, I have this beautiful bed. And before I get into it I do this long routine. I brush and floss, and shower, and wash my face, and put on moisturizer and zit stuff, and stuff for my elbows, and stuff for my feet, and then I go to my room. I pick out a new nightgown, it has to be pressed, and I go back to the bathroom and put it on, with fresh panties, and then I go to my bed [*pause*] and get the covers and go to the living room couch to sleep. I have a beautiful bed, and I've only laid down on it to fuck. I've never slept in it, by myself.

BRIAN: What's happening right now, Ruthy?

RUTH: Don't call me that.

BRIAN: What?

RUTH: Ruthy.

BRIAN: Whose name is that for you?

RUTH: Just shut the fuck up.

BRIAN: Why, Ruthy? Why? Why the couch?

RUTH: Stop that.

BRIAN: Ruthy?

RUTH: I slept on the couch because you didn't fuck with me there, mother-fucker. I could finally sleep. I could sleep and the TV would go and you, oh God, he. He couldn't make me. Go upstairs. Make me go upstairs, down the hall. As long as I sleep on the couch I don't have to stay awake in my room and listen for those steps. And if I lie very still. But you won't surprise me. Because I can sleep on the big brown couch and you can't make me go . . . you can't make me! I won't and you won't make me . . .

[*She breaks down into sobs.*]

BRIAN: I'm here, Ruth.

[*He moves cautiously to* RUTH.]

RUTH: I won't go anymore.

BRIAN: You don't have to anymore.

RUTH: I won't.

BRIAN [*touching her arm carefully*]: It's me, Ruth. Brian. You're safe here, Ruth. We're here, in my office, see. And you're safe.

[RUTH *falls into an embrace and cries softly while* BRIAN *holds her.*]

RUTH: Oh my God.

BRIAN: It's me, Ruth. You're OK. You're safe.

RUTH: I'm here. Please don't leave.

BRIAN: I'll be here, Ruth. I'm not going anywhere.

RUTH: What now?

BRIAN: Why don't you sit down and tell me what you need to tell me.

RUTH [*sitting slowly*]: I guess we need to talk about why my father raped me.

[*Light fades. Light rises on* JORDAN, *upset, playing something atonal, frenetic. She stops to address the audience.*]

JORDAN [*to the audience*]: I've reconsidered my position on practicing. It's true that something special happens right here, between us . . . this exchange of, of . . . this exchange. But it's not the music. Not just the music. It's true, I do make the music, with or without you. It's the experience. You make the rest of me . . . hopefully I give you something that you keep forever . . . We take care of each other. I'm pretty good at taking care of myself. My mother was vigilant about that . . . taking care of yourself because nobody else will . . . but when I play, and you hear, we take care of each other. And I like that.

[JORDAN *resumes playing. Light rises on* ERNESTO, *alone.*]

ERNESTO [*to the audience*]: Any philosophical principle or mandate will have a direct psychological correlate. Determinism, conventionalism, behaviorism, subjectivism, egoism, dualism . . . I could go on, but I'll spare you. These are the words of scientists, who through time have worked so hard to distill the essence of experience, as it relates to behavior, emotional well-being, and our universe. For every clinical observation I might make, there is an ism that can explain, contextualize, and attempt to, to fix it. I'm grappling with this. Because every so often an external object slams against us with such force, at just the right velocity and trajectory . . . and for these things there are no words, no worthy isms.

[*Light rises on* RUTH *in* BRIAN's *office, midsession.* JORDAN *continues to play.*]

RUTH: And then I do this like morning audit thing on myself, still half asleep, I go: OK, if I wear the beige slacks and brown T-shirt, I don't have to iron, which would give me fifteen minutes, and I can do laundry tonight, sleep another forty-five minutes, do my makeup in the car, never mind the nails, and still have time for Starbucks . . . And what happens is that no matter how much I mean all of this, I still leave the house, like, five minutes late because I couldn't find my other sandal or something, and I still don't get my extra forty-five minutes or Starbucks.

[JORDAN *stops playing.*]

BRIAN: That's cute.
RUTH: What does it mean?
BRIAN: That you have a gift for storytelling.

[*Pause.*]

Ruth, we've made more progress than this. This isn't why we're here on my day off. You paged me. Is it your dad?

RUTH: Always. But no. Not today. Worse. Brian, I can't breathe and tell you.

[*Lights come up on* ERNESTO, *dialing. The phone rings.* RUTH *takes her cell phone out of her purse or pocket and walks into new light as* BRIAN's *light dims slightly.*]

ERNESTO [*into the phone*]: We've got to talk.

RUTH: It's a bad day. Ever since I called my dad and asked him to come into town for a session, he calls drunk, like at two o'clock in the morning, every night. I can't sleep, and I have so much laundry, dishes, I just don't seem to be able to do anything during the week. How about next weekend, or maybe . . .

ERNESTO: Ruth, I need you.

RUTH [*to* BRIAN]: It's obscene how self-centered I am.

BRIAN: Breathe, Ruth.

ERNESTO: I'll pick you up.

RUTH [*excitedly*]: In the new Bug?

ERNESTO: It won't matter.

RUTH [*to the audience*]: It didn't matter. In fact, I don't remember how we got there, or where we went, what we ate.

[*Through this,* RUTH *joins* ERNESTO *at a table. She narrates, alternately to the audience and* BRIAN.]

I rambled on about stupid shit, stuff that I also can't remember that doesn't seem important now and was so unimportant then. [*To* ERNESTO] Oh, I love this restaurant, like my new dress? I saw it at Nordstrom's last season, three hundred dollars, I just got it off the rack for fifteen. [*To the audience*] And he just sort of sat there, not eating, getting more and more pale, which was kind of green on him, because he's sort of olive complected already.

BRIAN: Breathe, Ruth.

RUTH: He just sits there, and then this one big tear just balances in his right eye, and spills over the edge in slow motion, and I realize that through all the breakups and family tragedies and bad grades we've been through, I've never seen Ernesto cry. But that was it, just that one big tear. [*To* ERNESTO] I'm sorry. You broke up, didn't you? You and Bill?

[*Pause.*]

[*To* BRIAN] He didn't move, [*to the audience*] not even a nod. [*To* ERNESTO] I wouldn't worry about it too much, honey. I know it doesn't seem like it now, but there was something not quite right about him. I couldn't tell you what, but I think you can do better. Though I do like that he was a good cook. See if you can't do that again, get a culinary genius.

ERNESTO: I just got back my third test.

RUTH: Test?

ERNESTO: Hear me, please?

RUTH: I'm listening.

[*Pause.*]

Oh my God.

ERNESTO: The first time I knew it was a mistake because it had to be. See, he belonged to this study, this controlled study that I dropped him off at every week, at the hospital, every week. And he was in the negative group, right, that's what he told me. He said he loved me.

RUTH: No.

ERNESTO: So the second time I'm thinking, Oh my God, all the other tests have been wrong and I do have it and how will I tell him, how did they miss it before, and how will I possibly live with myself if he has it. And I swear I was going to kill myself if I'd given it to him. All I could think of was him. So on the third one I call him, from the doctor's office, from right there, and he calls me a bitch and whore and tells me how he always suspected and I deserved it and that's why he's always on top.

[*Upstage a silent* BILL *warms up for a jog. Neither* RUTH *nor* ERNESTO *acknowledges his presence.*]

RUTH: Oh my God.

ERNESTO: Please don't say that again. Please don't cry, not here, I can't hold it together if you break down here.

RUTH: But you used—

ERNESTO: Not once he said he wanted to marry me. I got myself tested once more for good measure, and we acted like any other engaged couple.

RUTH: Oh my—

ERNESTO: Don't—

RUTH [*to the audience and* BRIAN]: It was him. Bill had had it. Knew he had it. How did this stranger come into my Ernesto's life and change things forever, in just a second.

[BILL *jogs out. Pause.*]

[*To the audience*] And the thing is that right at that second I see this waiter who I know. This really cute guy who we went to school with, who would know us, and I feel so exposed. Normally we would have joked about if he'd figured out that he's gay yet, and how cute he's gotten, and we'd have called him over and had a flirting contest, since he was never officially gay. And now all I can think is, Please, God, please don't let him see us like this. Like he would know. Like if he saw us the whole restaurant would know. And if the whole restaurant knows then it must be true. As long as it's just us, it's not true. And Ernesto's talking on about the whole thing unraveling, by the time he'd gotten to his apartment Bill's things were gone, and everything glass was broken, and he had pissed on the walls and defecated in the middle of the living room floor—

ERNESTO AND RUTH: —where Princess was sitting, just staring at it.

ERNESTO: And the pièce de résistance, he's written "Die Fags!" on the wall in red fingernail polish. And still, all I can think about is, Where the hell did he get the polish? Why did he have red fingernail polish?

RUTH: And I'm hearing Ernesto, but I can't stop crying and looking at this guy. To this day I think about that guy, the waiter. And I can't breathe.

ERNESTO: I can't breathe.

RUTH: When I talk about it, I can't breathe.

BRIAN: Breathe, Ruth.

RUTH: Breathe, Ernesto.

RUTH AND ERNESTO: I can't.

BRIAN: I'm right here, Ruth.

RUTH: I'm right here, Ernesto.

[*Blackout.*]

ACT 2

SCENE 1

[ERNESTO *stands in tight spotlight.* JORDAN *plays.*]

ERNESTO: Several years ago I maxed out my credit card for an Aspen ski trip. Perfect snow. Perfect day. You know, fresh powder, hot sun. I was flying. No falls, no fears. It was a buddy trip. Just a bunch of friends hitting the slopes, checking out guys. So that night we're coming down for dinner, and the lodge has this huge-ass two-story stone and slate staircase, just suspended over all the freestanding fireplaces and leather couches in the lounge below. And we're laughing and talking and I'm on. I'm just cute and on and knowing it. And it happens. My foot somehow catches on the back of my boot and in a very fast slow motion my face is making its way toward the stone steps, and I hit, completely aware of my front teeth shattering. For an instant time stops, and then in fast-forward I'm falling again. Trying to grab something, a banister, a wall, and I'm ricocheting off like a rag doll. Seventeen or twenty-three seconds later . . . I'm perfectly conscious lying in a heap, looking up two stories, and before I black out I think, Wow . . . Antonio looks great in that sweater and Jesus, is that my blood? Five fractures, four breaks, one concussion, and several grafts later, I'm fine. My right shoulder hurts when it rains, my nose and teeth are better than they were before . . . But still, going on five years now, and I have not once walked down stairs without holding on to both banisters and looking at my feet. I'm an elevator man. But this. This is such a different kind of recovery . . . and I still don't know what to hold on to. For safety. And I can't find the goddamn elevator.

[JORDAN'S *music fades.* ERNESTO *leaves light as* RUTH *enters it.*]

RUTH: The decisions you would think of as difficult—getting married, buying a house, quitting a job, having a baby—are, I think, so much less difficult than the easy ones. Whether to do a load of underwear at twelve o'clock in the morning or just wash out a pair of panties by hand. To order the Taco Bell combo or just a burrito. Now that's a conundrum. But the really big solutions just come to me.

[*Pause.*]

In the time that I wasn't there for Ernesto it became more and more clear. And I wasn't there. I have not been there, really there for him since that day. For the first few months I called him, at least once a week, and we talked, around it. While I was confronting the horrors that had been my childhood with my dad, he was uncovering all of the horrors of the lie that had been Bill. He was, Bill, one big aberration.

ERNESTO: He was not a writer, had not been a musician, had never gone to— much less graduated from—Oxford, was not a Rhodes scholar . . .

RUTH: . . . did not have money, family, sanity, a soul. Ernesto kept going to work . . .

ERNESTO: . . . listening to housewives and househusbands drone on about their lack of self-confidence, cocaine addictions, affairs, suppressed memories. I listened and helped the same people I'd always helped, the narcissistic artists, people whose spouses were dying of breast cancer, prostate cancer, cervical cancer, AIDS. And for the time that I'm in that chair, I am alive, and well, and I have all the answers. And I care, I really do. I'm even good at explaining to the ones with less immediate problems why their problems matter, why it's important to address feelings of inadequacy, overeating, a temper.

RUTH: It was amazing and weird, but he was fine.

ERNESTO: She was doing OK.

RUTH: I had made it from the couch to the bedroom. I would sleep on the floor, halfway between my door and the bed.

ERNESTO: I didn't sleep for two months.

RUTH: At first I threw up every night at about 3:00 A.M. Now, well, I don't eat after five.

ERNESTO: The blackness, the darkness of sleep, felt like a void that would swallow me. Because I knew that eventually it would, it felt imminent and I just couldn't close my eyes.

RUTH: Hey, Ernie, how you doing?

ERNESTO: I'm handling it. [*To the audience*] It became very hard to get out of bed, even though I'd only had my eyes closed for a few minutes, and I was so lonely.

RUTH: Maybe we could get together [*beat*] sometime.

ERNESTO: Sure.

[*Beat.*]

[*To the audience*] I wasn't lonely for a boyfriend. I was lonely for a mate, a soul mate, and Ruth should have done that, been that . . . but I didn't make her. She would have risen to the occasion if I'd called and just said, "Hey, I need you to rise to the occasion." But it was not her arms I needed, it was Bill's. And I just couldn't tell her that. How does a mental health care professional explain being in love with his psychopath ex-boyfriend who has just given him a disease that won't go away. How do I explain why I didn't see it coming.

RUTH: The first several times I saw him, I would get this lump in my throat and not be able to talk. Actually it was more than several times so I saw him less and less.

[*She picks up the ringing phone.*]

ERNESTO AND RUTH [*staggered*]: I'm fine. I know how busy you are, let's do it next week.

[*Ring.*]

I'm fine. I'm really busy, maybe early next week. A movie. Great.

[*Ring.*]

I'm fine. I can't. Oh, yeah, me too. Real busy. Next week? I'm doing great. Really.

RUTH: Great.

ERNESTO: Great.

RUTH AND ERNESTO: Great.

[*Beat.*]

RUTH [*to the audience*]: My lump is still there, but now it doesn't feel like a lump. It just feels like the way I feel when I see Ernesto. So I worked extra hard to not be affected and used his spoon and drank after him and gave him hugs and kisses, because, after all, I'm supposed to be sophisticated like that.

SCENE 2

[RUTH *enters.* ERNESTO *sits at a small table in a coffeehouse. They make a strained attempt to hug naturally.* RUTH *plants an overly long kiss on* ERNESTO's *mouth. Both sit.*]

RUTH: So.

ERNESTO: So.

RUTH: This is like being kids again.

ERNESTO: Sort of.

RUTH: Isn't there this thing that happens to you in coffeehouses?

ERNESTO: I'd have to say no.

RUTH: This aloneness that goes along with the exposed bricks and classical music and bad art.

ERNESTO: And those kids behind the counter talking about alternative rock and Nietzsche.

RUTH: Yeah. It's this thing that makes you convinced that you're adorable and sad and alone.

ERNESTO: I know what you're saying. But for me the fantasy happens in bookstores. Not the mammoth sip-and-roam kind. A little lesbian-owned one with ferns and kittens. I'll round a corner and he'll be standing there, really engrossed in something like . . .

RUTH [*laughing*]: Danielle Steele.

ERNESTO: Come on, I indulged you.

[*Beat.*]

Anyway, he's lonely and smart, and sexy, and he's waiting for me.

RUTH: When you marry him I want to be your . . .

ERNESTO: I don't play that game anymore.

[*Uncomfortably long, awkward silence.*]

RUTH: You'll find someone.

ERNESTO: Please.

RUTH: I'm just saying . . .

ERNESTO: Don't. Don't say it. [*Turning awkward moment into a joke à la* Bullets over Broadway] Don't speak. Please, don't, don't speak.

[*He puts his hand over her mouth.*]

RUTH: I have something for you.

[*She removes a stack of small presents from her purse.*]

Birthday, Christmas, Cinco de Mayo . . .

ERNESTO: You know that's not a real holiday . . .

RUTH: I know. When I bought it I thought it would make you laugh.

[*She turns back to her purse.*]

I'm still working on the best gift. You have to shop carefully for what I'm planning.

ERNESTO: You didn't have to—

RUTH: Of course I did. I'm just sorry it's taken me so long to give them to you, we just never... OK. New topic. I'm quitting therapy.

ERNESTO: Why?

RUTH: It's time. I found myself spending more time worrying about what I'd wear than what I'd talk about, and I realized that it was time.

ERNESTO: You need to tell him.

RUTH: What?

ERNESTO: You need to tell him you have a crush. It's part of the process.

RUTH: But it's not necessary because I'm done with the process.

[*Lights come up on* BRIAN. RUTH *crosses to the therapy area.*]

OK, OK. I've been thinking about this. If I take a sleeping pill, like at seven, and . . . and go to bed later . . . I should be able to sleep in the bed until morning. And then I'm all better . . . I mean, that's really my only last big thing. Don't you think?

BRIAN: That's your concern? Sleeping?

RUTH: I guess.

BRIAN: Ruth, everybody and their mama has a hard time sleeping. That's not your problem.

RUTH: I think it is.

BRIAN: I beg to differ.

RUTH: Are you supposed to disagree with me?

BRIAN: When you're wrong.

RUTH: Look, Brian—

BRIAN: Just think about it—

RUTH: There's a slim possibility that sometimes I can know my thoughts better than you can . . .

BRIAN: If you'd just let me—

RUTH: I know your job is to—

BRIAN: If you'd just be quiet for a second, honey.

[*Pause.*]

RUTH: What did you just say?

BRIAN: If you'd just be quiet for a second.

RUTH: I thought you said something else.

BRIAN: You're not afraid of sleeping. You're not unable to sleep. You're tired. What are you afraid of?

RUTH: I'm afraid of what happens before I go to sleep.

BRIAN: And can that happen anymore?

RUTH: No.

BRIAN: Why not?

RUTH: Because I'm a grown-up and he's not in the next room.

BRIAN: Thank you.

RUTH: Thank you.

[RUTH *and* BRIAN *assess one another. The moment is too long and turns into awkwardness.* RUTH *continues to* ERNESTO.]

Yes. I think it's time. The process is over. I'm all better.

ERNESTO: You should tell him.

BRIAN: If you really think it's time.

RUTH: What, you don't?

BRIAN: No, actually you beat me to it.

RUTH: You *want* me to stop?

BRIAN: I didn't say that.

RUTH: What happened to "I'll always be here"?

BRIAN: Maybe you aren't ready for this?

RUTH: Sure I am. But what happened to "I'll always be here"?

BRIAN: Ruth, you don't have to stop.

ERNESTO: Really, you don't.

RUTH: I just think it's time.

ERNESTO AND BRIAN: Really?

RUTH: I mean, we've been working for so long and I understand my stuff. Right?

ERNESTO [*smiling*]: So, all better?

RUTH: All better.

BRIAN: You know this isn't an absolute. I don't give you magic beans and you're all better.

RUTH: But I'm equipped.

BRIAN: Yes, I think you are.

SCENE 3

[*Light rises on* ERNESTO, *standing alone, center stage. He addresses the audience.*]

ERNESTO: I tell my patients that time heals all wounds. It doesn't. Now, a year since I got the news, I still have big gaping holes, but they've developed scar tissue. My heart only hurts really badly when it rains. My soul, well that's another story. Still, at some point, with a lot of prayer and a great deal of help from God, a couple of months of heavy-duty antidepressants, and some truly amazing friends, I stopped waiting to die and started living. HIV is a strange thing, because it attacks your spirit and soul long before it touches your immune system. I'll never be quite who I was, but I've vowed to be as kind to the person I am now as possible. The day I knew I was on the right track is the day I called up Greg Louganis's publicist and asked if Greg was dating anyone. That night I stopped dreaming of what's-his-name, the psycho. Then I went to visit relatives I'd never met before in Colombia, and I went hang gliding, and I road a mule through the Grand Canyon . . . Oh, and I wanted you to meet somebody.

[ERNESTO *walks off left and enters holding* NOAH's *hand.*]

This is Noah. Noah . . .

[*He looks at the audience and gives up.*]

Never mind. Tell them where we met.
NOAH: A bookstore.

[ERNESTO *and* NOAH *laugh.*]

ERNESTO: I told him to tell you that. What do you think this is, a romantic comedy?

[RUTH *is sitting in a waiting room, talking to* ERNESTO, *who joins her as the light changes.*]

RUTH: I don't see why you're so leery about this.
ERNESTO: It's been proven that group therapy doesn't work for therapists. It throws off the dynamic, and I know all the tricks.
RUTH: It's just to let you meet people who're going through some of the things you are.
ERNESTO: Thank you, Dr. Ruth.

[NOAH *enters.* ERNESTO *and* RUTH *acknowledge to each other how attractive he is.*]

Hey.
NOAH: Hey.

[*The three are sitting in a row,* RUTH *in the middle.* NOAH *begins to read a magazine.*]

RUTH: Come here often?

NOAH: I beg your pardon?

ERNESTO: Excuse her, she hasn't had her shock treatments yet today.

NOAH: Oh, you too? That's what I'm here for.

[*Very awkward silence.*]

ERNESTO: I'm sorry, that was bad doctor's office humor. I'm Ernesto, this is Ruth.

NOAH: Noah. It's OK. I'm just getting to where I can talk about it. I appreciate that you two are so open about your treatments. [*To* RUTH] Are you outpatient, or do you stay at the hospital across the street too? It's cool, because after the treatments, I feel sort of woozy, so it's not very far. I should never have killed my brother.

[ERNESTO *laughs;* RUTH *looks befuddled.*]

RUTH: I'm sorry, I . . .

ERNESTO [*laughing hysterically*]: He's joking . . .

NOAH: I didn't kill my brother . . . I killed my dog, and it wasn't my fault, it's my illness, it's all in my head they tell me. Damned troublesome too. Shut up, Mary. So, what's your address?

RUTH [*just getting it*]: OK. You got me, but shame on you both. You can't make fun of mental illness.

ERNESTO: Well, I can.

RUTH: No, you can't.

NOAH: Well, I can. Because I'm mentally ill. [*Extending his hand to* ERNESTO] Hi, I'm Noah, [*sincerely*] posttraumatic stress and severe depression.

ERNESTO: Hi, Noah. Ernesto, psychologist and HIV positive.

NOAH: Oh, you're here for the group.

RUTH: Aren't you?

NOAH: No, I have an appointment with Dr. LeVance.

RUTH: Excuse me.

[RUTH *crosses to downstage left as lights fade on* NOAH *and* ERNESTO *enjoying their conversation.*]

So, OK. There are fairy tales. The trick really is not to anticipate the end, just to sort of go with it.

[JORDAN *enters, carrying her cello in a case and a suitcase.*]

JORDAN [*to* RUTH]: That's what I always try to do.

RUTH: I'm sorry?

JORDAN: Just go with it.

RUTH: OK.

[*Light fades on* RUTH.]

JORDAN [*to the audience*]: Miss me? Oh stop, you don't even know who I am. I just got back from West Africa. We were touring, Liberia and Ghana mostly. So, did I have culture shock? Hell no. Partially that's because I've been blessed and have had the opportunity to travel a lot, and I'm pretty fluent in most of the European languages, and, ass-backwards though I know it is, I'm just starting to learn Yoruba. OK. So, I've been to Harlem before. And I've spent quite a bit of time on the South Side of Chicago, and I thought I knew what it was like to be around people who are like me. But I didn't because, man, I got off that plane and as far as I could see there was blue sky and brown skin. And where there wasn't blue sky, where there were nothing but steel and glass buildings, there was nothing but steel, and glass, and brown skin reflecting off of the steel and glass. OK, OK, and every now and then a billboard of someone's really blond, blue-eyed Jesus.

[*Beat.*]

So, did I tell you how beautiful I was there? My skin turned this incredible honey brown red. And it just got darker and redder and, I swear to God, I glowed! So tell me how beautiful I was. That's OK. You missed it.

[*Light comes up on* ERNESTO *in bed with* NOAH. RUTH *sits on another side of the stage in her own living area.*]

ERNESTO [*to* RUTH]: I think he proposed.

RUTH: You think?

NOAH [*to* ERNESTO]: Did you think you'd ever end up with someone you'd love forever?

ERNESTO: Yeah, I woke up and he was just staring at me. It would have freaked me out but it wasn't like a weirdo love-stalker stare, it was like he was looking at me to see me, and did see me . . . and he's like . . .

NOAH [*to* ERNESTO]: Did you think you'd ever end up with someone you'd love forever?

ERNESTO: I used to . . . Yeah. I was pretty sure that I would.

RUTH: I always said you would.

ERNESTO: And then Bill happened.

NOAH: And so what do you think now?

RUTH: Yeah . . . now what do you think?

ERNESTO: I try very hard not to think about it.

RUTH: But you should . . . because you deserve to have love . . .

NOAH: As much as everyone else. It matters.

ERNESTO: To know . . .

RUTH: Who'll be there.

NOAH: Like forever.

ERNESTO: I'm not so good at long term, like forever.

NOAH: Forever's infinite.

ERNESTO: Infinite is finite for some of us.

NOAH: No. Life is finite, fine, I'll give you that. But love continues. Love is infinite and I like the idea of knowing who I'll love infinitely.

RUTH: He said that?

NOAH: Why wouldn't I say that?

RUTH: It's just so . . .

ERNESTO: The perfect thing to say. [*To* NOAH] So what are you saying?

NOAH: I'm asking you to let me love you infinitely.

ERNESTO AND RUTH: Forever?

NOAH: Forever.

ERNESTO: That's a lot of pressure. I'll have to be so wonderful that when I'm . . .

RUTH: If . . .

ERNESTO: That when I'm not here I'll live beyond whoever is.

NOAH: No. I'm just talking about you letting me reserve a special place for you in my heart that stays there forever. The heart has four chambers, I just want to give you, like, three of them for the rest of my life.

ERNESTO: How about three for while I'm here and two for the infinity part.

NOAH: Honey, you have all four already and we can negotiate the rest later.

RUTH: Then what?

NOAH: So you tell her everything?

RUTH: Then what?

ERNESTO: I cried and . . .

NOAH: Not everything please . . .

ERNESTO: Fair enough. [*To* RUTH] I cried.

[*Beat.*]

And then I showed him what infinity can feel like.

[ERNESTO *and* NOAH *kiss. Lights fade on them in bed.*]

RUTH [*to the audience*]: So, I've been spending all this time being disappointed because the princess may not be happy once she's on the horse, and that doesn't
matter so much. The here and the now of it is that she's on the horse, in the
arms of a man who is no longer a frog or a tree stump, and they're going to ride
somewhere and have fabulous sex. The fairy tale is happening, never mind
what comes next. Long story short. He's amazing. Noah is such a completion
of Ernesto that it makes me sad for when I was that. But I was never that.

[*Light comes up on* NOAH, *now in bed alone.* JORDAN *approaches and sits on the
edge of the bed.*]

JORDAN: That was beautiful.
NOAH: You were watching?
JORDAN: Oh . . . no, no. The proposal.
NOAH: It was beautiful, wasn't it.
JORDAN: He's very lucky.
NOAH: We all are.
JORDAN: I hope I have that, what you two have, one day.
NOAH: You will.
JORDAN: Thank you.

[RUTH *has crossed and stands looking intently at a painting in front of her.*]

RUTH [*to the audience*]: This whole new fairy-tales-really-do-happen philoso-
phy of mine is why I've taken to coming to the museum so much. It's a lot
easier to sustain a healthy, happy outlook if you're getting off the couch. The
impressionists really float my boat, which for a long time made me feel like
a sellout because they're so damn white.
BRIAN [*standing behind* RUTH, *who hasn't turned around*]: There's no race in a
pond full of lilies.
RUTH: Was I talking to you?

[*Beat.*]

Was I talking out loud? [*Seeing him for the first time*] Oh, Brian. Hi.
BRIAN: Hi, Ruth. You weren't talking out loud, I just knew what you were
thinking.
RUTH: Well, you have an unfair advantage that way.
BRIAN: I wouldn't have expected to see you at this exhibit. You know, I almost
didn't come over, it makes some clients uncomfortable.
RUTH: Clients?

BRIAN: Patients.

RUTH: Oh, but you're such a fan of Monet?

BRIAN: Well, yeah, I am, actually. And you're not.

[*Long beat;* RUTH *isn't following.*]

A patient.

RUTH: Oh. So, how've you been?

BRIAN: OK. I, um, fine. [*About to leave*] You take care, OK.

RUTH: But I'm not.

BRIAN: I'm sorry.

RUTH: I'm not your patient, so you don't have to run away from me.

BRIAN: You were my patient, so, yes, it was good to see you.

RUTH: I've missed you, Brian.

BRIAN: Well, you know, if you ever need anything, I've changed offices, I can give you my card, but I'm in the book. You take care.

RUTH: You're not allowed to say that you've missed me too?

BRIAN: I always miss clients when . . .

RUTH: Brian, I'm doing well, and it's largely because of you. Thank you for that. So, how many years after therapy does it have to be before you can tell your former therapist that you're in love with him?

BRIAN: That's part of the process, and we should have discussed that.

RUTH: But I never brought it up.

BRIAN: But I should have addressed it.

RUTH: Addressed what?

BRIAN: Your feelings.

RUTH: The feelings I wasn't telling you I was having?

BRIAN: I knew.

RUTH: Of course you knew.

BRIAN: Because it was my job to know—

RUTH: You knew because it was mutual—

BRIAN: That's called transference.

RUTH: Oh.

[*Beat.*]

I know.

[*Pause.*]

Here's my card, Brian. Why don't you call after you've had time to think about this. Because I'm seeing a kind of inflexible male sort of authority-driven block that you're having. This is all really very simple.

[*Lights come up on* ERNESTO *and* NOAH, *lounging on the couch.*]

ERNESTO: This is bad.

RUTH: No it's not, it's the fairy tale. Besides, he might not even call.

ERNESTO: Enough with the fairy tale already.

NOAH: *Mi hijo,* calm down.

RUTH: Listen to him. I'm happy and you're acting like a shrink. You're my friend.

ERNESTO: Did you ever stop to think how weird it is that you fell for a psychologist and your best friend is a psychologist and your father was a psychiatrist . . .

[NOAH *and* RUTH *groan.*]

RUTH: OK, OK. Sigmund. Lighten up. OK. So what if it's completely neurotic and emotionally unhealthy. So what. I don't get to be happy unless it's right? I mean who do you want me to meet and where am I supposed to meet him, not hanging out with you guys.

NOAH: OK, kids, can the boyfriend say something. Thank you. The boyfriend thinks you should meet him, Ernesto.

RUTH: Nothing's even happened. Yet.

SCENE 4

[RUTH *answers the phone in her bedroom.*]

RUTH: Hello.

BRIAN: Hello.

[*Long pause.*]

RUTH: You called.

BRIAN: You told me to, when you gave me your card.

RUTH: So. How have you been?

BRIAN: Fine. You? Has your dad been behaving?

RUTH: I haven't spoken to him in a year. He's not going to be able to handle a relationship with me on my terms. I'm dealing with it.

[*Pause.*]

So this was a business call.

BRIAN: No. I just wanted to clear up something.

[*Beat.*]

It probably shouldn't matter, but you asked once, and . . . I do believe in God. And she was black.

RUTH: God?

BRIAN: My wife.

RUTH: Was?

BRIAN: Was.

RUTH: And now she's . . . ?

BRIAN: Married to another man.

RUTH: I'm sorry.

BRIAN: Thank you.

[*Lights come up on* JORDAN *in her usual area. She plays something pointedly sentimental and romantic.*]

JORDAN [*to the audience*]: I met a man last week. We were in Munich, some kind of cultural-exchange thing with the city of Munich and New York. I have this terrific solo, a new composition, very cutting edge, very grand . . . The music swells, and there's a hush, and I come in under a light kind of staccato refrain that the piccolos start and the marimba picks up. I don't echo it, though, it's a new melody that I introduce . . . really very ethereal, and sooo beautiful. Anyway, I was coming down off of this postperformance buzz that I get sometimes, hanging out with some woodwind friends of mine in this Chinese restaurant down the street from the hotel. Oh and can I just say that in places where the people are superwhite, like translucently white, I get a lot of attention. I get really popular with the men. Which was great fun the first time—OK, the first few times—but became tiresome, because you can only be a country's collective sexual fantasy for so long. So, I'm sitting here, in Munich, eating the best Chinese food I've had since [*beat*] China, when this deep voice behind me says, "You're an incredibly gifted musician and you're beautiful." And I'm pretty flattered but still trying to figure out if I'm up to having saltines with my soy sauce, if you know what I mean, when this gorgeous black man sits down across from me and introduces himself to my friends—the very chic, very gay, very very Nordic oboist on my right and the very sweet and protective Filipino clarinetist on my left. We and about six others comprise the "color contingent."

OK, oboe man's an honorary member . . . I've digressed. His name is James. He was "in town" on business, don't know what that is yet, he lives in New York, loves the Philharmonic, has admired my work for some time, and is just so damn handsome. Handsome like superfine . . . like sooo beautiful it really kind of scared me. So, we have a date. Because he told me I'm talented.

SCENE 5

[RUTH *and* BRIAN *lounge comfortably on the couch, a lazy Sunday afternoon.*]

RUTH: It isn't bad, is it?

[*Beat.*]

Us?

[*Pause.*]

BRIAN: Do you think we're wrong?

RUTH: Well, you know, I have this nagging voice that tells me things are wrong even when they're not.

BRIAN: And your voice is saying?

RUTH: That it's the ultimate compliment if you'll have me despite the overwhelming disapproval.

BRIAN: When I saw you in front of that painting, I wanted to run up and give you a hug. I never felt that way when we were in session.

RUTH: Sure you did . . .

BRIAN: No. Maybe. No. Anyway, when I saw you my instincts told me to run away before you had a chance to see me, so I did. I tried to. I ran, and the next thing I knew I was standing right behind you.

RUTH: But you always say that we have control over our actions and feelings.

BRIAN: Sure. And my feelings and actions wanted you, just my intellect thought I should leave you alone. And what's intellect worth?

[RUTH *cuddles into* BRIAN.]

RUTH: Can't touch an intellect.

BRIAN: Certainly can't.

RUTH [*kissing* BRIAN]: Can't kiss an intellect.

BRIAN: No. No. You can't kiss an intellect.

RUTH [*beginning to unbutton his shirt*]: Can't undress an intellect.

BRIAN: Um, honey, where are you going with this?
RUTH: I'm trying to make a point.

[*She places her hand on his crotch.*]

Oh, but look, you've made it for me.
BRIAN: Just for you.

[RUTH's *mood changes abruptly. She sits up.*]

RUTH: God! Not even Ernesto thinks this is good.
BRIAN: Please tell me you didn't just kill the mood with Ernesto.
RUTH: But you know I'll put out eventually, so just hang in here with me. OK?
BRIAN: It's textbook. You're supposed to fall in love with your shrink.
RUTH: So you're saying it's not real.
BRIAN: I think it's real because I think ninety percent of relationships are based on whatever we bring to the table anyway... but until now, all I had was my professional pride. But I messed that up because everything about the way we've started is wrong.
RUTH: I thought you were telling me why this is OK.
BRIAN: For me it's finally OK because I'm happy and I see that I make you happy. I spend my day waiting to see you. I drive by a school and I smile because I can picture you in it. I remember the last time we ... and I get ... you know ... like a thirteen-year-old.
RUTH: Maybe I bring out the midlife crisis in you.
BRIAN: Oh no. I did that all by myself. That's how I lost my family.
RUTH: You slept with your secretary, didn't you.
BRIAN: Worse. I gave up. One day I looked at my wife and I couldn't remember why I loved her, and I looked at my kids and I didn't know why I'd had them, and I just didn't care. I left my family about a year before my wife left me.
RUTH: You still love her?
BRIAN: Sure, but in the context of what we had, and we can't have that anymore. It's done.
RUTH: Please tell me.
BRIAN: We were the perfect couple. I was an activist. President of the black student organization. We marched. We sat in. We were there in Washington. And she was beside me, doing all the quiet grunt work while I got all the credit. And she was beautiful, and articulate, and just radical enough ... but not hard.
RUTH: Sounds like Angela Davis meets Martha Stewart.

BRIAN: Sort of. Well, no. But man, I just got lost, you know. After the degrees and in between the kids, I got lost. My wife was this high-powered lawyer, and probably a good wife, but I decided she couldn't see me anymore. Then I had the prostate stuff . . . like every other fortysomething black man you'll ever meet. I don't know. Your plumbing gets screwed up, you face mortality, or, worse, maybe impotence, and I don't know . . . I just disappeared.

[*Pause.*]

So. Now she's with this guy who sees her *now*, not then, and loves her *now*. The way I love you.

RUTH: That should make me feel threatened, but it doesn't.

BRIAN: Why?

RUTH: I guess I understand somehow.

BRIAN: Do me a favor, baby?

RUTH: Uh-huh?

BRIAN: You were about to kiss the rest of my intellect, and you stopped to make a point.

[RUTH *laughs as she lounges into an embrace.* JORDAN *peeks her head in.*]

JORDAN [*to the audience*]: Pssst. Pssst. Over here. He's an architect. And his favorite color is blue.

[RUTH *crosses downstage and speaks to the audience.*]

RUTH: Brian and I decided together, after that first wonderful year. There I was, in the middle of my own love story, and he said . . .

BRIAN: I can't keep seeing patients, it would make me a hypocrite. I'll take that position at the university and you can take me. Forever.

RUTH: This is a proposal?

BRIAN: What do you think?

RUTH: I think I'd love to be Mrs. Dr. Brian Brennan.

BRIAN: Even though I can't have kids?

RUTH: It's kind of sexy. So yes, yes, if you'll make love to me on that big chenille couch, just once.

BRIAN: It's a deal.

RUTH [*to the audience*]: You've always known what happened, now you know how. And it's not as lurid and edgy as you expected, huh. I love my husband, and I love being married.

[*Light rises on* ERNESTO *and* NOAH *in the bedroom area.*]

ERNESTO: And she's having orgasms.

NOAH: We're very proud of her.

RUTH: Thanks, Ernesto. For sharing.

ERNESTO: Like they don't know everything else . . .

RUTH [to the audience]: It's true. All the time.

BRIAN: Many times!

SCENE 6

[JORDAN sits in her area, poised to play. BRIAN enters. They look at one another for a moment.]

BRIAN: We haven't met, have we?

JORDAN: Nope.

BRIAN: We're going to?

JORDAN: Sort of, I think, no, yes. We will.

BRIAN: Were you going to?

[He gestures toward the cello.]

JORDAN: Yes, um, no, you go on . . .

BRIAN: I'll be quick. [To the audience] So now I've got this great new office on this beautiful campus. Don't get me wrong, I do miss my practice, but here I don't have to justify my life, since most of my colleagues are sleeping with their students, next to whom Ruth looks like an old lady.

RUTH [from offstage]: Hey, hey, hey!

BRIAN: It's nice to set the high moral standard for a change.

JORDAN: If I may, I think you're a little too hard on yourself.

BRIAN: Do I know you?

[Light fades slowly on JORDAN as she plays. Lights rise on RUTH, BRIAN, ERNESTO, and NOAH at a restaurant table. JORDAN's music fades as the scene begins.]

RUTH: So. I have an announcement, but first we have to talk.

ERNESTO AND BRIAN: This better be good, honey.

[Both look at each other with annoyance.]

NOAH: I'm starving.

ERNESTO [to the audience]: I'd never seen Ruth's sense of drama played out to quite this extreme.

BRIAN [to RUTH]: This is a little much, even for you, don't you think?

RUTH: Look, it's like this. Noah, you suffer because of this almost as much as I do, and I think it's time we all set things right. [*To* BRIAN *and* ERNESTO] There's this animosity thing that you two have going on and it's just got to stop. Ernesto, grow up. He loves me, he's good to me, you should be happy for me. And, Brian, look, this is Ernesto. He's more to me than a best friend. You know this. When you do this, this attitude thing, it's like you're insulting me and my family.

NOAH: I think Ruth is saying that she'd like the men in her life to behave.

RUTH: Yes. Something like that.

ERNESTO: Point taken. Can we order already?

BRIAN: I'm with Ernesto, bring on the food.

NOAH: It can't be that easy.

RUTH: It won't be, but you have to try. I have a plan . . .

[*Lights fade on restaurant.* BRIAN *and* RUTH *move into their bedroom area.*]

SCENE 7

[BRIAN *speaks as they enter light.*]

BRIAN: It's the craziest thing that's ever come out of your mouth.

RUTH: No.

BRIAN: Well—

RUTH: Just listen . . . about a month ago I got out of my car at work and one of the faculty members, a second- or third-grade teacher, was throwing up. Something made me go over to her. Real young, really cute little white girl, probably twenty-four. You know, really sparkly diamond, new briefcase, little short bob. Can't tell you why this is important, but you see I'm drawing a complete picture here for you. Anyway, I asked her if she needed anything and she looks up, over her little red Chevy Cavalier, and says, "Oh, no, no, I'll be all right, first trimester, you know."

[*The following conversation exists both in the past, between* RUTH *and* ERNESTO, *and in the present, between* RUTH *and* BRIAN. *Many of* RUTH's *lines are or were for both men, and so one line may have more than one connotation.*]

And I don't know. I have no idea. And I said, "Yeah, yeah, I know." I was like, "It'll get better, just have some soda crackers and some ginger ale." But, Brian, I have no idea.

BRIAN: We talked about this.

RUTH: You talked about this, I listened.

BRIAN: We had an agreement.

RUTH [*to* BRIAN]: But if I had a baby for Ernie and Noah—

BRIAN: Remember, remember all of that, I'm not what you need, I'm old and I can't get you pregnant, and I don't want a family again. And remember you saying that was all right . . .

RUTH: If I can just be half as happy as I am now, I can survive whatever I miss. [*To the audience*] I did say that.

ERNESTO: You should think about this, you're young, one day you'll want to have babies.

RUTH: What about all of those people who can't?

ERNESTO: What about us?

RUTH: You know what I'm saying.

ERNESTO: Yes.

NOAH: Ruth, if we could have babies there's no way we wouldn't try.

RUTH: Oh my God, you make it sound so wrong.

NOAH, ERNESTO, AND BRIAN: No.

RUTH: Yes. You do.

BRIAN: Honey . . .

RUTH: Don't "honey" me.

ERNESTO: Honey . . .

RUTH: What?

ERNESTO: It's a big thing, what if you change your mind?

BRIAN: It's a big thing, but we talked about it.

NOAH: It's a big thing!

[*Beat. All look at* NOAH.]

ERNESTO [*to* RUTH]: Just make sure that you talk about it.

RUTH: I know.

BRIAN: Aren't we happy.

RUTH: I'm happy.

ERNESTO: I know you are, now.

RUTH: I am, honey.

NOAH: Will you be happy later?

BRIAN: You know I love you, and I'd do almost anything to make you happy . . .

RUTH: I want to be pregnant, and I wish you could make me. And you can't. And I don't blame you for that. Fine. But I could still be pregnant for us. I could have a baby for us, and then have one for them.

BRIAN: But I can't.

RUTH: No, you won't. It's like Biology 101. They have banks for this.

ERNESTO: One day you'll want to . . .

BRIAN: But I told you . . .

RUTH: It's not me. It's my body. My body aches to have a baby.

SCENE 8

[BRIAN *and* RUTH's *bedroom. Lights change. Time has passed.*]

BRIAN: You thought I'd be happy about it?

RUTH: It feels like a good idea.

BRIAN: Well, it's not. It's a bad idea. Why would you think that you getting knocked up by Noah would be a good idea?

RUTH: It's not like that . . .

BRIAN: How is it then?

[*Beat.*]

RUTH: It's not *with* Noah, it's just . . .

BRIAN: His spunk . . .

RUTH: That's disgusting.

BRIAN: My point exactly.

RUTH: I didn't expect you to like the idea, just to respect it and think about it.

BRIAN: Because I have a choice?

RUTH: Because you should want to support me.

BRIAN: So the choice is to support or not support my wife while she has someone else's baby.

RUTH: It isn't like that.

BRIAN: You tell me how it is then.

RUTH: You know that awkwardness when we're at a thing, like a social thing, gathering, and someone asks how we met.

BRIAN: This is not, has nothing to do with . . .

RUTH: Yes, but you have to agree with me about that thing that happens. That moment of silence that everyone fills with scandalous assumptions while you and I search for the words to make it right. The way to nicely package and present our love. As though it has to be made pretty and OK. Have you ever found the words, Brian?

BRIAN: Honey, it's different.

RUTH: Why?

BRIAN: Because it was a choice and we made it knowing how it might look. We decided together that it was worth it and it would only be our burden. Ours alone. Just us.

RUTH: No *baby*.

BRIAN: No *anyone* but us. But what you're proposing affects everyone.

RUTH: And you can't see where I'm coming from?

BRIAN: I see it, I just don't buy it.

SCENE 9

[NOAH, RUTH, *and* BRIAN *lounge on the couch.* ERNESTO *stands downstage center.*]

ERNESTO: Some would say she's insane. I prefer to call her a saint. Whichever, I've never been one to look a gift horse in the mouth.

[*He moves back into the group.*]

NOAH: Does anyone really know what that means?

ERNESTO: You mean the etymology of the expression.

BRIAN: I don't think an expression can have an etymology . . .

RUTH: I think it can, honey . . .

BRIAN: No. It think only a word can have an ety . . .

ERNESTO: You were making a point?

BRIAN: "Not look a gift horse" . . . It comes from horse trading, though I think it also has to do with the slave trade somehow.

RUTH: Brian . . .

BRIAN: No, no, honey, this is very relevant. Before you make an important investment of chattel, be it horses or humans, you'd want to examine the mouth, make sure there are no cavities.

RUTH: But a gift is something that you take, appreciate, don't question, particularly not in front of the one giving the gift.

BRIAN: But you can't give people anymore. Not since 1890 . . .

RUTH: You don't even know when it was.

BRIAN: Do you?

NOAH: The Emancipation Proclamation was signed in 1862. Anyway, I think it refers to the Trojan horse. If you get close enough to look into its mouth you could get killed.

BRIAN: Well, either way, I've made my point.

RUTH [*to the audience*]: You know I wasn't surprised that Brian was so unhappy, but I did think he'd come around. It seemed so damn reasonable. And I just knew that once he saw my dedication, my devotion to the . . .

BRIAN: It's a high-tech turkey baster, it's not rocket science.

RUTH: And so there I was, several times a week, certain times of the month, lying prone on a very hard, very cold, shiny stainless steel table, in an ugly green, thinner-than-a-sheet, harder-than-a-bread-box wrap while an intern inserted goo and metal and then a doctor inserted the important goo. Noah's goo.

NOAH: Poor thing . . .

ERNESTO: Why do they give you those ugly cover-up things right before they perform the most invasive procedures.

RUTH: Thank you for understanding.

BRIAN: Oh, I understand, I just have little sympathy.

NOAH [*to* RUTH]: I feel like I should be helping more. Be tired or something. [*To the audience*] Other than having a great deal of fun with Ernesto in an unusually sterile environment, not much was required of me. It felt weird. I offered to drive Ruth to her appointments, but she thought it would be a good idea if Brian did that.

BRIAN: I'm sorry, honey, I have a very pressing anything else to do.

ERNESTO: Are you sure we can't take you?

RUTH: Believe it or not, I do know to leave the envelope where it is once I've already pushed it too far. I wasn't going to beg Brian to divorce me.

BRIAN [*to* RUTH]: I'd never divorce you. I didn't get married so I could do that again. [*To the audience*] I just couldn't touch her. It felt like she was having an affair right in front of me. [*To* RUTH] I won't be a father again. I already screwed that up once. Don't act like you didn't know the deal.

SCENE 10

[JORDAN *enters, without her cello, and nervously sits in what had been established as* RUTH'*s therapy area.*]

JORDAN: Tell you about myself.

[*Pause.*]

Well. OK.

[*Pause.*]

You know it's hard to encapsulate a whole life. But you have to know me, right?

[*Pause.*]

Some people would characterize my life as unusual. It hasn't been so much for me . . . which seems like a contradiction. Normal life, my being here.

[*Light dims slightly on* JORDAN. BRIAN *enters the bedroom area, where* RUTH *sits on the floor, smoking. (Note: Lights may dim slightly to help shift focus, but all characters are visible in their areas at all times.)*]

BRIAN: Hey, baby, I just picked up some . . . What are you doing?
RUTH: Just sitting here.
JORDAN: OK. I'm a musician. A cellist. I have the second chair in the New York Philharmonic, a great boyfriend, James, who I suspect may be my husband soon, a really sweet dog named Butch, a really beautiful loft. It's my first thing, real thing, that I've owned. I've always had pretty much the best of everything. Oh, we weren't rich, but we were comfortable. In that upper-middle-class way that doesn't think of itself as privileged, but clearly has ninety percent more privileges than most Americans.

[*Shift to* RUTH *and* BRIAN.]

BRIAN: The cigarette. What's this about?
RUTH: Are you being my therapist or my father?
BRIAN: What?
RUTH: You're certainly not being my lover.
BRIAN: Your lover would not want to see his spouse killing herself.
RUTH: My lover would ask me what's wrong.
BRIAN: In an ideal world you can decide what your lover should say and he'll say it. But this is real life and I'm concerned. Besides, Ruthy, I'm not your lover, I'm your husband.
RUTH: You know, there's a reason why you're not supposed to marry your therapist.
BRIAN: I gave you a long list of those reasons.
RUTH: Look, I'm just tired. I'm so tired. Don't you see how important it was. It was bigger than a gift. It was part of me for Ernie, it was what I couldn't give before . . . It was all the time I didn't spend, all the recoiling, retreating. And I couldn't even do it. And now I have you. It's just you and me forever, and somehow that doesn't seem beautiful anymore.
BRIAN: I'm not your therapist, don't work this out on me and say things you'll regret.

[*Lights rise on* JORDAN.]

JORDAN: It was nice. We had a nice life. We went to church on Sundays, a different one every week. Mom wanted me to be able to choose for myself one day. She was liberal like that. A painter . . . I think she worked as a teacher for a while, before they got me, but then she stayed home and Tío and Noah built her a studio in the backyard. Really it's a studio on one side and on the other it's an office where Dad took his patients. He was a psychologist, a really well respected one. Mostly he wrote and researched, but I think he always enjoyed taking clients. I think it made him feel [*beat*] necessary.

[*Shift to* BRIAN *and* RUTH.]

RUTH: So what. So what if I say things that hurt you. We're married, Brian, sometimes you have to get hurt too. Jesus. Why isn't there an ashtray in this house?
BRIAN: Because we don't smoke in this house.
RUTH: Do you understand what I'm saying, Ernesto?
BRIAN: Talk to me. I'm the only one in the room.
RUTH: Don't you see what I'm saying?

[ERNESTO, BRIAN, *and* NOAH *all speak simultaneously.*]

ERNESTO AND NOAH: Yes.
BRIAN: No.

[*Lights rise slightly on* JORDAN, *fading on others.*]

JORDAN: Oh yeah, Noah and Ernie, Tío, I called him Tío. Those are my uncles, but it's weird, because really they were like a second set of parents. Tío picked me up from school every day, and they both kept me when Mom and Dad had to come to New York for one of her showings or vacations or whatever.
NOAH: Ruth.
ERNESTO: Are you breathing?
JORDAN: Tío was like the perfect other parent person, and Noah is this brilliant, gentle man who spoils me. It's because of Tío that I'm fluent in Spanish.
BRIAN: Breathe, Ruth.
JORDAN: All of my traveling that I did before the age of thirteen I did with Tío. We'd go to Spain for my birthday, and then, like, God, he took me to China for my eighth-grade graduation.

[*Lights rise on* RUTH, BRIAN, ERNESTO, *and* NOAH.]

RUTH: In between the moments of pure exhilaration and hurt there's this thing that I'm trying to be. I want to be something... necessary. And for Ernesto it can't be enough, and for you, you can't see it because I came to you in need of fixing.

ERNESTO: You don't owe me, Ruth.

BRIAN: You were never broken, Ruth. I love the healthy parts of you.

RUTH [*to* ERNESTO]: But I do owe you. [*To* BRIAN] I'm not whole.

BRIAN: You are.

ERNESTO: You don't.

RUTH: My dad stole something, something that communicates affection and love to my soul. And I thought Brian could cut through that, but he can't.

BRIAN: I can.

RUTH: No. Because I won't let you in there. [*To* ERNESTO] When he isn't in me, he's my enemy.

ERNESTO: And what does that make me?

RUTH: Safe, because you've never been there, that place that turns you into my foe. [*To* BRIAN] And I miss you because before, when it was just us and the couch, you were the one who could make me know that that place is a special but small part of me. That there's nothing between my legs that can make me vulnerable. And then I let, urged you into that space, and I can't see you right. You're skewed.

[*Lights rise on* JORDAN *and stay up on others.*]

JORDAN: Tío passed away right before I graduated from college.

[*Pause.*]

It's weird, because when I was really bad off, really missing him so much it hurt to go from the kitchen to the bathroom, I would think about this big African safari thing he'd planned and that would just make me sick because I knew how much he wanted that for me. We all knew that we'd have to give up Tío too soon, but that didn't make it any more bearable.

RUTH [*to* JORDAN]: I always knew I'd be a great mom. [*To* BRIAN] Remember I told you. I always knew I'd be a great mom.

BRIAN: What did the doctors say, honey?

ERNESTO AND NOAH: What did they say?

RUTH: That I can't do it. It won't take. We could try for three more years and it won't work because there's too much scar tissue. And it's been there since I was five or six, or eight. You know, it just kept getting worse because it just kept getting ruptured.

BRIAN: I'm so sorry.

NOAH: Oh, Ruth.

ERNESTO: Oh God . . .

RUTH: Here's the funny thing. I was going to have this baby even if I lost you, [*looking at* BRIAN] even if I couldn't stand to visit you [*looking at* ERNESTO] and Noah without having my heart break. It was going to be my contribution. My thing. The thing that would make it all right, because she would be safe. I was going to make this safe person, a gift just for you, Ernesto, just from us, Brian.

BRIAN: Breathe, Ruth.

ERNESTO: Breathe, honey.

NOAH: Breathe.

[*All characters stand in separate tight spots, with* JORDAN *still in the therapy area.*]

JORDAN: Daddy died a year later. I should have come in then, but we were on this world tour, and James was romancing me pretty hard, so between work and family I think I was doing OK. We all sort of just held each other up. I worry sometimes about Mom. She and Dad were so perfect. I swear, they were like a love story, or a movie or something. I was always a little lonely around them because it was like the Mom and Dad Club . . . not that they didn't make room for me. Oh, it was all about me. From the day the lady from the agency dropped me off, it was the Jordan show. I just hope that James and I will have what they did. So. Here I am. Partly because I promised my dad and Tío that if I ever needed to sort things out, I'd talk to someone, like you. So I thought, what the hell, and you're one of the names Tío had in his Rolodex. I don't know why, but it just seemed important somehow that I come to you, a woman, you know. I have girlfriends, but . . . I don't know, I think Mommy planted that in my head, something about the relationship being so important you shouldn't let there be room to get it confused . . . and Daddy would laugh at her and say that was crazy, that there are laws about psychologists and clients . . . Anyway, I just needed to talk to you about James, our relationship, I know that we'll want to have children soon . . . You see, it's like this. I always knew I'd be a great mom.

RUTH: I always knew I'd be a great mom.

JORDAN: Anyway, I knew this when I was a kid. It's not like I was discouraged from being a tomboy . . .

RUTH AND JORDAN: I was also taught to revere dolls. Dolls were little people, to be treated with care and respect . . .

[*Lights fade on* JORDAN, *talking into the darkness until her cello solo is heard.*]

JORDAN: . . . it all just must have been so much easier for Mom and Dad and Tío and Noah. Now everything is so complicated . . . what with my traveling and . . .

[*Lights fade to black.*]

KIWI BLACK

Shepsu Aakhu

First-Place Winner

2001–2002

PLAYWRIGHT'S STATEMENT

Entitlement, expectation, disappointment. As a parent, I have repeatedly seen each of them in my children's eyes. I am not yet comfortable with each renewed acquaintance. My greatest fear is that somehow the choices that I have made in pursuit of my own happiness, fulfillment, and peace of mind will negatively impact the lives of my children—the sense of entitlement that they have for all things luxurious, expensive, and fashionable—things I cannot provide. Also, the expectation that the world is warm, inviting, and invested in their personal happiness—a half-truth even during the best of times.

Perhaps worst of all is the disappointment of discovering that so much of what they want, believe they need, and are certain they cannot live without will be denied them because "Daddy failed to provide." Such is the life of artists and all those who live without the comforts that traditional wage earners often take for granted. Such is the way of all hustlers, regardless of the grift. In the end, I am glad to be counted among them.

PRODUCTION HISTORY

Kiwi Black, by Shepsu Aakhu, was first presented by the Columbia College Chicago Theater Department at the Gallery 37 Storefront Theater in February 2002. It was directed by Derrick Sanders, with set design by Mindy Fisher, costume design by Patricia Roeder, lighting design by Mary McDonald Badger, and sound design by Matthew Ulm. Andrew Glasenhardt was the stage manager.

Supervisor/Commuter	Douglas Amelianovich
Hustler/Commuter	Devin Bond
Bluesman (Drummer)	Brahm Fetterman
Joe Gratton	Christopher Franklin
Hustler/Commuter	Hugh Grady

Customer Service Rep/Hustler . . . . Curtis Jackson
Customer Service Rep/Commuter . . . . Kenya Kimball
Lennox Gratton . . . . Michael Pogue
Bluesman (Saxophone) . . . . Marcus Ranucci
The Suit . . . . Markieta Singleton
Bluesman (Bass) . . . . Mathew Ulm

The play was subsequently presented by MPAACT at the Victory Gardens Theater in Chicago in April 2003. It was directed by Mignon McPherson Nance, with set and light design by Shepsu Aakhu, costume design by Kanika Sago, sound design by the Ministers of the New Super Heavy Funk, and live music and scoring by Poh'ro. Leah Wintercastle was the production stage manager.

Bluesman (Drummer) . . . . Shepsu Aakhu
Commuter . . . . Derrick Anthony
Bluesman (Vocalist) . . . . Eddie Brown
Lennox Gratton . . . . Kevin Douglas
Commuter . . . . LaNisa Frederrick
Customer Service Rep/Hustler . . . . Simeon Henderson
Customer Service Rep/Hustler . . . . Elisabeth Isibue
Bluesman (Guitar) . . . . Aum Mu Ra
Joe Gratton . . . . J. David Shanks
The Suit . . . . Demetria Thomas
Supervisor/Hustler . . . . Sati Word

CHARACTERS

Joe Gratton
Drummer (of Bluesmen)
Guitarist (of Bluesmen)
The Suit
Lennox Gratton
Rep 1
Shell Game Hustler 1
Shell Game Hustler 2
Shell Game Hustler 3
Rep 2
Supervisor
Card Game Hustler 1
Card Game Hustler 2

The following multirole assignments may be made: The Suit/Rep 1/Shell Game Hustler 2; Rep 2/Shell Game Hustler 1/Card Game Hustler 2; and Supervisor/Shell Game Hustler 3/Card Game Hustler 1. There are also a number of nonspeaking roles for anonymous commuters and shoe-shine customers.

STAGING

The play is set in the present in Chicago, on and around the platform of the elevated commuter train known as the El. Parts of the city's train lines run on elevated tracks, but this section runs underground below Jackson Street.

ACT 1

SCENE 1: RED LINE

[*The sound of people hustling through on their morning commute is heard. A screeching subway train is heard approaching and then grinding to a halt. Lights come up on street musicians playing a tune for a dollar or a dime. The soundscape moves people aboard the crowded subway car. A shadowy figure meanders by the open instrument case and drops in some coinage. The musicians nod in appreciation, never skipping a beat. The sound is heard of the doors closing and the train moving noisily on toward the next stop, its screech fading. An occasional flash of blue light sparks up, revealing a lone man standing with a shoe-shine box. Lights fade in, illuminating the platform. A commuter approaches the shoe-shine man, JOE. He silently inquires about a shine. JOE holds up three fingers. The commuter hoists his foot to the box, his attention focused down the track, anticipating the arrival of his train. JOE preps, then shines one shoe at a time with skillful precision. The sound of a screeching subway train approaching and then grinding to a halt is heard. The commuter yanks the second foot from the box, drops three wadded dollars to the ground, and runs off.*]

JOE [*to himself while picking up the cash*]: I hate when they do that.

[JOE *picks up the money and his box and meanders over to the* BLUESMEN. *He leans up against the dirty wall. The sound is heard of the doors closing and the train moving noisily on toward the next stop, its screech fading. The* BLUESMEN *acknowledge* JOE *and continue to play.* JOE *soaks up the ambience, then speaks to the* DRUMMER.]

   You got a square?
DRUMMER: I'm tryin' to quit.
JOE [*to the* GUITARIST, *laughing*]: You?
GUITARIST [*abruptly stopping his playing*]: Kools?

[*He pops a pack of Kools out of his breast pocket.*]

JOE: That all you got?
GUITARIST [*offering the cigarette*]: Yeah.
JOE [*accepting the cigarette*]: I guess it's better than licking the pavement.

[JOE *lights up the cigarette with a fancy chrome lighter and then leans back against the wall, inhaling with deep satisfaction as his stress melts away. The* BLUESMEN *play on.*]

DRUMMER [*to* JOE]: Heads up . . . here she comes.

[JOE *looks down the long platform and sees a businesswoman approaching in a well-tailored men's suit. She is immaculate, right down to the black oxford men's shoes that she wears. He smiles with an impish grin and pats out the fire from the end of the cigarette, placing the snuffed-out cigarette behind his ear.* JOE *picks up his kit and heads toward* THE SUIT.]

THE SUIT: Hit me quick, Joe . . .

[JOE *hoists* THE SUIT'*s foot up onto the box, preps, and then shines one shoe at a time with skillful precision.*]

JOE: It ain't like you to be late.

THE SUIT: It's not like you to care.

JOE: You wearing down the heel on the right side . . . tension, most likely.

THE SUIT: If it were from the tension, I'd be barefoot.

JOE: Bring 'em by the shop tomorrow . . .

THE SUIT: I stopped by there last weekend, Harry said that you don't work there anymore.

JOE: We got an arrangement.

THE SUIT: Arrangement?

JOE: I still pick up shoes from time to time.

THE SUIT: What's in it for Harry?

JOE: Chicago tradition.

THE SUIT: What's that?

JOE [*smiling*]: A kickback. Anyway, you drop 'em there on your way home and I'll try to get them back to ya by Monday.

THE SUIT: No hurry, I'll just stop by Season's Best over the weekend and get me a few designer knockoffs.

JOE: So you do wear women's shoes from time to time.

THE SUIT [*flirting*]: Only for pleasure, never in business.

JOE: They gotta good product for the price. [*Flirting*] But then again, any old pair of mules would look good on you.

THE SUIT [*in mock offense*]: Do I look like the type of woman who would be caught dead in a pair of mules? Next you'll accuse me of not wearing clean underwear.

JOE [*ribbing her in mock surprise*]: So you wearin' underwear now?

[*She laughs in genuine amusement.*]

THE SUIT: You've still got your edge, Joe, I'll give you that.

JOE [*flirting*]: It don't get dull if you don't stop usin' it.

THE SUIT: How's your boy?

JOE: Trying to turn the corner on being a man.

THE SUIT: He comes from good stock. My mama always said, "A man is only as good as his seed."

JOE: He's just tryin' to maintain, just like the rest of us.

THE SUIT: At his age . . . he ought to be doing more than maintaining.

JOE: Things being what they are, him being near to grown . . . well, some lumps you gotta get for yourself, ya know?

THE SUIT [*looking down the platform in anticipation*]: You almost finished?

JOE: You'll hear it round the corner, fifteen seconds later it's here . . . by which time . . .

[*Sound is heard of the train beginning to screech around the corner.* JOE *picks up his pace and wipes off the shoe.*]

. . . I'll . . . beeeeeeeeeeeeeeee . . . done!

THE SUIT [*discreetly handing* JOE *three golden dollar coins as she examines the shine*]: Beautiful as always . . .

JOE: Thanks, princess.

THE SUIT: Every man should carry a little gold in his pocket . . . for good luck.

[THE SUIT *exits toward the suggested subway car. The sound is heard of the doors closing and the train moving noisily on toward the next stop, its screech fading.* JOE *opens his hand and looks at the three coins. He flips one into the air, then puts the coins into his pocket and smiles.* JOE *then picks up his kit and walks back to the* BLUES-MEN *and once again leans up against the wall.*]

JOE [*to the* GUITARIST]: One mo' 'gain . . .

GUITARIST [*abruptly stops his playing to retrieve the pack of cigarettes*]: You got one behind yo' ear.

JOE: Savin' it.

GUITARIST: For what?

JOE: When you ain't here.

[*The* GUITARIST *tosses* JOE *the pack.* JOE *lights up the cigarette with a fancy chrome lighter, returns the pack to the* GUITARIST, *and then leans back against the wall, inhaling with deep satisfaction as his stress again melts away. The* BLUESMEN *resume playing.* JOE *and the* BLUESMEN *remain lit in subdued tones. Seamless transition into the next scene.*]

SCENE 2: THE CALL

[*Lights come up on the apartment of* JOE *and* LENNOX. *The music of the* BLUES-MEN *fades out, and recorded hip-hop music fills the space.* LENNOX *is lying prone upon the floor with textbooks and papers spread out everywhere. He is wearing a set of earphones, attached to a Discman portable CD player, his head bobbing to the rhythm. He is lost in his studies when suddenly a shrill phone ring pierces the air.* LENNOX *is annoyed, but after a few rings he rises, removes the earphones, and is compelled to answer the phone. The hip-hop fades to a softer level.*]

LENNOX: Hello.

[*Lights come up on* REP 1, *a Global Credit customer service representative. She is squirreled away in some barely lit corner of the stage, the environment suggesting a cubicle in a warehouse collection agency.*]

REP 1 [*perky, reading text*]: Good day, sir or madam. This is Global Credit and I am your customer service representative, Cindy Weimer. Is Joseph Gratton available?

[*The music subtly shifts to blues while the lights fade up briefly on* JOE, *who is still smoking his cigarette with the* BLUESMEN.]

JOE [*to* LENNOX]: Tell them I ain't home.
LENNOX [*to* REP 1]: He ain't home.
REP 1: Very well, we'll try again later. Thank you.

[*The music subtly shifts back to hip-hop while the lights fade down on* REP 1 *and* JOE. LENNOX *returns to his studies and attempts to rededicate himself. He returns his earphones to his ears and the volume increases. After a brief bit of restlessness, he once again finds himself lost in his work. Once again a shrill ring pierces the silence.* LENNOX *is annoyed, but after a few more rings he rises, removes the earphones, and is compelled to answer the phone. The hip-hop fades to a softer level. Lights come back up on* REP 1.]

[*Perky, reading text*] Good day, sir or madam. This is Global Credit and I am your customer service representative, Cindy Weimer. Is Joseph Gratton available?

LENNOX: Just a minute.

[*He calls to* JOE *on the El platform.*]

Hey, Pop, it's for you!

[*The music subtly shifts to the blues while the lights fade up on* JOE, *who is now shining the shoes of another commuter.*]

JOE [*to* LENNOX]: Who is it?

LENNOX [*sarcastically*]: Ameritrade, Worldcom, ComEd, Mr. Ed . . . I don't know.

JOE: Tell them I'm dead.

LENNOX [*returning to the phone receiver*]: Hello.

REP 1: Mr. Gratton?

LENNOX: He's dead right now, so he can't come to the phone.

REP 1 [*reading text with false urgency*]: This is an urgent matter that needs his immediate attention.

LENNOX [*to* REP 1]: Just a second. [*To* JOE] She said she doesn't care how dead you are as long as you come to the phone.

JOE [*accepting payment from the commuter*]: Thanks. [*To* LENNOX] Tell them that dead men tell no tales. [*Laughs, self-amused.*]

LENNOX: Could you call back later?

REP 1: This is an urgent matter—

LENNOX [*interjecting*]: I can't get him to come to the phone, lady.

[LENNOX *hangs up the phone. The music subtly shifts back to hip-hop while the lights fade down on* REP 1 *and* JOE. LENNOX *returns his earphones to his ears and the volume increases. He returns to his studies and attempts to rededicate himself. After a longer bit of restlessness, he once again finds himself lost in his work. Once again a shrill ring pierces the silence.* LENNOX, *now highly agitated, tries to ignore the phone. He turns the volume up louder on his* Discman. *The phone seems to get louder along with the music. He is unable to shut out the distraction. After a few rings, he is compelled to answer.*]

[*Curtly*] Hello!

[*Lights come up on* REP 1.]

REP 1 [*perky, reading text*]: Good day, sir or madam. This is Global Credit and I am your customer service representative, Cindy Weimer. Is Joseph Gratton available?

LENNOX: Damn!

[LENNOX *holds the phone in his outstretched arm, beckoning* JOE *from the El platform.* JOE *enters, crossing directly into the apartment.*]

JOE [*to* LENNOX, *irritated*]: Haven't I told you how to handle these people?

[*He takes the phone.*]

Hello?
REP 1: Mr. Gratton?

[*In a highly agitated state,* LENNOX *begins to collect his papers and books.*]

JOE: Who is this?
REP 1 [*reading text*]: This is Global Credit and I am your customer service representative, Cindy Weimer. I'm calling regarding an urgent matter that needs your immediate attention. Are you Mr. Joseph Gratton?
JOE [*hanging up the phone violently*]: I'm dead.

[*Blackout on* REP 1. *Angry,* LENNOX *heads for the door.*]

Where you going?
LENNOX: Any place where it's quiet.
JOE: What? . . . Ain't nobody home but you.

[*As* LENNOX *turns to exit, the phone starts to ring again.*]

LENNOX [*turning to the phone, exasperated*]: You want me to get that?
JOE: No . . . I need to be dead for at least another half hour.

SCENE 3: BLACK KIWI, WHITE SHOES

[*The sound of an El train rumbles through. Flashes of blue light spark up, revealing* LENNOX *standing in his bare feet. He is approximately ten years old. Lights slowly fade up.* LENNOX *uses a chair to get the shoe-shine box off a high shelf. He places the box on the floor unopened, then takes a seat before it. He is hesitant but eventually musters the courage to open the box. He removes a three-ounce can of black Kiwi shoe polish, pries open the lid, and smells the polish. A faint smile creeps across his face. He pulls out an old rag and the horsehair buffing brush. He abruptly remembers to bring in his shoes. He jumps up eagerly and retrieves a pair of dingy white athletic shoes. He places a shoe on the footrest of the box, then gathers up some polish and smears it over the toe of the shoe. He spits on the polish and rubs it onto the shoe. Mimicking all the time-tested flamboyance of a skilled shoe-shine boy, he snaps the rag and buffs with exaggerated strokes. Then it dawns on him: the shoe is not shining but rather looks like he has pulled it from the muddy gutter. Suddenly panic stricken, he tries to undo his crime. He buffs the shoe harder, then tries to wipe off the polish. Finally he decides to return the kit to the shelf and hide the shoes. He grabs the shoes into his arms and runs toward the door, where he bounces off the chest of* JOE, *who is rounding the corner.*]

JOE: Where you off to in such a hurry?

LENNOX [*trying to conceal the shoes from his father*]: I . . . uhh, ohhh . . . nowhere!

JOE: Scored some free passes to the auto show . . . You wanna go?

LENNOX [*still hiding the shoes*]: Sure.

JOE: They got the Viper and the Batmobile. Now what ten-year-old boy wouldn't just die to see that?

LENNOX: The new Batmobile, right? Not that reject from the sixties . . .

JOE: Boy, do you wanna go or not?

LENNOX [*making his way around his father but keeping his back away from him*]: OK.

JOE [*taking him by the shoulders*]: Good, then go get your shoes.

LENNOX: Yes, sir.

[*He does not move.*]

JOE: What's this?

[*He reaches around behind* LENNOX's *back and takes the shoes.*]

You been in my stuff?

LENNOX: I was uhhhh . . . No . . . [*Summoning his courage*] Yes, sir.

JOE [*surveying the damage, mildly amused*]: When I was your age . . . this woulda been an ass whoopin' right on the spot. But I'm gonna do you better than I had it. [*Bending down to* LENNOX] The next time you want me to show you something . . .

[LENNOX *averts his gaze.*]

Look at me now . . . The next time . . . anytime you wanna know something . . . just ask me, OK.

LENNOX: But I didn't do . . .

JOE: Lennox!

LENNOX: I'm sorry.

JOE [*presenting the shoes*]: As it is, you'll have to wear these just as long as they last, regardless of what they look like.

[LENNOX *turns to exit, his head bowed, ashamed. Before he reaches the door, the sound of an El train rumbles through. The lights dim, leaving* JOE *and* LENNOX *in silhouette. Occasional sparks of blue light flash . . . Seamless transition to the next scene, back to the present.*]

SCENE 4: WHAT DOES THE FUTURE HOLD?

[*Lights come up on* JOE *and* LENNOX *in their apartment.* LENNOX *is still holding the knapsack full of books and papers.* JOE *stands between* LENNOX *and the door, blocking his exit.*]

LENNOX: You asked me to stay home, so I stay home. But I can't get nothin' done here, Pop! I gotta go.

JOE: What's the hurry?

LENNOX: Why you need me here anyway?

JOE: We ain't even had dinner yet. Hell, we ain't had dinner together all week.

LENNOX: I ate already.

JOE: So it would destroy you to sit down with me while I ate?

LENNOX [*sidestepping* JOE, *exasperated*]: Bye, Pop!

JOE [*pleadingly*]: Stay.

LENNOX: You want me in this crummy little apartment all the time . . . Why?

JOE: I can't work all day and not know where you are. It's distracting. If I'm distracted, I ain't makin' no money, and what's the point a workin' if ain't no money bein' made.

LENNOX: Your problem . . . why you making it mine?

JOE: It ain't safe for you to be runnin' the streets day and night.

LENNOX: Maybe I'd be at the library, you ever think of that?

JOE [*dismissively*]: Library? Yeah, OK . . .

LENNOX: This latchkey thing is gettin' old. Ain't like I can't be doing whatever I want right here.

JOE: Excuse me?

LENNOX: Ain't like you home no way. What's to stop me?

JOE: The fear of God, and my foot up your ass.

LENNOX: Anything that I wanna get into . . . I can get into it, and be done with it, before you ever got home. Why is it that parents think that we can't do the same things by day that you hope we ain't doin' at night?

JOE [*threateningly*]: Come again?

LENNOX: Nothing . . . Can I go?

JOE: Where you going?

LENNOX: The library.

JOE: Really?

LENNOX: Yeah, now move out the way.

JOE: Since when do you go to the library?

LENNOX: Since they don't have no phones there.

JOE: Why you interested in going to the library all of a sudden?

LENNOX: Why are you doing this?

JOE: Do I need a court order to talk to you?

LENNOX [*sarcastically*]: It would go nicely with this cross-examination.

JOE [*stepping out of the way*]: Fine. Go.

LENNOX: If I go now, you gonna trip for the rest of the week?

JOE: No.

LENNOX: Honest?

JOE: I swear . . . just answer me this one question: You really goin' to the library?

LENNOX: Yes!!! Why is that so hard to believe?

JOE: Ain't hard to believe from other people's kids . . . but the library ain't ever been your personal groove thang if you know what I mean.

LENNOX: I wanna go to school!!!

JOE: You got school five days a week—

LENNOX [*interjecting*]: College!

JOE [*surprised, pleased*]: Good . . . then go.

LENNOX: I need the grades, for decent grades I need to study, to study I need quiet.

JOE [*smiling*]: Hey, I'm sorry, by all means get your ass down to the library.

LENNOX: Thank you.

JOE [*discovering the thought*]: College cost money, books cost money, housing cost money . . .

LENNOX: I know.

JOE: Then you've thought about it?

LENNOX: One problem at a time.

JOE: If you don't solve that problem you ain't going nowhere.

LENNOX [*frustrated*]: That what you want, me to sit around on my ass and do nothing?

JOE: Excuse me.

LENNOX: What? . . . You mad 'cause I said "ass"?

JOE: White kids, they get to swear at they parents . . . You think you a white kid now?

LENNOX: I think I should be able to speak my mind.

JOE: This is still my house . . . If you feel that tall, then pack yo' shit and let the door hitcha where the good Lord splitcha.

LENNOX: Whatever, Pop.

JOE: Ain't room enough for but one man in this house.

LENNOX [*condescendingly*]: My fault, I didn't know I was supposed to be a little boy forever.

JOE: Shit, if you didn't eat so damn much . . . or if you had a job I could . . .

LENNOX [*turning to go*]: Bye.

JOE: Now hold on a second . . . I'm a hothead, you're a hothead . . . together, that just makes this house too damn hot sometimes . . . but if you give me a second . . . maybe I can figure out how to get you a student loan or a scholarship or something.

LENNOX: How you gonna do that and you can't hardly pay the bills around here?

JOE: Today is the first day I ever heard you make mention of *wanting* to go to college. Now I admit that it threw me for a second, but now, when I'm trying to get behind the idea, you wanna throw bills up in my face? . . . What you need is good hustle.

LENNOX: This is college, Pop! Ain't no hustle to this game. They wanna see the grades, they wanna see the test scores, and they want you to "show them the money."

JOE: Did I raise you?

LENNOX: What's that got to do—

JOE [*interjecting*]: This country was built on a hustle and that game ain't changed in over three hundred years.

LENNOX: That low-end ghetto mentality ain't gonna work in this situation.

JOE: Who you calling ghetto? Pack yo' shit and go then.

LENNOX: I'm gonna leave here soon enough . . . then you'll be alone. That what you want?

JOE: I want you to act like you got some backbone . . . quit whinin' all the damn time 'bout what folk will and won't let you do. You wanna go to college so bad . . . go to Loop City College then.

LENNOX [*correcting*]: It's Harold Washington! And I ain't going to no community college, I want to go to a university.

JOE: School is school . . . Them classes there ain't but a little bit . . . We can afford that.

LENNOX: I ain't going to no two-year I-couldn't-get-into-a-real-school city college.

JOE: Why not? You got something against sitting next to them low-end ghetto types? I wouldn't worry 'bout them none—'cause them immigrants is gonna be settin' the curve anyway. Or are they too low end as well?

LENNOX: Why you playing with me? Acting like what I want don't mean nothin'?

JOE: It means something . . . to you. For the rest of the world, they can't hear the noise that's fallin' from your face 'cause they got issues of their own. Actually they got problems. Issues are reserved for people who can afford therapy.

LENNOX: So you want me to get my hustle on just like you? Just get by . . . like you.

JOE: What you wanna go to college for?

LENNOX: An education!

JOE: Bullshit! If you valued an education you woulda done the work in school before now that woulda gotten you a scholarship. Politicians ain't turned the clock back so far as to get rid of academic scholarships . . . not so long as there's miners in Appalachia they ain't.

LENNOX: I got decent grades.

JOE: You fucked around for two years thinkin' you was in school to chase girls. It took you another year to catch up on the shit you shoulda been learning for the first two years, which left you with a year to try and impress somebody. Now ordinarily I would be crying them deep mournful tears of regret, knowing that I somehow failed you. I'd be on some trailer park talk show laying out my guilt for the world, or least the folks that don't leave for work in the morning, but I can't do that . . . 'cause I was the one trying to get you to go to class!

LENNOX: Yeah, but, Pop.

JOE [*quoting himself*]: "Lenny, you do your homework? Teacher says you have promise but won't apply yourself, could you work on that for me?" "Lenny, your paper is due tomorrow, ain't it? . . . Don't you think you should get started" . . . and what did you say?

LENNOX [*ashamed*]: "Don't sweat it."

JOE: You the one black child in all of America who can't find no money for school.

LENNOX: I could get a student loan if *somebody* had decent credit.

JOE [*emphasizing the point*]: So what do you want to go to college for?

LENNOX: I told you!

JOE: You said what you thought was a reasonable answer.

LENNOX: What you want me to say then?

JOE: You 'bout to die three times over, I just wanna know what it's for.

LENNOX [*reluctantly*]: A job, OK!

JOE: A nine-to-five, clock-punching, noon-lunching, three-sick-days-a-year J-O-B?

LENNOX: What's wrong with that?

JOE: Nothin'... for most folk. But...

LENNOX: But what?

JOE: They ain't handing out gold watches no more.

LENNOX: What makes you think I want one?

JOE: Do you?

LENNOX: Maybe I wanna do more than live hand to mouth.

JOE [*sarcastically*]: Paycheck to paycheck is all right though?

LENNOX: Top dollar being paid to folk with the right degrees, Pop.

JOE: Top dollar?

LENNOX: I knock them four years out, then the offers be just rolling in. I get my pick of the bunch. If they go on a bidding war for me, next thing you know I got a car thrown in, maybe housing, stock options. Then I knock out an MBA or something, that's six figures after taxes easy. Hell, I could be runnin' somebody's company in no time. Then I'm in charge, I'm callin' the shots.

JOE: If I was gonna build an empire and then turn it over to somebody, you know who I'd pick?

LENNOX: What empire you gonna build?

JOE: I'd look for the guy who thought like me, who came from where I came from, who wanted the same things I did. I would gift wrap my life's work and hand it over to the person who believed in the same principles I did. But most of all I'd give it to somebody who looked just like me...

[*Beat.*]

Who's running this corporation you want gift wrapped for you?

[*Pause.*]

Do you look like any of them?

[*Fade to black. During the blackout the sound of a train comes rumbling through, blue light flashes.*]

SCENE 5: THE BENCHMARK

[*The sound of people hustling through on their morning commute is heard. A screeching subway train is heard approaching and then grinding to a halt. Lights come up on street musicians playing a tune for a dollar or a dime. The soundscape moves people aboard the crowded subway car. A shadowy figure meanders by the open instrument case and drops some coinage. The musicians nod in appreciation, never skipping a beat. The sound is heard of the doors closing and the train moving noisily on toward the next stop, its screech fading. Lights come up on* JOE *standing with a shoe-shine box, beside him is his ten-year-old son* LENNOX.]

JOE [*to* LENNOX]: Honesty is not the benchmark of integrity. That middle-class ethics bullshit will have a black man starving to death over a concept. An honest hungry man is still a *hungry* man. That's why God invented the hustle, and I don't mean the dance. 'Cause God didn't mean for nobody to go hungry. You can tell more about a man from his hustle than you can from his shoes. There are darker paths . . . dealers, pimps, and what have you. But they all exploitin', most without boundaries. I ain't never met a dealer who wouldn't turn out his own mama for a dollar or a dime. Hustling in darkness like that just poisons your soul till you ain't good to nobody, and ain't nobody good to you.

[JOE *walks up to* SHELL GAME HUSTLER 1, *who is running the shell game with plastic soda caps and a small sponge ball.* SHELL GAME HUSTLER 1 *moves inaudibly through the routine of calling for suckers. He is flamboyant in his showmanship but silent in his delivery. A small group of commuters gathers round.*]

[*To* LENNOX, *indicating the hustler*] This cat . . . living in darkness . . . he got two problems.

[SHELL GAME HUSTLER 2 *makes her way toward the game, acting as though she were a mere commuter.* SHELL GAME HUSTLER 1 *mixes the caps around and signals to* SHELL GAME HUSTLER 2 *to pick a ball. The partner picks the correct cap and reacts with choreographed surprise and delight.* SHELL GAME HUSTLER 1 *hands over the money.*]

LENNOX [*to* JOE]: Yeah, he just lost some money.
JOE [*to* LENNOX]: Problem number one. He gotta split his money with this cat [*indicating* SHELL GAME HUSTLER 2]. The hustle don't work unless he got a setup girl. It's always best for at least one of the setups to be a girl.
LENNOX: Why?
JOE: Women make easy targets.

LENNOX: Why?

JOE: Couldn't say... but they are. Just like they're the ones that buy most of the lottery tickets, play church bingo... and vote.

LENNOX [*thinking it through*]: So he's splitting the loot with her... Where's the other setup?

JOE [*looking down the platform*]: You see that guy down there?

LENNOX: The one reading the *Trib*?

JOE: Nah, the one watching so intently but trying to act like he's not? The cat with the run-over Stacy Adams. He's down in the subway at commuting time but his shoes tell that he don't know what a nine-to-five is. A man don't show up at no office in those, he don't even do day labor in those. His eyes, they tell you that he's the second setup man. The cat whose job it is to get the suckers who are still afraid... to crack the leather open.

[*The man described,* SHELL GAME HUSTLER 3, *comes up to* SHELL GAME HUSTLER 1 *and places his bet. He wins his wager and responds with choreographed enthusiasm. The hustlers continue to mime the game.*]

[*To* LENNOX] See! That's how you know it ain't on the level. Nobody goes into the subway at commuting time to give their money away. The next person they get will be some kid on the way to school with his prom money or some mother headed to People's Gas with just enough cash to make sure there is heat for the winter.

LENNOX: It's a game, Pop. Don't nobody make them bet.

JOE: It's not a game. That's problem number two.

[SHELL GAME HUSTLER 1 *demonstrates the technique in slow motion.*]

Everything is cool until he stops mixing the caps. Then he tells you to choose.

[LENNOX *crosses and chooses a cap.*]

And it don't matter which you pick, 'cause if you get the right one, it's his job to make it the wrong one.

LENNOX: How?

JOE: He just pinches the sponge ball against the underside of the cap.

[*He takes* SHELL GAME HUSTLER 1's *hand and reveals the ball.*]

See, the hustler has fixed the game. And the sucker's money is gone. Any hustle that preys on kids, old people, or those struggling to live indoors is trouble waiting to happen. It's just a matter of time before somebody would rather see the hustler part with his life than part with their cash.

[*The hustlers pack up and discreetly blend into the action on the platform.* JOE *crosses to the* BLUESMEN.]

Now this, this is a noble hustle.

[*The musicians embellish the performance, basking in the glow of the attention.*]

LENNOX: What's so noble about sittin' in a dirty subway beggin' for money?

JOE [*agitated*]: That what it is to you? Beggin'? A cat gets up in the mornin' and he decides how much money he needs to make today. And he will work until that amount is made. He sets up his kit or what have you, and then he kicks back and does his thing. Working when and how he see fit, but he ain't a burden to nobody and he ain't trying to steal from you. He offers something up to the world, and the world, from time to time, it reaches into its pocket and offers up some appreciation. Everybody getting a little bit of what they need, and nobody really being hurt by the exchange. And that's why this is a noble hustle, 'cause it ain't beggin', and it ain't stealin'.

LENNOX: If you say so.

[*Fade to black.*]

SCENE 6: WANTS AND NEEDS

[*Lights come up on* JOE *on the El platform and* LENNOX *alone in the house. The two men are isolated by a gulf of darkness. Their lines are delivered as if they were talking to each other, but it is obvious that each is carrying on an internal monologue. They each pause and await responses from the other, reacting as if they are present with each other.*]

LENNOX: I used to watch you when I was younger . . . uneasy with the sight of you asleep in your clothes again.

JOE: I used to watch you when you were younger . . . just got lost in some kind of trance . . . enraptured to see you at play.

LENNOX: There was something about the way the couch, or the easy chair, or the floor just called to you . . . and there you would be . . . out like a light. I always wondered what kind of tired could make a man hold the hard floor like a soft pillow.

JOE: You had this way of getting into things. They talk nowadays about a child-proof home. Well, you couldn't Lennox-proof a house if you wanted to, 'cause you could do two things that could get you into anything: stack . . . and climb. Didn't much matter where we put things, you would use a chair to get the table, stack your blocks on top of the table, then stand on them to get at what you wanted.

LENNOX: Later I come to see that you got cozy with the floor 'cause mama won't have you in her bed . . . She thinks you're dead from the neck up, and so she's fed up with you and all your "A man's gotta do this, and a man's gotta be that." Ain't much longer before the floor ain't far enough away, and soon she's made her way out of here. Gone . . . leaving me alone . . . with you.

JOE [*laughing, self-amused*]: Nearly killed yo' mama once. Her heart near 'bout took its last beat when her eyes fell upon you teetering atop that "death pyramid" you built tryin' to get to the angel on top of the Christmas tree.

LENNOX: Twelve more years . . . alone with you.

JOE: At eighteen months you was fearless! Now you seem scared of everything.

LENNOX: I can see why she left. She wasn't getting what she needed.

JOE: Everybody is so goddamn needy. Know what I say now is true. People *want*! They spend most of the damn day coveting. Their little fucking eyes never stop flickin' from this thing to that thing. [*Imitating people*] "I can't be happy yet 'cause I don't have this thing." "Look at what so-and-so has. Once I get my hands on that then I'll be happy." "If I could just get one more of some stupid shit that I already own, then things would be great." But that ain't the fucked-up part. The shit starts to hit the fan when they start lookin' at you like it's your job to get them this thing that they *want*! And I do mean want, 'cause a body ain't got but a few simple needs. Food, shelter, peace, and companionship. Everything else is bullshit somebody invented to cause me *stress*!

LENNOX: You just got excuses for not—

JOE [*interjecting*]: You ain't missed a meal yet.

LENNOX: Maybe you ain't hold up your part of the bargain. Maybe Mama looked at all the stuff she *wants* 'cause you treated her like you treat me . . . like food and shelter is enough. Maybe she just needed her peace and companionship . . . but all you could hear is that she wanted you to get her more *shit*.

JOE: Maybe.

LENNOX [*sarcastically*]: Oh, now you can see that?

JOE: I can see why you see that.

[*The lights dim, leaving* JOE *in the shadows. Trains are heard rumbling by, kicking up occasional sparks of blue light and thus restoring the present. The lights shift to accentuate the* BLUESMEN *and* JOE.]

DRUMMER [*to* JOE]: You ain't makin' no loot holdin' up that wall.

[*The* DRUMMER'S *words seem to pull* JOE *out of his trancelike state. He takes a moment to survey the platform for business, then resettles against the wall.*]

JOE: Yeah, well . . . Everything ain't always about money.

[*The phone rings and the lights cross-fade back to the apartment.* LENNOX, *angered by the ringing phone, throws a shoe at it. The phone is knocked from its perch. Over the phone a faint voice can be heard. Lights up on* REP 1.]

REP 1: Hello, is anybody there? . . . Hello?

[LENNOX *walks over to the phone, picks it up, and gently places the handset back in the cradle. He exhales a deep sigh. Fade to black.*]

SCENE 7: MORNING RUSH

[*The sound of people hustling through on their morning commute is heard. Dim lights reveal street musicians playing a tune for a dollar or a dime.* JOE *shines shoes for one customer, then another. A shadowy figure meanders by the open instrument case and drops some coinage. The* BLUESMEN *nod in appreciation, never skipping a beat. The sound is heard of the doors closing and the train moving noisily on toward the next stop, its screech fading. Lights fade in.*]

JOE [*to the* DRUMMER]: You got a square?
DRUMMER: I told you I'm trying to quit.
JOE [*to the* GUITARIST]: You?
GUITARIST [*abruptly stopping his playing*]: Salems?
JOE: You got no brand loyalty.
GUITARIST [*offering the cigarette*]: I'm loyal to the cigarettes . . . any cigarettes.
    You got a problem with Salems?
JOE: Well—
GUITARIST [*interjecting*]: Then buy your own damn cigarettes!
JOE [*accepting the cigarette*]: I guess it's better than licking the pavement.
GUITARIST [*resuming his playing*]: Damn straight . . .

[JOE *lights up the cigarette with a fancy chrome lighter and then leans back against the wall, inhaling with deep satisfaction as the stress melts away.*]

DRUMMER [*to* JOE]: Heads up.

[JOE *looks down the long platform and sees* THE SUIT *approaching.*]

JOE: Damn . . .

[JOE *pats out the fire from the end of the cigarette and places the snuffed-out cigarette behind his ear.* JOE *then picks up his shoe-shine box and heads toward* THE SUIT.]

THE SUIT [*annoyed*]: What happened to you, Mr. Gratton?

JOE: I'm sorry 'bout—

THE SUIT [*interjecting*]: I stopped by Harry's yesterday to pick up my shoes and nothing!

JOE: I'm sorry . . . I intended to get them in day before yesterday but . . .

THE SUIT: This ain't you, Mr. Gratton. Now I come to you to get my shoes done partly because you do good work, partly because it's fast, and mostly because you make me smile. Do I look like I'm smiling, Mr. Gratton?

JOE [*apologetically*]: No ma'am.

THE SUIT: When all is said and done it's a business arrangement, Joe. I count on you to deliver, and you count on me to pay. If this is the way you're going to conduct business, I'll have to go elsewhere.

JOE: That ain't necessary. I ain't ever left you high and dry before . . . I promise it won't happen again.

THE SUIT: Well . . . OK.

[*She looks him over.*]

Is this place starting to wear on you, Joe? There's no bounce in your step anymore.

JOE: I'm maintaining.

THE SUIT: Look, it ain't really my business what you do with yourself but—

JOE [*interjecting*]: Really, I'm fine. But if it'll put you at ease, maybe I'll drop in on the clinic next week and let them give me the once-over.

THE SUIT: The day you want it bad enough, that's the day you make a change. Don't take no doctor to see that.

JOE: I wish the boy's mama was still around. She's the one that did all the worryin'.

THE SUIT: What's he doing that has you so worried?

JOE: It ain't what he's doing, it's what he might do, might not do, can't do, or don't know how to do.

THE SUIT: And you wanna fix that for him?

JOE: Yeah.

THE SUIT: But you can't?

JOE: Trying . . . but . . . No, it seems that I can't.

[*Beat.*]

The boy wants things . . . And it ain't like he wants all that much when you really look at it. He just wants more than I can get for him right now.

THE SUIT: You stand here how many hours a day?

JOE: Too many.

THE SUIT: And in that time you working hard to get over the hump, right?

JOE: Sure.

THE SUIT: He can't see that?

JOE: Nope.

THE SUIT: You want him to?

JOE: Just want him to get something of what he wants in this world.

THE SUIT: What did your parents give you for a head start? Wasn't much, was it? But you took it and did with it what you thought you could. Turned a little bit into a little bit more. That's what parents do . . . Lennox, he knows that. Don't spend so much time hurt over what you don't have to give him. Just be sure to give him a little bit more. The rest . . . that's between him and God.

JOE: I don't think he sees it that way.

THE SUIT: If he lives long enough, he will. The rest of the time you just get to keep on living.

[*Beat.*]

JOE [*indicating her shoes*]: You want me to hit them while you're waiting? Free of charge, of course.

THE SUIT: Not today, but I'll catch you in the morning, OK?

[*Fade to black.*]

SCENE 8: LIVING IN TWO TIMES

[*Lights come up on* JOE *and* LENNOX *in a voided space.*]

JOE AND LENNOX: We each living in two times . . .

JOE: . . . Oughtta be living in one.

LENNOX: Sometimes it feels like three.

JOE: Ever notice how the two times for grown folk be the past and the future? Past so strong it colors everything we do. Can't love without callin' up the memories of every love that came before. Weighin' the now against the then. Measurin' with the rula of how this once felt, or didn't feel.

LENNOX: Ever notice how the two times for young folk be now and later? I wouldn't say the future so much, 'cause the future is mostly some far-off place of "When I grow up I wanna be a millionaire" or "Someday I wanna have a big house with twenty-two rooms and a Jacuzzi." The now is the *now*. That moment when the only thing that matters is what's happening to *you* right *here*. That was the best part about being a kid. *Now* is what got your ass beat 'cause you didn't come home by dark. *Now* is what got you and Tanisha alone in a closet at a party, even though everybody knew what you was doing in there . . . and would be talkin' 'bout in school tomorrow. For a kid, there ain't nothin' more powerful than the now. The now makes your mind break down. Some part of it knows that if you ain't home by the time them streetlights come on . . . you gone get it. But you stay out anyway, 'cause whatever you doin' right then, it's got a hold to you and it don't let go until the now is your daddy's leather meeting your backside.

JOE: The future is another thing altogether . . . Gets so as you spend most of the day caught up in shit that ain't even happened yet . . . might not ever happen. You kinda like a driver trying to predict when the road gonna turn, how sharp the turn will be, and in what direction. Funny thing is . . . you ain't got no headlights. A whole day given to a road that turns at its whim, and the only reason you know it's turned at all is 'cause you done run your car into a ditch.

LENNOX: Later ain't no far-off later, it's an any-minute-now later. So it ain't the future . . . not really . . . it's just, you know . . . later. Sometimes your later be so close to your now that you can't even tell them apart. They flow into each other so smoothly. Like if I steal something from the candy store and get caught, I know a world a trouble is comin' . . . later. But it ain't that next-week kinda thang. It's that just-as-soon-as-my-daddy-gets-here kinda thang. That's all the future gaze that a kid's got. It don't matter how much you speak on what it's gonna be like when we grow up . . . what the grades mean . . . hangin' round with the wrong element . . . or being where we ain't supposed to be. We can't see that, we just see now and later. The rest of that is just too damn far away . . .

JOE: With so much energy given to the future and so much energy given to the past . . . we ain't got much left for the now. Funny how being a grown man moves you further away from living. If you think about it, with so much given to the future, even when the future get here, we won't be there . . . our energy will be given to the future that comes after that. I guess we don't ever get a now . . .

LENNOX: Guess that's how I know I ain't really a kid no more. I got a past . . .
   I'm worrin' about a future . . . and I'm losing my now.

[*A train rumbling through is heard, and occasional flashes of blue light kick up,
restoring the present. Seamless transition into next scene.*]

SCENE 9: WHISTLING

[*Sound of a train rumbling by, kicking up the occasional spark of blue light. Lights
come up on the El platform. The* BLUESMEN *are playing a lively number.* LENNOX
and JOE *sit on a bench.* LENNOX *has his earphones on and is grooving to a beat entirely different from that of the* BLUESMEN. *His hands are flailing in classic hip-hop
gestures.* LENNOX *watches a woman walk by. His eyes are fixed on her as she passes.
He whistles softly, indicating that he finds her quite attractive.*]

JOE: Take a picture, it lasts longer.
LENNOX [*still transfixed*]: What?
JOE: Take them phones off your face and maybe you could hear me.
LENNOX [*still transfixed*]: Huh?

[JOE *removes the headphones.*]

JOE: Live music, Lennox . . .
LENNOX [*still watching women go by*]: Yeah, Pop, live women!
JOE: Music! I said music!
LENNOX [*with a broad smile*]: Yeah, Pop, they are music, ain't they.
JOE: Why you wearing them headphones when the Bluesmen playing live for
   you right here?
LENNOX: I got my own sound track.

[*He watches another woman pass.*]

   It got a beat that goes with the [*imitating the sway in a woman's hips*] boom . . .
   boom . . . boom they got when they walk. The Bluesmen ain't got that
   sound.
JOE [*indicating the passing woman*]: You think she's good-lookin'?
LENNOX: Don't you?
JOE: She seems nice.
LENNOX [*smiling leeringly*]: Yeah, Pop, she's nice.

[*Another woman comes by from the opposite direction.* LENNOX *once again becomes
transfixed. He begins to poke* JOE *in the leg, trying to get his attention.*]

[*Calling to her*] Heeeeey, gurl.

JOE: Boy, act like you got some sense.

LENNOX [*still transfixed, shaking his head*]: Damn.

JOE: What'd you say?

LENNOX [*excitedly*]: Did you see that one? Damn, she looks good.

JOE: Now I know you done lost your mind. Cursing in front of me and on top of that actin' like you is.

LENNOX [*still enraptured*]: You don't look at them and just imagine all the . . .

JOE: It's one thing to think it and another to let the world see you think it.

LENNOX: Ain't no shame in my game!

JOE [*dismissively*]: Ain't no game in yo' game either.

LENNOX: You gotta show you appreciate 'em, Pop. That you got reverence for the female form.

JOE: Reverence? When did you start using words like "reverence"?

LENNOX: Females like a brotha with a vocab.

JOE: You doin' some kinda clinical study?

LENNOX [*becoming transfixed on the suggestion of another woman*]: Huh?

JOE [*puzzled*]: Females?

LENNOX [*sarcastically*]: Yeah, Pop, you know, like the opposite of male.

JOE: I know what it means, I just don't know why you would call a woman a female . . . Never mind.

LENNOX: It's just a word. Ain't like I called her a hottie or nothin'. You just wrapped too tight.

JOE: Subtlety.

LENNOX: Overrated.

JOE: Respect.

LENNOX: Overstated.

JOE: Courtesy then.

LENNOX: Undervalued.

JOE: I guess you got it all figured out.

LENNOX: I just know what females like.

JOE: And what is that?

LENNOX: A guy who ain't afraid to say what's on his mind.

JOE: Well that may be true with fourteen-year-olds. But grown women . . .

LENNOX: Females is females . . .

JOE: Would you quit saying that word!

LENNOX: Females?

JOE: Please.

LENNOX: What you want me to call 'em, then?

JOE: At your age they are just little girls.

LENNOX [*laughing*]: You see that girl down the track?

JOE: Which?

LENNOX: The one in the tight leather skirt . . . the one with the big . . . heart.

JOE [*laughing softly*]: Yeah.

LENNOX: She look good to you?

JOE: She's an attractive woman.

LENNOX: I think so too. You know who she is?

JOE: You know her?

LENNOX: You do too . . . That's Rene Ortega.

JOE: Get out of here.

LENNOX: Ninth grade, Pop! She's in my division . . . You said it yourself, that ain't no girl, that's a woman.

JOE: She's a girl dressed up like a prison sentence. But that don't make her no woman.

LENNOX: Would you even know a woman if she jumped up and bit you?

JOE: I've got appreciation for a good woman . . .

LENNOX: Since when?

JOE: Your mother.

LENNOX [*souring on the notion*]: Yeah, OK.

[*Beat.*]

It's not like I don't know what to do with a good female, Pop. But some females just made to look at, you know? I don't want every pretty girl I see to be my girlfriend. I'm just happy when they smile back at me. Some of them be too shy to smile back at first . . . they be trying to act like you ain't there. You know they can see you, but they be all about playin' the game. To them females, you say something . . . nothing too gross, just a "Heeeey, baby," "Come here, gurl," or a "Wassup," then they crack that smile they was guardin' like their mama's jewels and I'm happy. I get a little buzz off that and I'm floating for the next ten minutes.

JOE: What do you know about a buzz?

LENNOX: Not no drug buzz, man . . . just that feel-good you get that don't cost nothing. You act like I ain't got no sense. Anyway . . . they know it's a game, that's why they be playin' a brotha. I got maybe six seconds, right. They know I ain't gonna get up from this seat. The way I'm dressed, ain't like I'm gonna follow them down the platform. In six seconds she'll be in and out of range, and in that time, I gotta break her down . . .

JOE: Or what?

LENNOX: Or I'll come off lookin' like an idiot?

JOE [*ribbing him*]: No . . . never.

LENNOX [*spotting the suggestion of a girl approaching*]: Watch . . . Saaaay, sweet thang.

[*No response.*]

So you gonna play me like that . . . wit'cho fine self? That's all right then, take your sunshine home and brighten up somebody else's day.

[*He is pleased when she smiles, and he smiles back, turning to his dad.*]

See. Ten-minute buzz. Free of charge.

JOE: Do you act like this with girls you actually like?

LENNOX: Sometimes, when I like 'em, I mean that wanna-spend-some-money-on-them kinda like? Then I go the opposite, you know?

JOE: You zig where you useta zag?

LENNOX: Exactly.

JOE: You get shy and quiet?

LENNOX: Yeah.

JOE: And that's why you don't have a girlfriend.

LENNOX: I'm just waiting on the right one. The one that will recognize that I'm a diamond in the rough.

JOE: A lump of coal.

LENNOX: Maybe you're a lump of coal, but I'm a little further along than that.

[*Sound is heard of a screeching subway train approaching, then grinding to a halt.*]

JOE: Here's your train. So get yourself off to school.

LENNOX: All right.

[*He crosses toward the train.*]

Be safe!

JOE: Come straight home after class.

LENNOX: Whatever, Pop!

[*The soundscape moves people aboard the crowded subway car. The sound is heard of the doors closing and the train moving noisily on toward the next stop, its screech fading. The lights dim, fade to black.*]

ACT 2

SCENE 1: THE GLOBAL ANNOYANCE

[*Lights come up on the apartment of* JOE *and* LENNOX. *Recorded hip-hop music fills the space.* LENNOX *is lying prone upon the floor with textbooks and papers spread out everywhere. He is wearing a set of earphones attached to a portable CD player, his head bobbing to the rhythm. He is lost in his studies when suddenly a shrill phone ring pierces the air.* LENNOX *is annoyed, but after a few rings he rises, removes the earphones, and is compelled to answer the phone. The hip-hop music fades to a softer level.*]

LENNOX: Hello.

[*Lights come up on* REP 2, *sitting in the same corner occupied earlier by* REP 1.]

REP 2 [*reading text*]: This is Global Credit and I am your customer service representative, Alexander Lassiter. Is Joseph Gratton available?

LENNOX: Dad, phone.

JOE: Who is it?

LENNOX [*sarcastically*]: Your bookie, agent, dope dealer, flesh peddler . . .

JOE [*taking the phone*]: Hello.

[LENNOX *returns to his studies. He replaces the earphones, and the hip-hop music fades out.*]

REP 2: Mr. Joseph Gratton?

JOE: Who is this?

REP 2 [*reading text*]: This is Global Credit and I am your customer service representative, Alexander Lassiter. I'm calling regarding an urgent matter that needs your immediate attention. Are you Mr. Joseph Gratton?

JOE: What can I do for you?

REP 2 [*reading*]: First, Mr. Gratton, I would like to begin by noting that this is an official communication from our recovery systems division, a debt collection subsidiary wholly owned by Time Warner Global Communications, of the Murdoch Turner conglomerate formerly doing business as Illinois Bell and Famous Amos Cookies. As a wholly owned subsidiary we are licensed to conduct business through the Illinois Department of Foreign Affairs and the Delinquent Negroes Surveillance Program, which brings us to your accounts with Marshall Field's, Lord and Taylor, Kay-Bee Toys, Frederick's of Hollywood, and Kentucky Fried Chicken. We are required by law to inform you that this is an attempt to collect one or more outstanding debts now owned by this corporation; any information obtained will be used for that purpose.

JOE: Fine.

REP 2 [*dully*]: It says here on my screen, Mr. Gratton, that you are recently deceased. Is this in fact true, sir? . . . Because if it is, we will need verification by way of death certificate or DNA-validated cremains.

JOE: I'm alive and well, thank you.

REP 2 [*dully*]: Just one moment, sir, while I note this in your file . . . [*Typing and speaking to himself*] Rumors of his death . . . not verifiable. [*To* JOE] Thank you, sir. [*Typing*] OK, Mr. Gratton, now that we are up to date I need to know the answers to a few questions.

JOE: Shoot.

REP 2 [*suddenly blunt*]: When are you gonna pay this bill?

JOE: When I get some money.

REP 2: Do you know when that will be?

JOE: No.

REP 2: Work with me, sir, I'm only trying to be of assistance. Are you employed at present?

JOE: At present I am in my living room.

REP 2 [*typing*]: Yes, sir, living room . . . I mean no, sir, not living room, but rather do you have a job?

JOE: Yes.

REP 2: And your employer is . . . ?

JOE: Me.

REP 2: I see. [*Typing*] Not gainfully employed . . . [*To* JOE] Can you make a payment now?

JOE: No.

REP 2: We will accept a postdated check.

JOE: Why would I write you a check for money I don't have?

REP 2: It would be a showing of good faith.

JOE: It would be a showing of stupidity . . .

REP 2: Can you borrow the money from someone? . . . Family, friends, associates?

JOE: Why would I want to?

REP 2 [*caught off guard*]: Sir?

JOE: Have you ever borrowed money from your family or friends?

REP 2 [*becoming more passionate and abandoning the text*]: My borrowing habits are not at issue—

JOE [*interjecting*]: If I get money from someone I know, then I'll have to see them every day or thereabouts. They'd be lookin' at me funny, wondering where their money is, 'cause they got bills to pay themselves. Next thing you know, they ain't even speaking to me. Now I'm a broke man with no job, no family, and no friends . . . All in all, I think I'd rather just owe the money to Global Credit.

REP 2 [*flustered*]: But we must make some arrangement, Mr. Gratton.

JOE: How about this. When I get some money, I'll pay you. In the meantime, feel free to charge me loan shark interest.

[*The* SUPERVISOR *enters, listening in.*]

REP 2 [*growing annoyed*]: You're not really trying to resolve this matter, sir?

JOE: You're not really trying to resolve this matter either . . . [*recalling the name*] Alexander, right?

REP 2 [*summoning the* SUPERVISOR]: Could you hold, please . . .

[*The* SUPERVISOR *picks up the phone.*]

SUPERVISOR: Mr. Gratton?

JOE: Who is this?

SUPERVISOR: This is Mr. Pullman. I am a supervisor in the recovery systems division, a debt collection subsidiary wholly owned by Time Warner Global Communications, of the Murdoch Turner conglomerate formerly doing business as Illinois Bell and Famous Amos Cookies . . . What seems to be the problem, sir?

JOE: You're wasting my time.

SUPERVISOR [*checking the screen, pointedly*]: Well it says here, sir, that you are not gainfully employed, so I'm not quite wasting your time, am I, Mr. Gratton?

JOE: You the bad cop?

SUPERVISOR: Sir?

JOE: The other cat didn't seem to have a spine, so I figure you're the guy they call when they need a little backbone.

SUPERVISOR: We need to know how you plan to resolve this matter, sir.

JOE: Like I told the last cat. When I get some money, I'll pay you.

SUPERVISOR: That is not a satisfactory answer, sir. We need you to find employment. Are you even looking for a job?

JOE: Do I personally owe you any money?

SUPERVISOR: You owe Global Credit in the amount of—

JOE [*interjecting*]: Do I owe you personally?

SUPERVISOR: That is not the issue . . .

JOE: Of course it is. You need to thank me.

SUPERVISOR: For being a drain on this corporation and the global economy?

JOE: For getting you a job. The way I figure it, you got a gig 'cause I owe the Man . . . Now the Man, he gonna pay you whether I pay him or not . . . Your kids will be fed. They'll have little coordinated sweaters and pastel Hush Puppies for their first day at school . . . You got kids?

SUPERVISOR [*off guard*]: Ahhh, yeah . . . two . . . But, sir, we need—

JOE [*interjecting*]: Preschool age, right?

SUPERVISOR: Ahhh, yeah.

JOE: Private school?

SUPERVISOR: When they are of age, but I don't see what this has to do with your account.

JOE: College?

SUPERVISOR: Certainly.

JOE: Public or private?

SUPERVISOR: Mr. Gratton, this is a most unusual—

JOE: A word of advice. The Man will want to see a return on the debt. Maybe as much as forty cents on the dollar . . . If you don't make that, you won't be a supervisor for long.

SUPERVISOR [*confused and irritated*]: Excuse me?

JOE: You can't get blood from a turnip.

SUPERVISOR: Turnip?

JOE: It would be better if you rang the cat who could help you pick up that forty cents . . . 'cause I ain't that cat. But I'll tell you what I'm gonna do. When I get some money that doesn't have to go to my landlord, the grocer, or the guv'-ment . . . I'll drop you a line. Otherwise, kid, you're wasting time for both of us.

[JOE *hangs up the phone. Blackout on* REP 2 *and the* SUPERVISOR. JOE *sits down in a chair, spent.*]

LENNOX [*to* JOE]: You think that'll take care of 'em?

JOE [*to* LENNOX]: I give it a week . . . two max.

[*Fade to black.*]

SCENE 2: DECEMBER VOICES

[*Lights come up on* LENNOX *standing next to the* BLUESMEN *leaning up against the wall.* LENNOX *takes out a cigarette and lights it with a plain disposable lighter. He leans back against the wall, inhaling deeply, and then suddenly and violently coughs.*]

DRUMMER [*to* LENNOX]: That shit will kill you. Where you pick up a nasty habit like that?

GUITARIST [*to the* DRUMMER]: Don't look at me.

DRUMMER: Boy your age need to be careful which horse he hitch his wagon to.

LENNOX: It's just a square.

GUITARIST [*to the* DRUMMER]: The boy already got a daddy.

DRUMMER: So.

LENNOX [*to the* GUITARIST]: You sure you don't know where he is?

GUITARIST: Man come and go as he need to . . . Joe don't make a habit of tellin' me why or what for.

LENNOX [*concerned*]: How long he been gone?

DRUMMER [*to* LENNOX, *scolding*]: You need to put that butt out.

LENNOX: I can quit anytime I want.

DRUMMER: That's only 'cause you ain't learned how to inhale yet.

[LENNOX *looks at the cigarette, then tries to inhale. He coughs violently. The* BLUESMEN *laugh long and loud.*]

Burns, don't it!

GUITARIST: Once you get used to that . . . then you can be a chain-smoking bluesman. Once you a chain-smoking bluesman, you can't never quit.

LENNOX: Smokin'?

DRUMMER: The blues.

GUITARIST: Them cigarettes just be part of the persona. Hell, the only reason I ever picked 'em up in the first place was 'cause I thought I looked damn good with the smoke rising up while I sat with an ax in my hand. Billy Ray be wheeling his doghouse with that square hangin' there. See now, a bass player looks smooth as shit with that white stank rising up past his face while he lay down his fat-fingered rhythm. Shit, that smoke just be portable ambience. Billy Ray looked the part. Hell, his look made him sound better . . . Thanks to Billy Ray, I do a pack a day.

DRUMMER: A bluesman don't even know what it means to be a bluesman when he first start. But before you know it you in them dark-ass clubs, two in the morning . . . eyes heavy from the smoke that choke ordinary folk, but you breathe it like it's cool water for a thirsty man. Yo' health be damned. Don't matter if you smoke or don't, 'cause you suck down other folks' fumes and stale air without a care, and you'll step up to do it again . . . tomorrow, and the day after . . . even do four sets on Saturdays.

LENNOX: That why you down here? To get away from clubs?

GUITARIST: Come a point when a sewer feels cleaner than a club.

LENNOX: But you go back?

GUITARIST: A'course we do.

DRUMMER: You can't get it out'cho blood.

GUITARIST: . . . Don't even try no more . . . once you in the life, you in the life.

DRUMMER: It don't matter how long we play down here. At the end of the day we be at Mable's . . . 'cause Mable's got a score.

GUITARIST: . . . If we can't be there, then we be at the Mines, or Uncle Cholly-B's . . .

DRUMMER: Prob'ly die in this tube . . . or in some joint.

BLUESMEN [*in unison, laughing*]: But that's all right with us.

DRUMMER: Comin' and goin' . . . thems the perks of the life we lead . . . ain't no different for your daddy.

GUITARIST: Too true . . .

DRUMMER: Shit, he more addicted to his hustle than we are to the blues . . .

GUITARIST: What's wrong, boy? You got women troubles?

LENNOX: No.

GUITARIST: You got baby troubles?

LENNOX: Hell no.

GUITARIST [*laughing*]: Can't have them baby troubles without women troubles first, huh?

DRUMMER [*comforting*]: Don't mind him . . . he just pulling yo' leg.

GUITARIST [*laughing*]: That's what he tryin' to get him a woman for . . . to pull his leg.

[*The* DRUMMER *and* LENNOX *deliver a cold stare that quickly quiets the* GUITARIST.]

LENNOX [*to the* DRUMMER]: He ain't say nothin' 'bout where he was going?

DRUMMER: Why don't you head on home. Your daddy prob'ly won't be back here today. It don't matter how long you wait.

[LENNOX *looks to the* GUITARIST.]

GUITARIST: I told you all I know. What's got you so bent outta shape?

LENNOX: Sometimes I get this image burned into my mind that I can't shake, and then I have to come down here and see for myself.

DRUMMER: See what?

LENNOX: Whatever.

GUITARIST: Shit, boy, you sound 'bout like one a dem witchy women from out bayou way . . .

DRUMMER [*to the* GUITARIST]: Cut it out now, can't you see the boy is rattled?

GUITARIST: Over what?

LENNOX: Just a feeling I get . . . then I can't get nothin' done till I come see 'bout him.

DRUMMER: What kinda feeling?

LENNOX: Don't you ever feel like you can sense when somethin' ain't right? Like if you could just open your eyes wide enough you could see?

GUITARIST [*dismissively*]: No.

DRUMMER: See what?

LENNOX: They insides.

GUITARIST [*disgustedly*]: Like they guts and shit?!

LENNOX: Nah, just his uneasiness.

DRUMMER: What'chu see when you see what you see?

LENNOX: I don't know, it just be like . . . there ain't no sun here. No light to lift his night. I can see the sounds as they pass between his lips . . . misting then fallin' to the ground. Cold whippin' through the tunnel . . . Ramrodded by passing trains, cold slithering into his boots . . . wrappin' round his feet like a snake. Stinging . . . leavin' blisters that take days to fade. All those faces pass, never stopping to help him in his distress. Outside the moon hangs, staring at him through the concrete street, watching . . . knowing . . . he owns nothing. He can't even sell his soul . . . He's just got his hustle, dancing for nickels and dimes—as the El rolls by. Everybody's looking at him . . . fixated . . . Captured, enraptured. He is lecturing the cold, dank air. And he believes that it is listening to what he has to say.

DRUMMER [*concerned*]: You see him talkin' to himself?

LENNOX: Yeah.

GUITARIST: But not like for real, though, right? . . . 'Cause that would be some freaky shit. [*To himself*] You work in the hole, you think you know a motherfucker.

LENNOX: I just see it sometimes, that don't mean he do it . . . I just have to come see for myself. Make sure he's all right, you know?

GUITARIST: He was fine the last time I saw him. I'll keep a lookout, though. See if he be wanderin' around mumbling to himself.

DRUMMER: Get on home, Lenny. If your pops shows up, we'll tell him to ring you, OK?

LENNOX [*turning to exit*]: Yeah, I guess.

[*Sound of a train rumbling by, striking up sparks of blue light. Seamless transition into next scene.*]

SCENE 3: MARKERS

[*Lights come up on* JOE *and* LENNOX *in a voided space. The two men are isolated by a gulf of darkness. Their lines are delivered as if they were talking to each other, but it is obvious that each is carrying on an internal monologue. The* BLUESMEN *strike up a melancholy groove.*]

JOE: When you were little, you used to cry all the time . . . [*Laughs softly.*] Had to be the most sensitive kid in the world. I would pull you aside, hold your hand, and tell you everything would be OK. By the time you were four, I changed up my strategy. Decided I would toughen you up. 'Cause the last thing a little black boy needed was to go through life with the psychological equivalent of a glass jaw. I stopped picking you up with every whine. When you would fall I'd let you work through the pain . . . Thought I was helping you become a man . . . But you still cried at the drop of a hat. I wanted you to respond differently, but you just couldn't do it. And my wanting you to . . . pushing you to . . . was only making things worse. So I decided to let nature take its course. Figured that sooner or later the world would knock you upside your head hard enough to get your attention . . . and once you took note you'd figure out that what you needed was a little more courage and a lot fewer tears.

LENNOX: Courage don't mean that the tears stop. It just means that you hide 'em. From everybody . . . Maybe I just didn't wanna hide anything from you. Didn't want anything between us . . . not even that macho bullshit that lets other men think that they're close . . . when they're not. Batting averages, lineup changes, overs and unders, that don't make men close . . . Maybe them tears be like a river flowing from me to you, carrying the things that I can't say . . . but wish I could. Maybe them tears be for the things that ain't got no words at all. You, you still ain't cried . . .

[*Lights fade up on the suggestion of a cemetery.*]

JOE: It's just a little block of stone, you know. They won't even allow you to put up a suitable marker . . . Say that the mowers need to be able to roll right over the top of 'em. So each stone's gotta be lower than the mowin' height. I go some places, them old ones especially . . . they got shit rising up thirty feet in the air. Pretty as all get-out . . . some polished . . . some rough cut, some with symbols cut deep into 'em. You know, religious heavenly type shit, Latin I think. Them stone-cut angels dancing . . . cherubs . . . There is this pretty kinda way that the angels' faces smooth out . . . stone melted like hot wax . . . till you can't see no features in 'em . . . like you ain't supposed to know which angel is watchin' over 'em.

Can you imagine needing thirty feet of stone to say I miss you? I love you? . . . Don't leave me? . . . Woman wasn't much over five feet nothin' anyway . . . Thirty feet, that's a lot of rock. You think if one cat got thirty feet of marble that means he a better person than a cat with only ten? And the fella that ain't got no stone at all. What about him?

This clerk asked me, "Was she in the service?" Said that servicemen [*laughing uneasily*] or women, I guess, get stones courtesy of the guv'ment. Guv'ment don't care 'bout no stone if she ain't done a tour, though. "How much?" I ask him . . . and he looks straight through me and says, "Four hundred dollars." Four hundred dollars for a stone that can't be seen if the grass get high . . . a stone that sits below the mowin' height, 'cause the groundsman don't wanna get up off his fat ass when he's ridin' atop them blades. I might as well have asked him for a thirty-foot piece of granite with cherubs cut into it.

Your mama is still here . . . somewhere . . . resting . . . in an unmarked grave. I pray that she has some kinda peace knowing that it was a stone for her or some meals for you . . . I hope she ain't too upset that she couldn't have both.

[*Lights fade down on* JOE, *leaving* LENNOX *standing on the El platform in a trancelike state. Flashes of blue light spark up from a passing train, illuminating* LENNOX. *Lights gently fade in.*]

GUITARIST [*to* LENNOX]: Music that good, huh?
LENNOX: Huh?
GUITARIST: Good blues been known to do that . . . Like it best when it does that to a woman, but hey . . . we all vulnerable . . . [*To the* DRUMMER] Know what I mean!

[*They laugh.*]

DRUMMER [*to* LENNOX]: Get on home, Lennox, for this next groove make you wanna walk into an oncomin' train.

LENNOX [*distantly*]: Uh . . . yeah.

[LENNOX *exits. Fade to black.*]

SCENE 4: THE JOE SCHOLARSHIP FUND

[*Lights come up on* JOE *in the apartment.* JOE *is lying prone upon the floor with catalogs, handbooks, and papers spread out everywhere. He is lost in his research. The sound of a key rattles in the lock and* LENNOX *enters.*]

LENNOX [*irritatedly*]: I been down on Jackson waiting for you, where you been?

JOE: Home.

LENNOX: I called the house.

JOE: What, you keepin' tabs? . . . I just got back in a little bit ago.

LENNOX: The Bluesmen said you was down on the platform earlier but you left?

JOE: And?

LENNOX: Why ain't you working?

JOE: I am working.

LENNOX: I went by Harry's, he said he ain't seen you all day either, so exactly what kinda work you been doin' that you been nowhere near the work?

JOE [*excitedly*]: I got it figured out!

LENNOX [*annoyed*]: Where you been, Pop?

JOE: Just settle down for a second and check out—

LENNOX [*interjecting*]: You be 'bout to bust a gut if you don't know where I am, but you can drop off the face of the earth and I'm s'posed to be cool with that?

JOE: Lenny!!!

LENNOX: What?

JOE: Shut up and sit down.

LENNOX [*taking a seat*]: When you go to work, you work till you can't hardly stand . . . So where were you?

JOE: School.

LENNOX: We had a half a day.

JOE: Not your school . . . *the* school . . . as in the university.

LENNOX [*skeptically*]: Really?

JOE: You gotta make a choice.

LENNOX: Between?

JOE: Which you want more, the education or the fancy job.

LENNOX: Can't I have both?

JOE: Maybe, but I ain't got that much worked out just yet . . . So which is it?

LENNOX: Which what?

JOE: The education or the job?

LENNOX [*thinking*]: The . . . job . . . definitely the job.

JOE [*disappointedly*]: Fine.

LENNOX: You wanted me to say education?

JOE: I wanted you say whichever you meant.

LENNOX: Then why you look all broke over my answer?

JOE: I ain't broke.

LENNOX: You got a way for me to get an education?

JOE: If you got the nerve.

LENNOX: What's it gonna cost me?

JOE: A little pride.

LENNOX: I mean in dollars and cents.

JOE: Nothing.

LENNOX: Which school?

JOE: Where you wanna go?

LENNOX: I can't just choose which school I wanna go to, there's all this stuff to consider. They at least gotta choose me back. I gotta write essays, go on interviews . . .

JOE: Your first pick . . . which school?

LENNOX [*laughing*]: My number one would have to be Northwestern business school, or maybe the University of Chicago. You know what a brother could pull with paper from those business schools?

JOE: You're back on jobs again. Would you forget about jobs and money for a second and just think about the education part.

LENNOX: OK, fine.

JOE: If we could get you an education from Northwestern or the University of Chicago, free of charge, would you take it?

LENNOX: No loans?

JOE: None.

LENNOX: Hell yeah I would.

JOE: Would you go to class on a regular schedule, follow the curriculum until you finish all the required course work?

LENNOX: Is this a trick question?

JOE [*insistently*]: Your answer.

LENNOX: Free schoolin'? . . . No doubt, Pop, I'm there from the first day till the last.

JOE: . . . 'Cause the education is the most important thing?

LENNOX [*unconvincingly*]: Sure, Pop.

JOE: You gotta believe that or else it ain't gonna work.

LENNOX [*humoring him*]: Yeah, Pop, education, it's more important than anything.

JOE: More important than that high-powered job you talking 'bout, sweating for white folks and hoping they give you they company?

LENNOX: Yes sir.

JOE: Cool . . . Then you decide which school you want, and that's where you're gonna go.

LENNOX [*skeptically*]: You shittin' me.

JOE: Watch your mouth.

LENNOX: How, Pop?

JOE: You tell me which school you want. Tomorrow we'll stop by the—

LENNOX [*interjecting*]: Admissions office!

JOE: The counseling office.

LENNOX: Admissions first, then financial aid, then counseling.

JOE: This your plan or my plan?

LENNOX [*apologetically*]: Yours.

JOE: Thank you. So tomorrow we stop by the counseling office of the school of your choice, and we let one of them counselors pitch us why their business school is so great. I wanna hear right from their faces what the big deal is. Then we let them take us on one of them university tours where they show us their great library, and computer centers, and ivy-covered buildings.

LENNOX: OK, OK . . . then we go by the admissions office and pick up the application forms . . .

JOE: I went by DePaul today. I picked up a course catalog for fall semester, some student handbooks, and whatever else they had to offer. I brought them home so we could check them out.

LENNOX: You want me to go to DePaul?

JOE: I want you to go wherever you wanna go.

LENNOX: Then why you got all this stuff from DePaul?

JOE: I needed to test a theory.

LENNOX [*uneasily*]: Damn . . . you had me going for a minute . . .

JOE: I'm trying to help you.

LENNOX: If you don't wanna tell me where you been and what you been doing, it's only 'cause you hidin' something. What, you got some woman you don't want me to know about? Last time you had a woman you was creepin' for weeks thinkin' that that meant I didn't know . . . I knew.

JOE [*picking up a handbook*]: Here.

LENNOX [*reading the cover*]: DePaul University Student Handbook . . . No shittin'.

JOE: I'll find the money to buy the books.

LENNOX: Any school?

JOE: Any school.

LENNOX: How?

JOE: Whatever classes you want, you find them in the course catalog . . . they give you these things for free if you can believe that. Shit, they tell you who the professor is, what time the class meets, where and how often . . . they even got another book tellin' you what the class is about and what the other students think about the class and the professor.

LENNOX: Pop, you're ramblin'.

JOE: . . . I'm just in a rhythm . . . Pick out whatever classes you want . . . then go to class.

LENNOX: What good is that gonna . . . [*Catching on*] For no credit!

JOE: For an education!

LENNOX: Why you got me thinkin' I'm gonna be educated at Northwestern or U of C when all you got is this harebrained idea.

JOE: Professors don't ask students for ID to attend class.

LENNOX: How would you know what a professor does?

JOE: I went to class.

LENNOX: You?

JOE [*proudly*]: Sat in the front row.

LENNOX: What class?

JOE: Some shit, "Diffy-Q," the book says . . . means differential equations . . . some space-age math-type shit for engineers, I think. Can you imagine that? Me sitting in class with cats that's gonna build buildings and be technogeeks. You shoulda seen them cats workin' on them numbers . . . inspiring . . . and nobody asked me for a student ID.

LENNOX: So.

JOE: Had I wanted to know what the fuck a "Diffy-Q" was, I could have learned it today. Free of charge.

LENNOX: One class, Pop, that don't prove nothin'.

JOE: I'm feelin' the same vibe . . . like maybe I just got lucky . . . so I bounce down the hall and soak up some calculus . . . next hour I'm in some econ class . . . that means e-co-nom-ics.

LENNOX: I know what it means . . .

JOE: Same setup as before. But don't nobody ask me to prove I belong . . . Now this shit is startin' to work on my mind 'cause I ain't hardly lived a day on this planet that somebody ain't been lookin' to me to prove who I am and that I got a right to be where I am. First I think it might be my clothes, right, 'cause I ain't dressed like no preppie. So I look around and I'll be damned if these little prep-school fuckers ain't dressin' down. Like they ain't got no money. Clothes hanging off they ass, and I don't mean in that hip-hop style you be doin' with your underwear showin'. I mean they shit got holes in it. Their shoes! These cats' shoes are all run over, like they grooving on the feelin' of their toes meetin' the concrete. And that's when it all starts comin' together for me. So I hopped the train and did the same thing at the University of Illinois. Took French literature. [*Laughs.*] Don't know what the hell they was talkin' 'bout. But I'm fo' damn sure nobody asked me for ID.

LENNOX: They do take attendance.

JOE: Small classes do, big classes don't.

LENNOX: So I can only take big classes then?

JOE: You can take any class you want . . .

LENNOX: Sooner or later somebody's gonna put it together. What do I do in the small classes when the professor is looking at my chocolate face and wondering why if he ain't got but fifteen kids on the books, sixteen are in the desks?

JOE: It's just like any other hustle. Ninety-nine percent of the work is the right attitude and knowin' your mark.

LENNOX: They're professors. Ain't like I can just run game on them and expect 'em to roll over.

JOE: You act like I'm sayin' you should sit in a college class with a fifth-grade education. If I could afford to pay for the enrollment, you'd be sitting in his classes anyway. You don't look no different to him than any of them other kids. Hell, you look better, at least the clothes you got hanging off your ass are new.

LENNOX: It won't work!

JOE: You just gotta get inside the professor's head . . . think like he think . . . sooooooo . . . on the first day of class you have your smile and your freshly washed ass in the front row. You look him in the eyes when he speaks. You let him know that he may be wasting his time with everybody else in the room. But with you, in you, he has found the one student who wants to learn *everything* he has to teach. And when class is over, step to the fore and tell him that you are not presently enrolled in his class because your schedule does not permit. But you would like to sit in whenever you can.

LENNOX: And he'll let me?

JOE: Do you know what a learned man wants more than anything else in the world?

LENNOX: No, what?

JOE: Someone . . . anyone . . . to give a fuck about what he thinks and to listen to what he has to say. That professor, any professor, will lecture to you . . . quiz you, hell, he'll let you take the exams and tell you what your score was . . . but above all, he will never ask you for an ID.

LENNOX: Why not?

JOE: Because nobody in this country really wants to learn. Not for the sake of learning. We'll learn it if we think we can get ahead, otherwise we don't care . . . and that professor knows it. Them top-shelf prep-school kids ain't listening to him. Even the ones that look like they are, they just want the grade, not the wisdom. Gotta keep up that GPA. Ten minutes after a test, their mind is emptied. How many college kids do you think that professor has who come to class because of him? That's a buzz that few can pass up. Hell, if he ever figures out that you're not enrolled, it'll be 'cause you were too attentive. Too fuckin' interested in what's going on. And he still won't turn you in . . . because the buzz from you wantin' to learn *from him,* that's just too intoxicating. He'll figure out how it's OK for him to *give* to you what other kids pay thirty thousand dollars for. You can take that to the bank.

LENNOX [*dismissively*]: It's just another hustle, Pop?

JOE: And a damn good one . . . a noble one.

LENNOX: Without the degree, what good is it?

JOE: One hundred and forty years.

LENNOX: What?

JOE: One hundred and forty years ago a nigga would learn to read 'cause he knew that readin' was its own reward. Do you know how many people was killed just 'cause they was trying to learn to read?

LENNOX: Don't slip off into one of them—

JOE [*interjecting*]: Wasn't no degree in it for a slave, but I betcha they knew the value of an education.

LENNOX: News flash! Slavery is over!

JOE: That's all you see, ain't it? The piece of paper and job offers you hope to get if affirmative action is still up and runnin'.

LENNOX: You don't think I'm good enough to get a job in an open market?

JOE: You oughtta be figuring out how to have your own insteada trying to convince somebody else that you're worthwhile.

LENNOX: Even if I did do it. Four years later . . . me and *any* high school graduate would be standing in the same line trying to get a job at the post office.

JOE [*frustrated*]: You gotta think small, don't you?! Damn, boy . . . maybe you oughtta just quit then and cry 'bout what you ain't got like you always do!

LENNOX: It's on me now! You bring me this backwater bullshit, and because I don't buy into it I'm the one cryin'? Damn! Does everything have to be a hustle?

JOE: Life is a hustle.

LENNOX: That why you tryin' to hustle me? Trying to get me buzzed on Northwestern, so that I don't see that you the reason we sittin' round here hatchin' these crazy schemes in the first place . . . that you ain't take care of your business as the head of this house, so we ain't got no money . . . that you couldn't bear to have no nine-to-five 'cause you had to have the "noble hustle." Mama worry herself so hard that sooner or later she gotta pull back from everything 'cause the pressure was too strong. She pulled back so hard that she pulled back from me. Then she pull back from living altogether. If you cared for her you woulda stepped up like a man and did what had to be done insteada doing what felt good. You woulda carried the load like a man.

JOE: You don't know nothing about me and your mama.

LENNOX: I know she's gone . . . and that your hustling ass drove her to her death!

JOE: You don't know shit!

LENNOX: Maybe not, but I know what it smells like, and this plan stinks.

JOE: Get your shit and get out of my house. You so damn grown that you know what choices grown men have?

[LENNOX *begins gathering up his belongings.*]

LENNOX: I knew this day was comin' . . . the day you would tell me to get out and I would.

JOE: What you doing?

LENNOX: Getting my shit together.

JOE: I'll do you a favor. I'll let you keep the clothes you got on your back . . . but the rest of that shit I bought, bustin' my ass to provide. You don't get to insult the cook and still eat the dinner.

LENNOX [*shocked*]: I . . . Uhhh . . . Fuck it!

[*He tosses the Discman on the table.*]

Keep this too.

[*He grabs his jacket and heads out the door.*]

JOE: Go ahead . . . be the man . . . and live with the results.

[LENNOX *slams the door upon exiting. Fade to black.*]

SCENE 5: POX AND SIAMESE JACKS

[*An occasional flash of blue light sparks up, revealing a lone man standing with a shoe-shine box. The sound of people hustling through on their morning commute is heard. The sound is heard of a screeching subway train approaching, then grinding to a halt. Lights come up on street musicians playing a tune for a dollar or a dime. The soundscape moves people aboard the crowded subway car. The sound is heard of the doors closing and the train moving noisily on toward the next stop, its screech fading. Lights fade in on* JOE.]

JOE: So you figure, as you age, that a man gets only a few opportunities to invest in himself. There is only what you do and what you make. This place has more years than I care to remember invested in it. People you pour your craft into, hoping to make a mark that stays with them. You want it to be so that a man, he won't wanna get his shoes done no place else. A woman, you wanna make it so that she gladly lets you put a shine in her eye as well as her shoes . . . that she'll come back time after time. Why? Because a shoe shine is man's thing, and the fact that you let her into that world says that you see power in her that she may not see herself. And for that and the loss of three dollars she will nod, smile, and say job well done. Now I know this is a dingy platform that only serves any one person for five to ten minutes each day . . . but this is a world I help create. And for those that pass through it, well, they get a little piece of me.

The only other thing I ever helped create is Lennox.

[*Fade up on* LENNOX *in a voided space.*]

LENNOX: I look at him and all at once I love him and I hate him. It's a breath to breathe to believe in a man who has seen so much and yet so little. Yesterday I noticed that he had a chicken pox scar just below his hairline and another off center to the left on his forehead. He has another on his right cheek. If you look into his stubbly beard you can see the occasional ingrown hair, twisting inside him . . . making him swell. How can I see this now and not have seen it before? What else is there that I don't see? I hate . . . I love . . . No, I hate how he doesn't see me. How every word from his face is about him. What he wants from me, or the world, or from himself . . . If I can notice a scar that has been there for umpteen years . . . when will he notice the ones that I have?

[*A spark of blue light sparks up and snaps* JOE *out of his trancelike state.*]

DRUMMER: Joe! . . . Joe!

JOE: What?

DRUMMER: You got a square?

JOE: Thought you quit.

GUITARIST: He got that patch on but he's still fiending.

DRUMMER [*to the* GUITARIST]: Old habits, Bluesman . . . old habits.

[*Enter* THE SUIT. *She makes her way over to the* BLUESMEN *without being noticed.*]

JOE [*to the* DRUMMER, *indicating the cigarettes*]: I ain't got none . . . saving my pennies for textbooks.

GUITARIST: No shittin'?

DRUMMER: You going back to school?

JOE: Lenny gone need books come fall, and I gotta get him some.

GUITARIST: So you been holdin' out on us . . . 'cause I know business ain't that good.

THE SUIT [*to* JOE]: Got him going to college, do you?

[*The men are startled by* THE SUIT *and react accordingly.*]

JOE: You sneakin' up on people now?

THE SUIT: The day that I can make my way all the way down the platform and none of you fellas notice, well, that's a day I never thought would come. [*To* JOE] What, you don't want my gold this morning?

GUITARIST: He was just running his mouth . . . 'steada keepin' watch.

THE SUIT: What else is new? [*To* JOE] So what school are you sending him to?

JOE: We just talkin' 'bout it . . . ain't nothin' been decided yet.

THE SUIT: Got my shoes from Harry's . . . Nice work.

JOE: I do what I can.

THE SUIT: Can you hit me before my train comes?

JOE: Yes, ma'am. Always ready for a shine.

[JOE *hoists* THE SUIT'*s foot up onto the box, preps, and then shines one shoe at a time with skillful precision. A hustler* (LENNOX) *enters just out of* JOE'*s view. He is running a game of three-card monte. He sets up a small table and begins to move inaudibly through the routine of calling for suckers. He is flamboyant in his showmanship but silent in his delivery.*]

[*To* THE SUIT, *indicating the hustler he hears but cannot see*] Parasites!

THE SUIT: It takes all kinds to make a city . . . even the ones living in darkness.

LENNOX [*still pitching*]: People, people gather round. We got better odds than Vegas and pay out quicker than the state lottery. [*Demonstrating the game*] Just follow the Siamese Jack . . . Where is he? Is he on the left? . . . Is he on the right? . . . Is he in the middle? Who wants to pick? [*Flipping the card*] Bam! He's right here. [*Slapping the card to his forehead face up*] The Siamese Jack . . . one body, two heads . . . a sword in one hand and an olive branch in the other. War and peace . . . the two fists of fate . . . kinda like lady luck herself. [*Returning the card to the game*] Around and around he goes . . . where he stops nobody knows . . . Is the hand quicker than the eye? My oh my who wants to try? Five will get you ten, and ten will get you twenty, a little bit more can get you plenty. Come on, people, who wants to play?

[CARD GAME HUSTLER I *makes his way toward the game, acting as though he were a mere commuter.* LENNOX *mixes the cards around and signals to* CARD GAME HUSTLER I *to pick a card. The partner picks the correct card and reacts with choreographed surprise and delight.* LENNOX *hands over the money.*]

[*Taking the five*] There we have it . . . One brave soul who wants to roll the dice once or twice . . . [*Beginning the game*] Siamese Jack from front to back don't take no flack. Around and around and around we goes. Where he's at? . . . Nobody knows . . . Better odds than Vegas and we pay out quicker than the state lottery . . . Who's next!

[JOE *completes the shine on* THE SUIT'*s shoes. She takes her foot off of the footrest and turns around just enough to see* LENNOX. LENNOX *continues to pitch the game inaudibly.*]

THE SUIT [*to* JOE]: Ain't that your boy?

JOE: Where?

THE SUIT: Over there playing three-card monte.

JOE [*hardly looking*]: Lennox knows better than to throw his money away.

THE SUIT: Don't look like he's throwing it away, Joe . . . looks like he's taking it.

[CARD GAME HUSTLER 2 *strolls down the platform and offers up his wager.*]

JOE: My boy would never do nothin' like that. And even if he did, he definitely wouldn't do it here on my—

[JOE *stops in midsentence, realizing that* LENNOX *is running a card game hustle. He stands stunned for a minute, then his anger starts to build. He takes off, grabs* LENNOX *by the collar, and drags him, kicking and screaming, directly into the apartment. Seamless transition into next scene.*]

SCENE 6: SINS OF THE FATHER

[*Cross-fade up on the apartment.*]

JOE: What the fuck is wrong with you?

LENNOX: Ain't like you had to drag me down the street like I stole somethin'!

JOE: You are a thief.

LENNOX: I wasn't doin' nothin' but runnin' game . . . just like you. When you roll outta bed in the morning, the first thing that comes to mind is how you gonna make you some loot.

JOE: There's all kinds of ways to make a dollar.

LENNOX: It's all hustlin'. Ain't that what you said?

JOE: It ain't what I meant.

LENNOX: I ain't never seen you tell a man his shoes don't need a shine. Why is that? Does everybody that lifts their foot need a shine? . . . Or a new heel? . . . Or them damn taps you put on 'em to keep the sole from wearin' down? . . . Or do you put them on so you can hear the suckers comin'?

JOE: You cheatin' people.

LENNOX: Providing a service.

JOE: It's a stickup.

LENNOX: Game of chance.

JOE: Ain't no chance that they gonna win.

LENNOX: Three-card monte ain't like the shell game. The damn card don't get pinched to the bottom of a cap. That card be right there on the table . . . Any fool got a one in three chance of gettin' paid. Had you paid attention in your "Diffy-Q" class . . . you would know that.

JOE: They got a better chance of winnin' if they don't watch the shuffle at all.

LENNOX: So! What, I'm supposed to put up a sign tellin' a Joe how to win my dough? . . . And who said that they should watch in the first place? They got a chance to win . . . That's enough.

JOE: No it ain't.

LENNOX: Them just house odds, Pop! Just like at the boat. The casino can't stay in business if it gives away more than it takes in. But people still be linin' up to give their money away . . . State lottery tell you right on the back of the ticket you got a better chance of gettin' struck by lightnin' and dining with the queen of England, both in the same day, mind you, than you do of ever winnin' the lotto. Suckers still linin' up and givin' away they grocery money.

JOE: That don't excuse you.

LENNOX: Don't it! Did somebody appoint me the patron saint of stupid motherfuckers? When did it become my job to keep a fool and his money together?

JOE: I raised you better . . .

LENNOX: You raised me to be my own man . . . Well, I'll be damned if that ain't what I'm doing. Just 'cause you can't wrap your mind around it don't change that!

JOE: It's illegal.

LENNOX [*pointedly*]: You of all people ain't got no right to tell me about the law.

JOE: What's gonna happen to them big college dreams of yours if you get caught.

LENNOX: We do what we have to to survive . . . ain't that how it goes? Sometimes you so desperate that the law don't matter.

JOE: So you gonna give up?

LENNOX: You gotta get started in order to give up.

JOE: Your mother would—

LENNOX [*interjecting angrily*]: Would what? . . . Be disappointed in me? She wouldn't want this for me?

JOE: She wouldn't—

LENNOX [*interjecting*]: Mama had a big ol' soft spot for two-bit hustlers. The way I figure it, she will keep on lovin' me just like she kept on lovin' you. Maybe she moved your ass out to the couch, but she never pushed you out the door. Mama wouldn't give me up . . . just like she wouldn't give you up . . . And since she's already dead, I don't have to fret over drivin' her to her grave.

[JOE *is staggered by the venomous assault and takes a seat.*]

JOE: You tryin' to hurt me?

LENNOX: Ain't nobody tryin' to hurt you . . . That's just by-product.

JOE: From what?

LENNOX: Becomin' a man.

JOE: Bullshit!

LENNOX: I don't care what you think . . . world don't either.

JOE [*taken aback*]: It don't matter what I think?

LENNOX: Where did I sleep last night?

JOE: I don't know.

LENNOX: When was the last time I had a hot meal?

JOE: I don't know.

LENNOX: I been to school this week? . . . Last week?

JOE: No.

LENNOX: One for three!

JOE: All right, you made your point.

LENNOX: I'm just doin' what I gotta do.

JOE [*sincerely*]: You want me to say I'm sorry—

LENNOX [*interjecting*]: Why? You ain't. Maybe you sorry I threw it in your face. Sorry I drug yo' business down into the Jackson Street subway for your customers to see. But you wasn't sorry enough to come looking for me.

JOE [*pleadingly*]: Son . . .

LENNOX: I get to be your son again? Lucky for me, huh?

JOE: You never stopped being my son!

LENNOX: Yeah, I been thinkin' 'bout our fabulous father-son relationship for a couple of weeks now. [*Sarcastically*] It gives me warmth on the cold nights.

JOE [*calmingly*]: Can we just step back from this for a moment?

LENNOX: Ain't nothin' to step back from . . . I'm livin' the American dream . . . I'm growin' up to be just like my father. Ain't that what every son wants . . . to be just like his pop?

JOE [*pleadingly*]: I was wrong—

LENNOX: No shit!!!

JOE: You gonna let me get a word in?

LENNOX: What'chu gonna say that will change the last two weeks, or the last twelve years?

JOE: About the college thing . . . I was wrong . . . About putting you out on the street . . . I was wrong. I see that now.

LENNOX: You see it 'cause I put it in your face.

JOE: Maybe . . . but the point is that I see it!

LENNOX: Maybe it's too late for you to open your eyes. Maybe now I get to be the one to shut you out . . . let you twist in the wind wonderin' how I feel about you.

JOE [*sincerely*]: You don't know how I feel about you?

LENNOX [*emphatically*]: I been sleepin' outdoors!

JOE: I said I was sorry.

LENNOX: That don't take the chill off.

JOE: What you want me to say . . . I'm sorry, Lenny . . . I'm sorry.

LENNOX: I keep hearin' the words but—

JOE: But what?

LENNOX: Nothin'.

JOE: I made a promise to your mother—

LENNOX: Don't even—

JOE: She wanted me to raise you right.

LENNOX: I don't wanna hear no more about what Mama wanted you to do. When you gonna start doing what I need you to do?

JOE: I ain't sorry for how I raised you. Every step along the way there have been choices to be made. When the time came I made them.

LENNOX: But we both had to live with them.

JOE: When did you get to feelin' you were comin' up short? Like you ain't gettin' something you were entitled to? You ain't got no entitlements but my love, and I ain't never held back on that.

LENNOX [*sarcastically*]: Tough love, right?

JOE: Is there any other kind? You got it in your head that it's supposed to be easy?

LENNOX: Ain't it! . . . Somewhere along the way ain't it supposed to be easy?

JOE: It's supposed to be whatever it is.

LENNOX: Why ain't you helpin' me?

JOE: You want my help?

[*No response.*]

You seem to think that just 'cause somethin' don't work, that I didn't try. I always try. I tried with you, your mama.

LENNOX [*accusatory*]: She worried herself to death over you.

JOE: She got sick, Lenny. She squeezed all the life she could out of her soul, and when there wasn't nothing left she died . . . not because of what I did, or what I didn't do, but damn it, 'cause that was all that was left to do. I ain't gotta run you through every choice I made with your mama. I loved that woman and she loved me and that's all there is to that. I said all the I'm sorries I can for these last few weeks. You're looking for some I'm sorries for the last twelve years and I ain't got none of those. Every step of the way I chose for the both of us, the best damn way I could. Now the magical part is . . . you get to choose some shit for yourself . . .

LENNOX: You ain't gonna help me?

JOE: I give it my best shot and come up short . . . What you want me to do?

LENNOX: Something . . . I don't know . . . but I can't do this by myself . . . not and really get nowhere. Shit, every day I'm on the street I can see how what I want is slipping away and I can't do nothing to stop it 'cause all my energy is spent on finding a place to sleep and something to eat. You in my head all the time 'bout what I should do and what I shouldn't . . . but ain't none of it coming together enough for me to see how to make things work enough for me to get even a li'l bit of what I want . . . That's what I need the help with, Pop, putting it together enough to make it work.

JOE: I'll do what I can, Lenny.

LENNOX: Lennox. Lenny is a little boy's name. You switch back and forth all the time like you can't make up your mind who I am.

[*He crosses over and picks up the CD Discman.*]

JOE: I'll work on that.

LENNOX: You gonna let me come home?

JOE [*smiling*]: You wanna come home?

LENNOX [*holding up the Discman*]: You gonna let me keep this?

JOE: It ain't mine to take away.

[*The sound is heard of a train rumbling by. Flashes of blue light spark up. Fade to black.*]

SCENE 7: THE HARDEST TIMES

[*Lights come up on* JOE, *isolated in a pool of light on the El platform.* LENNOX *is likewise illuminated in a voided space.*]

JOE: Hardest day of my life . . . even harder than the day my wife died. There is a certain kinda desperation that comes from really needin' money . . . and not knowing where it's gonna come from. There are different kinds of broke. There's that "I can't afford a vacation in Fiji . . . this year" kinda broke.

Granted that's a kinda broke that I've only read about in magazines, but I'm sure for some people, the Fiji thing is a big deal. Then there's the "Which bill am I gonna pay this month" kinda broke. 'Cause can't but one of them get they money. Yes, I'm sure there are more than a few degrees of separation between that and the Fiji thing, but I only aspire to be that kind of broke. The worst kinda broke, that's the "My son is hungry, there ain't no heat in January, and I can't even sell blood" kinda broke. I got one credit card left . . . So I send my fourteen-year-old son to the electronics store to buy up every DVD, digital camcorder–type gizmo he can get in under the credit limit, all the while knowin' that they got the security cams just arollin'. He signs my name just like I told him . . . close, but not too close, to the way I sign. Then he comes home. Within an hour we sell just about everything for half price, take in maybe six, seven hundred dollars . . . then I call the police and report the card stolen. We get the cash, the credit card company takes the loss, and my son's blurry little image goes up on the wall of the room with the two-way mirrors. They never came for him . . . But I spent more than a few sleepless nights wondering what I would do if they did. Ain't nothing worse than realizing that you have sacrificed your own child . . . all the while tryin' to save him . . . I let him keep the portable CD player 'cause . . . just 'cause.

LENNOX: When does other people's shit stop being your shit. Hardest part about being a man is letting go of other people's shit. Start messing things up for yourself. It's all about the choices . . . making your own, I mean . . . Getting now so that I don't think he's completely crazy . . . but I know he ain't got it all together either. This is supposed to be the world I inherit. Given to me by a man who is a half hustle from homeless himself. Damn . . . but he's all I got.

[*Fade to black.*]

SCENE 8: FAREWELL

[*An occasional flash of blue light sparks up. The sound of people hustling through on their morning commute is heard. A screeching subway train is heard approaching and then grinding to a halt. Lights come up on street musicians playing a tune for a dollar or a dime. The soundscape moves people aboard the crowded subway car. A shadowy figure meanders by the open instrument case and drops some coinage. The musicians nod in appreciation, never skipping a beat. The sound is heard of the doors closing and the train moving noisily on toward the next stop, its screech fading. Lights come up on* JOE *standing with a shoe-shine box,* LENNOX *by his side. Lights fade in illuminating the platform.*]

JOE: What's the name of it again?

LENNOX: Parkland Community College.

JOE [*proudly*]: Yeah, Parkland Community College!

LENNOX: It ain't no big deal.

JOE: You could always go to city college right here at home.

LENNOX: The price of staying home is just a little too high . . . but you ain't
gotta worry . . . hell, ain't nothin' down there but corn. I ain't gonna have
nothin' else to do but study. I do my two years there, then bounce over to the
U of I and finish up.

JOE: Got something for you.

LENNOX: Come on, Pop, we been through this.

JOE [*pulling some small books out of his pocket*]: Take this.

LENNOX [*reading*]: Course catalog and fall semester timetable.

JOE [*smiling*]: Just in case you wanna get a head start over at the university.

LENNOX [*smiling*]: I gotta go or I'll be late getting over to Union Station . . .

[*They hug.* JOE *drops three golden dollars into* LENNOX's *pocket.* LENNOX *takes them
out.*]

What's this for?

JOE: Every man should carry around a little gold in his pocket . . . for good luck.

LENNOX [*looking at the coins and smiling*]: Thanks.

JOE: I'm proud of you.

[LENNOX *waves good-bye and then exits.*]

Call me when you get in.

[JOE *picks up his box, meanders over to the musicians, and leans up against the wall.
The sound is heard of the doors closing and the train moving noisily on toward the
next stop, its screech fading.*]

GUITARIST [*offering up a cigarette*]: You wanna square?

JOE: Nah, I'm doing just fine . . .

[JOE *pops a stick of gum into his mouth, then leans back against the wall, exhaling
with deep satisfaction. He tosses the chrome lighter to the* GUITARIST.]

Better keep this too . . .

DRUMMER [*to* JOE]: Heads up . . . here she comes.

[JOE *looks down the long platform and sees* THE SUIT *approaching. He smiles with an impish grin, then picks up his box and heads toward her. The sounds of the platform come rushing in. The subway moves to its normal rhythm.*]

THE SUIT: I'm runnin' late . . .

[JOE *hoists* THE SUIT'*s foot up onto the box, preps, and then shines one shoe at a time with skillful precision. Fade to black.*]

AFTERWORD

Chuck Smith

Thank you for reading this anthology. I would also like to thank the playwrights and my editorial staff, who have donated all royalties to the Columbia College Chicago's Theodore Ward Prize for African American Playwriting. This volume is the first in a series that will be published every three years. Its primary markets are American theater students and theater professionals across the nation. The series was created to exercise a lesson I learned from my mentor, Theodore Ward, to put together positive projects that will last after you are gone. In June 2003, the Literary Managers and Dramaturgs of the Americas held their annual conference in Chicago, and I was asked to deliver the keynote address at the Chicago Shakespeare Theater on Navy Pier. The following is an edited version of my presentation.

Most of us remember the first theatrical dollar we earned. I earned mine at the Goodman Theatre during the 1970–71 season. I was hired to understudy a role in a production of *The Night Thoreau Spent in Jail,* by Jerome Lawrence and Robert E. Lee, the same gentlemen who wrote *Inherit the Wind.*

The role was a runaway slave named Williams who encounters Thoreau at Walden Pond. Ira Rogers was cast as the runaway, and Christopher Walken played the role of Thoreau. Ira was the number one black guy in Chicago voice-over work in those days. He also had a one-man cabaret show, which is where *Thoreau* director Patrick Henry saw him. Henry was famous then as head of the popular Free Street Theater. I admired Chris Walken's work, particularly in the play *Status Quo Vadis* at Chicago's Ivanhoe Theatre, which was under the direction of another Chicago icon, George Keathley.

There I was, working at the Goodman Theatre with the likes of Ira Rogers, Christopher Walken, and Patrick Henry in a play by Jerome Lawrence and Robert E. Lee. Not bad; I should have had my camera. No camera, but I have a lasting impression of the great experiences and lessons learned. One particular experience is how well I was treated and supported by the Goodman staff. At the traditional Goodman closing-night party, some key staff members were there to say good-bye to the actors, and to me this was a class act. I really wanted to stay and made up my mind then that someday I'd be on staff at the Goodman Theatre and would be around to say good-bye to the actors on closing nights.

During *Thoreau* rehearsals, I got one of my first lessons in script development. In the play, the runaway slave I understudies makes it to the North, encounters Thoreau, and is so impressed by him that he offers to give up his freedom and become his slave. Ira confronted the writers, questioning the logic of an ill-treated bondman giving up his newfound freedom under any circumstances. The writers heard the case, agreed, and changed the text. That was December of 1970, and little did I know that I was experiencing my first lesson in dramaturgy.

This year I experienced yet another great Goodman Theatre moment when I was asked to serve as production dramaturge on the world premiere of August Wilson's latest drama, *Gem of the Ocean*. One of my favorite lines from the play was when the character Aunt Ester says, "You are on an adventure, Mr. Citizen. I bet you didn't know that. You're on an adventure and you didn't even know it."

My life, especially my life in the theater, has also been and continues to be an adventure. While writing this speech, I struggled with where to begin the story of my theatrical adventures. After some thought I decided the most appropriate place would be the Goodman Theatre, America's number one (ranked by *Time* magazine) regional theater. I want to tell you the story of how I became a staff member and, along the way, introduce you to black theater in Chicago, which is, in my opinion, America's number one black theater community. I have been a member of this community for thirty-nine years and a member of the Goodman artistic staff for eleven years.

For the record, I was born here in Chicago on March 7, 1938, at Cook County Hospital (the one made famous by the NBC television drama *ER*, which was originally a play that started here at Chicago's Organic Theater). I was raised on Chicago's South Side, where after two failed marriages I live today with my daughter Michelle, a professional cosmetologist. My one and only ambition as a youth was to join the United States Marine Corps, where after serving six and a half years I was honorably discharged in 1963 a few days after Dr. King delivered his famous speech. A year later I was ready to return to the Marine Corps but was instead persuaded to join a community theater group, where my life changed.

Chicago, known as the Windy City and the City of Big Shoulders, carries a large, rich history in theater. It is the home of three regional, Tony Award–winning theater companies: Steppenwolf, a company run by actors; Goodman, run by directors; and Victory Gardens, run by playwrights. Most of the city's 140 League of Chicago Theatres venues are located on the city's North Side.

Chicago also has six black theater companies. ETA Theatre, Chocolate Chips Theater Company, and the Chicago Theater Company are located on the South Side. On the North Side are the Black Ensemble Theater, Ma'at Production Association of Afrikan Centered Theatre (MPAACT), and Congo Square. MPAACT and Congo Square do not have a theater facility. All six companies are members of the African American Arts Alliance of Chicago and each produces a full theater season. All of this theatrical activity, plus the black productions featured regularly at the Goodman, Victory Gardens, and Next, along with sporadic ventures from the rest of Chicago's professional theater community including Steppenwolf and Northlight, make Chicago a national leader in the production of black theater.

Black theater has been in this city for a long time. The first play I remember seeing was in the early 1950s at the old Parkway Community House on Fifty-first and South Parkway, now known as King Drive. My grandmother took me there to see my aunt Willa perform in a play called *The Monkey's Paw*. The performance took place up in the center's loft, and the group was called the Skyloft Players, founded by Langston Hughes.

However, black theater in Chicago began long before that. In 1905, the Pekin, located at 2700 South State Street, first opened as a saloon and gambling den. The owner, Robert Motts, was encouraged by residents and city officials to make the place more respectable, so Motts transformed it to a cabaret-style setting. The Pekin Theater Temple of Music thus became Chicago's first local all-Negro show in the city's history. The legacy of black theater companies in Chicago lives on. Black theater stands tall today because we stand on the big shoulders of our ancestors.

Early in the spring of 1971, after finishing at the Goodman, I was invited to work with June Pyskacek of the Kingston Mines Theatre Company on North Lincoln Avenue, located just a block northwest of the current Victory Gardens Theater complex. The complex was then occupied by a theater company called the Body Politic, headed by Reverend Jim Shiflett and an actor named James O'Reilly. They asked a group of actors operating in Madison, Wisconsin, to come and use the downstairs area of the building. The invited group was the Organic Theater Company, run by Stuart Gordon. Organic was looking for a new home because it was being kicked out of Madison for slipping a nude scene into a recent production of its *Peter Pan*.

Organic took Chicago by storm. Some of its early productions included its adaptation of the classic *Candide;* its original production of *Warp,* a comic book–style action-adventure play; and *Poe* (as in Edgar Allan), a production that featured current Broadway actor André De Shields as the raven. One scene frightened me to the point that I had to check and make sure I could quickly get to the exit! André went on to be in the Chicago company of *Hair* and later originated the title role of *The Wiz* on Broadway. I first noticed *Designing Women*'s Meshach Taylor in Organic's *The Wonderful Ice Cream Suit* around the time the company moved to the Beacon Street Theater (current home of Jackie Taylor's Black Ensemble Theater). Organic's popular play about Cubs fans at Wrigley Field called *Bleacher Bums* went on tour on the West Coast. Both featured Dennis Franz of the popular *NYPD Blue* television series. Parts 2 and 3 of *Warp* were created and the trilogy went on to Broadway, but it didn't last. Of the few Organic shows that I missed, *Bloody Bess,* the pirate adventure, stands out. Many still rank it number one in Chicago theater favorites.

Organic later purchased a building on Clark Street, just south of Belmont, but could never seem to make it work. The only production that stood out was *E/R,* which went on to the "left coast" and originated the current successful television drama. Years later, the Organic organization teamed up with Ina Marlowe of Touchstone Theatre and is now producing out of Loyola University.

The original *Grease* was the hit running at Kingston Mines when I started working with them, and there were always long lines of people waiting to see shows at the Mines and the Organic theaters. That's when I realized that something was going on with this Chicago theater thing.

Kingston Mines was hoping for another popular show to follow the lively *Grease,* but unfortunately *Terminal* by Susan Yankowitz wasn't lively at all. In fact, it was all about death and not well received. We struggled through the run with the help of a wildly popular weekend midnight show called *The Whores of Babylon.* We were in the beginning stages of rehearsals for the next production based on King Tut when everything at the Kingston Mines Theatre folded.

I took an improvisation class at Second City on North Wells and then returned to the South Side troupe that I started with, the Dramatic Art Guild (or DAG, as we called it). It was an integrated community theater company operating out of Michael Reese Hospital, doing plays for the patients. In late 1971, a few black DAG actors joined a new group at the Parkway Community House called the Experimental Black Actors Guild, commonly known as X-BAG. They were working on a production of Ron Milner's *Who's Got His Own,* which featured a marvelous young actor named Douglas Alan Mann. I began working with X-BAG in 1972, and this was my first real experience with what we now commonly refer to as black theater.

Years later, Doug Mann and I would return to the Parkway Playhouse with two other actors, the late Michael Perkins and Charles Finister, to found the Chicago Theater Company. It was Chicago's first black company created under an agreement with the Actors' Equity Association.

My first show with X-BAG was *Day of Absence* by Douglas Turner Ward. I played the Announcer in whiteface. The company was run by a public school art teacher named Clarence Taylor, who, like so many black theater artists before me, had tried to work in Chicago's "legitimate" theater but was rejected because of his race. That rejection turned Clarence Taylor into a black theater revolutionary, and "Black Theater for Black People" became his X-BAG motto. Clarence Taylor spent hours preaching to Doug and me about the importance of practicing our craft in the black community.

My most memorable X-BAG adventure happened not onstage but when the Regal Theater (Chicago's Apollo Theatre) on Forty-seventh Street was being demolished. Clarence, Doug, and I went to the site and, with permission, tearfully removed many of the seats and installed them in our theater at Parkway. The following season, Doug became an X-BAG artist in residence and I was assigned resident stage manager as the company's popularity increased. We received countless requests to bring shows to locations throughout the city, so I put together two small productions that could travel easily. One was a collection of staged African American poetry that we called *Poetry in Motion,* and the other was a riskier one-act play called *Midnight Angel* by local playwright Oscar Griffin. We took these shows to churches, community centers, and schools throughout the city.

In the mid-1970s, we were doing *Midnight Angel* at a North Wells cabaret in Old Town called Club Misty, where I first met Jackie Taylor of the Chicago Black Ensemble (or Black Ensemble Theater). She had written this wonderful musical called *The Other Cinderella* that she was performing at Club Misty on a regular basis. A few months later, she moved into a 150-seat theater on North Wells. It was rumored that a gangster owned the venue. After he literally disappeared, she was able to stay there several years rent-free. Jackie and I had a lot in common and became fast friends. We first worked together at Victory Gardens and then later when she was operating in the studio of the new Organic space on North Clark. I directed two productions for Jackie—her one-woman show *Playsong* and *Fish Tale* by Charles Michael Moore.

Jackie later hooked up with drummer Jimmy Tillman (Jimmy has his doctorate in music and I sometimes refer to him as Dr. Cool), who became her music director. They started producing out of the now famous Jane Addams Hull House Center located at 3212 North Broadway, the declared home of Chicago's off-Loop theater movement. Together Jackie and Jimmy developed the documentary, cabaret-style musical that the Black Ensemble is known for today. Jackie writes and directs most of the Black Ensemble productions and recently has started to commission playwrights for scripts. When directing, she hates tech with a passion and knows that I love it. It's not unusual for me to get a call from her asking if I can stop by and hang out during her tech weeks.

The Chicago Black Ensemble moved into the Beacon Street Theater in the mid- to late 1980s, where they are currently located, and have begun raising funds to build a new theater. Jackie is currently touring nationally the ensemble's smash hit *The Jackie Wilson Story (My Heart Is Crying, Crying)*, which played in the 2001 National Black Theatre Festival in Winston-Salem, North Carolina, and the Apollo Theatre in New York.

Late in 1973, X-BAG's Clarence Taylor introduced me to playwright Theodore Ward. Clarence decided to do one of Ted's plays, *The Daubers*, and wanted me to direct it. At the time, my first marriage had recently ended, and I was living in a swinging high-rise bachelor apartment in South Commons on South Michigan. As it turned out, Ted Ward had a special friend living in the same building, and we spent many long nights there talking theater. Ted was a published playwright, and his play *Our Lan'* had been produced on Broadway. He liked what I did in directing *The Daubers* and encouraged me to forget about acting and focus on directing. He pointed out to me that there was only one black director active in Chicago's Equity theater arena at the time, a respected actor-director named Bob Curry. Ted was also impressed with the fact that I was then seeking a degree and had worked at the Goodman and Kingston Mines. Knowing how much I loved working with X-BAG, he told me that I should always keep strong ties with the black theater community but never be afraid to venture outside of it. He told me all the things I needed to hear and charted the steps I needed to take to launch a professional directing career. I was very proud to have him in the audience in the fall of 1978 when I directed my very first Equity production, *Eden* by Steve Carter, at the Victory Gardens Theater.

I came across *Eden* in 1976. I was emotionally suffering from the failure of a second attempt at marriage and decided to take my eight-year-old daughter, Michelle, to meet our relatives in New York. My uncle Abraham Booker, my mother's brother, served in World War II and when it was over decided not to return to Chicago but make a go of it in New York City. Later in the 1950s, he married Lois DeChabert, and they successfully raised her two children, Glenn and Hermione. Herm graduated from Hunter College in New York and the late Glenn DeChabert from Yale Law School and the University of Pennsylvania. I have traditionally visited them for Thanksgiving most of my adult life.

In 1976, Michelle and I visited Uncle Abe and his family for Easter weekend. Uncle Abe and Aunt Lois suggested that I see *Eden* at the Negro Ensemble Company. It was a good suggestion. After seeing the production, I knew this was the play for me to direct in Chicago to get things going. It took me almost a year to get the rights. At the time, I was a guest director at Loop College, where I had studied under Sydney Daniels for several years. I first directed *Eden* there in the Loop College Theatre in 1977 with a student cast. It went very well and even got a few positive press notices.

In August 1977, I got my bachelor's in general studies from Governors State University in Park Forest South, Illinois, and was asked to guest-direct a production of a play there called *My Sweet Charlie.* The show went up in the early part of 1978 and again got some favorable press.

Now armed with two productions to shop around, I went straight to Dennis Zacek, the artistic director at the Victory Gardens Theater. I chose Victory Gardens because they had just mounted a production of Lonne Elder's *Ceremonies in Dark Old Men* under Zacek's direction. While I was at the production, I noticed in their mission statement that they were committed to produce a black show each season. I hounded Dennis for an interview and he finally granted me one. Remembering all of my Ted Ward instructions, I had my "stuff" together and beautifully laid out. Dennis was impressed and promised he would read both plays and get back to me. Jackie Taylor was one of Zacek's former students at Loyola University and was then on the Victory Gardens teaching staff. She helped convince him that bringing me on board would be a good idea. After what seemed like forever, Dennis called me back and hired me to direct *Eden.*

In the 1970s, the Victory Gardens Theater was located down the street from Wrigley Field (Cubs park) at 3730 North Clark Street. Victory Gardens was in its fifth season and rehearsed during the day, six days a week, so I had to make schedule arrangements with my nine-to-five. I had been a computer programmer for the Illinois Department of Public Aid for more than ten years and, on Ted Ward's advice, had saved up a load of vacation days for such an occasion.

The 1978 production of *Eden* was a huge success, gathering four Joseph Jefferson nominations. Thus began my professional directing career and my relationship with Steve Carter and the Victory Gardens Theater that still exists today. My third season at Victory Gardens featured another Steve Carter play called *Dame Lorraine* and starred the late Esther Rolle, who was a close friend of Steve's from their early days at the Negro Ensemble Company. My most recent Victory Gardens production was *Knock Me a Kiss* by Charles Smith, which opened in January 2000. It was so popular that even Oprah came to see it, and I am currently working on getting *Knock Me a Kiss* and two other shows mounted at Woodie King's New Federal Theatre in New York.

The year 1978 was an important one at the Goodman also. It mounted its very first production of *A Christmas Carol* that year. Earlier that spring, associate artistic director Greg Mosher mounted a Stage Two production of *Sizwe Banzi Is Dead.* In the fall, the very first show he mounted after becoming artistic director was a main-stage production of Richard Wright's *Native Son.* A few years later, he really turned some heads when he staged a production of *A Christmas Carol* with a black Tiny Tim. I liked Greg Mosher; I heard him speak on a panel and remember him saying he couldn't understand why Chicago's professional theaters, which were suffering at the box office, weren't taking advantage of the fact that Chicago has a population of more than two million African Americans and a wealth of black theater talent. The following season after *Native Son,* he brought in African writer and director Wole Soyinka to mount a production of his *Death and the King's Horseman* in a coproduction with the Arena Stage in Washington, D.C. After the *Horseman* run in D.C., many of the Chicago cast members, now with Equity cards in hand, went on to New York City instead of coming back to Chicago.

Luckily, some did come back, including radio personality Bonnie DeShong, Jackie Taylor, and actor Ernest Perry, who currently has done more shows at the Goodman than any actor in the history of the theater. Returning from *Horseman,* Ernest got busy putting together a theater company called Amistad Productions and asked Bonnie and me to join. I was a bit reluctant only because they were meeting on Wednesday nights to read plays and set policy, and Wednesday was one of my nights to watch my daughter. But even in my absence, those Wednesday evenings became legendary. Every Chicago black actor who was around in those days has a story to tell about Wednesday nights at the Perrys'. Not only did all eat well because Ernest's wife, Alice, is one of the best cooks on the planet, those Wednesday readings led to Equity showcase productions from 1979 to 1982 that included *Black Picture Show* at Hull House, *Impromptu* and *Conversation at Night with a Despised Character* at Parkway, and a critically acclaimed production of *Suspenders* at Loop College. Fortunately, I was involved in each as stage manager, actor, or director. The late 1970s provided a wealth of productions from other members of the then-powerful Black

Theater Alliance of Chicago, including Kuumba Workshop, then Chicago's leading black theater company; LaMont Zeno Community Theater, under the artistic direction of Pemon Rami, the black theater community's most popular director at the time; Black Heritage Theatrical Players; Kusema; New Concept Theater; and Chicago Black Ensemble. In March of 1979, Ebony Talent School of Drama (now ETA) purchased a screen factory on South Chicago Avenue, becoming the first black theater company in Chicago to own its own space since the Pekin Theater in 1905. All of that activity gave Chicago black theater artists reason to look to the 1980s with promise. Unfortunately, the early 1980s saw the folding of my beloved X-BAG, and a new group called Black Visions began using the Parkway Playhouse part-time.

Around this time, a force of nature called Steppenwolf came upon the Chicago theater scene. These actors were young, extremely talented, and very smart. Plus they knew exactly what they wanted to do and exactly how they wanted to do it.

I saw the Steppenwolf group in the late 1970s when they first began in a Chicago suburb, Highland Park, with shows like *The Indian Wants the Bronx* and *The Glass Menagerie*. I was completely blown away by their tight ensemble work. They moved to Chicago to the Hull House space on North Broadway. I remember their prophetic ads, which read, "Steppenwolf Moves to Broadway." Those were the true glory days of the company to old-timers like me. Those days birthed Steppenwolf greats like *Of Mice and Men, True West,* and my all-time favorite, *Balm in Gilead.* They also did some funky late-night weekend shows there at Hull House. It was at one of those late-night shows that I first saw John Mahoney, famous now for his TV role as Frasier's dad. They brought in popular New York actor-director Austin Pendleton to direct them in *Say Goodnight, Gracie,* and he has been working with them ever since.

Sheldon Patinkin, head of the theater department at Chicago's Columbia College, mentored and hired many of the Steppenwolf players to guest-teach, act, and direct at the college so they wouldn't have to work nontheater day jobs. I remember one Saturday afternoon at a League of Chicago Theatres panel discussion held at Columbia College, Steppenwolf actor Rondi Reed, who was one of the panelists, was very late. When she arrived, she calmly apologized and explained that she was at a very important meeting where the Steppenwolf actors had just fired their entire board of directors. Again, they were very smart and knew exactly what they wanted to do and exactly how they wanted to do it, and they still do.

Personally, since seeing them in Highland Park, I have always been a Steppenwolf groupie, and I am happy to say that they have finally done an African American play on their main stage. This season the company mounted a fine production of Alice Childress's *Wedding Band* featuring members of the Congo Square Theatre Company and is scheduled to open its next season with Suzan-Lori Parks's Pulitzer Prize–winning *Top Dog/Underdog*.

In 1982, Sheldon Patinkin hired me to direct a student production of *Ceremonies in Dark Old Men* at Columbia College. When the run was over, he asked me to join the faculty. I told him that I wasn't a teacher and he replied, "None of us are," and I have been there ever since.

I was able to bring in Ernest Perry as a guest artist to play the lead in *Ceremonies*. Ernest and I had just completed the Equity showcase production of *Suspenders* by Umar Bin Hassan at Loop College featuring the then-popular award-winning actor Vince Viverito, with whom I had worked on *Dame Lorraine* at Victory Gardens. We did it at the Loop College Theatre to bring attention to the fact that the city was building a new Loop College but wasn't going to include a theater in the new facility. It was a great production, but our political efforts were in vain. The new Loop College, named after the first black mayor of Chicago, Harold Washington, still does not have a theater.

Soon after *Suspenders* closed, City Lit Theater Company asked the three of us to work with them in a staged reading adaptation of a short story about Pullman car porters called *A Solo Song for Doc*. To my surprise, City Lit's artistic director, Arnie Aprill, didn't want me to direct the work but to play the title role of Doc. The show sold out at the Illinois Institute of Technology. We then moved it to Hyde Park's Black Box Theater at Mandel Hall on the University of Chicago campus. We took a proposal to Greg Mosher to try to get it in the Goodman Studio, but it was booked solid. A few years later, in 1985, Greg Mosher suddenly left the Goodman to take over the two theaters at Lincoln Center in New York.

In 1983, I was introduced to Rufus Hill, Keithen Carter, and Phillip Brown, who had written a lively, upbeat musical called *Po'* (as in "poor"), but with no experience and no hard cash, they had no idea how to produce it. With all the Equity showcases I had done with Amistad, I knew just how to put it up.

We rented a loft at 806 North Peoria (the current location of Design Lab) and mounted the show under the showcase code. We played to packed houses, but no producers would bite, including Roche Schulfer, executive director of the Goodman.

Nevertheless, Roche Schulfer is a pretty amazing guy. Fresh out of Notre Dame, he started off in the Goodman box office and worked his way up to the very top. I first met him in 1978 when I took a summer class on how to produce theater at the old St. Nicholas Theater . Roche was the instructor. When he first walked into the room, I wondered why such a young kid would want to know about producing theater and was floored when I realized he was the teacher. Young and smart, Roche taught me a lot in that class, including the age-old lesson: Never judge a book by its cover. At a recent Goodman Board meeting, Roche was awarded a special presentation for thirty years of exceptional service.

Closing night of *Po'* was the beginning of the Chicago Theater Company. Doug Mann was at the closing-night party and quietly said to me, "Why don't we go home to Parkway?" That sounded like a pretty good idea to me.

The director who ran the Parkway Community Center was a wonderful brother named Karim Childs. We worked together on a few projects while I was at X-BAG, and when X-BAG folded, I sent him a letter to discuss the possibility of using his space. I worked there for years with X-BAG and had done a show there in the summer of 1980 with Ernest Perry's Amistad Productions, which turned out to be Parkway's first Equity performance. In late December 1983, Doug and I set up the meeting with Karim, and he agreed to let us use the space beginning in August 1984.

In January 1984, Doug and I brought in two other guys, Mike Perkins and Charles Finister, to help put it all together. Mike and I worked together with Amistad Productions. Mike was an all-around theater talent. He could do anything, and do it well—act, direct, stage manage, and design. Actually, he and Bonnie DeShong studied theater with many of the Steppenwolf members at Illinois State University in Bloomington. Like me, Mike's day job was with the Illinois Department of Public Aid.

Charles Finister was a producer-organizer type who studied theater at Roosevelt University in Chicago. He started a company called the Chicago Theater Company and had done some pretty good shows. It folded, however, and thinking that we could fool the funding community into believing that we were the same group with an established track record, the four of us decided to incorporate under the same name. It didn't work—we couldn't get a dime from anyone.

Harold Scablow, a friend of mine at the nine-to-five, loaned us five thousand dollars to get us started, and by January of 1984, we were meeting weekly and had assigned titles and responsibilities. Charles would manage the company, and I would be the artistic director. Mike was the resident stage manager, and he also wanted acting and directing options. Doug, whose voice-over career had really begun to take off, was associate director.

We came up with our first season. We would start with shows I had done before—shows that I knew worked and had gotten some press. *Po'* would be first, then *Suspenders.* The other two slots were to be determined. I made it clear, however, that after the first season, we should look for a larger space. I didn't want to live at the small, hundred-seat Parkway anymore.

In late January, I got a call from playwright Charles Michael Moore, who had written *The Hooch,* a play about Marines in Vietnam. I saw a performance when it played at the LaMont Zeno on Chicago's West Side and liked it. It was going to go up in New York at Woodie King's New Federal Theatre, and they wanted me as the director. I would be gone for four weeks in April but would be back in plenty of time to set up our first show.

New York is always an easy trip for me, sort of like going to Grandma's house. My aunt and uncle lived in a huge Harlem apartment where they raised two kids. My aunt Lois, whom I love dearly, lives there alone now, which is why I currently spend as much time in New York as I possibly can.

I arrived there in March 1984 to direct my first New York show, and my family was totally thrilled. My aunt and uncle were avid theatergoers at that time. One of their proudest collections is an original program from an early (preview or workshop) performance of *A Chorus Line.* I think they saw one of the very first public performances.

It was always difficult for me to explain to them that there actually is professional theater outside of New York City. To them, and to most New Yorkers, this does not compute.

The Hooch featured Kevin Hooks (son of Robert Hooks, cofounder of the Negro Ensemble Company) in the lead role, and the show went off without a hitch. At the same time, Steppenwolf's production of *True West* had taken New York by storm, and naturally I secretly anticipated the same success for *The Hooch.* But alas, lukewarm reviews put an end to all that. My family and friends filled the house the night after it opened, and my cousin Hermione and her young son Jonathan hosted a fabulous cast party. The following day I came home.

Po' opened the Friday after Labor Day in 1984 to great reviews. Word of mouth from the showcase the year before picked up right away and before we knew it we had ourselves a hit. Too bad, because starting on such a high meant everything was bound to go downhill from there. Mike and I were busy running the show and Doug was off into his voice-over career and not around very much. We were pulling in close to fifteen hundred to two thousand dollars per week profit, but somewhere near the sixth week, in mid-October, all the money disappeared. Charles Finister resigned from the company and signed a statement of liability for the loss, which was estimated between ten and fifteen thousand dollars.

We had already decided to extend the show, so we did so until the end of December. We closed and although everyone got paid, we couldn't pay back our loan and had no money for the next show. After wrapping everything up, Mike and I were standing on the corner of Sixty-seventh and King Drive waiting on his bus. We discussed our options, which really were to take the risk and go on or quit while we were even, with the exception of the loan, which we would pay out of pocket.

I wanted to quit, but Mike Perkins wanted to go on, so we went on. For the next year, every dime we made from Public Aid, Columbia College, and any other outside show we worked fed right into the company. During that time I directed *To Be Young, Gifted and Black* at Pegasus and *"Master Harold"... and the Boys* at Victory Gardens. We survived. Doug came back and we won a Jefferson Award for *Po'* and received a nomination for *Suspenders*.

Now, nineteen years later, Doug Mann is the only one of the original four who is still there at Parkway. Charles Finister and Mike Perkins are with the ancestors, and the ancestors, not I, will judge them both. As for me, I have completely recovered from my financial loss and I am where I want to be. So is Doug. I don't think he'll ever leave Parkway. He can't leave Parkway because he is a disciple of Clarence Taylor, just like I am a disciple of Ted Ward.

After staying with CTC for six years, I came to realize that the company intended to stay at Parkway forever, and I began working on plans to leave. One of my most popular shows there was in 1989, a ninety-minute, three-character drama called *The Meeting* by Jeff Stetson. It got extended several times and caught the eye of Robert Falls, the recently selected artistic director at the Goodman.

Years before, after graduating from the University of Illinois, Bob Falls came to Chicago as artistic director of the Wisdom Bridge Theatre, and he never looked back. His work at the Goodman is nothing short of ingenious, and his Tony Award–winning productions seem to back me up on this. During his days at Wisdom Bridge, his award-winning production of *Hamlet* was the one that garnered the most attention, but I especially remember a play he directed in 1979 called *Wings*, which hit me so hard I got lost driving home. Two others I can't forget are the powerful *In the Belly of the Beast*, with popular Chicago actor William Petersen (now TV's *CSI* lead), and a haunting piece he did with the St. Nicholas Theater Company called *A Sorrow Beyond Dreams*, featuring a young Steppenwolf actor named John Malkovich. Anyway, in 1989, Bob Falls selected my production of *The Meeting* as part of Goodman's 1989–90 Studio season.

After *The Meeting* closed at CTC, the lead actors Harry Lennix (recently seen onstage and in film in Julie Taymor's *Titus* and currently in the movie *The Matrix Reloaded*) and Greg Alan Williams (on TV in *Baywatch* and as one of the generals in *The West Wing*) started a company called Legacy. They invested in a set, props, and costumes and began touring the show. When they got a booking in Atlanta, they sent for me to help them get the show up. Right in the middle of a successful run, Greg was cast in *Baywatch,* and we replaced him with Percy Littleton, who also did the Goodman Studio run. *The Meeting* run at Goodman Studio in the fall of 1989 definitely rekindled my determination to work there as a staff member. However, in the spring of 1990, while I was still trying to come up with a quiet exit strategy from Chicago Theater Company, my uncle Abe died in New York.

By some strange but truly fortunate twist of fate, I was accepted for an Arts Midwest fellowship for which I had applied months before, and I was assigned to work in New York City with the Cornerstone Theater Company for five months. That blessing allowed me to be with my New York family when they really needed me there to help them stabilize.

The fellowship was called the Minority Arts Administration Program and was designed to help professional artists develop specific skills, of their choice, that would help forward their careers. I wanted to learn how to take shows on tour and program activities for a large theater space, like the Goodman.

The Cornerstone Theater Company is now based in Santa Monica, California, but in the fall of 1990 it was based in New York and had toured all over the country. Comprised of a young group of Harvard graduates, the company planted itself in small towns and staged local adaptations of the classics, integrating company and members of the community in major roles. Right before I joined Cornerstone, they were on the cover of the *American Theatre* magazine for staging *Romeo and Juliet* with a black Romeo and a white Juliet in Port Gibson, Mississippi. James Bundy, now based at Yale, was the company manager and taught me how to budget and manage a tour. The rest of the wonderful company members filled in the rest of my knowledge gaps. While working with Cornerstone in New York, I quietly mailed in my resignation from the Chicago Theater Company, effective January 1, 1991.

To accept the fellowship, Columbia College Chicago gave me a year's leave of absence. Fortunately, a few years before, I had already resigned from my nine-to-five; in 1988, my daughter declared that she no longer needed my financial support as long as she could continue to use our basement as a beauty parlor. That sounded like a no-brainer to me. The very next day, after twenty-one years of service with the Illinois Department of Public Aid, and at the ripe young age of fifty, I quit my job and became a full-time artist. I still had Columbia College as an anchor and two gigs lined up back-to-back. One was an acting job at Court Theatre in a production of *Playboy of the West Indies,* which got nominated for a Jefferson Award; the other was a television directing job for *Crime of Innocence,* based on the Emmett Till murder, which won me an Emmy.

After Cornerstone, my next fellowship assignment was with the Great American History Theatre in St. Paul, Minnesota. I arrived there in February 1991 in the thick of a snowstorm. Despite the bone-chilling weather, I fell in love with St. Paul, with its laid-back atmosphere and lively arts community, which includes my favorite black theater company, the Penumbra Theatre, where August Wilson developed his craft.

Lynn Lohr was the managing director at the History Theatre, and she taught me all I needed to know about running a six-hundred-seat space and, even more important, groomed me on how to handle myself correctly with company board members and members of the funding community.

I returned to Chicago in the fall of 1991 a free agent and feeling like a mercenary, armed and ready. The very first thing I did was begin working on a proposal to the Goodman.

I directed a production of *The Glass Menagerie* at Black Ensemble that got a lot of press with its all-black cast including Jackie Taylor. While setting up a tour of *The Meeting* to African American colleges in the South and working on a project with the Chicago Historical Society, I got word that the Goodman and several other major theater companies had received sizable audience-development grants from the Wallace Foundation to get minorities in their empty seats. Guess what my proposal was about?

The black theater community was furious, as it should have been. At least *some* of that grant money should have gone to them. If you want to know how to get black butts in theater seats, you should deal with the people who work at it full-time. I was furious, too, but furious or not, I knew Goodman had the grant, and thanks to my fellowship training and Ted Ward, I knew how to deal with it. I polished and dropped off my proposal the next day.

In the spring of 1992, I was called in for an interview and met with Michael Maggio, then Goodman's associate artistic director, and Steve Scott, associate producer. Artistic director Bob Falls was on a sabbatical and couldn't be there.

Steve had seen and complimented my production of *The Glass Menagerie,* and Michael and Steve both complimented me on the proposal. After discussing a few audience-development issues and a show I wanted to develop, the interview turned into a gossip catch-up session.

It seemed like just a few years before that we were all sipping cool ones up in Lake Geneva, Wisconsin, at a League of Chicago Theatres annual retreat. Bob Falls was artistic director of Wisdom Bridge, Michael Maggio was artistic director of Northlight Theatre, and I was artistic director of the Chicago Theater Company. Steve Scott, who has been with the Goodman Theatre since before time, used to hold legendary late-night drinking sessions in the resort hot tub. Michael was very frail during those wild Lake Geneva days, as he had been all of his life up to that point. But thanks to a recent lung transplant, he was now a new man, doing all the things his old life had denied him. Michael's exciting new life and early plans for a new Goodman Theatre facility are what I most remember about that interview.

Not long after in the summer of 1992, I joined the Goodman staff along with Mary Zimmerman as an affiliate artist. It had taken twenty-one years, but I was finally there. *Riverview* was playing on the main stage, and I saw it several times. I enjoyed sitting in the audience, randomly thumbing through the program, and coming across my name as an artistic staff member. My first assignment was as assistant director to Steve Scott in the 1992 production of *A Christmas Carol.* The following spring I assisted Frank Galati in *Cry, the Beloved Country,* and they gave me the 1993 production of *A Christmas Carol* for my very own. I directed *A Christmas Carol* for three straight seasons, and with the help of music director Larry Schanker and resident sound designer Rob Milburn, I changed it from a play with some music to a play with a lot of music.

During this time, Michael Maggio was training me on everything related to the Goodman Theatre operation, including Trustee Board meetings, artistic staff meetings, opening nights, Women's Board meetings, tech staff meetings, Discovery Board meetings, intern lunch meetings, closing nights, plus each and every social function. Few people realize that there is so much more to the Goodman Theatre than what is seen onstage, confirming that my 1971 instincts were correct—this was where I wanted to be.

In 1996, it was pointed out to me that Goodman had done all of August Wilson's plays except one, *Ma Rainey's Black Bottom.* I had seen several productions of *Ma Rainey,* including the acclaimed Chicago production at Pegasus Players, which featured my friend Harry Lennix, who had also become a member of the Goodman artistic staff. I was scheduled to direct and open *Ma*

Rainey in June 1997. It was a perfect show for me to do for three reasons—Harry Lennix, Rob Milburn, and Chicago. All of August Wilson's works take place in Pittsburgh, except for *Ma Rainey*. It's a play with music that takes place in Chicago, and I make no apologies for a certain spiritual connection that I have to all things black Chicago.

Harry Lennix and I were in perfect actor-director sync in those days. He taught music in the Chicago public school system, and we had worked together on countless productions of *The Meeting*. Rob Milburn was, and still is, the man of Chicago theatrical sound. Every production of *Ma Rainey* that I'd seen had one major flaw. The actors in the roles of the musicians couldn't play the instruments, and the audience always seemed to know it. I was sure that with Rob Milburn I could fix that.

All the band members we cast were actors with whom I had worked before, and we gave them each private music lessons. Harry was on trumpet, Percy Littleton on bass, Ernest Perry on trombone, and Tim Rhoze on piano. All of the music played in the play's rehearsal-room scenes was live, and the audience knew it. When action shifted into the recording studio, things changed. Thanks to Rob Milburn's wonderful sound design, Kimo Williams's music design, and the hot singing of Felicia Fields as Ma Rainey, no one cared if the band was live or Memorex. Harry had learned to play the trumpet so well that after the press opening, I gave him the option to play live in the studio scenes if he desired, which he did most of the time. A *Wall Street Journal* reviewer reported that "these actors are either playing their instruments or successfully fooling me." Artistic mission accomplished!

The Goodman production of *Ma Rainey* was seen by Chicago's mayor Richard Daley, Vice President Al Gore, and basketball legend Michael Jordan. August Wilson wrote me a note saying, "Thank you for the beautiful production of *Ma Rainey*. It is really fine, fine work. I haven't seen any better." August also latched onto my sound designer, Rob Milburn, and has used him in each of his premiere productions since. The show also set a Goodman Theatre box office record. Proposal mission accomplished!

After the Vice President Gore performance, Bob Falls and Michael Maggio both embraced me, and to this day, that was my finest Goodman Theatre moment.

That was the last show of mine that Michael Maggio saw. He died in August 2000 right before we moved into the new Goodman Theatre. In a publicity photo of all of us taken that spring there's Bob Falls, Mary Zimmerman, Mike, Cheryl Lynn Bruce, Harry Lennix, David Petrarca, Regina Taylor,

Henry Godinez, and me. It hangs on the wall in my Goodman office as a constant reminder that Michael will always be with us.

A Raisin in the Sun, The Amen Corner, and *The Gift Horse* are my other Goodman favorites. Like the plays before them and those that will follow, they each have their own stories.

Theater in Chicago has developed considerably since I listened to Ira Rogers passionately explain to Jerome Lawrence and Robert E. Lee that no black man would escape slavery, find his freedom, and then offer to give it up as if it were an item of clothing. It has certainly evolved since Ted Ward mandated that I always keep close ties to the black theater community.

Ted Ward died in 1983, and in 1985 Columbia College Chicago established the Theodore Ward Prize for African American Playwriting. In 1988, the third year of the prize, founders Lya Rosenblum, then dean, department chair Sheldon Patinkin, and playwright-in-residence Paul Carter Harrison asked me to facilitate the contest, and I naturally accepted. Next season, in 2004, the first volume of an anthology series of Theodore Ward Prize–winning plays will be published. I think he would like that.

Last month, I was on an assignment to review a show in Seattle. It was my first time there, and I thoroughly enjoyed my stay. I had the option to remain an extra day, but it was the final performance date of *Gem of the Ocean,* and I had to get back. I still try to make sure I'm there at the Goodman Theatre on closing nights to say good-bye to the cast.

"You're on an adventure and you didn't even know it." Those words ring in my head. I'll tell you one thing: I know it now.

CONTEST GUIDELINES

Columbia College Chicago's Annual Theodore Ward Prize for African American Playwriting

Sponsors

Columbia College Chicago Theater Center
Sheldon Patinkin, Chair, Theater Department
Paul Carter Harrison, Playwright in Residence
Chuck Smith, Facilitator

Goals

1. To uncover and identify new African American plays that are promising and producible.
2. To encourage and aid playwrights in the development of promising scripts.
3. To offer an opportunity for emerging and established playwrights to be exposed to Chicago's professional theater community through staged readings and/or fully mounted productions.

Eligibility

1. All entrants must be of African American descent and permanent residents within the United States.
2. Only full-length plays addressing the African American will be considered. One-act plays and musicals are not accepted (with the exception of a play with music).
3. Adaptations and translations are not eligible unless from works in the public domain.
4. All rights for music or biographies must be secured by entrant prior to submission.
5. One completed script per playwright will be accepted.

6. Scripts that have received professional productions are ineligible. "Professional" includes Equity Showcase and Waiver productions but does not include amateur and college productions.
7. All manuscripts must be typed and bound. Please include a brief personal résumé (with a telephone number), a short synopsis, and a script history. The script history should include information about any prior productions or readings.
8. Staff and faculty of Columbia College Chicago are not eligible. Winners cannot win in successive years.

Submission

All manuscripts must be typed, securely bound, copyrighted, and mailed to Chuck Smith, Columbia College Chicago, Theater Center, 72 East Eleventh Street, Chicago, IL 60605. Only scripts with self-addressed envelopes will be returned.

Prizes

The first-place winner will receive two thousand dollars and a fully mounted production in the New Studio season. The performance space is a seventy-seat black box theater that is a part of the Theater Center of Columbia College Chicago. The prize also includes transportation (within the continental United States only) and housing (maximum one week) during rehearsal period and performances.

The playwright must be willing to sign a contract with the college that obligates the playwright to (1) travel to Chicago during production; (2) acknowledge prize in future programs and publications; and (3) grant publishing rights to Columbia College Chicago. The playwright will receive future royalties of 1 percent (three-year time limit).

The second-place winner will receive five hundred dollars, a staged reading at Columbia College Chicago directed by a faculty director, and an audiotape of this reading.

Columbia College Chicago and the Theodore Ward Prize Advisory Board reserve the right to withhold the awards should the Advisory Board so recommend.

Deadline

Scripts will be accepted from April 1 to July 1. All scripts must be postmarked no later than midnight on July 1.

Columbia College Chicago

Columbia College was founded in 1890. In 1947, Mike Alexandroff became its president and instituted the principles Columbia is based on today: the use of professionals as teachers giving up-to-date and practical instruction, aiming toward success in the field after college. Today, President Warrick Carter carries on that proud tradition.

Columbia's Theater Department, chaired by Sheldon Patinkin since 1980, offers a program aimed at equipping its students with the skills needed to fully develop their careers. Performance is considered the key to progress.

The faculty and staff are all working professionals, active and prominent members of Chicago's lively theater community. The department stresses intensive one-on-one training in all aspects of the profession and supplies a multitude of opportunities for applying this learning in performance situations.

The Theater Department produces a six-show subscription season for general audiences. At the four-hundred-seat Emma and Oscar Getz Theater, fully mounted productions of two large-cast plays, or musicals, and one concert featuring our Faculty Ensemble as directors and designers are presented. In the seventy-seat New Studio, the season is rounded out with full productions of two smaller plays and one musical or concert. In addition, many all-student-directed workshop productions and recitals are presented each semester in the sixty-seat Classic Studio.

FIRST-PLACE WINNERS OF THE THEODORE WARD PRIZE FOR AFRICAN AMERICAN PLAYWRITING

1986–1987   Silas Jones, *The John Doe Variations*

1987–1988   Christopher Moore, *The Last Season*

1988–1989   Jeff Stetson, *Fathers and Other Strangers*

1989–1990   No winner

1990–1991   William F. Mayfield, *Sing Black Hammer*

1991–1992   No winner

1992–1993   Chuck Cummings, *The Negro Building*

1993–1994   Gloria Bond Clunie, *North Star*

1994–1995   Charlotte A. Gibson, *The Temple*

1995–1996   Duane Chandler, *The Trees Don't Bleed in Tuskegee*

1996–1997   Charlotte A. Gibson, *Lost Creek Township*

1997–1998   David Barr, *Black Caesar*

1998–1999   Benard Cummings, *The Grandmamma Tree*

1999–2000   Javon Johnson, *Hambone*

2000–2001   Lydia R. Diamond, *The Gift Horse*

2001–2002   Shepsu Aakhu, *Kiwi Black*

2002–2003   Leslie Lee, *Sundown Names and Night-Gone Things*

2003–2004   Mark Clayton Southers, *Ma Noah*

ABOUT THE PLAYWRIGHTS

SHEPSU AAKHU is a playwright in residence at the Ma'at Production Association of Afrikan Centered Theatre (MPAACT) in Chicago. In 2003, he debuted a new play entitled *SOST* for MPAACT. In January 2004, his most recent work, *Softly Blue,* was featured at the Goodman Theatre's Festival of New Plays in Chicago. The Griot Ensemble Theatre (GET) of Pittsburgh will produce a season of plays by Shepsu Aakhu (*Kiwi Black, Fascia,* and *SOST*) for its 2004 season. He received the Illinois Artist Fellowship Award for Scriptworks in March 2004. He has also been recognized by the Joseph Jefferson Committee of Chicago and the Black Theater Alliance of Chicago.

GLORIA BOND CLUNIE is a creative drama specialist in Evanston, Illinois. She is currently working on *Shoes,* which was developed in a workshop at Chicago's Victory Gardens Theater. The drama explores the 1963 Birmingham church bombings. Bond Clunie's novel, *Dear Cora,* was a finalist for the 2003 James Jones First Novel Fellowship, and her short story "Sweet Pea" was a semifinalist in the 2003 William Faulkner Creative Writing Competition.

LYDIA R. DIAMOND is a resident playwright at Chicago Dramatists and a part-time faculty member at Columbia College Chicago, where she teaches playwriting and acting. She is also a contributing editor at *TriQuarterly,* in which her play *The Inside* will be published. Diamond was the second-place recipient of the 2003 National Arts Club Kesselring Prize. Her plays *Stage Black* and *The Gift Horse* recently received staged readings at the Going to the River Festival at New York's Ensemble Studio Theatre.

JAVON JOHNSON is resident playwright and a founding ensemble member of the Congo Square Theatre Company in Chicago. He is a recent recipient of the Alabama Shakespeare Festival Commission. Johnson's recent productions include the world premier of *The House That Jack Built* at Congo Square Theatre Company, *Hambone* at the New Federal Theatre in New York and at the Village Theatre in Los Angeles, *TBA* at Black Repertory in St. Louis, and *Eighty-Six* and *Bones* at Penn Theatre in Pittsburgh. Johnson played the role of Calvin Sr. in the film *Barbershop 2.*

CHRISTOPHER MOORE is research coordinator for the Schomburg Center for Research in Black Culture in New York, where he recently served as curator of the Ralph J. Bunche Centennial Exhibition. Moore is chief writer of the Schomburg Center's critically acclaimed books *Jubilee: The Emergence of African American Culture* and *Standing in the Need of Prayer: A Celebration of African American Prayer Traditions*. Moore is currently writing a book about black soldiers in World War II.

CHARLES SMITH is head of the Professional Playwriting Program at Ohio University and a member of the Tony Award–winning Victory Gardens Theater Playwrights Ensemble. He was recently commissioned by Ohio University to write a play to celebrate its bicentennial. He has also been commissioned by Victory Gardens to write a play about Denmark Vesey.

JEFF STETSON resides in Marina del Rey, California. His first novel, *Blood on the Leaves,* was scheduled for publication in July 2004 by Warner Books. He recently received a commission from the Kennedy Center to write a play to be produced in April 2004, starring Debbie Allen and Phylicia Rashad.

Chuck Smith and Theodore Ward, 1972

CHUCK SMITH is a resident director at the Goodman Theatre in Chicago. He most recently directed *The Crucible* at the Timberlake Playhouse in Mt. Carrol, Illinois, and is currently directing *The Death of Bessie Smith* as part of Goodman Theatre's Edward Albee Festival.

THEODORE WARD, the sixth of eleven children, was born in Thibodaux, Louisiana, where his father was a teacher and principal of a parish school for fifty years. At the age of thirteen he hopped a freight to Omaha and ended up in Chicago, where he lived and nurtured his playwriting gift until his death on May 8, 1983. Sharing the literary and sociopolitical vision of his contemporaries Richard Wright and Clifford Odets, Ward was one of the most significant playwrights to emerge from the Chicago chapter of the Federal Theatre Project during the mid-1930s.

Following a period of study at the University of Wisconsin as a Zona Grey fellow, Ward had his first major play, *Big White Fog,* produced in Chicago by the FTP. During the early 1940s, he became cofounder of the Negro Playwrights Company in New York and with the help of a Theater Guild scholarship developed and produced his historical play *Our Lan'* on Broadway in 1945. The author of more that twenty plays, Ward was a recipient of the John Simon Guggenheim and National Theatre fellowships for playwriting and was one of the major role models who influenced the shape of the intellectual and cultural life of Chicago's African American community.

COVER PHOTOGRAPHS